MALTA
An Aviation History

ALFRED COLDMAN

MALTA
An Aviation History

Publishers Enterprises Group (PEG) Ltd

Published by
Publishers Enterprises Group (PEG) Ltd
P.E.G. Building, UB7, Industrial Estate
San Ġwann SGN 09

Web site: http://www.peg.com.mt
E-mail: contact@peg.com.mt

First published 2001

ISBN: 99909-0-283-6

Printed in Malta by P.E.G. Ltd

I dedicate this book to my wife, Josephine
My three daughters, and their families, in
Whom I've found Love, Life and Living
Wholesome
Till the very end ...

Acknowledgements

John & Reg Havers, Brian Goulding ARPS; Charles Waterfall; Peter Marson; Joe Vella of Victoria – Australia; R.C.B. Ashworth; the late L.A.C. Ken Cox, L.A.C. Les Davies & W.R. Elliott; Twanny Gauchi of MIACO; George Galea of MIACO; the late Phillip Vella, ex-N War M Ass. Secretary; Mr. John Agius MBE; Fredrick Galea – N. War M. Ass Secretary F. Galea; Richard Caruana; David Brown – author; Iain Mackie – Daily Mail Ass. M. Editor; British Red Arrows Base PRO; Roderick Smith – Canadian – ex-Malta Spitfire pilot; Ken Smy – Johannesburg – S. Africa; J.K. Arbuthnot; Major R. Pearce MBE.REME.- Vehicle Branch REME.; J. Portelli, Secretary, UTAL; Rev. Fr. Briffa-Brincati; Rev. Fr. C. Zammit; Mark Said; Joe Caruana.

Information Sources

British Ministry of Defence; Public Record Office, London; U.S.A. Force; Albert F. Simpson Historical Research Centre, USAF Maxwell A. F. Base, Alabama; Dept. of Defence (Air Office) Australia; Dept of the A. Force, Norton A. F. Base; Library of Congress. New York;

Personal Diaries & Flying Log-books

Diary of late Malta-Spitfire pilot, Canadian Jerrold Smith
Diary of L.A.C. W. E. Metcalf (Malta – 28/4/41 to 10/10/43)
Diary of G Hare (Malta, Sept. 1939 – May 1941)
Diary of Wg. Cdr. R.C. Jonas
Diary of Cpt. Des Vince Jones DSC; 806 Sqdn
Diary of Flg. Off. Peter Nash
Logbook of Sqdn. Ldr. Waters
Logbook of Sgt. A. H. Deacon
Logbook of Sgt. Pilot L. Davies

Logbook excerpts Sqdn. Ldr. P W. Lefevre DFC
Logbook of P. S. Simpson
Logbook of Plt. Off. Rod Smith
Logbook & letter excerpts Sqdn. Ldr. Whiteley
Logbook of Sgt. Pilot C. E. Broad
Logbook of J. E. Hall
Logbook of Flt. Lt. R. Hilton-Barber
Logbook of Flt. Lt. Sugden
Logbook of Plt. Off. J. Pickering
Logbook of Plt. Off. Knoble

Official Documents

RAF Base Malta – 1915/1927
Operation Order No. 52
31st Fighter Group (Advance Unit 3 Photo Recce Group) 12th Photo Sqdn. Detachment to Malta.
History of the Aviation Engineers in the Mediterranean Theatre of Operations, (Historical Section American AF Engineer Command).
Dept. of the US Navy – Naval Historical Centre – French Patrol Bombing Sqdn.

Operation Record Books

431 Flight RAF
228 & 230 Sqdns. RAF
185 Sqdn. RAF
01 Sqdn. S. African AF
21 Sqdn. S. African AF
40 Sqdn. S. African AF
450 Sqdn. R. Australian AF
69 Sqdn. RAF
148 Sqdn. RAF
249 Sqdn. RAF
12 Sqdn. S. African AF
24 Sqdn. S. African AF
03 Sqdn. R. Australian AF

Photography

National War Museum Association – Imperial War Museum – Times of Malta – Fotoforce – Charles Waterfall – Chris Ashworth – John & Reg Havers – Brian Goulding – Dr Joe Portelli – Colin Smith.

B. C. Allen – Kenneth Cox –Ray Sturtivant – Peter Marson – A.V. Gladstone – Imperial War Museum – R. Williams of Hants – R.W.Elliott – Ministry of Defence: R. Australian A. Force – Public Record Office: London.

Tony Gauci: MIACO – RAF: Malta – C. Ernie Broad – P. H. T. Green – W. S. Gooch — T. Fellows – Italian A.F – British Ministry of Defence – Richard Caruana – Malta Aviation Museum Foundation – J. W. Parsons – Mrs. Martin of Churchdown UK.

Author's Collection – D. R. Neate — Mr. W. L. Harding, Managing Director, Cassar & Cooper — George Barbara – Nicola Malizia.

Contents

Introduction

I can hardly recall the days when, as an aircraft enthusiast, I used to wander around Luqa aerodrome, logging and photographing military aircraft movements and activities.

Neither do I recall when I first felt the urge to start researching about past aviation movements over the island. When did the first aircraft actually appeared in/over Malta? How?

Thoughts that obsessed my mind with such intensity that from a present day aircraft spotter I became an amateur aviation historian.

My original enthusiasm for aircraft spotting at Luqa began to fade away.

A few years prior to the RAF's withdrawal from Malta, packing pen and note pad, I began spending most of my spare time writing, either at home or taking notes at the Public Library in Valletta, rather than with my camera at Luqa.

Henceforth, aviation-wise my attention was far more drawn towards researching about the past over Malta despite my occasional visits to Luqa.

Photography, apart from its basic use as a part-time job, began serving me to copy old time aviation pictures, depicting aircraft long gone, on sites that modern day progress had since obliterated for all time from the island surface.

What I am here passing on to you about this side of Malta's history, however, despite my pursuing it as a pastime, would not have been accomplished without the cooperation of diverse friends and colleagues, both locally and from abroad.

Communicating with the British Ministry of Defence, and the Public Record Office in London, unintentionally led me to become a member of Air Britain's International Association of Aviation Historians. I was soon promoted to a Maltese aviation enthusiast within their ranks.

By these means my name soon became associated with Malta's aviation history elsewhere.

I communicated with diverse overseas individuals with a common interest. Regretfully, however, many of these penpals, so to speak, were oftentimes after information rather than forwarding what I was expecting. Surprisingly, what I had by that date succeeded in accumulating related to past aviation in Malta exceeded what these individuals already had. However, I admit that these means were gradually filling in several of the blank spaces existing in my notes.

Others, with whom I eventually made great friends, without expecting anything in return, offered or posted me material, both text and photographs, for which I was constantly on the lookout.

Local newspapers provided their unexpected 'juicy' titbits as well. These were at times of great value as they occasionally led to sources which, with some further research, could supply you with more detailed information.

I communicated with wartime pilots who provided me with copies of either their personal logbooks or diaries. Some of these I met personally, of whom the one I recollect most is "Laddie" Lucas. A retired ex-RAF Spitfire pilot who flew over Malta during the war, he was a reputable journalist and a great author. He was one of the most interesting men to get along with, although I have every respect towards those others who I met during my research.

Nearly eighty years old he used to recall many of his wartime experiences with such clarity and enthusiasm that he could make his listener smile, or just as easily shed a tear.

Ex-RAF L.A.C.'s (Leading Aircraftsmen) who were in Malta during the war also had their own wartime recollections to spill. Some, like William Metcalf, had kept personal diaries, recording the action from their point of view shortly after it happened on the battleground.

The Ministry of Defence was also most cooperative.

Furthermore, I discovered that, location-wise, I was better off than any of my Air Britain colleagues. The Public Records Office provided me with numerous copies of official documents which, despite paying a nominal fee, were well worth the expence; unfortunately this beneficial procedure was eventually stopped. A means which was not provided to UK residents.

A few years later some friends of mine, members of the Malta National War Museum Association approached me. Having had their attention on my historical interests for sometime they encouraged me to join the Association as a committee member. I never regretted having said yes, for this decision proved to be a mine of information in my case.

Consequently, with the passage of years, information about which I had never dreamt, let alone read, turned up on my desk, often by post, but occasionally by hand.

This collection of manuscripts, and other literature, that I set out into chapters, open in 1915, the year in which appeared the first airplane in Malta, flying over the Grand Harbour area during the First World War.

This was succeeded by a greater aviation event when in 1916 construction of the Kalafrana Seaplane base began.

In 1918 was launched the first Malta Dockyard-built Felixstowe F.3 flyingboat, while the Marsa Sports Ground was used as a temporary airfield. From there, two DH.9As were operated to supplement the seaplanes at Kalafrana, when these were unable to take off operationally from inside the bay due to the roughness of the sea in bad weather conditions.

Despite the postwar military rundown, aviation movements and activities during subsequent years were at no time brought to a standstill.

Hal Far airfield was in the early 1920s constructed to accommodate carrier-borne aircraft when their floating bases were in Mediterranean waters.

To have civil aircraft movements separated from those military at RNAS Hal Far, local authorities in 1934 decided to construct Ta' Qali airfield.

At this time, with the threat of the Abyssinian Crisis, Britain had a concrete mirror radar built at Maghtab; however, by the time the British came to grips with Hitler's Germany in 1939 this construction had long been obsolete.

In the summer of 1940, when Italy declared war against Britain and her allies, Malta's position in the conflict only became seriously critical in 1941, just after the 'blitz' on the 'Illustrious', when Germany's Luftwaffe moved into the Mediterranean.

In 1942 the threat of an invasion hovered like death's scythe over the island.

Malta's fate remained in the balance until the Axis High Command, against the better judgement of some of their Commanding officers, refused to take Malta by 'storm', believing that their airforce was strong enough to keep the island aerially neutralized, without the use of such an exertion.

Some Germany officials might have rightfully taken into

consideration the island's topography as, the logistics of such an undertaking made it that much more hazardous.

However, Germany expected too much from the air superiority their Luftwaffe had gained in the region during 1941, and still commandeered during the winter and spring months of 1942. They failed to foresee that this asset would eventually be snatched away from them through the deployment of RAF Spitfire fighter aircrafts in Malta.

Numerous were the sacrifices made by FAA and RAF anti-shipping strike forces, operating from the island in detachments and full squadron strength at opportune intervals, striking at Rommel's lines of communication. However, despite the frightening losses to life and equipment suffered by these gallant aircrews in their relentless efforts to disable the enemy, the Battle of Malta remains a fighter aircraft's war.

Following the aftermath of the Second World War, the likes of which will hopefully never again be waged, aviation remained expanding and 35 more years were to pass before Malta watched the withdrawal of the British services from its shores. Nevertheless, much was to happen, aviation-wise, before, and after, that event.

During the years in which I pursued this hobby of mine I have never approached an authority on the subject to ask for advice as to how should I treat my work, perhaps because what I always had in mind was a pastime, despite the seriousness with which I took Malta's aviation history. Never have I ever foreseen that it would come to this, but now that I have come this far on my own it decided it would be best to keep it up.

To the literature mentioned above I also read every book I could lay my hands on about the subject, of which I possess a large number, including to those that I used to borrow from friends and the Public Library.

However, it was family and friends who eventually encouraged me to publish what I have dedicated so many years of my life writing about with such enthusiasm, and give interested readers an insight of what "Wings Past" was like over Malta.

Still, before concluding this introduction, I apologize to all my friends for any errors I may have unintentionally made. I blame no one for this but myself, and truly hope that I have taken the right step, and provide readers with as satisfactory a '*read*' as I have had a '*write*'.

Fred Coldman

Chapter I

W.W. 1 Aviation Era

Historical Outline – The Knights – The French – The British – WW.1 – HMS Ark Royal – Kalafrana Seaplane Base – Wyndham Levy Grech – HM Dockyard Aircraft Construction Unit – Kite Balloon Squadron – First Airfield – HP V/1500 H.M.A. Old Carthusian J1936

Historians assume that more than three thousand years ago the first invaders either drove out or annihilated the foremost inhabitants of Malta. But whatever happened afterwards was forever obscured in the mists of time until, by painstaking sifting of artifacts, and other discoveries, it was eventually disclosed that by the year 800 BC the Phoenicians were in possession of Malta. This occupation coupled with that of their Carthagenian relatives, lasted until 218 BC when, during the third Punic war, Malta was incorporated in the Roman empire. The Byzantine Greeks seized Malta in 535 AD while the Arabs, coming from Sicily, captured the island in 870. Beginning from 1090 Malta then passed under a succession of European kingdoms.

Towards the final stages of the Third Punic War, Malta became a colony of the Roman Empire, and remained so for the next seven hundred years, but sometime before the year 870 AD the Island had in some manner or another become an Arab state.

After the island fortress of Rhodes succumbed to a severe Turkish Ottoman siege the Knights of the Order of Saint John of Jerusalem were forced to wander aimlessly all over Europe. Finally, in the year 1530 AD, Emperor Charles the Fifth of Castille, concerned about the threat imposed upon his Empire by the followers of Islam, decided to offer the island of Malta to the Knight Hospitalliers as their new home and fortress.

During the next thirty years the island's features were changed considerably, and with Grand Master Jean Parisot de La Valette in office, Malta's defenses were strategically re-enforced, preparing it for the Ottoman invasion he was positive would be forthcoming. His forecast was not long becoming a reality for on 18 May 1565 hundreds of ships of the Ottoman Empire appeared over the horizon.

The ensuing battle lasted for nearly four consecutive months, with the outcome often in the balance, and when the besieged finally gained the initiative the price of victory was a costly one. In later years, however, the Turks shied off the Maltese islands, but other invaders were closer to home.

The tension that gradually developed between the Knights and the clergy resulted in civil unrest. Disquiet stoked further still by the infiltration of French Fifth Columnists whose main scope was to make it easier for Napoleon Bonaparte to take possession of Malta, a scheme which was finally realized in all its infamy in 1798 when the once proud Knights were driven out of the Island in disgrace.

Initially, following the French occupation, things for the Maltese seemed to take a turn for the better, but were shortly to develop into what is universally known as the calm before a storm. The French soldiers, under the command of General Vaubois, misbehaved and the Maltese rebelled. A full-scale uprising was organized, but Vaubois could not be budged from inside Valletta. This led to a meeting of the island's chief citizens on 4 September 1798.

At the suggestion of one of the members, a letter reminding the King of the Two Sicilies that he was Malta's sovereign, in an attempt to solicit his aid, was prepared and dispatched by a courier. Luigi Briffa was instructed to first locate the British Fleet en route, and implore Lord Nelson if he could possibly lend a hand by blockading the island.

The Maltese envoy concluded both tasks to the letter, but due to the fact that his ships were in a bad state of repair due to damages suffered during the battle of Aboukir Nelson directed Britain's allies, the Portuguese, to undertake the blockade in his stead.

On 3 October the British Ambassador in Naples received a dispatch from the State's Foreign Secretary. The contents were very brief and to the point:

> "His Majesty does not entertain any idea of acquiring the sovereignty of Malta."

Nelson apparently angered at his country's blunt refusal, sent an immediate reply in return.

> "Any expense should be incurred, rather than leave Malta remain in the hands of the French."

On 4 October, Nelson directed Alexander Ball, the captain of HMS Alexander, to sail for Malta in order to reinforce the Portuguese in the blockade, but although this strategy hemmed in the French, it failed to draw them out from inside Valletta. The backing of an allied power was a thing the Maltese could not do without now. What had been expected from the Neapolitan King was not forthcoming, and their country's freedom came first. So they turned to Britain for protection, and on 7 February 1799 they solicited King Ferdinand's consent to their request concerning the protection of their island by the British.

With permission finally granted, and Lord Nelson informed by a Maltese delegation to regard Malta as having been placed under his country's protection, action was expected to be taken immediately. But the French sat tight behind the formidable walled harbour defences and were determined to withstand a long siege. At this point in time even the Russians were prepared to take over the island at the first indication that the inhabitants were willing. The appearance of a French naval squadron in the western Mediterranean led to the temporary withdrawal of British warships from their blockading duties off Malta, as they sailed westwards to oppose this threat.

This turn in events was the cause of great concern to the Maltese as the French regained control of the waters around the Island. However towards the end of June a Capt. Dixon returned with four ships to resume the blockade and Ball's fleet sailed in shortly afterwards to strengthen Dixon's small force.

Early in August a Royal dispatch from the King of Naples reached Capt. Ball, informing him of his new post as Malta's first Governor.

Valletta proved to be as formidable as its founder and it was starvation that finally forced General Vaubois to capitulate on 5 September 1800. With the siege uplifted, the Maltese congress dissolved and all fortifications were manned by British troops.

The Royal Fleet lined the Grand Harbour, but Malta was not yet a British acquisition. Britain, initially, was inclined to denounce possession of the island. Its aid agreement was limited to the liberation of the inhabitants from under the French, so it was not prepared to commit itself any further. But the Maltese were determined to remain under the British crown, and in 1801 they presented a petition to the King through an influential Maltese delegation.

> "The Maltese have already began to experience the advantages and enjoy the happiness of being governed by His Britannic Majesty."

Although the British continued to occupy the island it was not until 1814 that Malta definitely came under British sovereignty by the terms of the Treaty of Paris.

Geographically located at the southern tip of Europe, Malta was always of great strategic importance. This has often been claimed by seafarers who, while traversing the Middle Sea, sought the island's indispensability as a stepping stone and a haven halfway to any coast in the Mediterranean basin. Prehistoric finds strengthen these facts, showing that this practice was in existence even in ancient times. But the island's importance as a stage station gained greater significance shortly after 1869, when the Suez Canal became operational, linking the Mediterranean with the Far East. The British Admiralty, aware of Malta's ever growing potential as a Central Mediterranean 'springboard', decided to build a proper ship repair yard. It had already established a naval base on the island precisely where the Knights used to berth their vessels before them and a dry dock was constructed inside the innermost end of where today is known as Dockyard Creek.

Steam engines were by that time outmoding sails and coal was indispensable to shipping. Progress on such an international scale was to affect Malta very favourably, and soon a coal station was brought into operation on the island. Shipping inside the Grand Harbour increased, boosting trade ashore.

By the turn of the century other notable events took place in Malta, but what is actually being dealt with here is the Island's outstanding aviation activities and other related occurrences. The first of these was an air balloon, brought along by a platoon of British Royal Engineers in 1904. However, it was Europe's political ferment that finally influenced Malta's future in aviation most of all.

Though more than half a century had passed since hostilities were brought to a stop after the Crimean upheaval, affairs in Europe were still unstable, straining under the influence of political differences to an extent that the threat of a world war became a reality.

At this time the airplane, the greatest invention of the century, was fast gaining in popularity, though, few, if any, could have foreseen its future potential as an instrument of war, one that, despite some changes to mankind, was to bring so much grief and destruction to this world of ours.

The spark that finally triggered off the First World War broke out in Serbia on 28 June 1914, when the Archduke of Austria and his wife were brutally assassinated while on a tour of the province.

In Britain the Royal Flying Corps was at the time just a little over two years old. Formed on 13 April 1912 the RFC consisted of four elements, a Naval and a Military wing, a Flying School and an aircraft factory at Farnborough.

On 1 July 1914, the Naval wing ceased to form part of the RFC and emerged as an independent military force, giving birth to the Royal Naval Air Service (RNAS), as if in preparation for the coming conflict.

Malta was spared the hardships that followed as Germany came to grips with France, pulling Great Britain into the conflict. Shortly afterwards Italy picked sides, and the war spread, engulfing most of Europe.

In 1918, however, Malta did contribute to the construction of the most modern instrument of the war, the airplane, but this was not its first glimpse of this ingenious flying machine, although positively one of the greatest chapters in the island's wartime aviation history.

Since before the war exploits like those of Henry Farman, Louis Bleriot, Glenn Curtis and others like them were being read about locally. Newspapers of the day kept their readers well informed of these great ventures and a few aviation-minded individuals, influenced by these events, aired their views with unusual enthusiasm.

A letter, suggesting the use of an aircraft to fly mail between Malta and Syracuse, appeared in the Malta Herald of 16 April 1914.

Another letter, signed 'Up to Date', appearing in the same newspaper on the 22nd, did not leave 'Look Ahead', who had signed the previous one, wanting. This individual wrote that the British Mediterranean Fleet should have its own aircraft based in Malta. He went as far as to quote, 'Our fleet without a plane service is plainly behind times.' An enthusiast's wish? With only two months prior to the breakout of hostilities it seems retrospect, to be more of a foretelling.

On 12 February 1915 HMS Ark Royal, the first British naval ship fitted with a 139 feet long flight deck forward of the bridge, as well as hangar space capable of accommodating ten parked aircraft, called at the Grand Harbour while en route to Gallipoli.

(In April 1937, a new carrier was launched and given the same name with the result that the original vessel, which was still in service for experimental aircraft work, was renamed HMS Pegasus to make way for the new arrival.)

Setting sail for the Dardanelles the ship had on board a full compliment of ten aircraft, of which six were two-seat single-engine fold-wing type floatplanes. These aircraft were:

Two Wight Type A.1 Improved Navy planes, Admiralty Nos. 172 and 173; pushers with 200-h.p. engines. Three Sopwith Admiralty Types.807, and a 200-h.p. Short Admiralty 135 Seaplane, No. 136, of which the ship had only one on board. The other four were single-seat Sopwith S.S.2 Tabloid Tractor Scouts powered by 80-h.p. Gnome engines, intended to be flown off from the forward located flight deck of the Ark Royal.

From records held at the Public Records Office, under reference

HMS Ark Royal inside Grand Harbour in February 1915 during it's few days' stop at Malta in transit to Gallipoli.

One of the first aircraft to appear in Malta on board 'Ark Royal', this Short-200h.p. Admiralty 135 Seaplane No. 136 was also the first aircraft to fly over the Grand Harbour on 13 Feb. 1915.

AIR 1/726/137/2, were noted these excerpts related to the first and second flights recorded in Malta.

Flt. Cdr. C.F. Kilner with Lt. Park, RNVR, as on 13 February 1915 flight-tested Short No. 136 over Harbour for 15 minutes.

Some 60 years later, the late Sir Hannibal Scicluna wrote in the Times of Malta that this event was during a flight sponsored by one of Britain's leading newspapers, The Daily Mail. But in a letter dated 39 August 1979, sent to me by Mr Iain MacKie, the newspaper's Assistant Managing Editor, there was this explanation:

> "Although the Daily Mail has had a traditional involvement with pioneering aircraft projects, I regret that we can find no trace of our having any part in the mention. Our reference library staff has made a careful search of our files, and I am sure that the event would have been recorded if the company had been involved in such a way."

On 14 February, a Sopwith Type 897 was test flown next. The pilot, Lt. Garnett, had with him Plt. Off. Marchand as passenger. While taxing around for a favourable upwind take-off position, a float hit the top of a wave and broke right off with the result that the aircraft turned over instantly, taking Marchand down with it. Garnett managed to pull his passenger out safely, from where both were shortly afterwards picked up by a passing boat. The fuselage and engine of the stricken machine were later salvaged. The next day the "Ark Royal" was en route to its destination.

To assist its Turkish ally, Germany began to send some of its submarines to the Mediterranean; the first group were sent by railway to Pola in March 1915 and in April the U-Boats began to pass through the Straits of Gibraltar.

The first indication that anything unusual was happening came to the attention of the British on 25 May, when the battleship Triumph was torpedoed and sunk by a submarine, followed two days later by the sinking of another battleship,the Majestic.

On 25 April, U-21 steamed from the Ems to inaugurate the launching of an expansion program intended for German submarine activities.

Proceeding on a bearing that brought it to the North of Scotland the U-boat was navigated on a southerly course down the North Atlantic and then passed through the Straits of Gibraltar into the Mediterranean reaching Cattaro on 13 May.

Completing a seven-day refit at this base U-21 resumed with the next leg of its experimental journey to the Dardanelles, sinking the two British battleships along the way, within two days of each another.

The success of this venture was the encouragement the German admirals needed to transfer more of their submarine force into the Mediterranean by this route following the sinking of the 'Lusitania'. By the end of 1915 some fifteen enemy U-boats were operating in the Central Mediterranean, taking a heavy toll of allied shipping.

The loss of the battleships alarmed the British no end they took immediate action to counter this threat to their Mediterranean shipping.

Limiting these movements in the region was their first precautionary measure. Then the Senior Officer Malta suggested basing a small airship on Malta to scout for the underwater lurking submarines. But the Admiralty was of the opinion that a seaplane, or a flying boat, would prove more effective in patrolling the region.

ASV (Air to Sea Vessel) was then still a thing of the future and human sight alone served as the crudest form of early warning system against this underwater threat. A lookout, equipped with binoculars, was posted to detect the vee-shaped patterns of moving ripples on a calm sea, stirred by anything sliding close to the surface of the water, or foam-flecked streamers left in the wake of a periscope, signs that were easier to detect from a low flying aircraft. So, in an effort to stem the infiltration and activity of the enemy U-boats in the Mediterranean, the Admiralty decided to establish an air base in Malta.

The Lords of the Admiralty advised the Senior Naval Officer on the Island, via Squadron Commander Bowhill, who was on his way to Mesopotamia, to select a site suitable for a base from where this type of aircraft could operate.

An area on the southern shore of M'Xlokk Bay was chosen and the Admiralty's approval for work to proceed with all possible haste on the seaplane base was received towards the end of January 1916. To further emphasize this urgency material, which had already been dispatched elsewhere from Britain, was diverted to the island while it was still en route to its destination. So work on the new station, under the auspices of the Royal Naval Air Service, began in earnest.

A slipway was constructed and the first seaplane shed took shape inside Kalafrana Bay, close to the Naval Torpedo Depot, where a repair station was already established, and by July the base was operational.

Aerial view of Kalafrana Seaplane Base. Constructed in 1916 this has today been obliterated by the Kalafrana Freeport.

Wyndham Levi Grech, first ever Maltese pilot who flew into combat on the Western Front during the First World War.

With the completion of these new facilities towards the end of the month five Curtis H4 Small America flying boats were shipped from Felixstowe. American built aircraft with which the RNAS had been equipping since the breakout of hostilities in Europe.

Personnel consisted of seven Flying, and two Warrants Officers as well as a group of mechanics under the command of Flight Commander J. D. Maude.

Shortly afterwards aircraft were airborne patrolling for enemy U-boats along the main shipping routes in seas around Malta.

That same month, albeit far off Malta's shores, the first of its sons was flying into combat for the British on the Western Front.

Under the British Rule students graduating from the Malta University needed to proceed to Britain for their final examination, and Wyndham Levy Grech was one of these promising young men.

Born in 1899 to Mr and Mrs. T. Levy Grech, Wyndham graduated in 1913 with honour in Doctor of Laws. Shortly afterwards he was in the UK where he succeeded in passing his final examinations, entitling him to be called to the Bar at Gray's Inn.

At the outbreak of the First World War Dr Grech, who was still in Britain at the time, enlisted into the Army.

In March of 1916, with the rank of Second Lt., Grech volunteered to join the Royal Flying Corps (R.F.C).

For an officer to be accepted for service in the RFC he had to be medically fit. Furthermore he had to have the consent of the appropriate military authority. But most important of all was the presentation of a certificate from the Royal Aero Club.

On 8 April 1916, Dr Grech joined No. 2 School of Aviation where, due to the crude and fragile aircraft of the times, and lack of safety measures available to trainees, casualties were high during training. However, Dr Grech succeeded in passing all his tests with flying colours and was granted his aviator's certificate number 7293. A month later he was flying with No. 7 Reserve Squadron.

Prior to being posted for active service, Dr Grech was given enough leave to visit his family in Malta.

As soon as he returned to the UK, Wyndham was on 9 August posted with 42 Squadron in France where, on 11 September, he shot down his first enemy aircraft in air combat on the Western Front.

While flying on a sortie Grech's aircraft was hit by return fire, killing his air gunner instantly and seriously wounding him. However Grech managed to fly his damaged machine back to base.

While recovering from his injuries Grech was posted with 75 (Home Defence) Squadron until he was on 22 February 1918 transferred to the 7th Brigade in Italy as a test pilot.

In May of that same year he was transferred to 98 Squadron from where he gradually found himself posted at HQ 14 Wg. in Italy in December 1918, when hostilities were near their end.

Mentioned in dispatches on several occasions, Dr Wyndham Levy Grech finally received the Italian Government's title of "Cavaliere della Corona d'Italia" on 1 April 1920.

Serviceable flying boats were intended to be kept anchored to moorings inside Kalafrana Bay, protected by a man-made breakwater stretching out from the shore to the eastern side of the entrance into the bay. However, it was found unreliable during the winter months, particularly when the sea was at its worst, stirred to mountainous waves by the south-east gregale winds, towards which the opening of the bay faces. During these periods aircraft were moored inside the bay opposite to that of Kalafrana, where it was far better protected by the Delimara Point promontory.

In March 1917, three Short 184s arrived at Kalafrana to cover losses sustained during the previous year, but by this time operational experience with the H4 had proven the aircraft's worth as a U-boat hunter.

In April Commodore Murray F. Sueter was appointed to organize the operation of British aircraft from Malta, including those at the recently established Otranto Station. He dispatched an immediate request for some more of the H4s, but partly due to the difficulties encountered in producing the machine in enough quantities, and the Admiralty's need for all the H4 to patrol over home waters, Sueter's request was turned down. This concerned the Commodore, for the safety of British shipping in the Central Mediterranean was his responsibility. The protection of these vessels depended on the best aircraft type available, which he lacked as no better substitute had yet been found to replace the H4. Somehow a solution had to be found.

Meanwhile earlier that same year Sqdn. Cdr. J.C. Porte of the RNAS had assisted Glenn Curtis with the construction of the Curtis H12. This was a larger version of the H4 with which to attempt a transatlantic crossing prior to the breakout of the First World War, from which he succeeded in developing the Felixstowe F.2A.

Commodore Sueter, one of the pioneer founders of the RNAS, informed of this development, proposed that provision be made for the building of this aircraft in Malta.

The Admiralty's approval to proceed with the plan was given in June, and the Dockyard Construction Unit was immediately established so that work in the building of the first twelve F.3 Patrol Tractor Biplane Flying Boats ordered under contract No. A.S. 14835 (BR86) from number N4310 to N4321 Malta Dockyard could begin.

Two small Italian FBA two-seat flying boats had meanwhile arrived as reinforcements on 27 June. In August, another three FBAs were transferred from RNA Station Otranto to supplement the six Short 184s that had arrived to make up losses so that more frequent patrols could be mounted for the ever growing number of enemy U-boats. There were now therefore five FBAs at Malta, four of which were numbered N1975 to N1978.

A delay in the shipment of cawdey, mahogany and Canadian elm for a while held up the construction of the Felixstowe flying boats. When the material was finally delivered to HM Dockyard in January 1918 it was unloaded at Boathouse Wharf, at the inner end of French Creek, and stored at the aircraft propeller establishment which had been built there.

When the prototype of the Felixstowe F.3 (N64) was first flown in February of 1917 it was powered by two 320 h.p. Sunbeam Cossack engines, but the power plants fitted to later models, including those built in Malta, were similar to those on the F.2A.

(The Rolls Royce 'Eagle' VIII model engine was capable of developing 345 h.p., but the Curtis H4 was powered by two 100 h.p. Anzanis.)

(The late Mr Giuliano, ex-HM Dockyard Chief Constructor, was told about all this by the man responsible of the Maltese carpenters working on the F.3s, Mr Spiteri Gonzi. During manufacture fish glue was the sole agent used between surfaces, before finally clinching them with specially made bronze nails. Wood was afterwards liberally painted over with burnt linseed oil as water repellant.)

The launching of the first Maltese built F.3, N4310, was held up due to a delay in the delivery of engines, but on 18 March 1918, 'Melita', as this flying boat was named, was afloat inside French Creek. From HM Dockyard the aircraft was then towed to Kalafrana where flight tests were carried out on the 22nd of the month.

At this time, aware of the flying boat's limited flying range, the C-in-C proposed the introduction of kite balloons for escort duties with the Mediterranean Fleet (i.e. watching for movement of enemy U-boats was the duty of observers inside gondolas lifted by the balloon which was attached by a cable to a warship.)

Duly approved, it was suggested that the unit be based in Malta. On 7 November three technical officers, under the command of Wg. Cdr.

The launching of the first Malta Dockyard-built Felixstowe F.3 flying boat, N4310; 20 March 1918.

H. Delacombe, were sent from Great Britain to find a suitable site on the island. They had to stay on there to supervise the erection of sheds. On 21 November, enough material for the construction of six sheds, large enough to accommodate just as many gas-filled balloons, arrived from Britain.

By the end of the year the nucleus of a Kite Balloon Squadron was formed at the head of Lazzaretto Creek, Ta' Xbiex. Balloon shelters and a gas-making plant began to take shape, as manpower was increased with the arrival of 100 ratings.

Meanwhile towards the beginning of the year it had become obvious that enemy U-boat activity in the Mediterranean was getting out of hand. In an effort to counter this threat, a new plan of operations was drawn up, and submitted to the Board of the Admiralty on 25 January 1918. The re-organization program decreed that the Mediterranean be divided into several strategic areas, from where air units could easily be directed to threatened spheres, Malta, Italy, the Aegean, Port Said and eventually Gibraltar, were to be self maintained bases. Equipped with their own personnel and aircraft repair shops, all said stations were to be controlled from Malta.

The four aircraft carriers proposed for the Mediterranean were small as carriers go, each carrying only four seaplanes. HMS Manxman, which had been commissioned in 1916, was the first to arrive in Malta and was later joined by 'Engadine', 'Riviera' and 'Vindex'. These were to serve, as mobile bases for aircraft to operate from, where shore based machines were unable to patrol due to their limited flying range. All aircraft brought to the island were to be allocated at Kalafrana for redistribution, and the main stockpile of stores and equipment was to remain in Malta.

On 22 February 1918, the Board of the Admiralty passed the expansion program directive and work started in earnest. Orders for an increase in aircraft production were soon relayed to the construction of the F.3 at Boathouse Wharf, with the result that the output of the flying boats was given immediate priority over every other type of work inside HM Dockyard. Thirty-eight machines additional to the original order of 12 raised the number of aircraft to 50.

At Kalafrana, the tests on the F.3 had meanwhile proved unsatisfactory. Sluggishness in the aircraft's performance was found to be due to it being overweight in excess of some two hundred pounds to the aircraft's specific 5.5 tons.

Initially it was suspected that the wood might have absorbed more moisture than expected, an inherent drawback that in later years led to the development of metal hulls.

According to Mr Spiteri Gonzi, via Mr Giuliano, when this possibility was eliminated, difficulties in tracing the cause forced local authorities to call in the aid of an expert from Britain.

A keen examination ensued and the conclusion reached at was that the cutting was being overemphasized by the builders. They were advised to keep all measurements down to the nearest inch with the result that delivery of the first F.3 was not effected until 24 April 1918. However, with work at the Dockyard Construction Unit in full swing, N4311 was on that same date also delivered to Kalafrana.

Delivery of the next three serials, N4312, N4313, and N4314 was effected at fifteen- day intervals during May, with N4312 delivered to Kalafrana on 1st May.

The next four, N4315/16/17/18, were during June/July 1918 all allocated to Otranto.

N4316 is recorded as being the first casualty, as it was wrecked by August 1918, although it was not struck off charge.

N4319/20/21, delivered to Kalafrana by June 1918, N4320 was shortly afterwards allocated to Otranto.

With the exception of N4317 and N4318, which were taken on charge by 268 Squadron at Kalafrana, all of the remainder went to 267 Squadron.

The next eight serials, N4322-N4329, were not allotted.

The seaplane station at Kalafrana underwent a full-scale expansion operation with the scope of carrying out the erection and repair of aircraft there. Storage space, however, had to remain as well to accommodate more machines as the number of seaplanes for use on the carriers and in reserve, was to be 36. This stirred up the demand for additional labour, and shortly afterwards it was proposed to recruit the service of Maltese youths, and training them as air-crafts-men.

In March, 778 Maltese ratings were enlisted into the RNA Service and based at Fort St Angelo. This scheme was received with great acclaim, and a training camp for Maltese recruits was established at Spinola, on the site that is today occupied by the hotel Malta Hilton.

These Maltese enlisted in the RAF as AC IIs for foreign service with Capt. Attilio Amato Gauci, Lt. Count Francis Sant Cassia and Lt. Philip Manduca of the King's Own Malta Regiment responsible for disciplinary and training purposes.

(According to records left by the late Lt. Philip Manduca, who was then Officer Commanding of Maltese RAF troops overseas, at the time of the Armistice, Maltese airmen were serving at Otranto, Taranto, Brindisi, Stavros, Imbros, Corfu, Constantinople, Mudros and Alexandria; all British bases.)

At this time antagonism and lack of cooperation between the RNAS and the RFC stirred up a great ferment within their sphere. The British High Command, as of 1 April 1918, decided to amalgamate the two, and place them under one command, which gave birth to the Royal Air Force. Consequently as of that date the Malta Seaplane Station, The HM Dockyard F.3 Construction Unit and the No. 1 Kite Balloon Base, each previously operating as a separate unit, became the Malta Group.

Towards the end of May the Kite Balloon Base was nearing completion. Personnel had also increased to 24 Officers and 120 ratings while three sloops, HMS Snapdragon, HMS Clematis and HMS Penstemon were provided for the embarkation of the balloons for at sea operations.

As has already been explained, in wintertime, bad weather conditions made flying off from Marsaxlokk Bay difficult, and at times impossible to execute.

Seaplanes were kept securely moored, protected by the Delimara promontory, or locked away in hangars at Kalafrana.

Inevitably, while these storms lasted, restricting flying from the bay, anti-submarine patrols were affected. Consequently the enemy roamed at will in territorial waters, causing the British so much concern that they decided to ship two DeHavilland 9As to the island to supplement the flying boats for emergency purposes. These were fitted with special large area type wings and 'PV' floatation gear, an improvisation for flying over open waters should they have to take over patrols from the flying boats.

With no airfield readily available for these two land-based aircraft, wartime exigencies led the Air Ministry to have part of the Marsa Sports Ground temporarily improvised as one. Lengthwise, east to west, the centre section was the area picked for use as an airfield as the boundaries were known to turn into quagmires in wintertime.

To further extend the strip, wooden planking was used to cover over those sections of the perimeter ditch at the eastern end of the strip.

Personnel to supervise the operation of this new station, designated No. 582 Flight, were provided from Kalafrana, and by late August 280 ratings and 22 officers were integrated in the flight with hangars erected near to the Ground's Pavilion, which the RAF used for administrative purpose.

Meanwhile the RAF had spread further afield on the island. A Stores Park was established at Sa' Maison to handle and supervise airforce material distribution in the Mediterranean. In July some 700 Maltese from the training camp at Spinola were certified ready for active service and 250 were immediately drafted for overseas duties.

During August a split-up in aerial forces was made at Kalafrana bringing into formation two separate units. One, No. 268 Squadron, comprised of two Flights, Nos. 433 and 434, was formed to separate the floatplanes from the other craft, and post them under one unit.

Space at Kalafrana became limited due to a number of Sunbeams that had to be kept on hand for the specific use of the carriers. No. 288 Squadron had to be relieved of eight of its original force of 12 Sunbeams. No. 207 Squadron was formed shortly afterwards to incorporate the first batch of twelve Malta built F.3s, N4310 to N4321, that consisted of 360 and 363 Flights. But this squadron soon found itself with 7 F.3's short. Four were transferred to the Adriatic, two had to be beached for repairs, and one was a complete write-off.

By September work on the second contract of F.3's was at an advanced stage with the first deliveries made later in the month.

Nine F.3's, N4360/61/62/63/64/65/67/68/69, were delivered to Kalafrana during October 1918. The following month these were all in transit to the Middle East with 15 Group.

The first F.3, N4366, which was delivered to Kalafrana in the New Year, went to 270 Squadron at Alexandria on 6 August.

Two "Certificates of Transfer" show that N4370 and N4371 were delivered to Kalafrana on 14 and 15 May respectively. These were most probably followed by N4372 that was on 3 July 1919 on transit to 270 Squadron at Alexandria, returning to Kalafrana, and 268 Squadron, on 27 August of that same year.

Details available relating to serials N4373 to N4387 is very sparse, hardly anything could be found.

Shortly afterwards, due to a noticeable decrease in U-boat activity in the Mediterranean, this final order was ratified with the result that N4388 to N4397 were immediately cancelled. So, from the original batch of 38 flying boats, N4360 to N4397, only 28 remained.

Additional units were established during October and November and the Malta Group was re-designated to No. 17 (MALTA) Wg. under the administration of the Mediterranean District Headquarters. At this time, the Wing's Malta-based units consisted of a Stores Park, 267 and 268 Squadrons, No. 562 Flight, a Construction Unit, the Spinola

Felixstowe N4370 of 267 Squadron. One of the last batch of 28 Malta-built F.3s under inspection at Kalafrana's south slip.

Training Camp and a Repair Depot, including the No. 1 Kite Balloon base.

With the approach of Christmas the last of the second and final order of 28 F.3's, N4360 to N4388, were nearing completion, and eventually brought the total number of Malta-built Felixstowe to 40.

For obscure reasons, the Marsa Sports Ground never again figured in British military plans for airfields after that one time in the First World War. Was it too valuable a sports ground for the British to spoil, when better sites were available at higher elevations?

The MSG is only feet above sea level, surrounded by high ground, made even higher still in later years by the addition of residential buildings everywhere.

This might have made the USAAF in 1943 shy away from it, when no more available space on which to construct airfields in Malta remained. Whatever the reason behind this, the fact that the MSG was kept in its original state increased its historical aviation value, particularly when in the winter of 1918, shortly after the cessation of hostilities, an unexpected visitor landed there one late December evening.

(This was to prove a great historical event as it marked the first transit of a military aircraft through the island while flying between Europe and the North African mainland. – Author.)

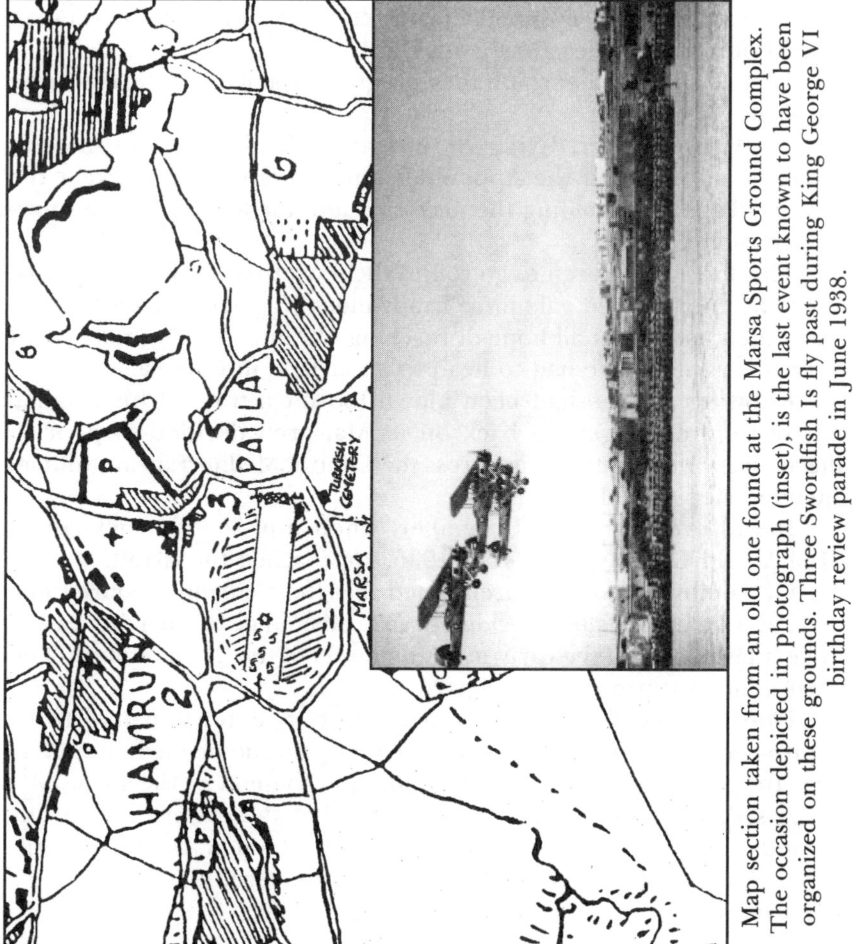

Map section taken from an old one found at the Marsa Sports Ground Complex. The occasion depicted in photograph (inset), is the last event known to have been organized on these grounds. Three Swordfish Is fly past during King George VI birthday review parade in June 1938.

Major A.S.C. Maclaren intended to start his flight to India on 8 December, but mechanical troubles, developing after some fifteen minutes flying, grounded the aircraft until the 13th.

The weather was against Major Maclaren and his group from the outset as well. From Martlesham Heat they flew almost blindly for nearly three hours, until they eventually managed to land safely at Bergues, an airfield only a few miles away from Dunkirk.

After that the farther south they progressed across France, the worse the weather became.

On 19 December, flying on a bearing leading to Otranto, as Maclaren approached the Appenines atmospheric pressure kept the Handley Page from gaining the necessary altitude to fly over the snow-capped mountains.

This forced Maclaren to go round them over the Straits of Messina, where he encountered gale force headwinds. This detour consumed so much fuel that he lost all hope of reaching Otranto. Furthermore night was closing in, and he had to head to an airfield in Catania.

Knowing that he had been blown too far astray off his original course to attempt getting back on it, Maclaren decided to plan an alternative route, southwards, across the Central Mediterranean, with an intended stop at Malta.

It was evening of 20 December, when h.p. V/1500 nicknamed 'H.M.A. Old Carthusian", serial J1936, approached the island.

On landing Major Maclaren noted that the elements favoured him here, and he immediately decided to take advantage of the fair weather while it lasted. So, in the early morning hours of the 21 December, "Old Carthusian' was prepared to depart.

Due to a westerly take-off, a temporary extension had to be improvised so that the heavy aircraft could gain the needed altitude to clear the administration pavilion standing at the end of the strip.

A section of the rubble perimeter wall at the eastern end of the grounds, near to where the Turkish cemetery is located, was temporarily removed to enable Major Maclaren to clear the Ground's Pavilion by a safety margin.

Chapter II

Armistice

Wars end – Rundown – The Fairey – Uprising – British Forces – Last of the F.3s – Hal Far – Opening ceremony – 481 Flight – Air Display – Defence of Malta Scheme Carrier borne aircraft – Air disasters – Imperial A/Ws – Archbishop's mishap – Air flying; a hazard – Visitors – Singapore G-EBUP – Air Pageant

With the approach of winter of 1918 the end of the war was immnent. Germany, at the brink of a major disaster, on 8 November decided to send an armistice commission to Compiegere where Marshall Foch received them in his railway coach, and offered them the severest terms ever demanded of a great power. The Germans protested, but Kaiser Wilhem had fled to the Netherlands, and on 11 November, the new government, given no other option, finally signed the armistice.

Shortly after hostilities came to an end Britain began to reduce her military strength in the Mediterranean. By the late spring of 1919, in Malta, 562 (anti-submarine) Flight, the Kite Balloon Squadron, the Spinola Training Camp, the Stores Park and the Construction Unit were all disbanded. The rest of 17 (Malta) Wg. was then split-up, reducing 267 and 268 Squadrons to one Flight each, and before Autumn had set in only one aircraft carrier remained in the Mediterranean.

In October 268 Squadron was disbanded, leaving 267 Squadron's single Flight with a disposal depot and workshops, while a meteorological station was set up. These dispositions, including the seaplane carrier HMS Engadine, which was in 1920 replaced by HMS Ark Royal, were

One of 267 Squadron's F.3s being dragged up Kalafrana's South slip shortly after an emergency landing inside the bay due to a windmill-driven pump failure.

kept stationed on the island to form part of the RAF Mediterranean Command. This was the smallest of the British RAF overseas commands with offices for AOC Air Commodore Charles P. Samson. CMG., 050, AFC., and his Senior Officer, Sqdn. Ldr. Harry F.A. Gordon ORE, in Valletta. At the same time the headquarters of the Mediterranean Fleet was also located at Malta.

Meanwhile, in accordance with the policy of discarding the F.3, of which quite a few were modified to F5s, 267 Squadron re-equipped with the F.2A, that was superior to the former. Some changes, however, had also given the F.2A a new face-lift. Horn balanced aerelons of constant chord were fitted to the flying boats to relieve the strain formerly experienced by pilots on long flights. Old glazed cabins were removed, serving a double purpose: to improve the aircraft performance and the view of those inside it. However, an inherent drawback remained where the failure of windmill-driven pumps frequently caused emergency landings. These often happened when crews failed to immediately operate the handpump installed in the aircraft to transfer fuel from the hull into the engines in emergencies.

No. 267's F.3s parked ashore in line astern at Kalafrana's South slip c.1919/20.

At that time these flying boats were all given individual names associated with astronomy: AQUILA, MERCURY, SATURN, SIRIUS, VENUS and NEPTUNE.

During the next few years these aircraft were operated on numerous naval and other military duties: aerial gunnery, torpedo spotting, bombing of floating targets and photographic reconnaissance.

In October 1920 command of 267 Squadron passed from Sqdn. Ldr. E. Osmond to Sqdn. Ldr. W.G. Sitwell who was in May 1921 succeeded by Sqdn. Ldr. P.A. Shepherd.

In December 1920, shortly after Sitwell took over command of the station, eight Fairey IIIc floatplanes arrived to suppliment the F5s. These were N9454, N9465, N9494, and N9567 to N9571.

The year 1921 was relatively calm, the only activities consisting of Army and Navy combined exercises in which the aircraft of 267 Squadron were always involved as this was the only RAF land-based unit in the Mediterranean at that time.

In spring of 1922 Felixstowe N4089, NEPTUNE, was shipped to Malta, assembled at Kalafrana, and earmarked for an experimental long-range flight between the island and Gibraltar. This was first attempted in April of that year, but was abandoned when bad weather forced the pilot to descend in the sea at Bona, in Algeria.

Engine failure caused another fruitless attempt made in the same flying boat on 22 May. Subsequently NEPTUNE was four days later lost at sea in a storm while it was loaded on a lighter under tow by HMS Spear.

In autumn 1922 internal political differences between Turkey and Greece developed into open hostilities, forcing Britain to intervene and strengthen her forces in the region.

On 22 September HMS Argus called at Malta for the first time, while en route to the troubled area. Before departing, five of 267 Squadron's Fairey IIIcs were embarked on the carrier, and another was taken on by HMS Revenge, leaving only the F.2As at Malta.

Group Capt. Bigsworth assumed command of the Mediterranean district on 12 March 1923, with Sqdn. Ldr. A.J. Miley taking over command of 267 Squadron.

Undeterred by the failures of the previous year, the squadron's personnel organized a further attempt to fly to Gibraltar and back. This time, however, two flying boats, N4085, NEPTUNE II, and N4086, SIRIUS, were to be used; the flight was under the command of Grp. Cpt.

A Fairey IIIC lands inside Kalafrana bay c.1922.

Disquiet between Greeks and Turks in 1922 led the British to embark equipment from Kalafrana in HMS Argus to strengthen their forces in the Aegean.

Bigsworth. Flt. Lt. Victor R. Scriven, who had piloted N4089 in May of the previous year, was to fly NEPTUNE II, while SIRIUS was to be flown by Flt. Lt. H. Stewart. During the flight, the two F.2As were to stop at selected refuelling staging points along the North African coast.

Early in the morning of 11 June, the two flying boats lifted off from Kalafrana, enroute to their first staging point, Bizerta, in Tunisia.

With the outward-bound flight a success, the two F.2As departed from Gibraltar early in the morning of 16 June.

Following an overnight stop at Oran, the two flying boats set off for Algiers in the morning, but, apparently inheriting its forebear's rotten luck, NEPTUNE II hit some sunken wreckage during take off which smashed a hole in its hull.

Arriving at Algiers it was immediately drawn up on a yacht slipway, where it took French mechanics two days to patch up the damage. On 20 June the two aircraft refuelled and departed for Bona where they arrived at mid-afternoon.

Nearly four hours later SIRIUS set off for Bizerta while NEPTUNE remained overnight at Bona, joining the former at mid-day of the 21st.

While preparing for the final leg to Malta one of NEPTUNE's

Grp. Capt. Bigsworth arriving at Kalafrana in "SIRIUS" lands inside Kalafrana bay.

engines refused to start, and the two aircraft remained overnight at Bizerta.

The next day SIRIUS, with Gp. Cpt. Bigsworth at the controls, despite some take-off difficulties, pressed on towards Malta, reaching the island that same day, having covered a flying distance of 2,052 nautical miles in 35 hours and 4 minutes.

Meanwhile NEPTUNE, encountering the same off shore blowing wind problems SIRIUS had overcome, in taking avoiding action over some trees while flying inland, the pilot turned out of wind, the aircraft lost height, crashed, and was written off.

The number of serviceable aircraft that 267 Squadron had on strength at that time were four flying boats and two Fairey IIICs. However, the Felixstowe, having already been certified as obsolescent, were in July of that year all withdrawn.

At that time, with the advanced development in aircraft carriers, more airplanes could be accommodated on board. This resulted that the original storage space at Kalafrana was shortly to become insufficient to either accommodate, or shelter, both the land-based and the ship-bourne machines, the latter deposited there at intervals by their ships to be collected at later dates, or when the necessity arose.

The British had been considering using Malta as a staging post for the transit of civil and military aircraft between the Continent and Africa since 1919. Consequently, with the advent of land-planes on board their carriers in the Mediterranean, the Air Ministry was interested in establishing an airfield on the island to compliment the Kalafrana Seaplane Station.

Early in January 1921, the Civil Aviation Department sent a Capt. Blandy to Malta for the specific purpose of choosing a suitable site for an aerodrome. The Daily Telegraph later reported what Blandy said:

> "When a regular service is established, London letters ..." for initially all airlines were at that time intended to convey mail, "... will be delivered here within twenty-four hours."

In Malta he had promised local authorities that he intended to include in his report the mailing difficulties the island was experiencing, and go as far as to suggest to the Air Ministry to consider the question of an air service between Malta to Sicily.

So, peacetime conditions and the world's general development in aviation generally, contributed not a little to the Air Ministry's decision to establish an aerodrome in Malta.

During the First World War Hal Far, after ages of comparative obscurity to the rest of the island, was saved from complete oblivion by a local publication, Inez Farrugia, an interesting and historical novel written by Antonio Emmanuel Caruana, a distinguished Maltese scholar and historian. Hence, by a literary incident, Hal Far was given prominence in a story which gave rise to the legend of Hassan's caves; today a tourist curiosity.

Again by a freak of fate Hal Far was destined to be given greater prominence, as the centre of an important new aerodrome though, as it was later discovered, Hal Far, from a constructional point of view, was a poor site to have chosen. In Malta solving the problem of finding a suitable piece of land for an airfield may have at first glance offered few favourable prospects. However, the nearness of Hal Far to the seaplane base at Kalafrana, some two miles south of the latter, and overlooking the sea from an elevation of nearly two-hundred feet, could not be ignored.

When early in 1922 work finally began, progress was slow during the winter months of the year, owing to the wetness of the ground. But, by the end of summer the 42 miles of rubble walls and 30,000 cubic yards of hard rock were nearly all torn down or broken up and the site began to rapidly take shape. Mister Xuereb, the building contractor, having a set work program to keep, pushed his labour force to greater efforts. This resulted that by the end of the year he succeeded in neatly spreading and packing the hewn rock, and broken down walls, to have the aerodrome-proposed ground leveled off and ready to be topped by a final layer of soil. Underneath this surface, a storm drainage was laid out by constructing an underground culvert leading down to the sea.

By inauguration day the top soil, reclaimed from the 75 acres of occupied ground, without a single cartload imported from anywhere else on the island, had been spread and levelled off over the 330,000 square yards of ground to a depth of eight inches. Couch grass, a weed with creeping rootstocks (present day turf) was planted on it and this was estimated to require close to a year to effectually bind the 68 acres of surface soil earmarked for flying off, and landing on, of aircraft.

At the opening ceremony on 16 January 1923, Flt. Lt. M.A. Simpson RAF made an address, in which were some very notable narratives:

> "... the progress of aviation generally in the world makes it clear to everyone who has fully studied the course of events, and was gifted with an insight into the future, that the establishment of an aerodrome of unlimited capacity was, in Malta, a work which could not be deferred."
>
> "... In getting this aerodrome the policy has never been confined to the needs of Military aviation: the requirements of civil flying and the prospects of passenger and commercial traffic involving, as they do, the higher interests of the whole community of Malta, have been constantly present. It is not forgotten that Malta may become ... a connecting link in the long chain of landing stations which are a condition precedent to the practical development of communication by air."

Mister Grose, the Superintending Civil Engineer, spoke next, giving praise to all those engaged in the excellent job done. Then, before proceeding with the inauguration ceremony, His Excellency the Governor delivered a splendid and appropriate speech from which these extracts were picked:

... "Few who saw the land where we now stand two years ago would have believed that in that comparatively short time it could have been converted into an aerodrome which, for size and surface condition, compares favourably with those in other countries ...."

... "And if I ask you to look farther ahead into the distant horizon of the future, will you tell me it is only a mirage if I say I can see Malta as a hive Industry. And being recognized as such, in view of her position as an important link connecting Eastern and Western Greater Britain, regarded as the hub from which the spokes of the great wheel of the Empire radiate."

... "These may be only dreams, but without dreams and ideals nothing great can be achieved, and in any case the inauguration of this aerodrome today makes the first chapter of that dream an accomplished fact."

A large Union Jack, to which a rope was attached, was spread on the ground. At the inauguration proper the rope was pulled and the flag

First Air Display over Hal Far airfield, 1923. Three F.3s fly past.

was hoisted up, flattering in the breeze to the strains of the National Anthem, uncovering a green patch of ground on which the name MALTA was made up of small white stones. Barely had the Union Jack reached the top of the flagstaff when three Felixstowe F.2As were seen approaching from the direction of Kalafrana, firing red, white and blue rockets. Then, circling over the crowd, the flying boats proceeded on their course.

On their return fly past a parachute, to which a bouquet of fresh flowers for the Lady Plumer was attached, was dropped from one of the aircraft. The short ceremony concluded those present were soon all astir. Vehicles conveyed the whole company to Kalafrana where, after first treated to another short aerial display over the base by the two Fairey IIICs, the guests were entertained by Air Commodore F. Sampson and other officers of the RAF in their large and beautifully prepared Mess Hall.

Early in August an RAF base was set up at Kalafrana, a self accounting establishment equipped with workshops, a headquarters of its own, and aircraft provided by disbanding 267 Squadron. Actually, this unit originated earlier in the year when HMS Argus embarked the squadron's Fairey IIICs, which were later detached on board the carrier 'Ark Royal' at the Dardanelles.

(With the First World War at an end, the Turks, having been allied with the defeated powers, lost all their now-Turkish territory. Greece surrounded its regions while British and French troops moved into Izmir and Constantinople. But Nationalist leader Mustafa Kemal, an army general, rallied his countrymen in opposition of the treaty.)

In 1922, fearing a full-scale confrontation with the new Turkish army, the British strengthened their forces in the area. However an agreement to ratify the armistice treaty was reached, and in 1923 the Republic of Turkey was established, resulting in the withdrawal of all foreign military forces from the country.

With the cessation of hostilities in Turkey HMS Ark Royal returned to the Mediterranean, just when the regrouping of aircraft on board all carriers had already come into effect, with Flights formed into four separate categories in the 400 series.

Towards the end of August the carrier visited Malta where, on arrival, No. 481 Flight, formed on board the ship on the 1st of the month, was transferred ashore to form the air arm part of the new RAF base.

With the British Mediterranean fleet inside the Grand Harbour and

Mid-1920s summer excursion to Mistra bay, inside St Paul's Bay, for 481 Flight.

Marsaxlokk bay military units on the island began to resettle at their old stations where, that autumn, the first cooperative military exercises were organized, introducing torpedo running, spotting, signaling and message dropping, as well as the bombing of floating targets.

In January 1924, the first Fairey Flycatcher to appear in Malta arrived, shipped from Britain. By the end of the month the land-based biplane fighter, N9672, was erected at Kalafrana. Doubtlessly the aircraft was then transported to Hal Far airfield, due to become operational as a Fleet airplane base, and flown tested from there.

To commemorate the airfield's first anniversary a flying demonstration was organized for 19 February, an aerial display which was to be the first of its kind to be held over the aerodrome.

Altogether different in appearance from present day aerodromes all that was visible then was a flat open stretch of grass covered ground for no buildings had up to that date yet been constructed.

At the invitation of Grp. Cpt. A.Wellesley Bigsworth CMG; DSO; AFC; commanding the RAF (Mediterranean), a large gathering attended at Hal Far airfield in the afternoon of Tuesday, 19 February 1923, to see the first official flight of service aircraft from the new aerodrome.

Among those present were His Excellency Field Marshall Lord Plumer and Lady Plumer. The Lt. Governor, and Mrs Robertson. The

Prime Minister. The Chief Justice, and Mrs. Mercieca. Sir Gerald, and Miss Strickland. Including members of the Legislative Assembly.

Proceedings opened with an inspection of the Fairey Flycatcher. The biplane, fitted with a high-powered Jaguar engine, was intended for operational service from aerodromes or carrier decks.

After various interesting points of the machine had been explained by Sqdn. Ldr. L.H. Slatter. OBE; DFC; DSC; (commanding RAF Base Kalafrana) one of his officers, Flg.Off. E.F. Waring, proceeded to carry out an aerobatic display in the aircraft. Five Fairey IIICs shortly afterwards appeared from the direction of Kalafrana, flying in formation to demonstrate the accepted method of resisting an attack from hostile aircraft. Then the seaplanes split-up and three of them climbed to an altitude of some 5,000 feet, from where they proceeded to enact the part of the enemy about to bomb the aerodrome.

The pilot of the 'Flycatcher' having received a signal that the 'enemy' was approaching was immediately on the alert, ready to intercept them. Soon the evolutions of an aerial battle were demonstrated to an awed audience. The 'enemy', however, proved too strong for the lone defensive biplane, which was shortly afterwards put out of action, to fall out of control in a dizzy spin. The 'enemy' aircraft then concluded the display by bombing the airfield, getting a direct hit on the specially erected canvas construction that went up in flames.

Like the previous year tea was afterwards served to the guests at Kalafrana in the officers' Mess.

Spring was soon giving new life to the land. In mid-April a Naval Review, held at the Marsa Sports Grounds, was brought to a close by a short aerial display over the grounds by naval aircraft.

In the summer a concentration of British naval forces in the Mediterranean led to an increase in local air movements and activities, particularly at Hal Far airfield.

On 7 June 1924 HMS Eagle arrived in Malta, disembarking the 'Seagulls' of 440 Flight at Kalafrana. The "Flycatchers" of 402 Flight, and some "Darts" of 422 Flight, which were flown off the carrier while it was still some miles off the island, were already at Hal Far where two large Besseneau hangars had been erected to one side of the aerodrome for storage purposes.

Throughout the rest of 1924 only on one other occasion was a flying demonstration given over Hal Far airfield and Kalafrana. This was on 10 July, to celebrate the arrival of Sir W.N. Congreve, VC, KCB, who that year succeeded Lord Plumer as Governor.

Towards the end of August a Defence of Malta exercise was put into practice. Launched early with the dawn of the 30th, while HMS Eagle was at sea off Malta, 'Darts' and 'Flycatchers' were flown off the carrier's deck and proceeded on a bearing leading towards the island, on which a mock attack was to be made.

From the Malta side, in cooperation with locally based land forces, aircraft were scrambled from Hal Far and their aircrews directed to the 'enemy's position, who they succeeded in neutralizing.

With the approach of winter the British Mediterranean fleet returned from its third summer cruise and ship borne aircraft began to gather in force at Hal Far. HMS Eagle released 402, 422, and 460 Flights, while 'Hermes' deposited 403 and 441 Flights. These units periodically sailed in the carriers for Fleet exercises involving torpedo attacks, spotting, photography, reconnaissance, Wireless Transmitting exercises, range finding, etc, etc, a precedent that set the pattern for the future function of Hal Far. So, with an aerodrome now available, the Fleet Air Arm put advanced methods of attacks from the air into practice in waters around Malta.

'Darts', flying from Hal Far, practiced torpedo running and dropping inside Marsaxlokk Bay. Flare dropping was also tried, to assess

In August of 1924 a concentration of British naval forces in the Mediterranean led to an increase in air movements and activities at Hal Far.

the efficiency of the equipment when used for observation purposes at night. But these were for obscure reasons postponed, though, night flying was encouraged, and take offs and landings were practiced on numerous occasions.

On 9 December, HMS Eagle returned to the Island, and entered the Grand Harbour. While anchored there six 'Seagulls' of 440 (Fleet Reconnaissance) Flight were flown round to the harbour area from Kalafrana, and descending in the sea they taxied in alongside the ship from where they were winched on board.

The next day, while the 'Eagle' steamed out of the harbour towards Kalafrana, 'Flycatchers' of 402 (Fleet Fighter) Flight were flown from Hal Far on to the carrier's deck. HMS Eagle then anchored inside M'Xlokk Bay where she embarked the complements of the two units taken-on earlier and additional aircraft spares and shortly afterwards the carrier wieghed anchor and departed for the U.K.

The first dummy torpedo attacks by 'Darts' flown from Hal Far were made on 28 November against HMS Queen Elizabeth. In January of 1925 more of these were tried against other naval vessels, on the 4th and 28th of the month respectively. But as the winter receded so did flying activities in general.

On 11 April, an official visit to the Kalafrana RAF base and Hal Far aerodrome by the Lord of the Admiralty three days later resulted in an unexpected Naval Review. The Fleet Air Arm organized this over both stations while his Lordship was being driven from Kalafrana to Hal Far on a tour of inspection.

That year three Italian Air Force S.16s visited Kalafrana. This flying boat had in 1919 been derived from its civil counterpart for the military purposes; at first it was powered by a FIAT A.12bis engine but in 1923 this was replaced by a Lorraine 400HP engine. This increased the aircraft's already fine characteristics and in 1924 established the standards requirements for a Sea Bomber and Observation machine.

In 1925 the legendary "Gennariello" De Pireda organized an expedition in which he crossed several continents in the S.16 and chose to make a stop at Malta.

During the following months 481 Flight's time was taken up on cooperative exercises with the ships of the 4th Battle Squadron and 3rd Light Cruiser Squadron, both based on Grand Harbour.

A Blackburn Dart from a British carrier carry out Torpedo running practice inside M'xlokk bay.

Italian military S.16s call at Kalafrana Seaplane base during "Gennarillo" De Pireda's 1925 expedition; the crossing of several Continents.

On 2 October, HMS Eagle returned to Malta, disembarking all her FAA Flights at Kalafrana and Hal Far.

On the 28th of the month, having finished his inspection of the performance of diverse aircraft during attack exercises against 'Eagle', the naval Commander-in-Chief, Admiral Sir Roger Keyes KCB, KCVO, CMG, DSO, was returning from the carrier. The Blackburn 'Dart' he was flying in suddenly developed engine problems which forced the biplane to descend in the sea. Fortunately, however, there were no casualties.

At this time a notable event was a short visit on 6 November by the King and Queen of Belgium. A fly past by aircraft of the Fleet Air Arm was organized over the Grand Harbour for the purpose of escorting the Royal couple as they were taken ashore; that was repeated when they were returning to their ship.

Shortly after this event, with Turkey threatening to attack Iraq, feverish preparations were underway in Malta as the British Fleet equipped itself for an expedition against Turkey. The carriers 'Furious' and 'Hermes' arrived from Britain, and joined forces with 'Eagle' to form a three pronged force intended to neutralize the Turks. However, before any action could be taken, peace returned to the region and up to the advent of the Abyssinian Crisis in 1935 the Mediterranean Basin remained relatively quiet.

During spring of 1926 the beginning of that year's cruise by the British Naval fleet again led to the usual shuffling and manoeuvering of all FAA Flights at Hal Far, as they were embarked in HMS Eagle, 'Furious' and 'Hermes', for at sea exercises.

Early in June three Fairey IIIDs carried out a long distance flight that took them to Corfu. The 481 Flight floatplanes returned to Kalafrana on 16 June.

Then, while the Mediterranean Fleet was on passage from Malta to Argostoli, between the 22nd and the 24th, an experimental flight was executed with a ship plane towing a Drogue Target sleeve 90 feet astern of it. No other planes practiced shooting at the sleeve on this occasion. However, this tentative experiment proved successful as no difficulties were experienced when the drogue was dropped prior to the biplane's landing.

In October, with the Fleet back in Malta, the command-training season commenced. The aircraft of No. 423 Flight were called to take part in the naval gunnery trails against HMS Agamemnon. The ship had joined the Mediterranean Station as a radio controlled target ship. Unfortunately, however, on 21 October, during a spotting exercise, an

Avro 'Bison' of 423 Flight crashed in the sea off Valletta and the crew of four on board all perished.

Just a few days before Christmas, on 22 December, the first two Imperial Airways Hercules, DH.66 passenger aircraft G-EBMW and G-EBMY reached Malta from Britain. One of the aircraft, flown by Pilot Woolley Dodd, had passengers on board who had paid a fare for the trip. So this can be taken to represent the first occasion in which passengers had payed to travel by air from London direct to Malta. Then on the 30th of the month a third Imperial Airways DH.66, G-EBMX, staged through Hal Far.

After the armistice aviation movements and activities were brought to a gradual rundown at Kalafrana until fear of an uprising in Turkey in 1922 led the British to move a strong military force back to the Mediterranean. Due to the location of the two British military stations at Kalafrana and Hal Far aviation activities in Malta were in the Twenties mainly concentrated around the eastern tip of the Island. However, aircraft were occasionally spotted flying over St Paul's Bay, up the island's north coast, where pilots of flying boats and floatplanes sought shelter when the waters inside M'Xlokk bay were too rough to risk descending on.

Bison N9848 of 423 Fleet Spotter Flight, HMS Eagle, Malta 1927.

By this time the vast distance that existed between Malta and Britain had finally been bridged by means of shortwave wireless communication. Then the construction of Hal Far airfield gave rise to the arrival of a gathering of wheeled ship-borne aircraft.

In retrospect, the tragic Bison crash of 21 October 1926 is looked upon like a dark omen for, from a historical point of view, a string of crashes dominated a good part of 1927.

Numerous aviation-minded individuals on the island tended to become more aware of the dangers these flying machines posed to those travelling in them.

Civil aviation had not yet been introduced at this time for only after SANA (an Italian airline) launched their trans-Mediterranean flight service in the early l930s, between Sicily and Tripoli, and in which Malta served as a stage station, did a few solitary Maltese travel by air as passengers. Still the fact remains that the first Maltese to travel by this means was in 1927, and what an eventful flight it proved to be for, in retrospect, it seems as if fate, through this incident, intended to give it greater historical significance.

As far as can be remembered when His Grace the Archbishop of Malta needed to visit Sicily, mostly in connection with ecclesiastical matters, it was customary for the Royal Navy to provide the necessary transport to see him across the sixty odd miles of water separating the two islands. However, early in 1927, the RAF for the first time proposed to convey His Grace across to Sicily by air. Although the aircraft used were not built to carry passengers this event can positively be taken to represent the first occasion in which Maltese civilians were flown half way across the central Mediterranean.

On 12 January two Fairy IIID floatplanes of 481 Flight took-off from Marsaxlokk Bay. On board were the Archbishop, Monsignor M. Caruana, and his chaplain, each in a separate aircraft. After seeing the priests off in Sicily the aircraft returned to base.

Five days later, on 17 January, another two Fairey IIIDs from the same Malta-based unit were dispatched to pick up the clergymen for the return flight to Malta,

The priests, having made the first crossing without mishap, took the one back in high spirits. However, while the aircraft were nearly within sight of the island one of them, developing engine difficulties, was forced to make an emergency descent in the sea. Due to the roughness of the water, and far from gentle a landing, the Fairey's two floats broke-off, and it began to sink.

Fly. Off. Pickering, in the second aircraft, had meanwhile remained circling overhead, awaiting developments. Noting the difficulties the pilot in the stricken aircraft was encountering, Pickering decided to assist his fellow officer.

Having succeeded in alighting his aircraft safely on the sea in very trying conditions, Pickering taxied his Fairey alongside the sinking machine, as near as safety permitted. The men inside the aircraft, who had already abandoned 'ship', swam across to the nearby floatplane whose pilot had risked so much to come to their rescue. The three men managed to climb on to its flat-topped floats.

At that stage everyone was, to a limited extent, safe. However, due to the state of the elements, and the extra weight of the three passengers on its floats, Pickering knew there was no hope of getting his Fairey airborne.

After nearly two hours of anxiety, a RAF motor launch finally arrived to their rescue. Picking up the two aircrews and their passengers the vessel returned to the island. Shortly afterwards a tugboat from HM Dockyard reached the spot and, taking the Fairey in tow, steamed towards the Grand Harbour, from where the biplane was later flown to Kalafrana.

The incident of 17 January, under different circumstances, might have ended in a tragedy, but it was brought to a herioc conclusion. However, the next day the unabated bad state of the weather was primarily responsible for the tragic accident that occured on Hal Far airfield.

The Bison, one of HMS Eagle's 423 Flight, took-off from the aerodrome at about 10.30 a.m., flying straight into a strong gusty 30 mile-an-hour headwind towards the edge of the high rugged cliffs round the island's southeast coastline. Rising sheerly up to some 200 feet from the sea, air turbulence was known to generate over these cliffs in stormy weather conditions. Furthermore a heavy downpour and limited visibility, and far from improved an already difficult situation while buffeting wind curtailed the Bison's take-off speed. These were elements positively hazardous to flying, and the pilot should have known this. Few aircrews, if any, would have taken the risk of flying any type of aircraft that day, particularly one with a full crew of four on board.

The Avro reached an altitude in the region of 50 feet then, progressing sluggishly, it could gain no more height. Finally, banking steeply to starboard, the biplane was slowly forced off course, away from the pilot's intended line of flight over Kalafrana towards open waters.

Evidently out of control the 'Bison' lost height rapidly after that. Suddenly its starboard lower wing struck the ground not far from the cliff-edge, broke right off on impact, and the stricken machine fell over into the sea nearly 200 feet below.

Local newspapers claimed that the aircraft failed shortly after it took off, when the pilot tried to land in very bad weather conditions. They might have a disputable point there. The 'Bison's banking away to starboard might have well been the pilot's final desperate attempt to fly clear of the cliffs to circuit about over the sea, so that he could perform a safe pre-landing approach upwind.

A Court of Inquiery organized an investigation to disclose what had caused the crash, whether it was due to some fault in the aircraft or human error, but neither seems to have been the case. Finally it was concluded that the crash could have only been caused by the bad state of the weather in which the biplane was flying.

Three of the victims' bodies, that of Flt. Lt. C.F. Brewerton, RAF Lt. E. Chafe, RN, and Leading Telegraphist G.W.Burton, RN, were recovered and interred.

However Lt. G.O. Owen Jones could not be found, and the search had to be finally abandoned.

Towards mid-afternoon of 1 February Lt. J.Y. Mills, flying in Fairey Flycatcher S1069 of HMS Eagle's 402 Flight, was involved in a collision with a Fairey IIID N9576 of 481 Flight over the sea beyond Benghajsa Point.

Engaged in air combat practice Mills, from an advantageous altitude to the rear of the seaplane, closed in to attack in a shallow dive. Most probably a little over enthusiastic, Mills must have gone in faster than he thought though with the result that when he tried to avoid the collision by rolling out of the dive, a manoeuvre that, had it been executed in time, would have proved effective, he might have by then been far too close to his 'adversary.' His aircraft sheared off the IIID's tail section, and in the impact he lost his own Flycatcher's wing which sent his aircraft plunging straight into the sea where, with the exception of a small amount of wreckage, the rest of the biplane sank immediately, taking the pilot down with it.

The crew of the floatplane was far more fortunate. The pilot, Wg. Cmdr Cooke, managed to keep control of his aircraft long enough to make a safe descent in the sea. Despite the extensive damages inflicted to the IIID, of the crew of three Flg. Off. Hewlett escaped unscathed. Cooke suffered a broken nose and the Flt. Sgt. a smashed leg.

The destroyer HMS Wren picked up the survivors, who truly had a close call with death.

'The City of Jerusalem', another of Imperial Airways DH.66s G-EBMZ staged through Hal Far on 25 February. Then on 12 March, G-EBNA, 'The City of Teheran', followed next.

Alone in DH Moth G-ABOT, Mr Dennis Rook, an ex-RAF officer from Australia, after accepting a wager, left Croydon on 24 May. Flying by means of 200 and 300 mile 'hops' across Europe, Rook reached Malta in the morning of the 31 May and landed on Hal Far.

Escorted by two RAF floatplanes, which were expected to accompany the Moth for the first 100 miles, Mr Rook departed from Hal Far in mid-afternoon, expecting to reach his destination, Australia, in three months time.

A few days later, exactly on 9 June, while flying a 'Flycatcher' in a bombing practice run, Lt. Cmdr HMS Forbes, DSC, RN of 402 Flight went into a nose-dive and crashed into the sea, sinking immediately. The body of the pilot was later recovered and interred.

A visitor worthy of note seen at Hal Far during that year's summer months was a privately owned DeHavilland 'Moth', G-EBPO, belonging to Lt. L.G. Richardson, RN who, accompanied by his brother, ventured on a flight from Britain to Malta and back.

Starting from Kentchurch on 1 August Richardson arrived on the Island on the 8th. The trip was taken in stages, just as others had flown theirs, hopping from one airstrip to the next across France and Italy. Serviced by RAF personnel the 'Moth', escorted by two military aircraft, departed the next day.

A month later, on 8 September, another DHMoth, G-EBSO, with Lt. R.R. Bentley at the controls, staged through Hal Far airfield enroute to the Cape via Italy from Britain. However, it was 21 November when the arrival of yet another pioneer of aviation heralded the beginning of one of the most memorable struggles in Malta's history of aviation.

It was after nightfall when a searchlight was switched-on onboard HMS Queen Elizabeth anchored within the seclusion of St Paul's Bay. An unusual act for a naval battleship to do, without a good cause. The beam of light, long and finger like probed the darkness sweeping back and forth over the entrance of the bay.

Eventually the distant drone of aero engines was heard through the raging storm. The ship's light had served its purpose well, as a homing beacon to Sir Alan Cobham whose Singapore I, G-EBUP, flying boat had been forced off course by heavy squalls blowing from a north-easterly direction while en route to Malta via Bordeaux.

The shadowy, almost obscured, silhouette of a large low flying aircraft finally materialized through the murky darkness approaching over the sea, boat-shaped undersides parting water as it descended inside St, Paul's Bay.

Afloat inside the bay, with no visible moorings in the darkness of night, Cobham sought out the assistance of the man-of-war. Shortly afterwards, with the ship's searchlight illuminating the operation, a naval pinnace had the Singapore on tow. It was then led towards the battleship's stern in the heavy swell where it was made fast for the night and, before long, Queen Elizabeth's, searchlight turned-off and St. Paul's Bay was again shrouded in darkness.

The next morning there was little change in the weather but Sir Alan Cobham was determined to continue with his Survey Flight. He had the Singapore towed away from the battleship's stern towards calmer waters inside the bay from where, with the Short's two 700 h.p. Rolls-Royce 'Condor' engines roaring, he took off from St.Paul's Bay shortly after the break of dawn, and set course for Marsaxlokk Bay.

Cobham's Singapore taking leave of the shelter HMS Queen Elizabeth had provided for the night in 1927.

Fifteen minutes later Cobham was circling over Kalafrana Bay at the southeast end of the island.

Extremely exposed to southeasterly gale force winds the sea was rough with a high swell running inside the bay. However, as previously arranged, an RAF pinnace waited inside St George's Bay to direct the Singapore to the smoothest landing spot.

A white rocket was fired from the pinnace as a pre-arranged signal to which circuiting once Cobham had the flying boat in the water moving up alongside the boat.

Shortly afterwards Cobham was given directions to taxi across the bay towards Kalafrana's seaplane base, but estimating that the sea was rather rough to risk the crossing under the Singapore's own power he asked if he could be taken in tow and, engines shut off, they were on their way.

Towing an aircraft the size of the Singapore in rough seas, with a swell running, is no easy matter. As long as one keeps head on to it the flying boat can ride it fair and square. The real danger was in moving along the swell and, despite Cobham's efforts to keep this from happening to his aircraft, an unexpected manoeuvre from the pinnace brought the Singapore's hull parallel to the waves that sent it rolling and rocking alarmingly.

The lower starboard wingtip and float began to disappear under the waves. The side-pressure over the whole length of the float must have been so great that its supports, unable to stand the strain, broke and it was wrenched away. To avoid sustaining further catastrophic damage three of the crew on board the aircraft rushed out along the footpath of the port lower plane to weigh the wing down and lift the unfloatable side out of the water.

The Singapore was again turned into the swell but this resulted in diverting the aircraft away from the shelter offered by the camber at the Kalafrana Seaplane. As no other shelter existed elsewhere except right across the bay, under the lee of the Delimara Cliffs, it was decided to turn into the heavy swell and head for it.

After a terrifying effort in the storm, this was reached and the Singapore was securely moored below the cliffs without further damage.

There, in order to keep the aircraft's unfloatable wing out of the water, the port-side wingtip was weighted down with 200lbs of sandbags.

The Singapore remained there for the next two days then, at dawn on a Monday morning, with a fair change in the weather, the aircraft was safely towed and berthed inside the Kalafrana seaplane base camber, ready to be taken on an improvised trolley and hauled out of the water for repairs.

Treacherous underwater currents, however, were increasing to an already high sea swell and the dreaded gregale was again returning in force.

Despite the sheltered seaplane base, where the Singapore remained at anchor all day long, the swell was getting right round the jetty and into the inner waters of the camber.

The next morning the winds were at their worst, with waves breaking right over the jetty, and as the morning wore on these were flooding two feet deep over the top of the concrete pier protecting the camber. The swell surged right up on to the tarmac, and was occasionally breaking over the concrete passage in front of the hangars.

The Singapore was at this stage riding head on into the wind with the swell running parallel to her hull, rocking her severely, putting undue strain on to the remaining float which was seen to be getting lower into the water.

Removal of the sandbags had no effect whatsoever. The float appeared to have become waterlogged for it kept on sinking inch by inch until the lower plane was all but touching the water.

The alarm was given for something had to be done if the aircraft was to be saved. Unexpectedly, with the lower wingtip now touching water, a heavy swell surged against the remaining wingtip float and tore it off and the lower port plane began to sink. The sea inside the camber was so rough that all hope of getting alongside the flying boat in a skiff was hopeless, but a line had to be taken from the shore to the Singapore at all cost. Suddenly, without any warning, Bonnet, the expedition's cinematographer, plunged into the sea and, taking a line with him swam out to the stricken aircraft. Others took the example and some half-a-dozen Air Force men dived into the swirling waters, all managing to climb on to the Singapore. Attempting to manoeuvre it towards the shore proved to be a desperate attempt. With the weather still at its worst dragging it up to the comparative safety of the trolley on the slipway was a feat of strength. The mighty swells surged round some one hundred servicemen, lifted the flying boat into the air and washed away the trolley right off the slipway. Men were knocked overboard in all directions.

Landing the Singapore on the slipway without a trolley would positively seriously damage the aircraft. But salvaging and damaging risks were better than letting the flying boat sink inside the camber.

Heavy breakers rolling over the slipway, at times dragging the men

Cobham's Singapore sustains heavy damages from the storm and rough sea he encounters inside Kalafrana Bay.

off their feet, and the difficulties encountered in handling the large aircraft manually resulted in inflicting further damage to the biplane. The rescue party was unable to control the Singapore in spite of their efforts, until, by sheer luck, a huge wave lifted the Singapore bodily some six feet into the air and dropped it right on to the slipway. When the next breaker surged up the slipway with a mighty pull the men dragged the aircraft up the slipway on the side of its metal hull, sliding it on its keel and chine, over the concrete to temporary safety. However, with the submerged wing overhanging the side of the slipway, just a few feet from the sea wall, the wingtip rested on the rocky shallows. This had to be lifted over the top of the wall otherwise, with the tail still thrust down into the water on the sloping slipway, and the sea getting worse, the hull could easily get twisted off the trolley.

The strength of three hundred men was needed to bring the submerged wing over the sea wall and drag the Singapore higher up on to the tarmac, assuring the temporary safety of the aircraft, but ruining the lower wingtip in the process.

Finally, all that could be done was weigh the flying boat down with stacks of ballast, have it tied with ropes, and leave it guarded for the night.

The next morning gale force winds raged on worse than ever. Waves broke over the Singapore where the sea flooded the tarmac. The hangars, which were fifty feet away from the sea wall, were swamped out. It was evident that if the aircraft was not dragged farther up the slipway it was in danger of being washed away by the sea. By sheer manpower the Singapore was dragged over the tarmac towards the hangars, away from the force of the breakers, at the cost of a smashed lowerplane.

Later in the day the wind died down and the sea abated, but the damage had been done. A new lower port plane, two new wing-tip floats, new elevators, and a general overhaul of the hull was needed if the "Sir Charles Wakefield Flight of Survey round Africa" was to continue. Cables were sent off to Britain and, aided by Air Force personnel, the aircraft was jacked up on to a cradle into position for repairs.

The Singapore was too large an aircraft to go into a hangar, so all of the work had to be done in the open on the tarmac.

This Singapore, ordered in 1925 to specification 13/24, was first flown on 17 August 1926 under military serial N179. When Sir Alan Cobham planned the 23,000mile flight round the African Continent the Air Ministry loaned him the flying boat, which was given a civilian registration, G-EBUP, for the duration of the flight. So the builders, Short Brothers, were called upon to undertake all necessary repairs and, after several arrangements, both at Kalafrana and at Messrs Short Brothers, of Rochester, by Christmas a ship arrived from England with all the new spares on board.

Just before Christmas a terrible gale suddenly sprung up in the night, slewing the flyingboat off its cradle and damaging the rear spar. However repairs were effected in time to fit the new wing on Boxing Day.

By early January 1928 the Singapore was ready to be launched once more, and the Air Force personnel at Kalafrana managed the affair.

Test flights were carried out on 8 January 1928, and it was found that the aircraft was perfect in every way, after which preparations were made to continue with the expedition, but fate seemed to dog Cobham at every turn.

On 10 January, while the Singapore was riding at anchor inside St George's Bay for the night, where it was considered a safer anchorage than Kalafrana, another storm broke out. Gale force winds tore the flying boat adrift from its mooring and before it could be recovered the aircraft

Further storms wash G-EBUP ashore inside St George's Bay, Birzebbugia; after damages from the first mishap were repaired. (Opposite the Al Fresco Restaurant.)

was washed ashore inside the bay. Luckily it had drifted on to a sandbank, but it was soon discovered that one of the floats was ruined, and a spare was needed before the aircraft could be refloated. But the only float available was one of the old ones, which had been partly repaired, and needed some five or six hours more work before it could be fitted on.

Work was carried out on the spot in the storm without much ado, in an effort to get the job done in time so that the Singapore could be launched and taken to a safe anchorage before darkness fell.

It was dark when the aircraft was ready and by a super human effort towed afloat without sustaining heavy damages in the raging storm, and, with both engines working, Cobham taxied his Singapore into the inner confines of St Georges Bay, and moored the aircraft there for the night.

The next day dawned beautifully calm and it was decided to lift the Singapore out of the water and inspect the hull for any damage. For this purpose HM Dockyard, where a huge crane was available on the quayside at Somerset Wharf, alongside No. 3 Dock, was approached and

Damages found to be slight, Cobham lands inside
the Grand Harbour at dawn on a fine day.

every arrangement was made to have the harbour area cleared for the landing.

The damages found to the hull needed to be repaired and in about two days the Singapore was once more ready to resume with her flight. But, owing to the bad state of the weather locally, and at Benghazi, the flyingboat had to remain moored inside the Grand Harbour for another three days.

Finally, on 21 January 1928, the dawn brought with it a dead calm, and shortly afterwards Sir Alan Cobham and company were taking off from inside the Grand Harbour to resume with their flight of survey.

Meanwhile that same month a new unit, No. 448 Flight, equipped with Avro 'Bisons', was formed at Hal Far for communication purposes and other duties, while No. 440 and No. 481 Flights operated Fairey IIID landplanes and floatplanes respectively.

On the civilian side, however, with the exception of Cobham's misadventure, there was only H.J. Hinkler who, in his attempt of the first crossing from England to Australia in 1928, included Malta to his route, and on 8 February he transited through Hal Far in his Avian 581E, G-EBOV. So the most notable event that year was attributed to the military.

At Hal Far new outbuildings were erected on the northern side of the airfield, while older quarters were demolished. During this change

Air Commodore R.H.Clarke Hall, CMG, DSO, and other officers decided to organize an aerial pageant over the aerodrome, one the general public could attend.

The privileged few who could afford cars of their own arrived early. Others, lacking this luxury, arrived either on foot, horse-drawn cart, bus or whatever was most convenient as transport, came to Hal Far until, by mid-afternoon, a large crowd had gathered to the land-ward side of the airfield. Finally His Excellency the Governor of Malta and Lady Ducane arrived and that historical afternoon of 18 May 1928 the air display was declared open.

Layers of low cloud limited visibility from the air to about two thousand feet, however, none of those present were disappointed even though an increase in wind velocity failed to clear the hazy atmosphere.

Bisons, Fairey III.Ds, Darts and Flycatchers from locally based and ship-borne units, amongst which were No. 481 (Coastal Reconnaissance) Flight and No. 402 (Fleet Fighter) Flight, circled over Hal Far in one massed 'vee' formation.

A shot, fired from a Very-light pistol, was the signal for the formation to break and split up into separate flights, each flying across the airfield from different directions.

During a combat sequence between a Bison and two Flycatchers one of the latter was 'shot' down, and to make the action appear more

The Grand Finale to the Air Pageant held at Hal Far on 18 May 1928.

realistic the aircraft spiraled earthwards, to disappear below the level of the cliffs trailing rigged-up flames and smoke. Far more authentic was a dummy dropped out of the biplane at the beginning of its 'death'-dive, swinging beneath a mushrooming parachute, to simulate the pilot's escape from the 'stricken' biplane, that floated down to safety over the airfield, to the relief of many a shocked spectator.

A relay race was soon forgotten in the excitement of an aerobatic display put up by three Flycatchers, and the passage of time went unnoticed by all until more than an hour had elapsed. Then the aircraft parade flew past overhead.

To give this number more life two parachute suspended dummies were dropped over the airfield. The pageant literally came to a close with a bang. As it has earlier been explained old buildings on the airfield were being demolished to make room for the construction of more modern quarters. However, one particular structure was left standing and used at this precise moment for the climax to the whole show. The building was arranged to represent an enemy 'fortress' towards which five Bisons approached. As the biplanes flew past over the 'fort', explosives, set up

Blackburn 'Iris' III, N185, with Sqdn. Ldr. C. L. Scott at the controls, accompanied by Flt. Lt. Martin as co-pilot, stops at Kalafrana on 8 November 1928, in transit to Karachi.

inside the building in advance, were detonated giving everyone the impression that bombs were dropped on it from the air.

On 11 June eleven Blackburn 'Darts', of Nos.463 and 464 Flights, on their first ever hop off HMS Courageous, landed on Hal Far. Twelve machines were being expected to arrive on the airfield, however, it was later disclosed that one of the aircraft hit the carrier's superstructure during take off and crashed in the sea.

On the 25 June, during 'Eagle's' first days inside the Grand Harbour, a Blackburn Dart of No. 463 Flight crashed, killing the pilot. Fly. Off. J Nicholson RN had just taken off from the carrier's deck, a torpedo attached to his biplane when, hitting the ship's funnel with a starboard wingtip, he lost control of his aircraft and dived into the sea a short distance away from St Elmo's Light.

Later in the year, precisely on 8 November, a Blackburn Iris III, N185 touched down inside Marsaxlokk bay. With Sqdn. Ldr. C L Scott at the controls accompanied by a Flt. Lt. Martin as co-pilot, the flying boat was en route to Benghazi on an attempted record flight from Felixstowe to Karachi, and back. The three-engine seaplane departed from Kalafrana on 10 November.

Chapter III

202 Squadron

Visiting squadrons – Kalafrana Air Pageant – HMS Courageous – Kalafrana assembled aircraft flown to Hal Far – SANA – CAMs S.55 of the French AF – Egyptian AF DH.60 Moths – Hal Far movements – HMS Glorious – In Flight re-fuelling – Concrete Mirror Radar – Imperial Airways at Kalafrana – Eagle, Courageous & Furious – Malta Sports Ground Review – First ground-based RAF units at Hal Far – The Elements hit Hal Far – Nyon

In January 1929, all existing flying-boat flights were raised to squadron status. As a result No. 481 Flight was disbanded and 202 Squadron, which had just been reformed, succeeded it, taking over its equipment. But before taking up from this transition a summary of the latter's history deserve mention as that of 481 Flight had already been treated in the previous chapter.

No. 202 Squadron acquired this number with the formation of the RAF in 1918, when all naval units were renumbered by the addition of 200 to their current designation. Then, placed at the disposal of the Army with other units, 202 Squadron remained under the control of the Navy when two, out of the five that formed the 61st Wg. RAF, were moved to the Western Front.

For a time, 202 moved from the Belgian coast to Dover with their DH.4s; but later in 1918 returned to Belgium. With the armistice then imminent the squadron was transferred to Varssenaere, from where it was immediately engaged on spotting enemy positions as the German forces retreated over the Meuse.

Early in 1919 the squadron was withdrawn to the UK, and stripped of all its equipment. A year later, while posted at Eastburn, it was finally disbanded.

The postwar period was one of uncertainty for the RAF, and the Navy was in no better state. The Mediterranean was evacuated of aircraft units. Many squadrons were disbanded. Others, withdrawn to the UK, were to suffer the same fate. But the RN Fleet, wanted to have a seaplane unit in attendance at Alexandria so an RAF Flight, still stationed there, was in April 1921, raised to squadron status, resulting in the reappearance of 202 Squadron. Unfortunately, however, this was more of a false front than a show of force as there was only one aircraft on strength; a Short 184. Then, before it could become fully effective, another change of policy led to the disbanding of the unit on 16 May 1921. The result of this action in the Middle East left 267 Squadron the sole air guardian in the Mediterranean, so when HMS Argus stopped at Kalafrana in 1922, en route to the Dardanelles, the unit was embarked in the carrier.

Later detached to HMS Ark Royal, in August 1923 it became 481 Flight, and by the end of the month the new unit was disembarked to Kalafrana complete with personnel, Fairey IIICs and other equipment, where it remained until 1 January 1929.

No. 202 Squadron, which was supposed to have had flying boats on strength, remained flying the Fairey IIIC for the next six-and-a-half years.

Due to the location of the bay heavy swells frequently prevented the seaplanes from operating, particularly during the autumn and winter months, posing a serious drawback.

The squadron for the first time provided five of their now Fairey IIIDs for the Air Pageant of 25 May 1929. This was held shortly after Hal Far was upgraded to become an RAF Station on 29 March, resulting in the forming of the RAF Base Miscellaneous Flight (Which was in the early war years to become known as Station Flight: Malta) with Wg. Cdr. C.W. Nutting OBE, OSC, as Station Commander.

In July 1932, 202 Squadron received its first few Fairey IIIF.Mk.3M with which it was to replace its old IIIDs. As a substitute to fill in the post of a very much-needed flying boat this new biplane, basically a carrier and land-based aircraft, was the only one of type with the RAF specifically fitted with floats. Meanwhile many of 202's counterparts were

A few of 202 Squadron's Fairey IIIFMs, S1373 in the foreground, on detachment to Mistra Bay during the early 1930s.

already operating with flying boats, an aircraft which the Malta-based unit did not receive until May, 1935.

Advancement in British aircraft design had meanwhile made great progress since the war. This resulted in sealing the seaplane's fate on carriers, because, the flying boats ability to navigate over long distances, and fly large payloads over short ones, as well as the low cost needed to construct terminal facilities, scored in its favour. Other favourable factors were its obvious chances of survival in a forced descent on water. Neither were any landplanes with a comparable payload/range performance yet available, which enabled seaplanes to flourish during that period. These facts had been constantly kept in perspective since the war, and given greater attention in 1925 when the Southampton, a replacement for an earlier flying boat, the Felixstowe F.5, the last of the type, was introduced. Although the latter's attacks on enemy U-Boats were seldom effective, and few conclusive sinkings were ever reported, the presence of the Felixstowe served to keep the enemy submerged. Under water the U-Boat's cruising speed was limited, resulting in giving the Admiralty time to divert their cargo ships from the danger area and to direct their warships to converge on the enemy for a hydrophone search of the lurking submarines.

After the war the F.2s, F.3s and F.5s became the RAF's standard maritime reconnaissance equipment, and remained in service until the mid-1920s when the derivative of Supermarine's Swan, the Southampton, came into service in August 1925.

(The Southampton was the flying boat which led to the development of a string of similar types during the ensuing years, until the advent of the Second World War.)

In March 1925, the civil Supermarine Swan was adapted to meet specification R18/24, and on the 14th flew for the first time as military prototype N218. Within a few months the first production batch, N9896-N9901, were being delivered as the Southampton.

The first deliveries, like their predecessors, had wooden hulls but, no matter how well protected, these still soaked up enough water to increase an aircraft's weight by as much as 400lbs and affect its overall performance.

Eventually, after corrosion problems were overcome, metal hulls were introduced, and contributed significantly to the flying boat's performance.

Two of the flying boats, the Mk.IV and Mk.V, were christened the Scapa and Stanrear respectively and overseas units that equipped with the type were 203 Squadron at Mt.Batten, later stationed at Basra. No. 204 Squadron at Mt.Batten and Kalafrana, and 205 Squadron at Seletar.

No. 202 Squadron missed having the Southampton on strength. Neither was it given an option to equip with the Rangoon, a long-range flying boat produced to replace the former in tropical regions. But this fact did by no means keep this aircraft from casting its shadow over local waters. Of the above two the Southampton 1 appeared first, with two of the type, S1038 and S1039 reaching Malta via Britain on their first flight with the RAF in July, 1926.

On 8 November 1928 a newly built Blackburn R.B.1B Iris III, S1263, staged through Marsaxlokk Bay, northwest-bound, via North Africa, with two VIPs, Under Secretary of State for Air Sir Phillip Sassoon CBE, CMG, MP, and Air Commodore A.M. Longmore, CB DSO, who were on a tour of RAF Stations in the Middle East and the Mediterranean.

Four months later, in March 1929, a further three Southamptons, S1298, S1299 and S1300 of 223 Squadron, transited through Kalafrana en route to Basra.

At that time the RAF was preparing for an air pageant they were to hold over Kalafrana. The date was set for 25 May, and to add to an already full program the band of HMS Courageous was to be brought ashore to offer musical entertainment right through the afternoon.

Demonstrations in formation flying by separate Flights from resident units, and those from the carriers Eagle and Courageous, presenting a variety of aircraft types, all maneuvering according to a pre-arranged plan, launched the display.

Arranged to fall into six separate events, the second one, a mimic aerial combat between a Fairey IIID and two Flycatchers, must have reminded some of those present of the tragic air collision nearly four months earlier. A Fairey IIID S1108 of 445 Flight made a nose-dive in shallow waters close to Kalafrana's Seaplane base slipway, when the pilot tried to avoid some aerial cables. Although there were no casualties, it must have caused some anxious moments. In this number an enemy scout, a Fairey IIID approaching the coast, was immediately intercepted by two Fairey Flycatchers and 'shot' down in 'flames'.

Fighter aircraft attacking a target from low altitude formed the third event of the afternoon. Executed by two Flycatchers in perfect sequence, to minimize risk of collision, both biplanes performed steep climbing turns as they pulled away from the target.

The Fairey Flycatcher that first appeared as a land-plane back in 1924 later reached the amphibious stage.

A short break, in which the RAF treated their invited guests to tea, preceded event four, which consisted of aerobatic flying. A variety of flying stunts were breathtakingly executed, from inverted flying, looping-the-loop, falling like a leaf, rolling, to either downward or upward vertical spins. It was truly a masterpiece for its day.

Event five was a massed fly-past formed of all the different types of aircraft that took part in the pageant, and typical of the RAF the most spectacular number was left for the last. An 'enemy' force appeared attempting to land troops from an auxiliary vessel escorted by a submarine cruiser. The base, duly given a wireless alarm, had fighters and torpedo bombers scrambled to intercept the invaders. The vessel, now under attack, is finally driven off, and the submarine cruiser is seen to blow up, ending the pageant.

On 22 August 1929, with the carrier HMS Courageous anchored inside the Grand Harbour, an attempted take-off by a drogue towing Fairey IIID N9490 from the ship's deck ended in a forced landing, wrecking the biplane, but causing no casualties.

Fly. Off. Owen Cathcart-Jones, flying a Fairy Flycatcher from Hal Far, made history when, on 25 November 1929, he performed the first night deck landing in a fighter aircraft on HMS Courageous while it was anchored inside Grand Harbour.

Cooperation duties during combined military exercises and routine flying increased to the squadron's flying hours under the command of Flt. Lt. C. Brymphray DFC. Furthermore, in June of 1929, after the squadron was successfully engaged on submarine spotting exercises its CO was promoted to the rank of Sqdn. Ldr.

On 28 January 1931 the Station Command changed hands, with Sqdn. Ldr. R.H. Kershaw filling the post.

That year 202 Squadron suffered its first tragic loss when, on 5 June, one of its Fairey IIIDs S1178, for obscure reasons spun into the sea from an altitude of some 3,000 feet, killing the pilot, Flg. Off. R.F. Francis and his passenger.

In July the squadron received a Fairey IIIF S1374, though, by September, due to the shortage of type, the unit still needed to be fully re-equipped with the new biplane; this re-equipping was done gradually during the ensuing months.

Then on the 29th of the month three Farman Goliath floatplanes of the French Navy staged through Kalafrana en route to Beirut via Bizerte.

Departing for Navarino Bay, Greece, the next day, they reappeared

Fairey IIIF which was used for Target Towing duties during the early 1930s.

on 25 October, during their return flight back to base at Bizerte. However, bad weather delayed their departure by four days.

Then three days later, escorted by Fairey IIIFs of 202 Squadron to a point some 50 miles north of Gozo, the French aircraft were en route to Bizerte.

On 10 March 1931 two Blackburn Iris III, S1263 and S1264, of 209 Squadron inaugurated the first Mediterranean crossing between Malta and Sollum. Air Chief Marshall Sir John Salmond, Chief of Air Staff, who

Blackburn Baffins under assembly at Kalafrana's north slip prior to their being flown off from the Seaplane base to Hal Far.

Blackburn Ripon, S1359, preparing to take off along Kalafrana's north slip hangars' apron.

Kalafrana north slip. Arrow marks indicate direction assembled land-based planes took off from the Seaplane base during the 1930s.

was on board one of the flying boats, inspected the Station before departing to his destination.

In April, three Rangoons, S1435, S1436 and S1433 of 203 Squadron, of which the latter was in March 1936 taken over by Imperial Airways to become G-AEIM for air pilot training, staged through Kalafrana via Naples, on transit to Basra.

On 15 March, Fairey IIIDs newly assembled at Kalafrana, were for the first time flown from there to Hal Far, instead of transported. These aircraft, amongst others, were launched under full power off the eastern end of the 'North Slip' apron down along its length westwards.

Flying across to Naples on 14 July 1931, 202 Squadron crossed over to Corfu, Greece, on their first cruise, an activity which they annually adopted, until the war finally put a stop to it. This trip reached as far as Aboukir, Egypt, but two of the biplanes fell by the wayside. One aircraft, S1382, suffering from engine problems, made a forced descent in the sea shortly after departing from Kalafrana, and had to be towed back to base by a RAF Pinnace.

Towards the end of the tour, S1380 had to be left behind at Corfu until repairs had been effected, so that it could be flown back to Malta. By the 29 July they were all back to base where Sqdn. Ldr. H.W. Evans became the squadron's new CO

On 16 February 1932 Fairey IIIF S1384 of 202 Squadron was dispatched to search for a stranded Dornier Wal of the Italian airline SANA some 52 miles off Malta, shortly after an SOS signal was received. Once the flying boat was sighted HMS Brilliant was homed in to the stricken aircraft which was taken in tow. However, just outside Marsaxlokk Bay, the Dornier capsized and had to be cut loose while the passengers, having been taken on board the ship, were brought ashore.

The flying boat was later relocated where it had drifted to, some 15 miles off shore, by another of 202 Squadron's Faireys. Recovered, it was brought to Kalafrana where SANA was flight proving another of the type prior to its introduction on the Syracuse-Malta-Tripoli route.

On 6 May, eight C.A.M.s 555.2 of the French Air Force broke waters inside Marsaxlokk Bay. Scheduled to participate in co-operative exercises with French naval forces steaming in the eastern Mediterranean, the twin-engine flying boats formed the strength of two separate escadrilles, Nos.3 and 4, one based at Berre, the other at Bizerte.

Aeronavale (French Navy) visitors at Kalafrana on 6 May 1932.
CAM.s 55.2 of Escadrilles 3 and 4 make transitory stops at the seaplane base.
(*Above* CAM. No. 6 of Esc. 3).

No 3Escadrille	No 4Escadrille
3E I No. 2	4E I No. 1
3E I No. 3	4E I No. 2
3E I No. 4	4E I No. 3
3E I No. 6	4E I No. 4

The aircraft stopped overnight and departed the next day. Neither was this their only stopover in Malta. They passed through again on 7 June while the two French AF units were on the return flight to their respective bases.

Arriving in two separate groups the units finally took leave of the island on 9 May.

Meanwhile, on 29 May, another five biplanes, float-equipped DH.62T Moths, E.121, E.122, E.123, E.124 and E.125, transited through Kalafrana. This resulted from the fact that in 1931 Egypt, having organized its own air force on a basis similar to that of Britain's own RAF, was equipping itself with British-built aircraft. So these five seaplanes were en route to Cairo, for the Royal Egyptian Air Force. A sixth aircraft, E.126, construction number 1199, was delivered at a later date.

Constant experimentation in night flying practice that month led to the installation of night flying facilities at Kalafrana. Floats from those used on Fairey IIID aircraft, each fitted with battery illuminated lights, were anchored to create a flare path about 250 yards long, making it possible for night flying to become a regular practice.

Four of 202 Squadron's aircraft left on 22 June on an expedition to Khartoum via Aboukir. A flight during which crews gained valuable experience in mooring, beaching, picketing and refueling before returning to Kalafrana in mid-July.

Anti-submarine exercises were organized later in the year, and under the command of Sqdn. Ldr. A.H. Wann, turned up some successful results.

On 15th and 16th of August respectively two Southampton Is of 204 Squadron, of which one was S1044, made a seven day stop at Kalafrana before moving on again, while at about the same time four Fairey IIIFs of 202 Squadron were flown as far as Khartoum, Sudan.

Early in June of 1933 a Southampton IV, S.1648, arrived at Marsaxlokk Bay. This flying boat, issued under specification R20/31, was Supermarine's latest machine to meet with Air Ministry's requirements. However, in view of the few evident differences between this aircraft and its predecessor, the Mk.1, the name of Scapa was adopted by the Mk.IV, and the scope for which it was brought to Malta was to have it undergo finalization trials before going into production.

To add more interest, on 10 June a Blackburn Iris III, S1593,

Blackburn Iris, S1593, being brought up Kalafrana's south slip for a hull inspection in 1933.

Zephyrus, later to become the Perth prototype, carrying modifications to take a 31mm gun, visited Kalafrana.

The flying boat called again on 5 July, and after a forthnight's stay, during which it was flown on a number of proving flights, it departed on the 21st.

While the Kalafrana RAF Seaplane Base attended to both civil and military flying boats that shuttled through the station movements, and activities at Hal Far were not restricted to carrier-borne aircraft. Heavier land-based airplanes staged through the airfield on transit to British military bases elsewhere in the Mediterranean and the Middle East particularly during the course of the Abyssinian Crisis. As early as 1933 troop carrying Valenzjas of 70 Squadron were noted stopping at Hal Far on transit to the Middle East; K2806 and K3195 appear to have been the first of type to land on the airfield on 14 October, departing two days later.

Some movements, however, remain obscure. A case in point was when a fortnight later an Armstrong Whitworth Atlas AC (Army Cooperation) aircraft staged through Hal Far, about which no more information could be found. But on 24 November, another two of

Aerial view of Hal Far airfield in 1929, with an unusual array of aircraft parked opposite a newly built hangar space.

70 Squadrons Valenzjas, K2800 and K4643, each carrying troops, were noted staging through the airfield on transit to the Middle East.

The Fairey IIIFs of 202 Squadron had that year flown out as far as the Adriatic, making stops at Kotor and Split in Yugoslavia. The squadron was once again involved with the Italian airline SANA when, on 7 November, as it was landing inside Marsaxlokk Bay, Fairey S1385 collided with Dornier Wal I-AZDZ. About a week later another Wal was reported stranded between Malta and Sicily, and a naval pinnace was dispatched to tow it to Kalafrana. Another Wal was involved in a similar mishap in March of 1934.

In April of 1934 there was a change at Hal Far Station Command with Wg. Cdr. E. R. Prettyman DFC, being relieved by Wg. Cdr. R.L.G. Maris DSO. Then the next day, 17 April, there was an inspection of the Station by ACM Sir Edward Ellington, Chief of the Air Staff.

A week later the Station had another visitor, AOC Air Commodore C. E. Rathbone.

Although carrier-based Flights still continued to fly frequently ashore to Hal Far, the majority of these had by this time disappeared. The Fleet Air Arm units which had been disbanded in April 1923 to form the 400 series Flights of 6 aircraft each were re-introduced in April 1933. This resulted in the amalgamation of Flights to form squadrons in the 700 and 800-series, each operating either nine or twelve aircraft.

Spotter reconnaissance and Torpedo bomber units had begun equipping with the Fairey Seal as their Blackburn Ripons were gradually withdrawn to be converted into Baffins, of which new ones were also under construction.

No. 812 Squadron was the first of these units to arrive at Hal Far, having flown off HMS Glorious in April with Blackburn Baffins.

Official records at the PRO in London would positively produce far more information related to air traffic movements and activities through both RAF stations in Malta in 1934 than does local newspapers. However a Valenzja, K3168, of 70 Squadron, is reported staging through Hal Far airfield on 18 August in transit to the Middle East.

In September 1934 was executed over the island part of one of the most notable aviation events in history.

Present day in-flight refueling is a highly sophisticated operation. It requires great flying precision, but modern technology makes the transfer of fuel from one aircraft to another simple compared to its initial stages of development. Like most other types of inventions, its beginning

A Ripon of 480 Flight releases a torpedo off Kalafrana in June 1931.

was crude, and extremely dangerous to execute. However, that is history in the making.

As expected, due to its strategic location in the Central Mediterranean, Malta was chosen to serve as a refueling point along the planned route in this venture by Sir Alan Cobham.

An h.p. W10 took off from Hal Far airfield at exactly 16.00 hours on 22 September.

Meanwhile an Airspeed Courier, G-ABXN, was approaching Malta from the direction of Sicily. The two aircraft were scheduled to meet over the island at precisely 16.15 hours where the h.p. W10 was to air refuel the smaller Courier, so that it could proceed on to its next refueling point.

Much was written regarding Sir Alan Cobham and his exploits, but nothing exposes more about him than his own deeds. Columbus chose the high seas to explore, while Cobham's main scope in life was to exploit air travel. Considering the airplanes of his time, and the distances they were relied upon to fly, occasionally in very trying conditions, the unexpected was a constant hazard on all his flights. Yet through his

Another of Cobham's daring attempts, in 1934, was to fly non-stop from Britain to India by the then still crude means of air-to-air refuelling.

failures, and astounding achievements, his attempts to set up new records, or break older ones, finally set the pattern for some of the present day progress both in civil and military aviation. Cobham seemed to favour Malta on the majority of his Mediterranean flights and this was no exception, but as on his 1928 flight, lady luck seems to have abandoned him again over the island.

At the opening phases of this attempt to fly non-stop between Britain and India, Cobham was confident he would succeed for when he departed from Portsmouth in his Oxford Courier, early in the dawn of 22 September, every step of the way had been carefully planned in advance. The first air-to-air refueling attempt over British soil had been a success. Then Cobham proceeded flying on a south-easterly bearing over France, down the boot of Italy, onwards to the Central Mediterranean, where the next in-flight refueling operation was scheduled to be executed.

The W.10 climbed steadily on an easterly course while the lighter single engined Courier approached on the tanker's starboard wing, finally falling into formation at an altitude of some 2,000 feet, the W.10 flying above the other.

During the refuelling operation the Courier rose unexpectedly, seemingly out of control, towards the W.10 that was flying steadily above it, endangering them both. Then just as suddenly the smaller aircraft lost height again, as if to avoid a collision. Something appeared to be terribly amiss with Cobham's machine.

Later, according to his own report, at that precise instant Cobham realized that something in the Courier's throttle linkages had gone awry.

Loss in altitude was fast after that. The Courier's engine, although still in perfect trim, was uncontrollable. Only gliding skills would keep the aircraft airborne for a limited period of time, during which Cobham hoped to coax it as far as Hal Far airfield, otherwise it would have to be ditched in the sea off Marsaxlokk Bay. However, Cobham's own flying expertise was the one factor that finally tipped the scales of fate in his favour. Keeping the undercarriage of the Courier retracted he remained airborne, flying just above Hassan's caves, nearly scraping the cliffs which rose some 200 feet from the sea. He cleared some fields, and their treacherous rubble walls, by a hair's breadth.

Moments before the Courier crash-landed on Hal Far airfield, sliding on its undersides, Cobham switched-off the engine to lessen the chances of a fire breaking out, albeit the aircraft had very little fuel left at that stage.

Damages to the Courier were minimal, while the cause of the temporary interruption to Cobham's venture was found to have simply been a loose throttle linkage pin that had fallen out of place.

Despite this unfortunate misadventure the fact remained that the feasibility of in-flight refuelling could not have been more clearly demonstrated to the aviation world.

Following a decade in the experimentation and development of an early warning system against the approach of enemy aircraft, the Air Defence Experimental Establishment in Britain had that year under construction a chain of large acoustic concrete mirrors around the southeast coast of Britain.

The Royal Engineering Board had at first baulked at the great expence needed to have these built but the Air Ministry had agreed to finance a third of the cost. Then, shy of Mussolini's aggressive anti British politics, and his great thirst for power in the Mediterranean, it was decided to have one of these mirrors constructed in Malta, their base nearest to the Italian mainland. So on 8 November 1934 a War Office contract was drawn, calling for the installation of a re-enforced concrete mirror and forecourt.

In the shape of a curved wall 200 feet long, and 25 feet high, this acoustic mirror needed to have three banks of microphones to go with it.

The 1934 annual cruise for 202 Squadron was an elaborate flight that began in July, with four aircraft leaving for Khartoum with a first stop at Syracuse. From Sicily the Faireys flew to Corfu, Athens, Rhodes, Famagusta in Cyprus, on to Haifa across to Aboukir and Helwan in Egypt and finally Khartoum. This was a five-week tour during which the squadron gained further experience.

In mid-October it was announced that 202 Squadron would soon be equipping with flying boats; however, in January 1935 its Faireys still performed patrols and searches in cooperation with the Mediterranean Fleet, although the post of CO had by then been taken over by Wg. Cdr. J.H. Jones.

Aviation traffic, particularly due to Italy's threatened invasion of Abyssinia, that was finally launched in October, and the breakout of internal trouble in Greece, that forced Imperial Airways to divert their aircraft from Athens to Malta for about a week, was far more motivated in 1935.

Four Short S.19 Singapore IIIs, which had been delivered to 202 Squadron in pairs in July and November 1934 respectively, all developed to Air Ministry Specification R3/33, were in February 1935 dispatched on a round the globe flight.

The first of these flying boats, K3592 and K3595, departed about the mid-February. On the 15th, the two Singapores became separated. One, K3592, arrived safely inside Marsaxlokk bay, but, K3595 had crashed into the mountains near Messina, killing all on board.

On the 22 February, the second flight of Singapores, K3593 and K3594, reached the island and four days later the three remaining flying boats resumed with their flight eastwards.

Singapore K4581, an ex-230 Squadron aircraft, staged through Kalafrana on 28 July on transit to the Far East as a replacement for K3595, to bring 205 Squadron, based in Singapore, up to strength.

With the exception of 267 Squadron, which flew flying boats during WW1 and the early 1920s, the only other Malta-based unit that had flying boats its on strength was 202 Squadron in the mid 1930s. Having been given prior claim to re-equip with the Scapa, a flying boat built to specification 19/33 and of which fifteen, including the prototype, had

Saro London II, K9682, of 202 Squadron at Kalafrana.

been completed in 1935, 202 Squadron received the first production machine, K4192, on 1 May of that year, after six years operating floatplanes. At this time the squadron's strength had risen to ten Fairey IIIFs amongst which were S1381, S1517, S1804, S1854 and S1865, which had reached Kalafrana via Syracuse on 21 July 1934.

Scapa K4193 arrived towards the end of May, and was on 12 June followed by K4194. In July, Scapa K4195 arrived next, with an additional two, K4196 and K4200, the latter an ex-201 Squadron aircraft, reaching Kalafrana towards the end of August 1935, bringing 202 Squadrons final replacement of its Fairey IIIs. However, the squadron's complete establishment of 4.IE and 2.IR aircraft was not concluded until May 1936, with the arrival of the sixth Scapa, K7304.

During this period visits from diverse carriers at Malta, particularly when the British Naval fleet was in the Mediterranean, activity generated on Hal Far airfield was so intense that ground crews based there refused to accept it. Shortly after Rear Admiral Ramsey visited there on 5 February 1935, however, this problem was somehow solved, easing the pressure on the overworked ground personnel.

On 6 May, activity shifted to the Marsa Sports Grounds where a review was organized to celebrate His Majesty's King George V's Jubilee;

on 9 June 1938, another birthday celebration was to be held for the then recently crowned HM King George VI.

Taking part in the celebrations were Hal Far-based 447 and Station Flights as well as ship-borne 812 and 825 Squadrons.

As a follow-up to the daytime action, the Baffins of 812 Squadron carried out illuminated night flying, and a show, in illuminated aerobatics was performed by two Avro Tutors of Hal Far Station Flight.

In June, for the benefit of local army searchlight operators, Hal Far-based aircraft were again involved in more night flying exercises, carrying out mock bombing runs.

On 1 August, two Valenzias, K4634 and K4635, staged through Hal Far loaded with troops on transit to the Middle East.

All the necessary gear needed to have the acoustic concrete mirrors constructed in Malta was loaded on the SS Fabian on 31 July 1935 and arrived at the island on 17 August.

By the end of September the mirror was declared to be completed, and the training of personnel from the 16 Coy began on 6 November 1935 under the supervision of Mr Ferquson and Mr Handford from the Air Defence Experimental Establishment, Biggin Hill.

Concrete Mirror Radar.
Constructed in 1935 it was never used operationally.

Trials on the mirror were terminated on 6 November after which two 24hour tests were carried out between the 2-3 and 5-6 December.

Its function was to track the sound of approaching aircraft by means of microphones set up at the fore-court across the mirror's line of focus. Built at Maghtab, north of the village of Naxxar, some two kilometres inland the coastline at sea level, the mirrors line-of-shoot was towards Sicily, the direction from where the British expected the enemy to come should Italy decide to attack Malta.

In a report dated 6 January 1936 during trials and training a Fairey IIIF Short Scapa, Hawker Osprey, Avro Tutor and a Vickers Vildebeeste were used.

More official extracts from test reports were issued in July 1936 and as late as April 1938 the mirror was reported still in use. However, by June 1939, the mirror had been abandoned because it was replaced in Malta's defences by Radar Station AMES241, which began operating in April 1939.

Observers during RAF exercises in UK were of the opinion that ... "... as a positive means of early warning system the mirror's reliance on sound direction, in relation to the ever increasing speeds of modern aircraft, was useless." In fact, so great was the advancement in the development of Radio Direction Finding (R.D.F) by this time that the Air Council immediately suspended the construction of anymore *acoustic mirrors*.

Meanwhile on 16 September two Singapore IIIs of 203 Squadron, K4582 and K4583, passed through Kalafrana where they made a two day stop before moving on to their destination.

These were on the 23 September followed by another three flying boats, a Singapore, K4585 of 230 Squadron, and two Scapas, K4191 and K4197, of 204 Squadron. The latter were on 26 September joined by a third Scapa, K4198, and were that very same day on transit eastwards.

The next day 230 Squadron arrived with the rest of its Singapores, K4578, K4579 and K4582 later joined by K4585 on the 28th; all four flying boats left en route to Aden.

September, with Italy poised to invade Abyssinia, was a highly motivated month in 1935. Britain, suspecting that Mussolini might turn his attention on Malta, had some RAF units shipped to the island to compliment 202 Squadron. These were that summer still familiarizing themselves with the large flying boats, while the British War Cabinet was planning on how to react best to the Middle East crisis that threatened their country's interests in Egypt.

Mussolini, whose dictatorship had been established years before, had risen to become a powerful contender in European politics, a pedestal upon which he found himself by bringing organizationto Italy, a country that the First World War had left in almost complete chaos. But Il Duce, a nickname he had bestowed upon himself, was a man whose senses succumbed easily to self importance, looking ever forward, ready to grasp at every opportunity that promised to increase to his popularity and stoking up his pomposity.

By 1935 he was almost incensed into believing that he would soon restore to his country the empire which it once had possessed, a boast which was to eventually cost him his life less than a decade later.

To start off with his conquering spree Mussolini picked Abyssinia to quarrel with. This East African state, bordering on Italian occupied Somaliland, made things that much simpler to him. He was never known to throw caution to the winds by taking undue risks, so finally determined to move into Abyssinia nothing the League of Nations said could change the Duce's mind. Unimpressed by the League's verbal warnings the Dictator kept concentrating troops and supplies, in preparation for an invasion with which he was soon to proceed, unopposed.

Britain was truly concerned about this situation. All her possessions in the Middle East were at stake, and she did not trust the Italian dictator to keep his hands off elsewhere once he was on the rampage. Precautionary measures were immediately taken. The British Mediterranean Naval Fleet, based in Malta, was signaled to sail for Alexandria, a move that would leave the island defenceless. However, the Ministry of Defence decided that provisional reinforcements should first be provided to protect their Central Mediterranean stronghold before the Fleet sailed to the Middle East.

Various infantry battalions, as well as RAF reinforcements were dispatched from Britain to supplement Malta's defences.

The method by which the drafting of the latter was worked out was motivated with one scope in mind, to mislead the enemy. In an effort to minimize the actual magnitude of these movements the Air Ministry, instead of transferring a whole RAF unit, which might have attracted immediate attention from spies and given rise to unwanted speculations, detachments from different squadrons were picked out. These included the equipment and personnel from numbers 3. 23, 32, 54, and 56 Squadrons, the Balloon Centre, the Anti-Aircraft School, coming from RAF Calshot, Eastchurch, Henlow, and

Leuchars. The Units from which RAF personnel-over one hundred men, between officers and airmen – were picked were all fighter aircraft squadrons. It was also stressed that the contingent should be a fully trained one, with a minimum of at least two years service experience, requirements motivated by the decision to have Hawker Demon Is sent to Malta.

During the drafting of personnel a number of Demons were flown straight to Sealand from various RAF bases in Britain. The Packing Depot then took on all sectional dismantling of these biplanes at this station. Original squadron markings were left untouched. Engines, contrary to general packing procedures, were left installed and, while undercarriages and centre sections were taken on board ship in situ, all movable parts were packed in light wooden crates. This, in fact, was another unorthodox crating procedure, but due to the haste with which the Hawker Demons were to be re-erected on reaching their destination this packing procedure had to be adopted.

With the troopship Neuralia out at sea none of those on board the ship, with the exception of the Commanding Officer, knew right off where they were bound. But word soon leaked out that the Mediterranean was to be their destination. It was also disclosed that most of those on board came from Demon equipped squadrons. Then realizing that nothing official had thus far been released regarding the number to be given to this newly established unit, as sometimes happens under these circumstances, someone took the liberty of using his imagination to christen it. Most probably without intending it to, when it was first suggested, the nickname Demon Flight gained in popularity to the extent, that by the time the 'Neuralia' reached Malta the name had been firmly adopted.

On 9 September, the S. S. Maihar, the ship on which the crated biplanes had been delivered to Malta, dropped anchor inside Marsaxlokk Bay, but due to the heavy swell lighters could not be maneuvered alongside for disembarkation to begin. So the task had to be abandoned, and postponed for the next day, if the weather permitted. But the dawn brought little change to the disturbed elements, and it was decided to take the 'Maihar' round to the Grand Harbour. There a 200 ton floating crane, the 'Clive', property of HM Dockyard, supplemented the ship's own derricks to hasten unloading.

By the afternoon of 17 September a substantial number of aircraft sections were transported overland to Hal Far and the next day eight Demons were rigged up, four of them ready for tuning.

Two days later the first of these were air tested and on 22 September the unit was provided with eleven serviceable aircraft.

Assembling finally concluded, the Hawker Demons were split up into three separate flights.

'A' Flight under the command of a Flt. Lt. Brooks, flew four: K2847 / K2853 / K3770 / K3784.

'B' Flight, operated five of the biplanes: K2850 / K2905 / K3767 / K3772 / K3777, under the command of Flt. Lt. Halling-Potts.

'C' Flight, commanded by a Flt. Lt. Pearson Rogers, had only K2846 / K3769 and K3773, with the post of CO over all three occupied by Sqdn. Ldr. H.G. Crowe.

Unbelievably, however, although these machines were on hand, ready to be flown at short notice, the fact remained that not a single one of them was ready for combat. None were fitted with any armament, not that the equipment was unavailable, but regrettably it was disclosed that it was badly in need of servicing, apart from other minor defects which required special attention.

(A similar case in point occurred in 1942 when more than forty Spitfires, just ferried to the island via the United States carrier USS Wasp, arrived with defective armament.) Further still, certain spares were also found missing, and at least a week was expected to elapse before these bits and pieces reached the island, and the guns on the aircraft could then be operated. Another difficulty that the unit found itself up against during the following weeks was shortage of life jackets. Oxygen gear was also in demand. Spare engines were non-existent, and realizing that the chances of receiving replacements was remote, flying was immediately restricted. This negligence, resulting from all sectors responsible for the transfer of the Hawker Demons, might have weighted down the scales of war in favour of the enemy had he decided to attack Malta at that time.

Back in 1918 when DH.9As were brought to Malta to supplement the F.3 flying boats these were equipped with a special type of floatation gear, in case of emergency landings in the sea. So, although the Scapas of 202 Squadron were ever present to patrol over territorial waters, in 1935 all RAF biplanes were equipped with the Youngmann dinghy-type floatation gear, to ensure the safety of pilots should they have to ditch in the sea.

Early in October, just for experimental purposes, local pigments were applied to one of the Hawker Demons to have it painted in camouflage.

On 9 October, 202 squadron for the first time had a Scapa airborne patrolling over Malta's territorial waters in search of Italian warship activity and plot their movements, duties that were extensively practiced during the crisis. Another squadron activity was exploratory cruises down the East African coast in search of bays suitable as flying boat bases in case of war with Italy.

While Mussolini's ambition to extend his influence farther afield in East Africa led him to launch his armies to invade Abyssinia on 12 October, that same day more RAF reinforcements arrived in Malta. These comprised of the Coastal Artillery Co-operation Flight and No. 22 Squadron, equipped with an array of torpedo carrying Vildebeests, Ospreys and Fairey IIIFs to which was included the ground personnel of 65 Squadron.

No. 22 Squadron was at the time still seeking to officially establish an emblem of its own. The sketch was eventually finished in Malta with the result that a Maltese eight-pointed cross was impressed into it, as a backdrop to a drawn mathematical Greek equation of 22/7, or 'PI'.

The 'Demon Flight', the name under which it had been functioning since its arrival in Malta, had meanwhile received a signal on 14 November that it had been operating as 74 Squadron since 3 September.

On 16 January 1936 Singapore K6907 of 203 Squadron, and Scapa K4565 of 204 Squadron, departing from Mountbatten en route to Aden and Alexandria respectively, staged through Kalafrana.

Then on 2 February Singapore K6908, another 203 Squadron aircraft, arrived from Calshot on transit to Aden.

That month, envisaging sustained daylight attacks on the island, assisted by a bombardment from enemy surface craft, preparatory for a night time invasion, a combined Navy, Army and RAF exercise was organized. This was on 11 March followed by a Civil Air Defence exercise to test the measures adopted for passive defence, for which the aircraft of 22 Squadron filled in the role of attacker, while the Demons of 74 Squadron defended.

On 23 March, the Editorial of 'Il-Berqa', Lord Strickland's Maltese counterpart to the 'Times of Malta' newspaper, under the title of 'Malta as an Air Base', had this in print:

> "We think our reasons in last Saturday's issue were clear enough to show Britain that she need not think of having her naval fleet in Malta withdrawn and base abandoned to have another established elsewhere east of the Mediterranean."

"Today we want to show that Malta's importance as a fortress have never diminished in the least. Every one admits that Malta can never be conquered by any seaward invasion force. Neither does the island need a naval force of any magnitude to neutralize such an assault should the necessity arise."

"However, today aircraft are in existence, with which Malta can be threatened at any time, but these can just as effectively be used by the British, for which a powerful RAF base, something of inestimable value to Britain, must first be established on the Island. For this purpose, however, numerous changes and alterations must be made on existing aerodromes. Hangars need to be dug underground where aircraft can be sheltered and protected from air attacks."

"It is a fact that the aircraft has increased the chance of Malta being more easily reached and assaulted twicefold, but aircraft can also provide the Island with greater importance as an airforce base than it had ever enjoyed as a naval one."

On 5 April, the arrival of His Excellency Sir Charles Bonham Carter, KCB, on board the S.S. Strathmore, gave rise to some unexpected aerial activity when, while the vessel was still some miles off the island, aircraft

A Drone Queen Bee, K5107, of A2 Gunnery Co-operation Flight taking off from inside M'Xlokk bay c.1937.

from Malta-based units provided her with an escort, these were eighteen biplanes from 22 and 74 Squadrons and three Scapas of 202 Squadron.

On 7 April, No. 2 Gunnery Co-operation Flight equipped with remote controlled Queen Bees and Swordfish target aircraft arrived from Alexandria. This was a year later given the title of No. 3 Anti-Aircraft Co-operation Unit (3 AACU).

Joining 202 Squadron the Flight's duties were to provide their aircraft to the Navy and Army gunners during exercises. For this purpose the aircraft were alternately used either with or without floats. However, in 1937, once it lost its original title, a 'B' Flight, flying float equipped Queen Bee aircraft was formed and used extensively on naval gunnery practice both in Malta and Alexandria. 'A' Flight, on the other hand, operating Swordfish from Hal Far for Army gunnery practice, occasionally had floats fitted to the aircraft.

A change in the Station's command took place on 29 April when Grp. Cap. Maris was relieved of his post by Wg. Cdr. W.L. Taylor AFC, by which time Hal Far was returning to its normal function as a Fleet Air Arm base.

Meanwhile it was becoming more apparent that the Middle East crisis was gradually diminishing, loosing most of its original threat.

A float equipped Swordfish of No. 3AACU at Kalafrana.

However all RAF units stationed on Malta had been kept on the alert, and frequent combined exercises continued unabated. Night flying had been encouraged as well as ground dispersal, scrambling, strafing attacks and bombing practiced, but the Abyssinian Crisis, who many feared was the prelude to another world conflict, finally dissolved.

Before the end of July 74 squadron was returning to Britain, with 22 squadron following it home in August.

In mid-July four Fleet Air Arm (Catapult) Flights had been formed, all shore-based at Kalafrana:

No. 701, formed from part of 447 (Catapult) Flight, flew Ospreys from ships of the 1st Battle Squadron serving with the Home and Mediterranean Fleets. Its biplanes were embarked periodically in the battleships HMS Barham and Malaya.

No. 705, formed from part of 444 (Catapult) Flight, was equipped with Swordfish floatplanes serving on ships of the Battle Cruiser, Squadron attached to the Mediterranean Fleet.

Absorbing the remainder of 447 (Catapult) Flight No. 711 inherited its Ospreys, with which it was attached to the 1st Cruiser Squadron, embarking periodically on HMS London and Devonshire.

Then, the fourth Flight, No. 713, was formed by simply renumbering 445 (Catapult) Flight. With the Ospreys on strength, the Flight was chosen to serve the 3rd Cruiser Squadron with periodical embarkation on HMS Arethusa and Galatea.

These four units, that were by 1939 elevated to the 700 series squadron status, disappeared in January 1940 as they were absorbed into other FAA squadrons.

On 27 July 1936 two Scapas of 204 Squadron arrived at Kalafrana from Alexandria on transit to Mountbatten. However, the two flying boats were unavoidably delayed due to technical problems.

Three days later Singapore K4580 and K6912 of 230 Squadron also arrived from that direction en route to Pembroke, in Britain. Then during the first week of August the rest of 230 and 204 Squadrons passed through Kalafrana on their return flight to UK, where the latter commenced re-equipping with Londons.

On 17 October three Singapores of 230 Squadron, of which two were K6192 and K4585, reached Kalafrana from Berre, and the next day, just as these couple departed, another two landed inside Marsaxlokk Bay. On 19 October the three remaining Singapores took leave of the island.

That month 202 Squadron were off on their annual cruise, their first with the Scapa, a four-aircraft tour of the Adriatic and Aegean Seas.

Another was made on 12 December when two of the squadron's flying boats K4194 and K4195 flew to Algiers. This tour, called a West African Safari, started from up the north coast to Freetown, where one of the two flying boats, K4194 and K4195, developed engine trouble, and had to be delayed. The second Scapa, however, continued on its way to Takoradi, then on to Lagos, Nigeria. But on 23 January 1937 both aircraft returned to Kalafrana.

Meanwhile, since the departure of the two RAF units from Hal Far activities on the airfield during the following months slackened considerably, then on 24 November 1936 calamity struck.

Unusually heavy storms over Malta at winter time are scarce, and tornadoes the likes of which struck across the island's south coast just a few years prior to the breakout of the second world war are a rarity.

Mr Lawrence Lateo, employed as a barber at the Royal Naval Air Station, Hal Far, had temporarily closed shop, and was on his way for a short break at the NAAFI's canteen. He was hardly halfway there when an exceptionally cold bite to the buffeting wind made him look in the direction from where it was blowing. He recalled that:

> "The heavens were ominously dark, choked by leaden grey mass of billowing cloud – the likes of which I don't ever remember seeing. Bolts of multiple jagged lightning streaked earthwards amidst reverberating claps of shattering thunder. But most frightening of all was an eerie whistling noise that increased in volume the nearer the wind-whipped tornado got."

Lateo ran for the nearest cover just as the first wind-swept hail hit the airfield.

> "The tornado swept across the airfield at frightening velocity. Luckily I was not in its path."

It hit the three large hangars that were on the airfield with devastating effect. They were ripped off their anchorage like so much chaff, and in a matter of seconds their rooftops simply disappeared without trace. All that the storm left in its wake where the hangars once stood, as it kept on blowing farther inland, were piles of twisted metals.

Damages to private property were inflicted in the village of Ghaxaq,

The pile of Baffin aircraft wreckage in the wake of a Tornado that hit Hal Far airfield on 24 November 1936.

to the northwest of Hal Far. Large hail swept across the countryside ruining acres of cultivated fields in the area, and seriously injuring two farmers.

At Hal Far, miraculously, there were no reports of casualties, but where the hangars once stood all that remained were masses of twisted girders and smashed naval biplanes.

HMS Glorious, following the completion of a major refit at Davenport, England, was recommissioned on 23 July 1935. Returning to Malta in August the carrier joined the Mediterranean Fleet, of which the warship had been part since June 1932, a prominent participant in the Navy's periodical cruises in the region. During the last quarter of 1936 Glorious had 812 and 802 Squadrons on shore transfer to Hal Far airfield, and the Baffins of the former were on that fateful 24th November day parked inside one of the storm-struck hangars. Number 812 Squadron was literally wiped out. Eight of the Baffins were found to be complete write-offs and these:

K2884 / K2885 / K2886 / K2887
K3559 / K3590 / K4776 / K4778

were eventually struck-off-charge. The following year 812 Squadron re-equipped with the Swordfish.

On 1 January 1937, dispatched on a cruise of the Mediterranean, four Saro Londons of 201 Squadron, of which three were K5259 / K5262 / K5909, landed at Kalafrana on transit to Algiers, to where they departed two days later.

Four Singapores of 210 Squadron arrived on 17 April and remained at Kalafrana until the 20th.

That same month all carrier-based units at Hal Far were withdrawn to UK to participate in the Royal Review of the Fleet at Spithead.

This movement left at Malta only the 3 AACU, which kept sending regular detachments to Alexandria and Gibraltar, and Station Flight. However, shortly after the Royal Review was over naval aircraft began arriving at Hal Far just as their carriers returned to the Mediterranean.

More Singapores appeared on 22 May, those of 209 squadron, under the command of Wg. Cdr. G.W. Bentley, DFC. Making an overnight stop the flying boats departed next day.

Saro Londons K5910 / K5911 / K6927 / K6929 of 204 Squadron arrived at Kalafrana from the UK via Gibraltar on 11 August.

Attached to Mediterranean Command the squadron carried out intensive training in night flying, as well as other exercises with naval units during a forthnight's stay in Malta. The flying boats of 204 Squadron departed on 27 August.

On 19 September the Short Singapores of 209 Squadron returned from Britain to participate in the Piracy Patrol Scheme, set up under the 'Nyon' Agreement with French forces, to discourage Italian submarines, which at this time were suspected of sinking ships supporting Communist-backed forces in the Spanish Civil War. This operation continued during the following months until December when 209 Squadron finally returned to their home base in the UK.

'Nyon' drew French-built aircraft to the island which, in cooperation with their British counterparts, patrolled over the Mediterranean. The types were mostly Loires H-257bis, a float-equipped torpedo bomber. Operating from a base in Karouba it formed the backbone of Escadrille 452. The Loire 72, a flying boat built for maritime reconnaissance purposes, also based in North Africa, formed the strength of Escadrille E7.

The Scapa's time with 202 Squadron was a comparitivelyshort one for on 24 September the unit received its first two Saro Londons, K6931 and K6932.

On 7 October, Scapa K4200 crashed inside Marsaxlokk Bay just as it was taking-off, and on 22 November, the type flew its last patrol with 202 Squadron, which recieved its last two Londons on 12 December.

On 5 October, leaving Mountbatten for Australia, five Londons of 204 Squadron stopped at Kalafrana where they made a three days stop. Just as these moved on to their destination, Singapore III K4583 of 203 Squadron, expected at Pembroke Dock for an overhaul via Sollum, arrived at Kalafrana on 8 October and, after making an overnight stop, departed for Bone.

No. 202 SQDN'S SARO LONDONS
K5259 / K6931 / K6932
K9682 / K9683 / K9684 / K9685

On 22 December 1937 the Londons of 202 Squadron were stopped from all operations, by which time the squadron had flown more than a hundred Scapa/London sorties in intensive anti-submarine search and rescue and various other exercises.

The year 1938 was one of troubled uncertainty in Europe. Britain, troubled over Germany's aircraft numerical strength, had increased her own production level to equal that of Hitler's.

During September, to oppose the German long range striking force of some 1,200 modern bombers, Fighter Command could muster, including all reserves, only 93 of the new eight-gun fighters. All the remainder of its 666 aircraft were outdated biplanes. No Spitfires were yet in line, and the Hurricane, being without heating for its guns, could not fight above 15,000 feet, even in summer.

With the breakout of hostilities in 1939, however, more than five hundred of these Hurricane fighters were ready to go into battle. But none of all this was to have any effect on Malta until late summer of 1940.

All those who knew about these activities in 1938, and read of Hitler's Nazi atrocities againt Jews and left-wing Germans, were alarmed at their implications. Actions which could easily result into a to second world war. Neither did the Spanish Civil War, which had erupted in 1936, augment well for the peace which the majority of European countries desired. In retrospect many historians described the Spanish conflict as the rehearsal for World War II. Three European powers were involved in Spain, Fascist Italy, Nazi Germany and Russia. By taking sides they used the civil war as an excuse to put their new weapons to the test. The Fuhrer that year marched his troops into Austria as well, and without any evident signs of violence, annexed the country to Germany. Then, taking advantage of the Munich Pact, an Agreement which he made with Great Britain and

France that same year, Hitler was also permitted to annex part of Czechoslovakia, which he later over-run.

The only RAF unit stationed in Malta at that time was 202 Squadron operating Saro Londons. Following an urgent call from London, two of these flying boats were employed to convey the Governor of Malta, Sir Charles Bonham-Carter, and his legal secretary to Berre, France, from where the two resumed their journey to London by train.

At Hal Far, with the exception of No. 3 AACU, no other units were established there, and carrier-based biplanes were getting scarcer, particularly with only HMS Glorious in the Mediterranean. However, during some large scale combined exercises, organized on 2 and 3 June 1938, the carrier had Nos.822, 812, 823 and 825 Squadrons, joined by 202 Squadron, involved.

Meanwhile, on 10 June, Sunderland L2159 of 230 Squadron, the first of type to appear in Malta, staged through Kalafrana on transit to Seletar.

Official calls were that month exchanged between AOC. RAF Mediterranean and Admiral A. Ricardi, commanding the Italian Squadron on the occasion of the ship's visit to Malta between the 21st / 24th. No. 822 Squadron escorted the Italian ships during their departure.

Sunderland I, N9021. Another of the type to stop at Kalafrana, 1939.

On 28 June, the FAA units of Glorious were again airborne on an exercise meant to test Malta's air defences against the possibility of a sea-borne invasion.

On 16 July, another of 230 Squadron's Sunderlands, L2161, flown by Fly. Off. Ainsley, staged through Kalafrana.

At Hal Far that same month a Fairey Seal was attached to the Station's Flight for spotting purposes as part of a coastal defence program against the threatening situation in Europe. The new buildings, which had been projected to replace what the 1936 tornado had destroyed, were that year completed, and a Bellman hangar included. Then on 8 August 3 AACU lost a Swordfish when K8384 crashed into St Paul's Bay.

That month 202 Squadron was also frequenting the bay as an advance base.

Shortly afterwards a period of emergency was held on Hal Far airfield between September and October, during which a flow of RAF aircraft were recorded as having been through on transit to the Middle East. However the first of these were noted to have passed through Kalafrana on 4 September, when 228 Squadron, equipped with their new machines, five Stanrears, K7280 / K7290 / K7292 / K7294 and K7296, was en route eastwards.

No. 202 Squadron was on, 22 September, ordered to reach a state of preparedness, and three days later a movement order was received. With embarkation of ground crews, stores and spares in HMS Maidstone completed the ship steamed for Alexandria, and after 27 September the squadron's Londons were for a period gone from Kalafrana.

At Hal Far, on 22 October five Ansons of 4 FTS Flying Training School landed on the airfield on transit to Abu Sueir, while five more passed through on 26 October. These were:

L7973 / L7974 / L7975 / L7976 / L7977
L7991 / L7992 / L7993 / L9145 / L9146

In between these two Anson transits, on 24 October, five Wellesleys:

L2637 / L2638 / L2639 / L2682 / L2681

from LROU (Long Range Development Unit) led by Wg. Cdr. R. Gayford and Sqdn. Ldr. R. Kellett, landed at Hal Far on transit to Ismalia, from where three, L2638, L2639 and L2680, were to fly on to Australia.

The aircraft moved on to their destination after an overnight stop.

Meanwhile, with 202 Squadron back at Kalafrana live bombing practice on Filfla was carried out by the squadron's flying boats. Other duties performed by the Londons during November were searches for suspected shipping and updating of all photographs of Italian ports in North Africa.

On 26 January 1939, with the ongoing threat of hostilities, two of the squadrons aircraft flew to Casablanca via Gibraltar to carry out an exercise in the Western Approaches.

In March two of the Londons flew across to Athens for a short visit. Then towards the middle of spring it was rumoured that the Saro Londons of 202 Squadron may soon be withdrawn, to be replaced by the Sunderland. Nevertheless, the news proved to be unfounded. Although two of the squadron's flying boats flew to UK on 30 April, where their crews were supposed to receive initial training on the Sunderland, and two of the type did visit Kalafrana during this interval, it was 228 Squadron which finally re-equipped with the large four-engined flying boat.

Kalafrana Seaplane Base late 1920s, with Hal Far in the far background.

Meanwhile tension the in Europe increased as, in the early days of April, Mussolini invaded and conquered Albania. Defence posts were immediately manned, and a state of emergency was declared, while 202 Squadron was kept in a state of readiness. Further precautionary measures taken by Britain in the Mediterranean was the forming of No. 86 (General Reconnaissance) Wg. to have control over 202 and 228 Squadrons. The ship S.S Domana was provided to serve as the Wings' mobile base, and towards the end of the month she steamed for the Middle East.

On 24 May the Fleet Air Arm, which the Admiralty had been striving to have under their control, was officially handed over to the navy with all its squadrons and their aircraft.

Meanwhile in June four Londons were picked for that year's cruise; this proved to be 202 Squadron's last cruise because the following year war broke out in the Mediterranean. The Londons, departing on the 12th, toured the Aegean where they visited various Greek bases, before returning to Kalafrana early in July.

During the next few weeks night flying was frequently carried out, and by the end of August full war preparations were in force. On 2 September, an air raid warning practice was organized as a counter measure should Italy become involved in the war.

At about this time Wg. Cdr. J.S. Fall relinquished Hal Far's Station Command to Sqdn. Ldr. W.L. Houlbrook, former CO of 3 AACU.

With the Sunderlands of 228 Squadron based at Alexandria, and Britain now at grips with Germany, the former, suspecting that Hitler might be tempted to maneuvre his U-Boats through the Straight of Gibraltar, moved 202 Squadron to patrol over that part of the Mediterranean. This resulted that the Anti-Aircraft Co-operation Unit was turned into an operational unit, performing anti-submarine and close reconnaissance patrols over Maltese coastal waters. Meanwhile Station Flight and Station Hqtrs personnel were all absorbed into No. 3 AACU.

(The RAF had by the end of 1942 formed units operating long-range land-based aircraft for reconnaissance purposes. So 228 and 230 Squadrons remained the only two British units operating flying boats in the eastern Mediterranean. At the western end 202 Squadron had at Gibraltar been re-equipped with the Catalina, a twin-engined American-built amphibious aircraft.)

Chapter IV

Malta Gladiators

The Legend – An Island defenceless – Gloster Gladiators – HMS Glorious – 802 Squadron – Station Fighter Flight – Hostilities – Britain's only hope – The Hurricane – Out of the Ashes: "Faith" – Presentation – Museum exhibit

Stripped of its equipment by the British War cabinet, nowhere was the RAF as unprepared for the coming conflict in the Mediterranean as it was in Malta in 1940.

Had it not been for the handful of Fleet Air Arm biplanes, loaned by the Admiralty, with which to improvise a temporary fighter aircraft unit of sorts, the RAF would not have had a single aircraft with which to offer any resistance to the Regia Aeronautica. The Italian air force was armed to the teeth when Italy entered the war, as of midnight of 10 June 1940.

In later years these same Sea Gladiators received a tremendous amount of publicity, their actions being accepted widely as fact. The story of 'three' indestructible Gladiators, 'FAITH' – 'HOPE' – 'CHARITY', their pilots flying them constantly against overwhelming odds, throttles at maximum boost, 'right through the gate', to provide Malta's solitary air defence, could not fail to give a romantically dramatized, though hardly accurate, reading.

Actually the Malta Gladiators' primary line of defence lasted until 2 August with the arrival of the first 12 Hurricanes ferried via HMS Argus, composed of 418 Flight with which Fighter Flight Malta was amalgamated to form 261 Squadron.

Earlier still, on 21 June to be exact, a handful of Hurricanes on transit to the Middle East were kept on the island to supplement the biplanes and robbed most of the highlight the Gladiators had been enjoying.

Despite its shortcomings, and short-lived existence, however, the Gladiator served a notable purpose. It led Regia Aeronautica pilots to believe that there were more of the biplanes than there actually were. Furthermore its pilots succeeded in achieving the destruction of the first enemy aircraft of the war over Malta.

Malta, with its strategic location in the Central Mediterranean, have always been observed with great interest, but the island's isolation, and its dependence on overseas trade for survival, were against it in times of stress. To Britain, however, with the rise of Nazism and Fascism looming ahead, Malta acquired another dimension with the result that in 1939 the Committee for the Imperial Defence approved the introduction of a long-term air defence program for the island.

After Britain's hopes for peace with Germany were shattered, when Hitler broke all the promises made between the two countries, first by invading Poland, then turning his armed forces on more of his neighbouring countries, serious doubts remained as to whether Malta was worth defending. The island's isolation and its proximity to Italy were doubtless against it in such a situation.

Air Commodore F.H. Maynard, AOC; Malta.

The observer countries present at Versailles, when strict disciplinary terms were dictated to Germany in 1919, had long observed these arrogant actions by the Fuhrer. However, none of them had dared to enforce them upon the Nazi dictator when he first came into power in 1933. Four years later it was far too late to do anything about it.

By the end of March 1940, Air Commodore F.H. Maynard, who was in January appointed

AOC Malta, lost all hope of receiving the promised squadrons. With the exception of the few Swordfish in use by No. 3 AACU (Anti-Aircraft Cooperation Unit) for target-towing duties, and a solitary radio-controlled DeHavilland Queen Bee, as far as he was aware, there were no other aircraft on the island. But Group Capt. N.G. Gardner, Chief Administrative Officer, knew otherwise and informed Maynard that there were a number of crated naval aircraft in storage at Kalafrana.

In 1938, when the aircraft being considered to succeed the main Fleet fighter, the 181mph Hawker Nimrod, was still a year away, the Navy was in need of an immediate replacement for the biplane. A small number of Gloster Gladiators were first obtained from the RAF on an extended loan then an order for 80 Sea Gladiators was put forward by the Navy of which deliveries began early in the Spring of 1939.

On 21 March 1939 Glosters delivered 24 brand new biplanes to No. 38 MU, a batch carrying serials N5512 to N5535. Packed in wooden crates at Ellesmere the Gladiators were shortly afterwards shipped to the Mediterranean onboard the freighter Nailsea Court.

On arrival at Malta on 30 April six, N5512 to N5517, were moved on to Alexandria while the remaining eighteen, N5518 to N5535, were stored at Kalafrana.

These 18 biplanes, which were all meant for HMS Glorious, were immediately taken in hand for assembling which went on well into May, after which the Gladiators began operating from Hal Far airfield as 802 Squadron.

Of these N5534 on 19 May became the first casualty when, engaged in a simulated air combat, it stalled while climbing from a low altitude. The pilot, Sub. Lt.William A. Sykes, had no chance to recover control of the biplane and it crashed into the sea near Filfla.

Meanwhile on 14 May, HMS Glorious had returned to Malta from Alexandria, bringing with her three of the six Gladiators delivered there earlier. These, N5512, N5513 and N5517 were immediately assembled to join the others with 802 Squadron at Hal Far.

On 6 June Glorious departed for Alexandria and the 20 Gladiators were landed on board the carrier off Malta.

N5512 was in August sent to China for deployment onboard on HMS Eagle.

On 3 September 1939 Britain declared War against Germany and three days later the Gladiators of 802 Squadron were practicing air to air firing in earnest. The next day they were busy exercising on

HMS Glorious entering Grand Harbour in March 1940.

Squadron Air Drill and fighter attacks. But what was most notable was the "Crash Embarkation" movement from Dakheila to HMS Glorious on 11th September.

The next day a long session of Air Surveillance Patrols was launched, lasting for three consecutive days, but there were no reports of any sightings.

These activities were late in the afternoon of 14 September followed by dummy machine gun attacks on HMS Warspite. Then two days later 802 Squadron was disembarked off HMS Glorious at Dakheila.

On 9 October the aircraft carrier departed from Alexandria to carry-out anti surface-raider patrols in the Indian Ocean, leaving all of the 19 Gladiators in Egypt.

A second casualty was suffered on 11 October, when Gladiator N5528 crashed in Lake Mayrut killing Sub Lt.T E Clark.

Shortly after this incident the remaining 18 biplanes were dismantled, returned to their crates, and shipped to Hyeres in France, where they were reassembled and for the next two months flown on operational training.

Towards the end of December 1939, the biplanes were again packed in their crates and returned to Malta. Arriving on the 23rd of the month they were immediately stored still in their crates at the Kalafrana aircraft repair section.

Early in March 1940 eight of the biplanes, N5518, N5521, N5525, N5526, N5527, N5530, N5532 and N5533 were assembled and began operating from Hal Far.

At this time, due to the deteriorating situation in the North Sea the British War Cabinet decided to withdraw HMS Glorious from the Mediterranean and have her replaced by HMS Eagle, which was still stationed in the Far East.

This movement ultimately led to the splitting up of the Sea Gladiators between the two aircraft carriers. It was decided to deploy eight on HMS Glorious and ten on HMS Eagle.

While HMS Glorious was approaching Malta from Alexandria, en route to the UK, all the assembled Gladiators at Hal Far were flown on to her.

The remaining ten still in storage at Kalafrana were earmarked for HMS Eagle with the result that Malta was left literally defenceless against air attacks should an enemy decide to mount any against her.

It was the 10 Gladiator which Gardner indicated to Maynard as being in storage at Kalafrana and Maynard immediately asked the Navy for the loaning of some of these fighters.

The Chief of Naval Staff's attitude towards the AOC's request proved favourable. After consultations with his Staff Admiral Sir Andrew Cunningham, then Commander-In-Chief Mediterranean, who had the Island's safety at heart, gave his permission to the RAF for the loan of specific Naval articles from the stores at Kalafrana.

Early in April measures had been taken to have RAF Station Hal Far provided with a Station Fighter Flight, under the command of Wg. Cdr. G. R. O' Sullivan.

On 19 April 1940 four of the Sea-Gladiators, N5519, N5520, N5524, and N5531 were finally transferred to the RAF. These biplanes were taken in hand by Flg. Off. Collins, Officer-in-Charge of the Aircraft Repair Section at Kalafrana, who had them assembled and delivered to Hal Far where they were to form what was to become known as Fighter Flight, Malta, which was operational by 23 April.

Collins, who was aware that his services would now be needed, joined by a handful of eager British and Maltese servicemen, volunteered to man a badly needed maintenance crew.

Three of Malta's Gladiators at Hal Far early in June 1940.

Although jubilant by these few biplane fighter aircraft, Commodore Maynard knew that this gain was far from solving all his problems, as no trained fighter pilots were then available on the island. But hardly had word spread when volunteers began to gather.

Flt. Lt. G. Burgess, Air Commodore Maynard's personal aid, was the first to volunteer. From Hal Far's original staff came Sqdn. Ldr. A. C. Martin. Two other members from Martins own group, Flg. Off. W.J. (Timber) Woods and Flt. Lt. P.G. Keeble, enlisted as well. Two other volunteers were Flg. Off.s J.L Waters and P. Hartley both from No. 3 AACU. Another pilot, a member of the radio-controlled Queen Bee Experimental Flight, Plt. Off. B. Alexander, also joined.

'Timber' Woods. One of Fighter Flight's pioneers.

Of this group only Flg. Off. J. Waters had any experience in Gladiators. An ex-No. 3.AACU pilot, he had in March spent a week on HMS Glorious training in the biplane with 802 Squadron.

On 23 April, R/T and armament training, as well as live bombing, was

Waters, Hartley and Alexander, another three stalwart volunteers of Fighter Flight (Malta).

carried out in cooperation with 3 AACU. A few days later, however, with the Flight personnel in high spirits, news that the RAF transport ship Dumana would early in May be calling at Kalafrana to pick up the ten Sea Gladiators, spoiled their day. The biplanes were reportedly to be transported to Alexandria for delivery to HMS Eagle.

On 29 April, the four biplanes were dismantled and, their morale shattered, the small RAF group watched them being returned to their crates, and the recently formed Fighter Flight was dissolved.

Meanwhile, however, the Navy evidently seems to have been considering the situation. They decided that only three of the Gladiators would be of any use on board HMS Eagle. So on 4 May, when Dumana departed from Kalafrana, it had only three of the crated fighters, N5513, N5517 and N5535, in its hold.

This resulted that with the packing procedure barely over, counter orders were given to Flg. Off. Collins. The effect this movement had on Fighter Flight's personnel was remarkable as on 3 May they were regrouped under a reformed Fighter Flight to receive the return of the biplanes.

The new Gladiator jockeys were soon experiencing minor difficulties. More adept to slower, and heavier, types of aircraft they were discovering that their new mounts were too agile for them, but with permission to increase the pilots' hours of flying practice granted, the situation improved.

A number of modifications were ultimately made to the Gladiators, mainly motivated by suggestions made by the pilots themselves. The most outstanding feature was undoubtedly the addition of armour plating. Wg. Cdr. Louks recalls that:

> "I had taken a template to the Dockyard for an armour plated shield behind the pilot."

HM Dockyard had these shields made from the lightest gauge material and fitted to the cockpit bulkhead for pilot protection. Ironically, however, this vital addition increased the aircraft's overall weight, so revisions to the biplanes' structure had to be made as a remedy. This led to the removal of the arrestor hook, dinghy compartment, and a few other features.

That month Germany was advancing on France, causing great concern all over Europe at the realization that this might prove too tantalizing an opportunity for the likes of Mussolini, who had long been a Nazi sympathizer.

In fact the Dictator was highly impressed with the progress the Fuhrer was making. Other countries, however, watched with great anxiety, suspecting that if Italy joined the conflict this would surely spread to the far reaches of Europe and the Mediterranean.

War Headquarters – Malta took immediate precautionary measures against the possibility of an invasion by Italy. Airfields were littered with all sorts of bulky junk available, keeping a single flight path clear of obstructions on Hal Far airfield. Aircraft movements were restricted to solitary take off and landing in the daytime. Furthermore, unless a pilot knew of this pathway, it was not easy to spot from the air, making landing hazardous. Then, in the evening, when all flying was over for the day, obstacles were shifted to obliterate all traces of this solitary landing strip.

By the middle of May Fighter Flight was prepared as far as it could possibly be, albeit a very poorly equipped unit from whichever way you looked at it, should hostilities break out in the Mediterranean.

Due to the limited number of aircraft and personnel on strength a re-organization program had to be adopted by Fighter Flight. The unit was split up into two, so that it could operate in a sort of shift system. This brought into operation two flights with three pilots each. One was intended to take off soon after sun up, and another early in the afternoon. This was to be followed by the first, if the need for an extra patrol was required later in the day. It was also established, for economical purposes, that only two of the Gladiators were to be kept airborne at any one time.

Meanwhile, under pressure from their French ally, in one desperate effort to tempt Mussolini to remain neutral, Britain nearly offered Malta, along with some of her other colonies, to Italy as a peace token. This was on a proposal put by the then French Premier Paul Reynaud, who suspected Italy was preparing to join forces with Germany.

Winston Churchill invited his colleagues to consider what terms Italy would probably demand of Britain. Uppermost in his own thoughts were the neutralization of Gibraltar and the Suez Canal, as well as the demilitarization of Malta, including the limiting of British naval forces in the Mediterranean. Churchill believed little would be gained from such an approach, still it was for the War Cabinet to decide.

Some of the ministers were initially tempted, believing Mussolini was against a Hitler dominated Europe.

"If Britain was capable of obtaining terms which would not interfere in her independence..." Noted down one minister in his diary, he claimed he was ready to jump at the opportunity. "...if we could get out of this jam."

Having earlier decided that the island was indefensible the British War Cabinet was at first of the opinion that Malta could readily be dispensed with. But with Reynaud's departure for France, Churchill, now with greater freedom of speech, said:

> "... If France could not defend herself, it is better that she should get out of the war rather than she should drag us into a settlement which involves intolerable terms!"

On 27 May, while the debate was still unresolved, the French Ambassador, Rene Corbin, reminded the British War Cabinet of Reynáud's proposals, stressing the need for an early settlement, giving specific "geographical precision".

The War Cabinet Ministers shied guiltily at the reminder and what it implied, confessing that such bartering would be a grave crime indeed, if they were to be found out and exposed. If Mussolini accepted, Hitler would soon get to know what they had done, giving rise to consequences too terrible even to think about. But Mussolini had by then already decided to join Nazi Germany, and France was abandoned to her fate, with all thoughts of bartering British territories forgotten.

Although the Duce had been observing Germany claim victory upon victory with great interest, and not a little envy, since the invasion of Poland, it was the 'blitzkrieg' of 10 May 1940 that finally robbed him of all reasoning, and dreams of power and glory got the better of him. The fact that his airforce was not prepared for war, due to the modernization and re-equipment program it had just embarked upon, deterred him little. However the Regia Aeronautica still presented an impressive force, even though many of its aircraft were all but absolete.

The outbreak of hostilities in the Mediterranean was at that time imminent, while Malta's state of defence, particularly her airfields, on which, with the exception of Hal Far, aircraft were non-existent, was frightful.

Of these there were three:

HAL FAR:

Complete with hangars and outbuildings, this was the only airfield fully equipped as such. But due to lack of any surfaced runways it had the tendency to become bogged down very easily in places after heavy downpours.

TA' QALI:

Established in the mid-1930s as an airport for civil aviation, it was located on the site of what had once been an ancient lake, with the result that heavy rainfalls could easily turn its surface into a quagmire.

LUQA:

On this aerodrome runways were given a top layer of bitumen macadam more than two inches thick. This was built with one scope in mind, the exclusive use of strike aircraft, but it was understood that, in the event that the other two airfields became waterlogged, any aircraft operating from them at the time was to use Luqa.

Sited on high ground, the aerodrome overlooked the Grand Harbour. Work on it was started in October 1938 by a specialized construction team who, shortly after the breakout of hostilities with Germany in September 1939, was withdrawn from Malta and moved to France.

Designed for heavy aircraft, construction difficulties were many due to the levelling off of hills and quarries. It can only be left to the imagination what problems were met by the locally organized labour force, unassisted by modern equipment, to finish the aerodrome after the British constructors departed.

The first landing on this aerodrome was performed in a Swordfish of No. 3 AACU, flown by Flt. Lt. G. Burgess, in June 1939, but Luqa was not completed before Spring of 1940, to become an RAF Station on 1st April. A week later, on 8 April, a Flamingo, R2784, on transit to the Middle East, landed on the aerodrome.

When, in June 1940, 830 FAA Squadron was established at Hal Far with their Swordfish, and Hurricanes arrived on the island, Fighter Flight made a move to Luqa on 28 June.

After many of the civilians engaged there had left, manned by a skeleton crew from Kalafrana and Hal Far, an independent RAF headquarters were set up.

The Admiralty, due to the island's poor ground, and poorer air defences, ordered the withdrawal of their fleet from Malta. Worse still was the fact that none of all these movements could have possibly gone unnoticed by Italian civil aviators. These still staged through the island on flights which were permitted to go on regularly up till 5 June, shortly before Italy declared war against Britain as the armies of the Reich penetrated the Siene, and France began to crumble.

Radios in Malta were kept tuned for days on end at this time as people waited expectantly for news of Mussolini's intentions.

As usual Kingsway in Valletta on 10 June was crowded. As usual people laughed and chattered away merrily. Suddenly these sounds were hushed down. A new cry was taken up, spreading like wildfire as it passed rapidly from mouth to mouth.

"War ... Italy have just declared war."

The crowd's noisy chattering began to fade away as people gradually vacated the streets, excited and apprehensive, to return to their homes.

Shortly afterwards out of the darkness of night crept an uneasy silence that settled on the island until the dawn.

People woke up to go about their business as usual, albeit with furtive, anxious, glances skywards, many hoping that what they had listened to the evening before was nothing more than a bad dream.

Others were of the opinion that Italy was unprepared for a military

Palace Square, Valletta, 10 June 1940, Italy declares war.

confrontation with the British. However few, if any of the islanders, were aware of Malta's own state of unpreparedness.

(Author's recollections of that unforgettable morning:

"I was rudely dragged out of bed into sudden, blurry, semi-consciousness, one small wrist firmly held in my mother's grasp. On her right arm was my baby sister.

Terrified, she scurried down two flights of stairs, dragging me after her. All three of us were still in our underwear, bed sheets streaming in our wake. Finally the closed street door must have brought my parent to her senses. Our mad rush was abruptly abandoned.

At that time I was too young to understand what all the panic was about. However, I can still recall hearing, and feeling, very distinctly, the sounds and tremours, not unlike those made by distant thunder, while my mother mumbled incoherent prayers under her breath.")

This must have surely been one of the numerous confused scenes that must have heralded the dawn of Tuesday, 11 June 1940, the morning Italy launched her first air bombardment of the war in the Mediterranean – over Malta. Seven formations of five SM79s attacked in just as many waves, their objectives the Grand Harbour, Hal Far airfield and Kalafrana.

The first two Gladiators took off from Hal Far airfield, grabbing for elevation where some enemy Macchi MC200 fighter aircraft were visible weaving about above the bombers.

Although Sqdn. Ldr. Martin and Flt. Lt. Burgess reported making a few fleeting passes at the formations nothing resulted from their efforts. One of the things they discovered was that the SM79's three-motors propelled it faster than their Gladiators in level flight.

In the afternoon another attack ensued, its pattern similar to the previous one, on the same targets, with the exception that the number of escorting fighters was noticeably less.

Fly. Off. Woods planned to exceed the altitude of the enemy bomber formations. He knew that by gaining this altitude he could match the speed of the faster SM79s by diving from above them.

When nearly at this advantageous position, however, Woods was

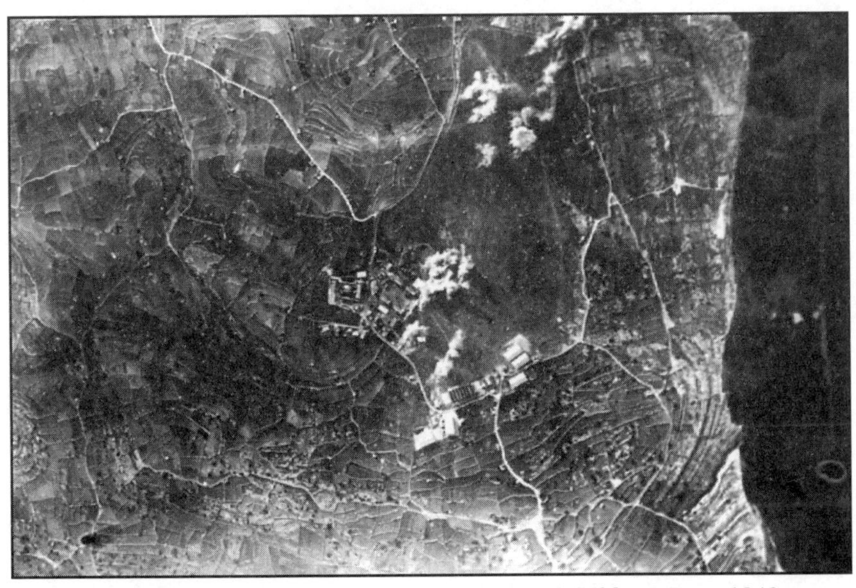

First enemy bombardment was on Hal Far airfield, 11 June 1940.

suddenly pounced on by an enemy fighter. He later wrote about this encounter.

Recorded here are the final lines of his air combat report:

> "...suddenly I heard machine-gun fire from behind me. I immediately went into a steep left-hand turn and saw a single-engine fighter diving and firing at me. For quite three minutes I circled as tightly as possible and got the enemy in my sights. I got in a good burst. Full deflection shot, and he went down in a steep dive with black smoke pouring from his tail. I could not follow him down, but he appeared to go down in the sea."

In later years it was ascertained that the Macchi actually managed to reach the coast of Sicily safely, on almost dry fuel tanks which, in effect, were drained during the Italian's own evasive action in the engagement with Woods. This was an issue that few have ever really questioned, the destruction of an enemy fighter by a RAF biplane, on the very first day of the fighting. In retrospect, however, Woods did state in his report that his opponent, "...appeared to go down in the sea."

After this couple of day's consistent enemy attacks it was considered desirable to increase the Island's fighter aircraft defenses. Hence, on 14 June, an additional two biplanes, N5522 and N5529, were transferred to the RAF. Unfortunately, however, anyone flying in any of these two Gladiators had to do so without the benefit of protective armour plating.

Fortunately Malta was given secondary importance by Italy, and remained so until the latter surrendered.

This was a strategic error that later proved disastrous to the Axis in the battle for North Africa. Mussolini's primary objective then was France, and the territory it was still occupying in Tunisia. Consequently, shortly after launching his first offensive on Malta, the Dictator concentrated his main airborne forces against Tunisia. But the French resistance there proved weaker than expected with the result that strike units of the Regia Aeronautica soon returned to Sicily. In fact on 10 July, Italy resumed with her attacks on the Island. Four bomber formations, totalling some twenty SM79s, bombed various locations around the Grand Harbour area. On this occasion CR42s, which were to escort the bombers, arrived nearly an hour early with the result that they ran low on fuel, and had to return to base when they were most needed by the bombers. Consequently the RAF Hurricanes intercepting the latter had a field day. They struck hard shooting down three of the SM79s and damaged several others.

The Gladiator pilots were constantly on the alert during this period, rising to intercept the enemy each time he made an appearance. But the chances of engaging the elusive SM79s, or their escort, were remote due to the high altitudes at which they flew, and speeds superior to their own biplanes. Surprisingly, however, their presence, in effect, did spoil the aim of a number of attacking bombers. So the gallantry of the men of Fighter Flight did succeed in confusing the enemy.

The withdrawal of these two biplanes from Kalafrana now left in storage one solitary Gladiator, N5523, which was most probably shipped to Egypt on one of the ships of convoy MF-4 in January 1942.

June 21st was not a lucky day for the Gladiators of Fighter Flight. Sqdn. Ldr. Martin and another pilot, scheduled to undertake the morning's first patrol, ran into trouble. During take off the undercarriage of Martin's biplane hit one of the numerous obstacles littering Hal Far airfield and crashed. This accident to Gladiator N5531 so early in the day was not an encouraging start. Then in the afternoon P. Hartley damaged the undercarriage of N5522 in a similar mishap, but succeeded in keeping the biplane airborne. However the damage done to its undercarriage led to its collapse as the aircraft was landed and crashed.

Neither one of the pilots was injured but Fighter Flight suffered a severe blow.

A survey of the two wrecked biplanes showed Commanding Engineering Officer, Sqdn Ldr A.E. Louksthat one good Gladiator could be put together fromthe remains. One biplane, N5531, sustained heavy damages to the front end of its fuselage and the other, N5522, had a mangled stern end; which seems to have resulted to the disappearance of this number from that date onward.

Late in the evening of that day Berlin radio announced that the Regia Aeronautica had succeeded in destroying harbour installations and bombed Britain's naval base in Malta out of action.

To verify this report a SM79 was the next day sent on a photoreconnaissance sortie over the Island.

Flt. Lt. Burges, and Flg. Off. Woods were scrambled to intercept the unescorted aircraft. They succeeded in reaching an altitude above 14,000 feet, by which time the enemy, flying nearly 3,000 feet below their height, was over Marsaxlokk Bay, heading towards the Grand Harbour.

Reassured that neither of them needed to cover the other from any escorting enemy fighters the two Gladiators dived on the unsuspecting SM79.

Burges recalls:

> "'Timber' went in first but I did not see any results. I managed to get right behind it and shot off the port engine. I was told this happened right over Sliema and Valletta and caused quite a stir in the population. The aircraft caught fire and crashed in the sea off Kalafrana."

Of the crew of six on board the aircraft only two baled out. These were later picked up from the sea just off the Grand Harbour to be taken prisoners, Malta's first airmen in the war, Lt. Francesco Solimena and Wireless Operator Nunzio Torrisi. The stricken SM79, 'MM22068', crashed into the sea off the island.

This was Fighter Flight's first victory.

The next day Burges was to achieve another success when, paired with Woods, they were scrambled to intercept an incoming raid. Flying in N5519, to which repairs had been rapid1y made, Burges was involved in a dogfight with an MC200, which he out maneuvered, using the Gladiator's nimbleness, and shot down. The pilot baled out safely.

In the afternoon of 23 June, a Gladiator, N5529, piloted by Flg. Off. Woods, collided against a parked Queen Bee where, it had been placed as an obstruction, inflicting minor damages to the biplane.

That same day a flight of SM79s, escorted by some MC200s, mounting a raid on Hal-Far airfield, were given a hot reception by the Island's ground defences whose concentrated barrage damaged an enemy fighter, forcing the pilot to crash-land on the outskirts of the village of Mqabba.

Five Hurricanes, P2614, P2623, P2629, P2645, and P2653, which had been on transit to the Middle East, were on 21 June, kept in Malta to supplement the Gladiators. To these was included a Lockheed Hudson I, flown by Plt. Off. V. Davies, that arrived with the fighters as a navigational aircraft.

Twenty-six unescorted SM79s, in waves of fives, dropped their bombs from extreme altitude round the Grand Harbour, Kalafrana and Hal Far areas on 26 June.

Four days later military installations were again the primary objective of yet another sixteen of the bombers.

George Burges, 22 June 1940, claims his first victory and Malta's first shot down enemy aircraft.

For the first time Hurricanes were scrambled to intercept them, but this maneuvre was more for the benefit of the new pilots to gain practical experience in air combat, rather than to get them directly involved with the escorting gaggle of MC200s.

Although Italy intended to replace the antiquated Fiat CR42 by the Macchi MC200 shortly after joining in the conflict, due to two consecutive crashes suffered by the latter, and the difficulties encountered in tracing the fault, the MC200 was grounded by the end of June. This resulted in the biplane remaining the Regia Aeronautica's frontline fighter until autumn, debuting over Malta on 2 July. That was the day when the Hurricane was for the first time scrambled to intercept the enemy, but after a short encounter the Italians withdrew, and neither side reported any claims or losses.

On 3 July two SM79s approached the island for reconnaissance purposes, escorted by nine CR42s. Intercepted by Waters in one of the recentlyarrived Hurricanes he succeeded in shooting down one of the SM79s. But as the RAF pilot came in to land he was set upon by CR42s and his aircraft was so badly shot up that he was forced to crash land, wrecking the Hurricane.

The Italians, unsettled about the presence of the new British monoplane, the next day twenty-four of their CR42s struck at Luqa aerodrome, obviously intending to catch the Hurricanes on the ground. All they succeeded in doing, however, was extensively damage one of the fighters.

In the afternoon two SM79s, sent to photograph the morning's results left by the Fiats, fell foul to two patrolling Hurricanes, which shot down one of the bombers into the sea.

This must have further worried the Italian High Command for the RAF fighter appeared as a threat to their efforts to neutralize the island. But on 8 July thirty enemy bombers attacked local airfields in three separate waves.

The next day ten more, escorted by nine CR42s, bombed Luqa and Hal Far airfields, intending to kill two birds with one stone by destroying as many as they could of the Hurricanes and the Swordfish on the two aerodromes. But again the Regia Aeronautica failed miserably, and lost a bomber to the guns of two patrolling Hurricanes in the attempt.

Conserving equipment and keeping his men alive was the AOC's main concern and this lent its weight to the fighter limit on patrol. When either Hurricanes or Gladiators were sent up during air-raids this was to distract the bombers, and create aerial confusion among them, rather

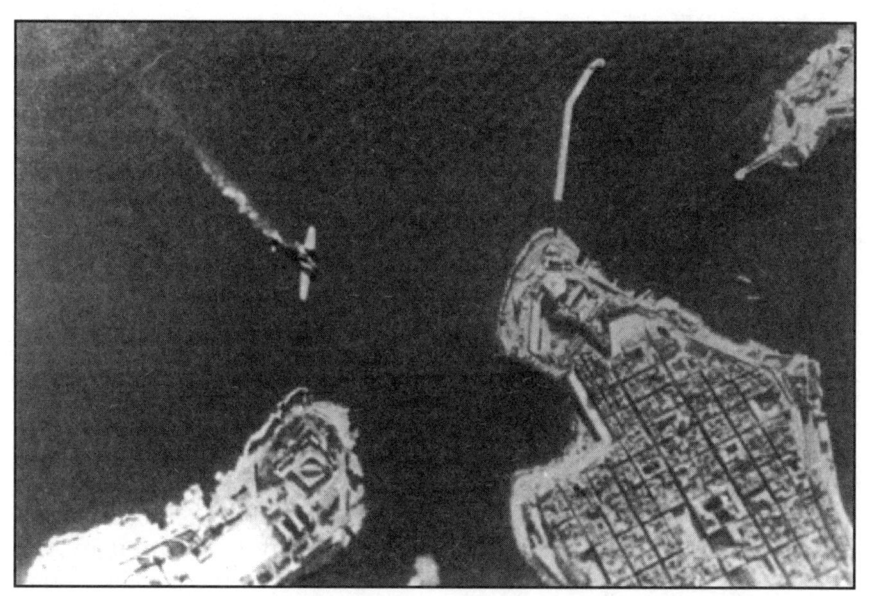

SM79 suspected to be that of Sottotenente Felice Filippi of 195a Squadriglia, as it went down within the Grand Harbour area on 10 July 1940.

than to get his pilots involved in actual combat, particularly with the knowledge that at no time were the odds in favour of his men. Although fuel was still abundant and ammunition was not short, both had to be conserved. Furthermore, when a Hurricane was damaged, Collins and his crew were encountering problems when it came to repairing this fighter. These repairs were proving complex on the monoplane, both due to lack of technical experience and specialized equipment.

Occasionally, however, the 'inevitable' happened. The RAF pilots came to grips with the enemy now and again, resulting in tentative encounters, which unavoidably encouraged them to get 'accidentally' involved with him more often, hoping for a successful engagement. However, the luck of the Malta pilots was not destined to last out indefinitely.

On 18 July Fighter Flight (Malta) was blooded for the first time.

As usual only two aircraft, a Gladiator and one Hurricane, were that day spared to hustle the dozen CR42s that came in to the attack, outnumbering the RAF fighters by six to one.

The two were in difficulties from the outset, hard-pressed by the small, agile, enemy biplanes. The encounter developed into a long drawn out full-scale battle. Aircraft chased one another all over the sky. The RAF pilots, as expected, became separated. It was every man for himself after that, each intent on making as difficult a target of himself as he possibly could, looking for any opening through which he might blast his way through the gaggle of CR42s hounding him at every turn, twist and dive.

In his Gladiator Burges succeeded in eluding his nemesis and escaped. Keeble, however, albeit in a faster and sturdier aircraft, failed to outmanoeuvre the two biplanes stuck doggedly to his rear. Over open waters he managed to shake off one of the two pursuers.

Shortly afterwards the remaining combatants crossed the coastline round the Grand Harbour area at zero altitude. Flying over the undulating countryside, the Italian was apparently determined to finish off the RAF fighter before breaking away.

The Hurricane's nose shot suddenly skywards, momentarily obstructing the CR42's'flightpath, whose pilot, trapped by the suddenness of this manoeuvre, had no chance to avoid the collision that followed, destroying the two aircraft and killing both pilots.

A few days later Burges was to become the first Malta pilot to recieve the Distinguished Flying Cross (DFM). A distinction that was published in the London Gazette of 19 July 1940, with the citation reading:

> "Although normally a flying-boat pilot, and only transferred to fighter duties since the commencement of the war with Italy, Flt. Lt. Burges has shot down three enemy aircraft and so damaged three more that they probably failed to reach their base. He has shown great tenacity and determination in seeking combat, usually in the face of superior numbers."

Then, on 31 July, escorted by some dozen CR42s, a lone SM79 flew over the island on a reconnaissance sortie. RAF fighters were scrambled to intercept and in the ensuing encounter Gladiator N5519 was pounced on by one of the enemy CR42s, flown by Sergente Tarantino, and shot down in flames. This was the first of type to get lost in air combat with the enemy since the breakout of hostilities. The pilot, Fly. Off. P. Hartley, who succeeded in baling out of the biplane, was so severely burnt that his flying days over Malta were terminated.

In the same encounter, however, flying in Gladiator N5529, Woods in turn succeeded in shooting down one of the CR42s.

The Hurricane should have overshadowed the Gladiator since its arrival in Malta on 21 June. However, the monoplane was considered too complex a machine with the result that many were in favour of improving the overall performance of the Gladiator, on which experiments had already consumed numerous hours in the summer of 1940.

Pilots were strapped in their cockpits, just before the buildup of an attack, to cut down on scrambling time.

Later still, in an effort to improve the biplane's performance, modifications were made to the aircraft itself. The airplane's boost override was brought into operation to increase the thrust needed for that extra bit of speed. An encouraging improvement was immediately noted during acceleration tests. Wg. Cdr. Louks recalls:

> "I tested the first one, Sea Gladiator N5529, on 21 September 1940, to 10,000 feet in a shade under 5 minutes."

But the excessive stresses upon the engine resulted in increased wear.

Experimentation with the Gladiator became more complex with each successive day. A Mercury XV Blenheim engine was brought out of storage from Kalafrana. Then, painstakingly converted into a Mk.VIII, this was installed to Gladiator N5529, to which a three bladed variable pitch propeller was fitted in place of the

Sqdn. Ldr. A. E. Louks;
the brains behind most of the
Gladiators' modifications.

Gladiator's original two bladed 'fan'. But contrary to expectations, with trials on the biplane at an advanced stage, the Hurricane was shortly afterwards established as the RAF's frontline fighter on the island, an event which came about early in August when more of the aircraft were for the first time ferried to Malta as reinforcements via the carrier HMS Argus. With this swing in favour of the Hurricane the ambition to improve the Gladiator further began to show signs of flagging.

> "The first objects that attracted my attention as I stepped out of my Hurricane cockpit were three pitifully worn out biplanes."

This was the comment of one of the Hurricane ferry pilots soon after landing at Luqa on 2 August 1940. He was referring to Gladiators N5520 – N5524 – N5529, which were waiting to be serviced.

With newly formed 261 Squadron equipped with Hurricanes the remnants of Fighter Flight were absorbed into it and the latter was disbanded.

The epic of the Malta Gladiator in the war was actually terminated with this event, but the Gladiators were still around.

On 17 September Woods succeeded in shooting down another CR42.

Then on 25 September, two Gladiators were scrambled alongside three Hurricanes to intercept an incoming raid.

On 27 October two Gladiators were again scrambled to assist six Hurricanes in intercepting some MC200s.

Air Headquarters Malta left recorded that by the end of October only one Gladiator was lost, while another was badly damaged on the ground.

Later still, on 2 November 1940, flying in Gladiator N5520, Burges assisted two Hurricanes in intercepting a formation of 20 SM79s, escorted by MC200s. Burges, however, identified the formation he attacked as CR42s, of which he believed he shot one down. But as he did not see the aircraft crash, he could only claim a damaged.

At the end of December 1940 four Gladiators, N5520 – N5524 – N5529 and N5531 were reported as still being on strength of 261 Squadron.

On 19 January 1941 a Gladiator was reported operating with six Hurricanes and one Fulmar during the 'blitz' of the carrier 'Illustrious'. In fact three were on 25 January scrambled in response to a radar plot.

An AHQ subsequent report also shows that four Gladiators were still with 261 Sqdn. as late as 31 January 1941, which were then transferred to 806 FAA Sqdn. In fact it is reported that while Sub. Lt. Sewell of 806 Sqdn. was airborne in one of the Gladiators on a meteorological flight, he noticed tracer passing by his starboard wings. These were a moment later followed by a Ju88 diving towards Hal Far. Sewell immediately gave chase, and reported shooting down the intruder off the coast.

The next day more action was recorded from Hal Far as two Fulmars and three Gladiators were scrambled from the airfield, but there were no reports of any contact with enemy aircraft.

On 4 February 1941 one Gladiator, N5531, received a direct hit on the ground and was burnt out while two more were damaged in combat.

(It is interesting to note that OKW did credit the Luftwaffe with shooting down two Gladiators while operating over Malta during 1941.)

The two damaged biplanes were in all probability N5520 and N5529 for on 12 April Flg. Off. W.R.C Sugden crashed in N5524 when, coming in to land, burst a tyre, sending the biplane into a violent spin. A wingtip hit the ground, and the Gladiator sustained Cat. R damages.

Meanwhile, in March 1941, 806 Sqdn. had taken leave of the island enroute to Egypt with three Fulmars, evidently without taking along the remaining serviceable Gladiator, N5520.

It seems that when the decision was taken to prepare a Gladiator to have on hand for Meteorological Flight duties, N5520 was found to have the soundest frame from amongst the remains of the last three damaged biplanes; N5520 – N5524 – N5529. But in June 1941 this Gladiator, piloted by Flt. Sgt. Jolly of 185 Squadron, sustained heavy damages while landing on Hal Far airfield. The late Kenneth Cox, then an L.A.C. (No. 053831) with the same unit, recalled:

> "At the time of the crash I was waiting on the runway, ready to refuel N5520, painted silver all over. Flt. Sgt. Jolly came out of it in one piece. We then righted the aircraft by lifting the tail up as low as possible, pulling it over with a length of rope that had already been attached.

The Gladiator was in a sorry state. Both wings sagging to the ground and we had quite a job pushing it the 200 yards or so to a place between two damaged hangars. The engine fitted to N5520 was a Blenheim's Mercury with a three-bladed variable-pitch propeller."

From copies of pilots' logbooks found in Malta, however, it is recorded that Flt. Lt. P.G.St.D. Jeffries of 185 Squadron air tested and flew a Gladiator on the following dates:

01 September 1941	Gladiator	Air Test
02 "	"	Met Flight
12 "	"	"
15 "	"	"
20 "	"	"
26 "	"	"

Apparently the damages inflicted to the biplane were not as bad as Cox at first thought, N5520 was duly repaired and re-issued for Meteorological Flights.

FAITH, HOPE and CHARITY, the nicknames that had at sometime during the war become household names in Malta, began to be mentioned at this time.

From reports found the Gladiators which carried these nicknames, N5519/'R' was CHARITY, N5520 was FAITH, and N5531, HOPE.

George Burges was retired, and an elderly man, when he recalled:

> "During this period none of us ever heard the aircraft referred to as 'Faith', 'Hope' and 'Charity', and I do not know who first used the description."

Early in 1941, John Pain, a newly arrived Australian Hurricane pilot, had these notes entered in his diary:

> "All the hangars (at Hal Far) had been hit but there were a few aircraft in them and in one was 'Hope' of the famous Malta trio. She was in the throes of becoming a six-gun Gladiator (under Sqdn. Ldr. Louks, the Command Engineering Officer) the only one in the RAF, but she received a bomb smack through the centre-section and that was the finish of her."

Referring to Gladiator N5531, this statement indicate that this biplane was the by-product of the two that crashed on 21 June 1940.Obviously it had undergone several modifications during reconstruction under Sqdn. Ldr. Louks, but it was destined never to be flown in anger in its modified state.

"Faith" at Ta' Qali airfield in November 1941,
ready for Meteorological Flights.

Entries in the flying logbook of Charles Palliser indicate that he flew in Gladiator 'Faith' in November 1941. No aircraft serial is given, but this is the first recorded instance of such a name being applied to any of the biplanes.

(It is quite probable that the Serial number was not painted on to the biplane at that time.)

> "FAITH": In his book "Faith, Hope and Charity, published in 1954, Kenneth Poolman credits the naming of the Gladiators to Flg. Off. John Waters. Contemporaries of his, however, have since denied knowledge of any such names at the time, attributing these to journalists at a later date.

The presentation ceremony of the Gladiator "Faith" was held on 3 September 1943 at the Palace Square, Valletta. Air Vice Marshall Sir Keith Park, on behalf of the Royal Air Force, presented N5520, the sole surviving Gladiator, to Chief Justice Sir George Borg who received it on behalf of the people of Malta.

When this Gladiator was being refurbished at RAF Luqa in 1974,

Chief Technician 'Curly' Alcock, who was technical adviser, discovered the number 5520 on the bottom fairings, to the rear of the tail wheel, after the aircraft was stripped of old paint and fabric. (See "After the Battle" – Issue No. 10, Malta GC).

The armour plating, still evident behind the pilot's headrest, also proves that this could only have been one of the first four Gladiators assembled as these were the only ones fitted with this protective shield.

The last report found related to N5520 was in January 1942. This is further strengthened by an entry in the Flying Logbook of Sgt. F.G. Shepperd of 185 Squadron, recording that he flew the biplane on Met. Flts, that same month.

Possibly the Gladiator was badly damaged at some later date during the Malta 'blitz' of 1942, and the remains subsequently removed to the disused quarry at Kalafrana, from where the derelict was eventually recovered by a fitter at Ta' Qali, Corporal William Brown, in the summer of 1943. The late Leslie Davies, then an RAF L.A.C. at Ta' Qali, recalled:

> "Late in August we were given charge of the Gladiator's remains. There were three of us restoring the biplane at Kalafrana, where we finally inscribed our names on a plate near to the tail wheel. We do not know whatever became of it."

The discarded remains of Gladiator N5520 in a quarry at Kalafrana, 1943.

"We could not have painted the remains any other colour but silver. It was the only dope we had in stock then." Concluded Davies.

During the restoration of N5520 in 1974, Alexander Maxwell, a Propulsion Mechanic servicing Canberras at the time, recalled:

> "While some elevator fabric was removed to facilitate repair to frame damage we were astounded to find old patches signed and dated by wartime riggers who applied them."

Treated to slight and hurried repairs, a Bristol Mercury Mk.XI engine with a two-bladed propeller was fitted to the wingless fuselage. Then with a few final decorative touches Gloster Sea Gladiator N5520 was presented to the People of Malta on 3 September 1943.

"Faith" at the Palace Square, Valletta, on Presentation Day, 3 September 1943.

Mr Charles Waterfall inside the Palace Armoury, December 1946.

As far as can be ascertained Malta's Gladiators claimed at least nine air combat victories, with at least a further five enemy aircraft as damaged. Of these claims probably three, possibly four, are credited to pilots flying in Gladiator N5520.

The Grand Masters Palace, situated just behind the Palace Square, housed a collection of war relics of the period of the Order of St John's rule in Malta (1539-1798), better known as the 'Palace Armoury', together with other later 19/20th century artifacts.

Following the presentation the Gladiator was to be placed on permanent display there. At that time, however, with the building partly in ruins, it was necessary for the place be cleared of all rubble beforehand.

The Gladiator was then moved inside the Armoury through a bomb-blasted opening in one wall and an improvised one, made from corrugated sheeting nailed on to wooden battens, was erected until a proper rebuild was effected.

This conclusion was reached after one particular photograph, taken by a friend, Mr Charles Waterfall in December 1946, inside the Palace Armoury, came to light. Depicted in the background of this picture is a wall of corrugated sheeting fixed to timber battens.

In a letter that Mr Waterfall wrote to me, dated 8 April 2,000, he recalled:

> "I had been at Hal Far since early 1948 when I eventually heard about "Faith" having been preserved at the Palace and decided to try and gain access."
>
> "The main doors on Kingsway (now Republic Street) were closed so we went round the street corner to the right; Archbishop Street. There we came to a doorway in the wall and I rang the bell."
>
> "A gentleman opened the door. I don't know if he was an official of the church or Palace staff, but I do remember he was wearing a black cape or cassock. He was very polite."

(Actually he was one of a number of Greek priests who were at the time given temporary quarters on the premises as there own church nearby was bombed. – Author.)

"When I mentioned our wish to see the Gladiator he invited us in. I seem to remember a short pathway through a small garden from where he took us to the Armoury. He said "Faith" had been there since 1943,

"Faith" inside the Palace Armoury after the war.

so I doubt very much if it had been elsewhere since its presentation," concluded Mr Waterfall.

At the end of August 1960, the RAF organized an air show at Ta' Qali to commemorate the 20th Anniversary of the Battle of Britain, wherein they included a Battle of Malta static display. It was planned to have the Gladiator 'Faith' exhibited, and have it partly refurbished before being put on display at Ta' Qali. But first it had to be taken out of the now rebuilt Palace Armoury. This entailed the removal of the engine and its tailplane, so that it could be manoeuvered through a window overlooking Archbishop Street and craned down below.

The only way the biplane could be moved out of the Palace Armoury.

From there N5520 was transported to RAF Safi where No. 183 Maintenance Unit was engaged to undertake the work.

Returned to Valletta on 31 August, RAF airmen tried to get 'Faith' up the curving staircase leading to the Armoury so that it would be put on display in time for the Great Siege Commemorative Exhibition held during the first twelve days of September 1960. However, their efforts proved futile and they finally had to park the aircraft within the Palace confines until a crane was provided to lift it back up through the window in Archbishop Street into the Armoury.

(In retrospect, from old photographs, it is noted that the gunsight, with which the Gladiator had left the Armoury, was missing on its return. However, had this been removed outside of the Palace Armoury, or inside it?)

Some years later the display of the Gladiator, and other World War l and II artifacts alongside the armour of the Knights of Malta, were deemed not to be in keeping with their surroundings. So it was decided to have them removed from the Armoury and stored at Fort St Elmo inside a drillhall, pending the opening of a proposed War Museum.

"Faith" at Lower St Elmo Drill Hall in 1972, prior to the opening of a planned National War Museum.

The RAF requested the loan of 'Faith' as a backdrop to the Battle of Britain church service to be held in September 1974. The museums' department did not lose the opportunity to have 'Faith' restored following the recovery, in 1973, of Spitfire BR108, from Marsalforn Bay, Gozo.

When AOC Malta and Luqa station commander gave the go ahead for the restoration 'Faith' was moved to RAF Luqa, where Chief Technician Alcock assessed the situation.

The fuselage was stripped of old paint and fabric. Missing stringers were repaired or replaced, including ribs, etc. Panels, fairings, flying wires and gunports were manufactured on site. Major items included the making of a rudder, spinner and a canopy.

Sergeant Bill Feeney, a painter and doper by trade, carried out the work of installing a covering of fabric completely encasing the aircraft fusealage and spray it in its original naval wartime finish.

Corporal Rajan, an engine fitter, also assisted in various aspects of the work and the Armament Flight restored the two remaining machine-guns to full working order.

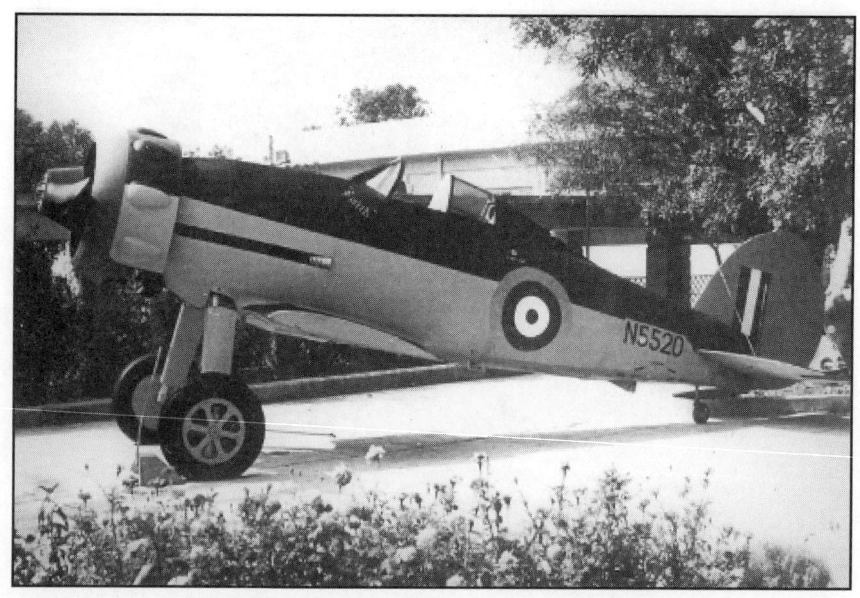

"Faith" after restoration by the RAF for the Battle of Britain display outside the Officers Mess at RAF Luqa, September 1974.

The aircraft was returned to the newly opened War Museum in 1975 where it can still be seen to this day.

The seven officers found listed here are the pilots who volunteered to fly the Sea-Gladiators in defence of Malta against Italy's Regia Aeronautica at the outbreak of hostilities as of 11 June 1940:

Sqdn. Ldr. Alan C 'Jock' Martin
Flt. Lt. G. Burges
Flt. Lt. P.G. Keeble
Flg. Off. W.J. 'Timber' Woods
Flg. Off. John L. Waters
Flg. Off. Peter W. Hartley
Flg. Off. Peter B. Alexander

Chapter V

Fighter Plane Fund

"Malta" – "Ghawdex" – Spitfire Ferrying – Spitfire Presentation

In retrospect, considering the times and the circumstances, it cannot be justifiably concluded that Malta bought her own Spitfires in the Second World War. This would, in truth, be a misinterpretation of the facts. Malta boasted of no air force. Neither were any of her men qualified as pilots. So why buy fighter aircraft?

In the summer of 1940, when operation codename 'Sea Lion' was planned, Britain had the might of the German Luftwaffe to contend with. She could spare no fighter aircraft to send abroad, particularly to the Mediterranean. With Italy's involvement in the war in favour of Nazi Germany, a new front had been opened. But this was, to an extent, the lesser of two problems facing the British War Cabinet at the time, both related to their fighter aircraft defence strength. Manpower to keep airplanes coming off the production line, trusting Britain remained financially stable, was available. Unfortunately, however, expences to run the war were phenomenal and could easily result to bankruptcy whether employees worked on a voluntary basis or not. But the countries of the British Empire, observing Britain's difficulties, each in their own way voluntarily subscribed towards providing additional funds with which it could have the equipment required, as part of their effort to help terminate the war in the shortest time possible; Malta was no exception.

Since the outbreak of hostilities in the Mediterranean the Island was keenly observant of the effort put up by the RAF. This was evident in the few British pilots who flew the three absolete biplanes against the Regia Aeronautica in defence of the island with such gallantry. As a gesture of appreciation, the council of the Anglo-Maltese League organized a 'Fighter Plane Fund.'

A Mister Ercole John Valenzia Presided. As Honorary General Secretary was Mister A. C. Crockford, and Mister Joseph Cassar was Honorary Treasurer.

'The Fighter Plane Fund', Malta, was launched on 30 July 1940. As an encouragement to others the Anglo-Maltese League contributed the first £100 out of its own funds, while an appeal to the people of Malta for contributions, in order to present a fighter plane to the British Government for service over the Island, appeared in local newspapers. By this gesture the Anglo-Maltese League was convinced that it was fulfilling the earnest desire of all the Maltese, and English, people on the island to express their gratitude and admiration to the RAF.

By the time this news reached the public the fund had already risen to £240. The Staff and Messengers of Barclays Bank (DC & 0) Ltd;

From left to right – Treasurer, Mr Joseph Cassar – President, Mr Ercole Valenzia L.P. – Secretary, Mr A. C. Crockford. The three major representatives of the 'Malta Fighter Plane Fund'.

Valletta and Sliema, had between them collected £40, and Allied Newspapers Ltd, had contributed the other £100.

On 3 August, a Saturday, by which date numerous firms and individuals had already turned in their contributions at the prescribed offices of Barclays banks and Allied Malta Newspapers, the President of the Anglo-Maltese League addressed the people of Malta and Gozo via the local cable broadcasting system, the 'Rediffusion'.

He again appealed to the Islands' population, insisting that they give their assistance in any way they possibly could, to ensure, the growth of the 'Fighter Plane Fund'. Mister Valenzja's follow-up speech gave an account of the war in which Malta had become involuntarily involved, and the experiences it was going through. How the Italians had once boasted that if they would ever shower Malta it would be with nothing less than flowers; however, since Mussolini declared war against Britain it was bombs they had been dropping on the island.

He emphasized on the close ties existing between the people of Malta and the British. The messages of great import received from High Officials serving in Britain's military services to the people of Malta and Gozo, and concluded his message with the following encouraging praises:

> "We, with our courage and ability, will forever remain unconquered. Our stand must be firm, not unlike that taken by other countries of the British Empire. Some doubted whether the Anglo-Maltese League would ever succeed in collecting the £7,000 needed to buy this fighter aircraft.
>
> I, who know well how the people react to patriotism, can tell these few that the Maltese will not only succeed in buying one aircraft, but two and if the need arises, even three. The League feels indebted towards all those who were instrumental in backing this project, which we launched knowing success was ahead, and when concluded it would become an honour fitting to these islands. The Anglo-Maltese League is positive of the people's will to back this venture. And towards such a cause no sacrifice is too great. Every workman, whatever his trade, should not therefore find it too hard to subscribe half a day's earnings, or one or two hours worth of overtime, in aid of the 'Fighter Plane Fund'."

This plea was not ignored. The country's response must have surely been beyond expectation. Patriotism drove the people to any sacrifice. Organizations readily offered from their funds, adding to an ever-escalating collection. Theatre owners ran feature shows for the same purpose, while football clubs organized matches, with one organized in Gozo as late as 27 October.

By 5 August, the fund had risen to £2,485-6s-6d, and was still gathering momentum, to an extent that by the end of the month this had gone up to £8,937-ls-6d. Of this amount £6,000 were on 22 August, transferred to the Officer Commanding, RAF Headquarters, Lord Beaverbrook in Britain, for the purchase of the first fighter aircraft for the defence of Malta.

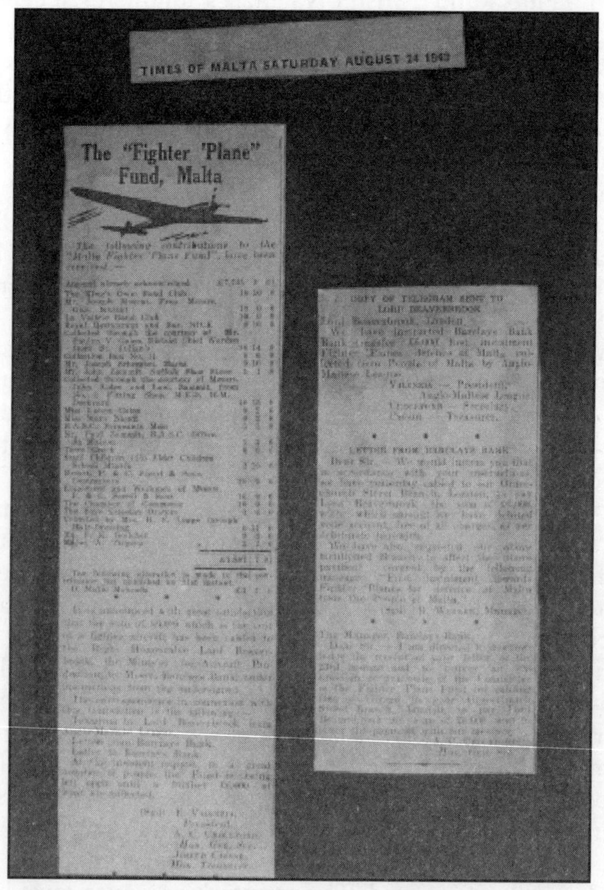

TIMES OF MALTA SATURDAY AUGUST 24 1940

The "Fighter 'Plane" Fund, Malta

COPY OF TELEGRAM SENT TO LORD BEAVERBROOK

LETTER FROM BARCLAYS BANK

Newspaper cuttings listing a few of those who gave donations to help raise the first 7,000 Malta pounds, and other related correspondence.

Air Commodore Maynard, Commanding RAF Malta, praised the Maltese for their patriotism, and extended his gratitude and sincere appreciation to all those involved in the organization of the 'Fighter Plane Fund'.

The President of the Anglo-Maltese League also received this message from Lord Beaverbrook himself:

> "The attractive sum of money your Island fortress sent for the airplane touched the British Nation to a man. We respect the resolution and believes with which Malta, loyal towards her untouched traditions, confronts the enemy. Yours is an example to the world for your courage and loyalty: now it is our duty to get from our factory a fighter aircraft to fight, and destroy those who dare to attack the island fortress."

The company of HMS Fermoy organized a dance in aid of the fund. This was held on 18 September at the Vernon's Club, by which date the sum of £10.957-8s-lld had been collected.

A further £4,000 were on 13 September sent to Britain as part payment towards a second fighter aircraft.

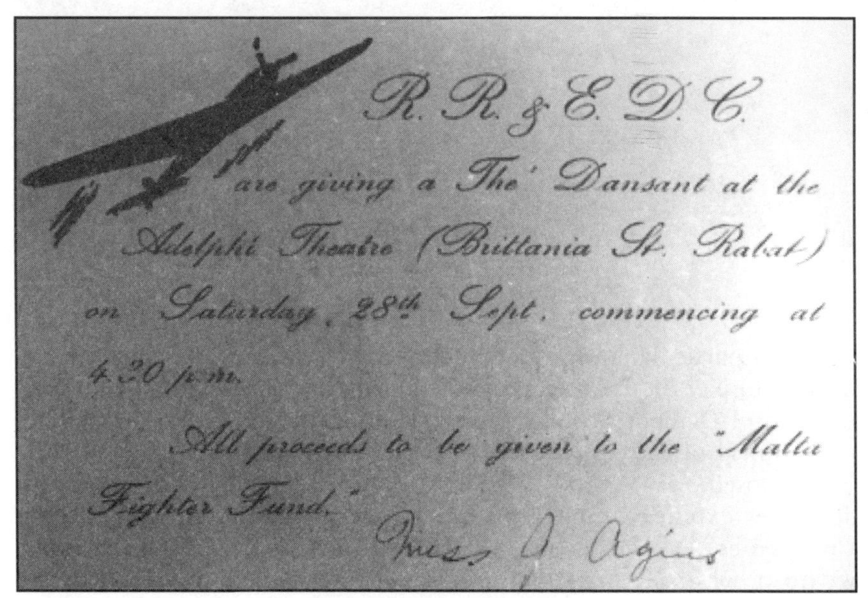

R. R. & E. D. C.

are giving a The' Dansant at the Adelphi Theatre (Brittania St. Rabat) on Saturday, 28th Sept. commencing at 4.30 p.m.

All proceeds to be given to the "Malta Fighter Fund."

A self-explanatory photograph.

By the beginning of October it was estimated that only another £370 were needed to collect the predetermined sum, and in an attempt to resolve the matter the council of the Anglo-Maltese League met on the 10 October. The committee's decision was to organize street collections, from a suggestion made by the Secretary. Permission duly granted by the Commissioner of Police collection tins and boxes were on 20 October in circulation throughout Malta and Gozo.

Original fund raising collection box.

Two particular individuals, who preferred to remain anonymous, offered to pay the balance needed to terminate the Fund, but towards the end of October this was found to be unnecessary, and on the 29th the Council of the Anglo-Maltese League declared the 'Fighter Plane Fund' closed.

They extended their gratitude to everyone, Maltese and British, Companies, Organizations and Institutions, as well as individuals, without whose contributions the Fund would not have been successful.

Contributions deposited at:

The Anglo-Maltese League – £3607-6s-10d.
Allied Newspapers Ltd – £4467-5s-02d.
Barclays Bank (DC & 0) Ltd – £4013-8s-00d.

The smallest denomination amongst these contributions was a farthing, equivalent to our present day 'mil', while the biggest was that of £500.

Listing the name of each and every contributor would turn this chapter into a roll-of-honour, space needed for other interesting historical content, but the people of Malta and Gozo should be thankful to their forefathers for so generous a gesture in aid of the Allied War Effort.

The two fighter aircraft paid for by the people of Malta and Gozo came off the production line in mid-1941, and at the request of the people of the two Islands were given the names 'MALTA' and 'GHAWDEX'. Regrettably, however, neither of the two Spitfires ever saw service over Malta at any time during the war years, or later.

The two representatives Spitfire Vbs were received by No. 8 Maintenance Unit on 14 and 16 May 1941 respectively, and released to 74 Squadron on the 18th.

'MALTA', serial W.3210 was lost in action over France on 27 June credited with two Me109s, a probably destroyed and a damaged during its brief operational service.

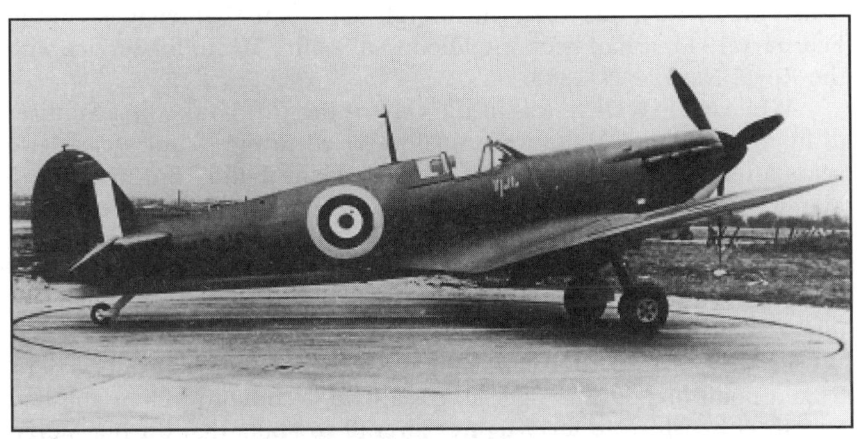

Spitfire W3210 – "Malta".

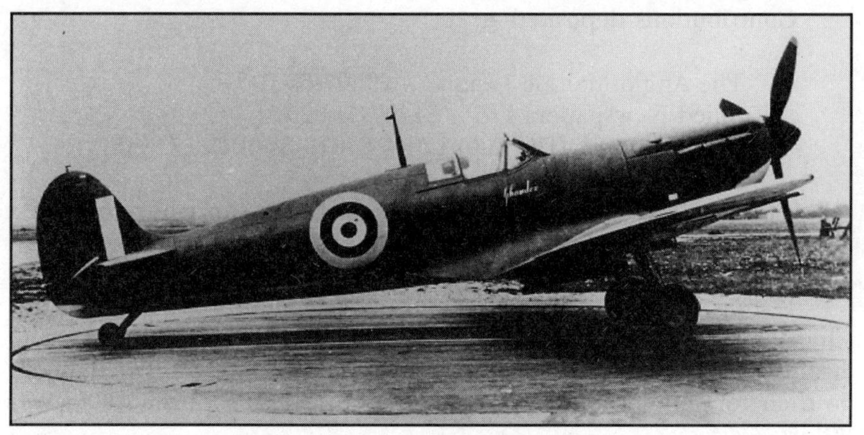

Spitfire W3212 – "Ghawdex" (Gozo).

'GHAWDEX' faired better. The fighter, serial W.3212, with a Me109 probably destroyed to its credit, was passed on to 92 Squadron on 25 September 1941.

On 6 February 1942 all of 92 Squadron's Spitfires were flown from Digby to Colerne to No. 417 Royal A.F Squadron.

On 10 February, faulty fuel gauges led to 'GHAWDEX' running out of fuel with the result that it had to be force-landed on Charmy Down.

Taken over by a Civilian Repair Unit the Spitfire was eventually re-issued on 26 May, but when the aircraft left No. 9 Maintenance Unit in February 1943, it had been modified to a Seafire Mk.Ib for service with the Royal Navy as NX.883.

While 'GHAWDEX' was in the care of the C.R.U. the first Spitfires to fly in defence of Malta were finally ferried to the island, nearly two years after the launching of the 'Fighter Plane Fund'. So, when on 7 March the fighters landed on Ta' Qali airfield it was history in the making in more ways than one for these were the first of type to go on operational service abroad.

Ferried to Malta via HMS Eagle the first Spitfire Vc of this batch of fifteen was flown off the carrier by acting Sqdn. Ldr. Stan Grant.

By December of 1941 launching of Hurricane fighters from carriers, from a point just off the Algerian coast, had become so well established a method by which to ferry fighter aircraft to Malta that during March 1942, 31 Spitfires were flown to the Island via HMS Eagle.

During this interval, however, Malta was provided with a secondary fighter aircraft to replace the absolete few Gladiators then defending the island against the Regia Aeronautica.

However, that is another story, more elaborately treated in the next chapter.

Meanwhile, so effective had been the British anti-shipping offensive from Malta during the final half of 1941 that by the end of the year the Axis High Command had decided to put a stop to it all by seizing the island in one coordinated invasion.

The Hurricane, having shouldered the brunt of the battle during the past months, could not possibly cope with what the enemy was planning.

Luftwaffe units had been arriving in Sicily since mid-December 1941, where by the end of March 1942, over 400 aircraft, mostly Ju87s and Ju88s supported by some 100 Me109s, had gathered.

However, even the Spitfires which had been flown to the island by the end of March were clearly too few to defend Malta against the 'Luftwaffe's expected 'blitzkrieg'. Furthermore, with HMS Eagle laid up for repairs, neither could more of the fighters be ferried to the island due to the Spitfire's fixed wing configuration as none of the other naval carriers could be used in the same way as 'Eagle' was.

Winston Churchill immediately explained the situation to President Roosevelt in a personal telegram on 1 April, and on the 20th U.S.S. Wasp was ferrying fighters in the Mediterranean, launching a consignment of 47 Spitfires to Malta in an operation Code-named 'CALENDAR'.

A further 125 Spitfires were ferried to the island in July and August in four separate operations, enabling Malta-based fighter units to go over to the offensive. However, following operation 'BARITONE' on 17 August, AVM Keith Park received this signal from the Air Ministry in London:

> "Now that 'BARITONE' is completed it is intended to dispense with further carrier operations for these reinforcements and to make deliveries of Spitfires from Gibraltar to Malta by air carrying 170 gallon jettisonable tanks."
>
> "Commencement of these delivery flights from Gibraltar to Malta is to await instructions from Air Ministry."

AVM Keith Park advised that for this purpose Spitfires should be disarmed of their cannons and carry only two Brownings and 350 rounds of ammunition per gun while they should always proceed in pairs. Nevertheless, following a relative period of quiet during September, and the early part of October, a run of anti-shipping successes by Malta-based RAF units resulted in the Luftwaffe's return in some force.

In mid-October the Air Vice Marshall was forced to inform the Air Ministry that:

> "When the present battle began on 10 October we had 141 Spitfires of which 113 were serviceable. The last five days intensive fighting has reduced total strength to 119 of which 55 are serviceable. In addition to the absolute losses of 22 Spitfires in the last five days a further 25 are beyond our capacity to repair before the end of October, making a total wastage of 42. If the enemy maintains his present scale of attack for another week we shall not be in a position to put up any effective fighter defence owing to lack of serviceable Spitfires. Therefore the twelve Spitfires promised by the end of October are totally inadequate as previously reported."

With the first Spitfires still not ready to make the direct flight from Gibraltar to Malta, to make good the losses, one last carrier ferrying operation, code-named 'TRAIN', was made on 29 October, in which 29 Spitfires reached the Island via HMS Furious.

The very next day the first two Spitfires expected from Gibraltar also arrived after 5 hours 15 minutes flying time.

By the first week of December 15 Spitfires had taken off from Gibraltar en route to Malta, out of which only one failed to reach the island. But at this time, with the turn of events in North Africa, and the siege over Malta expected to be lifted, there was no longer the need to keep the island supplied with more fighters for its defence so the Gibraltar flights were discontinued. By the end of the year nearly 400 Spitfires had been ferried to Malta in batches from the decks of British, and twice from one American, carriers.

The Hurricane had its merits but it was with the Spitfire that the RAF finally succeeded in breaking the Luftwaffe's air superiority over Malta during those bleak nine months of air warfare in 1942.

Despite the fact that the Hurricane spent nearly two years defending Malta against the Axis air force, the Spitfire's nine months were far more hectic. The decisive outcome remained doubtful for weeks on end due to diverse factors until mid-summer when air superiority began its reversal process. However, in October the Luftwaffe returned with unabated ferocity to wipe out the RAF defenders who had by that time become too strong for the enemy to overpower.

But for more elaborate details about these historic air battles over Malta it is suggested to refer to subsequent chapters farther on.

The number of Spitfires ferried ran to a total of 382 out of which 362 reached Malta safely, all in a period of 8 months. Of the 18 that failed to show up on the island, proportionately, the heaviest loss was that sustained in Operation 'STYLE' when Me109s, diverted to Pantelleria for the purpose, intercepted the incoming 31 fighters and shot down four.

In the majority, except for one abortion, in Operation 'BOWERY', whose pilot landed back on USS Wasp, all those lost failed to reach their destination.

The first Spitfire to appear in Malta, however, remains that of 19 January 1941 when an unarmed Type 'D', P.9551, flown by Flt. Lt. P. Corbishly arrived to photograph targets in Italy. After having flown one successful mission, however, while out on a second one on 1 February, Corbishly's aircraft was shot down and he was taken prisoner. But as this features aerial reconnaissance from Malta during the Second World War a separate chapter has been reserved for it.

Presentation of Spitfire Mk.IX EN199 to the Air Scouts of Malta on 27 May 1947.

Commemorative plaque found
at the Anglo-Maltese League in Valletta.

Just after the end of the war, with a large surplus of all types of aircraft in hand, the Air Ministry was able to present countries worldwide with one type or another, and Malta ended up with a Spitfire Mk.IX, the EN.199.

On 27 May 1947 Air Vice Marshall K.B. Lloyd CBE, AFC, on behalf of the RAF, presented the aircraft to the Air Scouts Headquarter in Floriana.

The Spitfire remained there for a number of years, until it was subsequently taken over by the Civil Defence Organization for their training program.

Regrettably, however, the fighter was so badly misused that by the time the C.D.O. were finished with it the pitiful remains were abandoned.

(Had local authorities preserved the aircraft just as the Gladiator 'FAITH' was since 1943, it would have saved Mr Ray Polidano and friends two years strenuous labour to restore it to its present state. Furthermore Malta would today have had an original Spitfire exhibited alongside 'FAITH' at the War Museum; wherever that might have been allocated. – Author.)

Chapter VI

The Hurricane

(Part 1)

Operation 'Hurry' – 261 Squadron – Operation 'White' – Ta' Qali – Wellington night – 'Illustrious' – The 'Luftwaffe' – The Me109E – 'Winch' – 'Dunlop'

Had it not been for the timed arrival of the Spitfire in the Mediterranean the probability that the British and their Allies would have won the war in North Africa is unlikely.

In 1940, when a fighter-plane fund was raised as part of Malta's war effort, this was ultimately for the purchase of two Spitfires. The Maltese may or may have not expected to see these in action over the island by the end of the year. However nearly two years had to pass before the first of the type arrived in some force to defend Malta. For a short period it was the Gladiator, thanks to Italy's concentration of air power elsewhere, that managed to hold its own against the Regia Aeronautica. Then, for eighteen crucial months, the Hurricane absorbed the brunt of the Axis air power, serving to pave the way for the arrival of the Spitfire, that materialized in time to tip the scales of war in favour of the British in the battle for the Mediterranean.

The first few Hurricanes, which were in June 1940 kept in Malta to supplement the outmoded Gladiators after they landed at Luqa, were originally intended to stage through the island on transit to the Middle East. Lack of spare parts, however, limited their operational flying. But like the Gladiator, despite this discrepancy, the Hurricane immediately made its presence felt, until the beginning of August when more of the type arrived.

With Germany's advance into Southern Europe the Central Mediterranean, particularly Malta, appeared to lose most of its strategic importance to Britain. But when France succumbed to the Nazi jackboot, and Mussolini joined forces with Germany, to partake of the spoils of war in French North Africa, the Island immediately regained its strategic values. All British holdings in the Middle East were threatened, their defences at a disadvantage. However they were not going to abandon Egypt without a fight. Malta was now their only remaining outpost in the Mediterranean, halfway across the sea separating Alexandria from Gibraltar. The British War Cabinet now began to realize that, like the proverbial chain link, at that stage in the war Malta, due to their own neglect earlier in the year, was found to be in a similar state. But it was now their solitary means of communication with the Middle East. Possession of this tiny fortress in the Central Mediterranean now proved to be a Godsend and hurried preparations to fortify the island were underway.

Despite June's few Hurricanes, kept in Malta to supplement the Gladiators, the Island's air defences remained weak, unable to have the desired effect upon the enemy whose attacks had been on the increase since the small force of naval Swordfish was established at Hal Far.

During July the Regia Aeronautica was to take its toll of Malta's RAF fighter defences.

On the 3rd of the month, flying in Hurricane P2614, Flg. Off. John Waters shot down an SM79, an encounter in which his aircraft was badly shot up by escorting CR42s.

On 12 July Plt.Off. Dick Sugden, one of the pilots who was on 21 June 1940 supposed to have gone on to the Middle East, in Hurricane P2653, accompanied by a Gladiator in which was Flt. Lt. George Burges, were scrambled to intercept some 13 CR42s. However the two British aircraft were almost swamped by the gaggle of enemy biplanes. Both RAF aircraft returned to base safely but once on the airfield Sugden noted that his Hurricane had been hit several times in the encounter. Then he was called to the telephone.

"Sugden, you've already been warned – so have the rest of the fighter boys – don't get mixed up with any enemy fighters." That was Air Commodore Maynard, the Air Officer Commanding, slamming down the phone at the other end.

Yet, boys will remain boys for on 16 July, with Burges flying in a

Gladiator and P. Keeble in Hurricane P2623, both were scrambled to scatter a gaggle of some 12 CR42s.

These enemy biplanes had come over for reconnaissance purposes, but all were armed. The two RAF fighters were attacked by the FIATs and a long drawn out battle ensued.

When it was all over Keeble's Hurricane had been shot down, the first of type to fall in defence of the island. Many may have been expecting a Gladiator to become the first RAF fighter to fall to the enemy but it was this Hurricane, P2623.

Unfortunately Keeble was not only the first RAF pilot to get killed in action, he also happened to be one of the pioneers of Fighter Flight, Malta.

Burges's luck still held out. He succeeded in eluding the enemy fighters and returned to base safely.

Early with the dawn of 2 August 1940 12 Hurricanes, equipped with underwing long-range fuel tanks, were flown off the British carrier 'Argus' from a point some 450 miles west of Malta and, provided with two Skuas for navigational purposes, were led to the island.

August 1940. Hurricane ferry operation code-named "Hurry". HMS Argus's flat top makes it identifiable from other carriers.

It was a long flight and the sun was setting by the time the leading section of 418 Flight caught sight of the island. The first fighter aircraft reinforcements ferried specifically for Malta had finally arrived.

These were:

N2484, N2622, N2672, N2673, N2700, N2701, N2715, N2716, N2717, P3730, P3731, P3733

The aircrews were:

Flt. Lt.s. D. W. Balden, R. N. Lambert, A. J. Trumble, & J.Greenhalgh;

Flg. Off. H. F. R. Bradbury;

Sgts. E. N. Kelsey, H. W. Ayre, R. J. Hyde, O. K. Ashton, F. N. Robertson;

O R Bowerman, R. O'Donnell, W. J. Timms and J. Pickering.

At RAF Luqa the Hurricane ferry crews, who were expecting to be returning back home, were shocked to learn that they were to remain on Malta, due to the shortage of pilots on the island. What was expected

Group photograph of pilots of 261 Squadron at Ta' Qali.

of them was to learn the basics of air combat, to prepare to fly their aircraft into combat. This system kept on recurring with each successive batch of ferried fighter aircraft, irrespective of whatever they were told prior to the ferrying operation. Fly. Off. Albert Anderson, who arrived in Malta on 6 June 1941 with 46 Squadron, was expecting to be moved on to the Middle East. When he wrote to his relatives back in the UK he had this explanation included to his letter:

> "I expect the address will surprise you, as much as it did me when they decided to keep us here. How long we shall be stuck I don't know."

Flt. Lt. A. Anderson, the sketching artist, in the cockpit of a Hurricane.

On 8 August two submarines, the Pandora and Proteus, arrived inside MarsaXlokk bay and disembarked the rest of 418 Flight at Kalafrana.

The next day Fighter Flight was amalgamated with the former and 261 Squadron, the 1st RAF fighter aircraft unit to operate from Malta since the breakout of hostilities in the Mediterranean, was officially formed.

Britain was at about this time organizing yet another strategic operation, one for which the strengthening of Malta's fighter aircraft defences was now essential.

The original route by which strike and fighter aircraft reinforcements were reaching the Middle East, where Wavell was expecting their support, was taking too long. So, while very little else could be done to speed up the ferrying of fighters, except by the method already adopted, strike aircraft, which were capable of flying longer distances, had to be found a shorter route to negotiate. One that, despite it being flown with the maximum of safety should take the shortest time possible.

It is found reported that such a route was established during the early days of August 1940 when Blenheim T2049 reached Gibraltar directly from Britain. Flown almost to the limit of its endurance the aircraft landed on the 'Rock', from where the first phase of a new three-stage ferrying operation across the Mediterranean was launched.

The gallant crew had to first fly their Blenheim across to Tunis. From there was then undertaken the most hazardous second leg of the flight. This was to reach Malta, flying within range of enemy held bases, before resuming with the final leg to their destination, Alexandria.

The success of this venture led to the opening of a new chapter in the Mediterranean Air War. It had by this time also been decided by Britain that Malta should be defended at all cost for the balance of the scales of war in Africa depended on the island's soundness as an operational base.

Listed below is a list of the Hurricanes issued to 418 Flight at Abbotsinch, which served to form the backbone of 261 Squadron during August of 1940, including some relevant details:

N2622 – N2701 – N2715 – N2716 – N271

All five aircraft listed above had either been lost, Struck off Charge, or otherwise destroyed by the end of February 1941.

N2700. Crashed on arrival at Luqa on 2 August 1940.

P2623. Another 2 August casually. This was one of the June Hurricanes which made a forced landing after returning from a standing patrol. It was SOC on 4 Aug.

N2484 – N2672 – N2837

The above three survived the Luftwaffe blitz of 1941, and saw further service with 185 Squadron after 261 was disbanded.

P3730 – P373 1 – P3732 – P3733

The above were the remaining four Hurricanes which are recorded as having been issued to 418 Flight.

Italy, her armies stretched out along the whole length of the North African coastline, from the Western desert at Libya as far as Egypt, struggled against Britain's 8th Army who, although on the defensive, was determined to keep the enemy out of Egypt.

Italian troops were repeatedly relying upon the support of their air force, demands that affected the performance of the Regia Aeronautica elsewhere, draining from its original strength in Sicily, resulting in a decrease in enemy air activity over Malta.

The Regia Aeronautica organized their first night raids over Malta on 20 June 1940. However, as the RAF were at that time unequipped to take counter action, the ground defences dealt with the enemy. But on 1 August Flt. Lt. Roger Hilton-Barber for the first time flew in Gladiator N5529 on night flying practice.

Six days later he also practiced this in Hurricane N2701.

On 9 August he was again airborne practicing night flying in co-operation with local searchlight units. However, when he first encountered the enemy, on the night of 13 August, despite being out of the range of the island's searchlights, he reported that he succeeded in shooting down an SM79 in Hurricane N27l6.

SM79 on a solitary reconnaissance patrol over the island above cloud and anti-aircraft smoke puffs.

The first daytime bloodstained encounter for the Hurricanes of 261 Squadron came on 15 August, just two days prior to the unit's official recognition, when five of the RAF fighters intercepted ten SM79s escorted by CR42s.

It was later disclosed that the arrival of August's Hurricane reinforcements had eluded the detection of the enemy, with the result that the appearance of so many of the fighters on this occasion took the Italians by surprise. Still it was the latter that drew first blood, shooting down Hurricane N2716.

Due to the aircraft replacement problem on the island 261 Squadron did not fly more than six of their Hurricanes at any one time, two being the normal average. Although still few, it was a significant improvement when compared with what had previously been flying against the enemy.

The Regia Aeronautica sorted out airfields during August with Zl007bis mounting bombing attacks from extreme altitude.

On 2 September one of two Fulmars of 806 Squadron, on patrol off HMS Illustrious, was damaged in an encounter with enemy aircraft. As it happened to be nearer to Malta than to the carrier it was escorted by the second to Hal Far airfield, to become the first of type to appear on the island.

The month also heralded the return in force of the Regia Aeronautica; however, the most notable attack made by the Italian air force was during the night between 3/4 September. This was not due to its severity, but because of the aircraft type debuting over Malta, the Ju87, with which were both BR20Ms, and Z1007bis.

During the last days of August, Germany, having kept Italy's progress under surveillance, did not fail to note the difficulties the Regia Aeronautica was experiencing due to the shortage of strike aircraft operating out of Sicily. To the Fuhrer, assisting his ally was a matter not to be taken lightly; however, he was still considering it when an urgent dispatch reached him from Italy.

Unable to wait any longer for the production of a competent dive-bomber from his own aircraft industry Mussolini turned to Germany for a supply of Stukas. With these aircraft in hand the Regia Aeronautica, eager to press them into service, launched their first few against the island. So this German dive-bomber, manned by Italian aircrews, made its operational debut over the Mediterranean. Towards mid-day of 7 September Ju87s bombed the dockyard, sinking a tug-boat and damaging buildings in Senglea. The number of escorting fighters on this raid, however, gave the impression that the Italians' confidence in the

Stuka's reputed invincibility was doubtful where fighter aircraft could get at it.

The advent of the Stuka over Malta seemed to have encouraged the enemy to go to greater lengths, spreading his attacks to various military installations. This activity proved beneficial to the defenders as it left them free to go about repairing airfields and erecting blast-pens at dispersal points. These walls were in great demand as they protected parked aircraft. But the freedom with which all this useful work was progressing was a short-lived one. Attacks on enemy targets in Sicily by the Swordfish of 830 Squadron were not taken lightly by the Italians.

On 15 September two formations of six Ju87s to each, escorted by more than a dozen fighter aircraft between CR42s and MC200s, the latter having just been pushed back into operational service, sorted out Hal Far airfield.

Up to that time the pilots of 261 Squadron had been facing unfavourable odds. However these were to an extent balanced by the fact that the enemy was operating with a fighter aircraft inferior to their own. But the return of the Macchi MC200 meant that they now had a fighter that matched their Hurricane in performance to contend with.

On 17 September a similar enemy force was reported approaching from Sicily. The two formations of Ju87s flew on a bearing directly in line with Hal Far, obviously intending to hit the Swordfish of 830 Squadron on the airfield.

The Hurricanes of 261 Squadron were scrambled to intercept the enemy. Heavily outnumbered they still flew into combat, engaging the Macchis which, although matching the performance of the Hurricane, lacked some of its firepower.

In this encounter Flg. Off. R. Hilton-Barber claimed the destruction of a Ju87 while a CR42 was reported shot down by Fly. Off. Woods in a Gladiator. But as the latter failed to see this crash he could only claim a damaged.

On 25 September two Gladiators were scrambled alongside three Hurricanes when a formation of nine patrolling MC200s was reported approaching the island. An enemy fighter was shot down in the ensuing battle.

On 4 October, 261 Squadron's fighters intercepted more MC200s, another encounter in which the Hurricanes reported shooting down two of the enemy aircraft.

Then on the night between 16/17 of that month, flying in Hurricane P2845, Waters succeeded in shooting down another SM79.

A MC200 on a surveillance patrol of Hal Far airfield on 27 October 1940.

Ta' Qali, where the August Hurricanes moved to from Luqa in December 1940.

The rest of the month was relatively quiet, then towards its close, with the expected arrival of the first RAF strike aircraft, the Hurricanes vacated Luqa, moving to Ta' Qali airfield under the command of Flt. Lt. A. J. Trumble.

The enemy, mistaking this movement for further fighter aircraft reinforcements, organized his first attack on this airfield on 2 November, but the Italians did not press on with their offensive after that, and the defenders enjoyed several days quiet.

November 17 proved to be a dark day to the RAF when another attempt to ferry further fighter aircraft to Malta failed disastrously. The twelve odd Hurricanes, predominantly due to human error, flew astray, and missed the island.

In the summer of 1940 flying fighter reinforcements to Malta was a two-fold problem for Britain. At that time every available aircraft was needed as the Battle of Britain was at its peak. Secondly, no allied airfield was within normal flying range of the island from where Hurricanes or Spitfires could be flown to it. These two fighters could only be flown to

Malta from the UK across Europe by means of refueling stops en route. But since France had fallen this ferrying method could no longer be accomplished.

However a system for the embarkation of fighters on an aircraft carrier, to get them within flying range of the island, from where they could be launched, was eventually perfected.

These air-ferry operations, as they were to become known, were primarily the responsibility of Admiral Somerville who had his headquarters at Gibraltar, and, generally speaking, their history is one of effective co-operation between Navy and Air Force.

The first air-ferry operation, Code-named 'Hurry', which could not have been more appropriately called, executed early in August 1940, was reputed to have been an unqualified success for the smooth running of later trips was achieved at the price of human lives.

Operation 'White' was the Codename of the second attempt to ferry fighter aircraft to Malta, which was destined to become one of the most distressing ferrying operations of the Mediterranean Air War.

On 15 November 1940, an impressive looking Force 'H' escorted HMS Argus out of Gibraltar towards the Central Mediterranean. This was operation Code-named 'White', during which twelve more Hurricane reinforcements were scheduled to be flown to Malta.

Unexpected mishaps were encountered en-route. Towards mid-day a Spanish civil airliner was spotted flying past some way off over the fleet. As suspected the pilot, whether unintentionally or otherwise, exposed them to the enemy as shortly afterwards news reached Somerville that Italian naval forces were gathering in the Gulf of Sorrento.

The next day the weather turned foul. Anti-submarine patrols had to be called off. So were the Malta-based aircraft originally sent to patrol over the Gulf.

Sommerville was in a quandary, about which he later wrote:

> "It seemed to me that the Italians were probably aware of our departure from Gibraltar. And they might well consider engaging Force 'H" with their superior forces in the hope of balancing their recent losses at Taranto."
>
> "In view of this I deemed it advisable to fly off the Hurricanes from a position as far to the west as weather would permit. In reply to an enquiery, 'Argus' informed me that with the wind as at present the Hurricanes could be flown off from Latitude 37°40'N, Longitude 6°40'E. Since all available meteorological information indicated a

continuation of the westerly winds I decided to accept this as the flying-off position."

But things did not work out as every one hoped they would despite the fact that the Hurricanes were flown from a position more than 450 miles from Malta when, according to Air Ministry Handling Notes, their range, in still air, was 521 miles. But bearing in mind the following wind it was obviously clear that the aircraft were to encounter difficulties en route to their destination.

Flying through low cloud one flight of six fighters, led by a navigational Blackburn Skua, did not meet the Sunderland that was meant to escort them to Malta as this failed to take-off from Gibraltar.

The second flight led by Skua L2882, also failed to make contact at their rendezvous point over Galita Island with the Sunderland sent out from Malta for the same purpose. However an error occurred that resulted from the fact that where the Hurricane pilots worked out their distances in miles Flt. Lt. Woodwards, the Sunderland pilot, worked out his in knots.

At one point the navigator of Skua L2882, corrected his bearings. The leader of the sub flight to his rear, Flt. Lt. J.A.F. MacLachlan, DFC., though only 21 years old, was an experienced pilot. He formed up beside the Skua and caught sight of the rest of his sub-flight strung out to his starboard side. Shortly afterwards the aircraft came into contact with Woodward's Sunderland. Woodward, observing two of the six Hurricanes ditching in the sea, immediately went to the rescue. He succeeded in picking up one of the downed pilots, but could find no trace of the second.

Eventually only four of the original twelve Hurricanes flown off HMS Argus managed to reach Ta' Qali, where they all landed safely, albeit on literally dry fuel tanks.

By 23 November 261 Squadron had enough men and equipment on hand to scramble eight Hurricanes to intercept an approaching attack, but there were no reports of any encounters.

On the 26th, however, although reported destroying a CR42 during an enemy fighter sweep involving MC200s and CR42s, 261 Squadron lost Hurricane N2701 and its pilot.

The next day the Hurricanes shot down an SM79 and damaged others, an encounter in which the squadron suffered no losses.

In confrontation with this opposition the Regia Aeronautica again withdrew. However they reverted to solitary night intruding, most probably to avoid daytime patrolling RAF fighters. These tactics, albeit succeeding in that aim, inflicted little damage to military installations.

Meanwhile the pilots of 261 Squadron, who had been braving this difficulty since August, when Hilton-Barber was credited with the destruction of the first enemy aircraft at night shortly after the Italians organized their first sporadic night attacks, rose to the occasion by working in cooperation with Malta's searchlight units.

Finally, on the night of 18 December, Flt. Lt. F.N. Robertson, in Hurricane P3731, managed to fly up close to an unsuspecting SM79 caught in searchlight beams and succeeded in shooting down the enemy bomber, his first night victory, in the sea east of Marsaxlokk Bay.

With the end of the year drawing to a close 261 Squadron was credited with a substantial number of victories. Between destroyed, probably destroyed and damaged the number had gradually exceeded forty enemy aircraft. However, the most outstanding claim credited to this Malta-based unit was recorded on 9 January 1941.

To Mussolini Malta remained a rocky outcrop in the Central Mediterranean, its value too insignificant to lure him into exhausting his Regia Aeronautica on.

Materially Greece, to him, was far more profitable to conquer. Riches and glory, the dictator's main weaknesses, again robbed him of all strategic reasoning, blinding him to the island's true value in the Central Mediterranean. So during October he prepared his forces for an assault on Greece.

In Sicily the units of the Regia Aeronautica which were kept there for the purpose of keeping Malta subdued, had in fact little effect on the buildup of RAF forces on the island during the ensuing weeks.

On the night of 8 October, following a half-hearted attack on Kalafrana by five SM79s, of which one was shot down and another damaged by an RAF Hurricane, air raids waned, and shortly afterwards came to a halt. Then on 27 October nine CR42s were intercepted by two patrolling Hurricanes, whose pilots later reported that they had shot down two of the enemy biplanes.

Italy invaded Greece on 28 October, and Britain responded by immediately approving a plan to organize a full scale offensive against supply ports in Southern Italy and Sicily. A decision that was reached in the light that the island, having safely sheltered the passage of medium range bombers to the Middle East, might as well have some of the type operating on a temporary basis from Luqa.

Unfortunately this second attempt to raid enemy military objectives in Sicily and further north into southern Italy opened with a disastrous note.

On the night between 3/4 November 1940 two of the operational Wellingtons crashed shortly after taking off from Luqa aerodrome.

The first crashed within the uninhabited limits of Tal-Handaq and burst into flames. The pilot, Sgt. R. Lewin, despite the presence of explosives inside the aircraft, and wounded, risked his own life to drag clear and carry the unconscious second pilot from the wreckage shortly before the bombs on board exploded. Nevertheless, Plt. Off. D. Allen did not recover from his injuries.

The other Wellington, R1094, also crashed, and caught fire, but on the outskirts of the village of Qormi on top of some residential houses. This aircraft broke in two. The front end broke free and fell into a nearby quarry while the burning rear end remained on top of the ruins. Rescuers discovered that a seriously injured crewman was down the bottom of the quarry, trapped inside that part of the wreckage. A Police Constable, Carmel Camilleri, volunteered to be lowered down into the

The scorched remains of one of the Wellingtons of 3 November 1940. This one, crashing on buildings in Qormi, killed some civilians.

quarry, from where he succeeded in pulling the RAF officer clear and, with the assistance of others, had him pulled out to safety, despite the fact that he later died from the injuries he sustained.

That night seven people perished, of whom two were civilians. From Wellington R1094 only the wireless operator, Sgt. D Palmer, survived.

Mussolini, his ambition to invade Greece finally appeased, soon realized that he had committed yet another of his wartime blunders. So demanding had the assault been on his airforce that it was left wanting elsewhere. The pressure under which Malta was supposed to have been kept was further eased during that period.

Meanwhile, in the Western Desert, General Wavell's Army of the Nile drove Marshall Graziani's Army out of Egypt, a battle in which the latter had some 30,000 troops taken prisoners. These misfortunes, however, which the Italian dictator had brought upon himself, were to have unforeseen repercussions upon the British and their allies.

Italy's position in the Mediterranean and North Africa late in 1940 was the cause of great concern to the Fuhrer. The air war on this front had been confusing from the outset, resulting from the dismal inferiority of the Regia Aeronautica. The British naval fleet in the Mediterranean went unchallenged for months on end while Italian battleships sought the seclusion of their bases, where anti-aircraft shore batteries offered them additional protection, laying bare the impotency of their own airforce.

Hitler, who was up to that time occupied with his widespread successes across Europe, was prevented from taking notice of the region where his partner was at war. When his attention was finally focussed on the Mediterranean, however, he was unable to dismiss Mussolini's incompetence and neglect. With the Continent at that time under his control the Fuhrer decided he could spare aircraft ideal over inhabited cities where little, if any, defences existed. So, during December, 1940, he had Fleigerkorps X moving down through Europe from Norway to airfields in southern Italy and Sicily, where they began to settle in while the Italians, true to their old traditions, grounded their Regia Aeronautica over the week to keep the Christmas peace.

Some have not excluded that Hitler's decision might have been motivated by the fact that, having failed to crush Britain on its own home ground, albeit subjecting it to a severe mauling at great cost to his own Luftwaffe, partly to vindicate himself he backed his partner's cause in the Mediterranean. There, he was aware, having driven Italy out of

North Africa, Britain had gained greater freedom of passage to her convoys, reaching out to each and every corner of the Mediterranean. A success that, if not checked, would more than likely result in a British Allied victory that would seriously threaten his recent plans to invade Russia.

Possessing no naval power with which he could come to grips with the British naval fleet, the Fuhrer meant to use his Luftwaffe to obtain control of the Mediterranean basin. In December 1940 he had Fleigerkorps X, under the command of General Hans Geisler, moved to Sicily, their priority to neutralize Malta and the British Fleet, to safeguard Axis sea lanes to Tripoli.

By the end of January 1941 Luftwaffe strength in Sicily had risen to 141 aircraft, reaching a peak of 243 by May.

At this time measures to strengthen Malta's defences further had already been taken, in preparation for what action the enemy might take. When in August 1940 Blenheim T2049 was flown from Britain to Alexandria, via Gibraltar and Malta, it did more than represent the beginning of an association between the RAF's 2 Group and the Middle East.

Meanwhile reports that Germany intended to involve itself in the Mediterranean further exposed the RAF's weakness in Malta, and the Air Ministry's failure to prepare the island against such unforeseen hostilities earlier in the year.

Fighter aircraft with 261 Squadron by the end of 1940 numbered 16 Hurricanes and 4 Gladiators.

Wellingtons, belonging to recently formed 148 Squadron, there were 16. These, supplemented by some 12 Swordfish of 830 Squadron, represented the island's offensive strength.

To cater in general reconnaissance and other diverse duties were provided 4 Glenn Martin 'Marylands' that formed 431 Flight and just as many Sunderlands of 228 and 230 Squadrons.

Early in 1941, while General Geisler's Fleigerkorps X prepared themselves for the conflict over Malta, the majority of Italy's strike forces were concentrated in North Africa. Consequently the Regia Aeronautica had to commit a good number of its Macchi MC200s to the fighter-bomber role over the island.

On 9 January, twelve of these MC200s, escorted by a number of CR42s, made a concentrated attack on Luqa aerodrome, while some Ju87s picked out Kalafrana's Seaplane Base.

The Hurricanes of 261 Squadron rose to the occasion, and came to grips with the enemy fighters. Flt. Lt. Mac Lachlan shot down two of the Macchis.

The next day another of the enemy fighters was badly shot up in an encounter with Hurricane V7474.

Plt. Off. MacLachlan.

Early with the dawn of 10 January, while the British fleet was engaged in covering activities of great importance in the Mediterranean, of which one was the passage of a supply convoy eastwarde, Britain's naval power had its first encounter with the Luftwaffe.

Ju87s and Ju88s came in wave after wave upon the whole fleet, but were noted making directly for HMS Illustrious. These were shortly afterwards followed by torpedo carrying Italian SM79s.

With no sign of escorting fighters the few patrolling Fulmars of 806 Squadron had a field day for a short while. However they were soon to realize that they could not possibly intercept the large number of attacking enemy aircraft.

Ammunition was what they ran out of first. Fuel ran short next and, due to the damages the 'Illustrious' had already sustained in the attack, landing back on the carrier was impossible. Bombs, which were unable to penetrate the ship's four-inch thick armour-plated flight deck, were unluckily dropped right through the opening of the carrier's after-deck lift while it was being lowered, with disastrous results.

The explosion had set fire to the hangar below deck where some Fulmars, fully loaded with fuel, contributed to the conflagration. So, with all hope of getting rearmed and refuelled at sea gone, the Fulmars turned to the RAF base nearest to their position, Malta.

On arrival at Hal Far the pilots broke the news of the conflict to the AOC.

As had been recurring in Malta since the breakout of hostilities, due to lack of aircraft technicians and adequate equipment, every time a new type of aircraft on which work was required reached the island there were, as one could expect, unavoidable delays. So the arrival of the Fulmars, although two had recently called at Hal Far, was no exception. Rearming and refueling the naval fighters took longer than their pilots expected, but an hour or so later they were airborne once more, flying out to sea in defence of the 'Illustrious'.

Over the island fighters of the Regia Aeronautica kept 261 Squadron occupied, engaging the Hurricanes to draw their attention from the besieged convoy. But before the sun had set below the horizon the RAF pilots had the satisfaction of bagging a few more enemy aircraft. It was also noted that, in the confusion of battle, the Italians had failed to spot the arrival of the FAA Fulmars. This served the latter to good purpose for they were enabled to fly back into combat again and again, without any undue interference from the enemy fighters, as they traversed back and forth between island and convoy.

For the first time in history the German Luftwaffe was challenging a naval power, once declared the ultimate weapon, for the supremacy of the Mediterranean.

The battered hull of HMS Illustrious finally appeared over the horizon, but darkness had fallen by the time the carrier reached the harbour breakwaters. Listing to port, and badly down at the stern, HMS Illustrious moved painstakingly slow, albeit still under her own power. Fires, which still raged out of control in the ship's after hangar, glowed eerily in the night through a break in the deck as, assisted by harbour tugs, the carrier was labouriously manoeuvred inside French Creek alongside Parlatorio Wharf, where she was finally made secure.

Expecting the enemy to appear at the break of dawn the defenders prepared themselves for the onslaught in great haste. However the state of the weather kept the enemy at bay, waiting for more favourable conditions before resuming with his attacks.

Unfortunately, however, in a case of mistaken identity, a low flying Hurricane, N2622, is suspected to have been shot at by local anti-aircraft gunners on the outskirts of Ta' Qali. However doubts remain whether this was the case.

Mr J Galea recalls that he was on the rooftop of his house when he heard the sound of an engine coming at speed over his village, Siggiewi (On the opposite side of a rise in the ground south of Ta' Qali).

> "As it passed overhead in the direction of Luqa it just turned over and spun into the ground. The pilot baled out at too low an altitude and his parachute never opened. His body was only a short

distance away from the aircraft. I could see the name 'Timms' on his jacket."

Sgt. Jim Pickering, another 261 Sqdn. pilot, who was watching events from the ground, also recalls:

"Timms' must have been experiencing some difficulties with the aircraft just before he crashed."

The island's RAF fighter aircraft strength did not number more than a dozen Hurricanes or so, including the unserviceable, with the few surviving Fulmars of 806 Squadron providing additional backing. However MV Essex, having just arrived with the convoy, had crated Hurricanes on board, but it was doubtful whether these could be assembled and prepared in time for the coming conflict.

The Luftwaffe appeared over Malta for the first time on 16 January 1941 and, as was expected, their primary objective was HMS Illustrious. More than fourty Ju87s arrived for the purpose, escorted by no less than a score of fighters between CR42s and MC200s. Twenty Bf.110s were also in attendance, escorting nearly just as many Ju88s.

The attack was a spectacle terrifying to behold. Smoke gathered and settled like some huge shroud over the Grand Harbour. Columns of water rose stories high from the depth charge-like explosions of numerous bombs, their thunderous noises flowing into one continuous deafening sound, through which could still be distinctly heard the blood-chilling scream of the Ju87s as they swooped down out of the sky.

Aircraft came as thick in number as the barrage puffs of bursting anti-aircraft shells which sought to pluck them out of the smoke-choked sky.

Oblivious of the hail of steel rising to meet them the enemy bombers dived almost vertically through the inferno, from which none were shot down by gunfire in this raid.

HMS Illustrious was most of the time hidden from view by the monstrous upheavals of smoke, dust and water that spewed skywards all around it.

Only seven British fighters were that day scrambled to intercept the enemy bomber formations. Of these four were Hurricanes of 261 Squadron and three Fulmars from the "Illustrious's" own 806 FAA Squadron.

Hopelessly outnumbered, and aware of the folly of chasing after the

HMS Illustrious under attack at Parlatorio Wharf.

Germans where anti-aircraft shelling was thickest, the British fighter pilots sought safer and more strategic tactics. While the Hurricanes flew above the gaggles of enemy fighter aircraft way up high over the Grand Harbour the Fulmars chased the waves of approaching bomber formations.

Although Malta's defences that day claimed the destruction of ten enemy aircraft, only one was actually shot down; by a Fulmar.

On 18 January the enemy made it obvious that both Malta's RAF strike and defensive forces were affecting him badly. HMS Illustrious was ignored and some one hundred Axis aircraft between Ju87s, Ju88s, Bf.110s and MC200s concentrated their attention on Luqa and Hal Far airfields.

Five Hurricanes and three Fulmars, of which one was shot down in the sea, were scrambled to intercept the enemy. However, although few in comparison, there were so many of the enemy that between them these RAF and FAA fighters and the ground defences that day accounted for eleven more enemy aircraft.

The enemy returned on 19 January, his attention once more turned upon HMS Illustrious. In this attack there were more than forty Ju87s and some thirty Ju88s escorted by a mixed gaggle of Bf.110s, MC200s and CR42s, an air raid that shook the island to its very foundations.

All the fighters 261 Squadron could get airborne to engage this superior number of Axis aircraft were five Hurricanes, one FAA Fulmar and an obsolete Gloster Gladiator.

Due to the daylong blitz many of the RAF pilots flew into battle several times before the sun had set, by which time they and the ground defences had between them shared the destruction of nineteen enemy bombers. To these were included a CR42 and a Cant Z5O6B, the latter spotted flying offshore probably on ASR duties, for the loss of Hurricane P2829, and a FAA Fulmar which was reported missing.

Sgt. J Pickering, who arrived with the first batch of Hurricanes ferried off HMS Argus on 2 August 1940 flying in Hurricane N2715, had his first hot encounter with the Luftwaffe on this day.

Flying in Hurricane V7548 he reported attacking a Ju87 and a Ju88, and a Cant Z506B, which he claimed only as probable due to lack of confirmation.

The Luftwaffe must have rued the day they had laid eyes on HMS Illustrious. In spite of the heavy casualties they had suffered the scope for which so great a sacrifice was made had failed. The carrier after which they had been chasing for the past two weeks with such deadly intent was still afloat.

The three-day blitz had cost the Axis nearly fourty aircraft, to the defenders' four.

Before the sun had set that evening of 19 January reports reached General Hans Geizler that his Fleigerkorps X had failed to sink the 'Illustrious'. All loss in life and equipment expended throughout the whole operation had been a tragic waste.

Large-scale attacks were temporarily brought to a stop, and Malta's defenders enjoyed a few days respite. Meanwhile Dockyard workers increased their efforts to finish the temporary repairs to HMS Illustrious. Then on the night of 23 January they had the satisfaction of seeing the carrier steam her way out of the Grand Harbour en route to Alexandria.

HMS Illustrious on 22 January 1941.
Still down by the stern due to the damages sustained

The enemy's formations of attacking aircraft during the 'Illustrious' blitz was partly to blame for his heavy losses. During the final quarter of 1940 those suffered by the Regia Aeronautica were due to lack of adequate fighter cover. However, with the advent of the Me109, when the RAF Hurricanes became the target of this superior Luftwaffe fighter, very few of them were able to get within shooting distance of the attacking Axis bombers. When one or two of the latter was shot down this was more than likely hit by artillery fire.

(Shortly after the departure of the 'Illustrious' many of our elders foolishly believed that the Luftwaffe would not return but ... – Author.)

From an expected large number of pilot reinforcements only a few arrived by Sunderland on 20 January. Then on the 29th two 38 Squadron Wellingtons, in which were three fighter pilots as passengers, accompanied by six Hurricanes, arrived from the Middle East and landed at Luqa. Their arrival coincided with an enemy air raid and the RAF fighters, although their guns empty, mounted dummy attacks on the enemy aircraft, scaring them off.

Towards the end of the month a few more pilots arrived by flying boat.

Early in February 1941, the enemy again began returning in force. Sometime around mid-day a few Italian aircraft made tentative attempts to attack military objectives, but patrolling Hurricanes scared them away.

Sgt. Robertson, flying in Hurricane V7116, recorded that shortly after attacking a reconnaissance SM79 a number of CR42s attacked him in turn. In the ensuing encounter Robertson succeeded in shooting down one of the biplanes and badly damaged the SM79.

Flt. Lt. F. N. Robertson, Hurricane pilot.

Towards evening, however, some Ju88s, escorted by fighters, attacked Luqa aerodrome. Hurricanes were immediately scrambled to intercept them with the result that the encounter soon developed into a running battle. Flg. Off. Peacock Edwards recorded that in this chase he succeeded in shooting down one of the enemy bombers.

Plt. Off. Pain, who was flying in Hurricane P3731, also reported that he attacked one of the Ju88s off Gozo, and the last he saw of the enemy aircraft just before it disappeared into cloud, was that its starboard engine was ablaze.

A Wellington of 148 Squadron was on 3 February destroyed on the ground.

The next day more Ju8Ss were in the evening turned loose on local airfields. Eight Hurricanes and two Fulmars took to the air to intercept them, and succeeded in shooting down two of the enemy aircraft, but not before they had taken their toll of a FAA Swordfish and a Gladiator, both parked on Hal Far.

From 7 February, like the Regia Aeronautica before them, due to lack of an adequate fighter cover, the Luftwaffe shifted the majority of their attacks to hours of the night. However local searchlight units found it difficult to follow the German bombers as, contrary to their Italian counterparts, they took evasive action. Approaching on long glides they released their bombs without any undue delay and flew away.

On 8 February, however, it is reported that, assisted by searchlight illumination, a Hurricane accounted for two Ju88s confirmed and a third damaged during four separate raids between 15.00 hrs and 00.54 in an alert that lasted nearly 7 hours. This was the same date in which Rommel began embarking the equipment of his two frontline Divisions towards Libya.

Shortly afterwards reports that squadrons of Luftwaffe aircraft were withdrawn from Sicily in support of Rommel's move to North Africa bolstered the morale of Malta's defenders. However they were in for the shock of their lives.

A detachment of 14 Mel09Es of 7/JG2S, flown by war hardened veterans, had arrived in Sicily. The German fighter aircraft possessed numerous features that the Hurricane lacked, maneuverability, speed and firepower, posing the first real threat to the existence of the RAF's defences on Malta.

On 12 February the Me109 made its debut over the island, and immediately overshadowed the RAF fighter. Hurricane N2715 was shot down during that first encounter. P3733 was reported missing and a third RAF aircraft was badly shot up. Fortunately, however, only one of the pilots went missing, Flt. Lt. G. Allen.

On 15 February, Plt. Off. Knoble recorded that Plt. Off. P. Lowe was killed.

The next day, in another encounter with Bf109s, a further Hurricane was shot down, severely wounding Flt. Lt. J.A.F. MacLachlan. So desperate was the pilot situation in Malta that any RAF and FAA officers capable of flying aircraft were called to fly Hurricanes.

Flg. Off. G H Bellamy, who used to serve with 3.AACU was at this time posted to Ta' Qali. " I was given cockpit drill in a Hurricane. The only monoplane I had flown was a few hours in the 3.AACU Magister. This was supposed to make me fit to fly a Hurricane."

A few days later Pickering had this recorded in his logbook:

> 20 February – McDougal was killed.

A newspaper report claimed, however, that RAF fighters damaged two Ju88s.

Hurricanes attack Luftwaffe Ju88s. (An Anderson painting).

On 24 February, engaging patrolling Hurricanes the Luftwaffe 109s for once failed to shoot down any of the RAF fighters. The number of serviceable Hurricanes at this time was nineteen, with about half as many needing repairs. Needless to say the morale of the RAF pilots was badly shaken at the arrival of the Mel09. Excerpts, drawn from a report by Wg. Cdr. Jonas, gives this situation greater emphasis:

> "... ever since Italy entered the war these boys, often in obsolete aircraft, had carried out bravely, and unquestioning, any task that they had been called upon to perform. Then Hurricanes had arrived, and encouraged by successes, morale had risen ... to almost unbelievable heights ...".

But shortly after the arrival of the German Me109 ...

> "... not only were many of the Hurricanes tired and scarred, but the pilots themselves were tired. No new fighters ever seemed to come now, no fresh and eager faces appeared in the Ta' Qali mess. Instead there were empty places at the table ...".
>
> "To anyone interested in physiology the effect of the 109 on the Hurricane pilots was obvious ...".

The handful of Bf.l09s operating out of Sicily had opened a new phase in the Mediterranean Air War. They laid bare the impotency of Malta's RAF defences.

Sgt. Plt. Les Davies, who, on 25 February, attacked some Do.215s in Hurricane V7771, recorded that he fired a good burnt at one of the bombers but was unable to see the result owing to hits sustained by his aircraft's fuel pump from return fire.

Plt. Off. Walsh suffered an engine failure and crashed in the sea. He was duly picked up, but was to die later in hospital.

The next day the Luftwaffe mounted another full-scale attack. Wave upon wave of Luftwaffe bomber formations, amongst which were spotted Heinkle He.111s and Dornier Do.17s, bombed Luqa aerodrome.

The pilots of the eight Hurricanes which were scrambled to intercept the enemy had more than a score of Luffwaffe fighters to contend with, mostly Me109s.

After the raid was over two Ju87s, however, were claimed to have been shot down, but the destruction left behind by the enemy at Luqa more than vindicated this action. Six Wellingtons of 148 Squadron were burnt out, and another so badly damaged that it was later written-off. Of the remainder four needed extensive repairs, so the Malta based bomber unit was left with only two serviceable aircraft. Furthermore three Hurricanes of 261 Squadron were shot down, with the loss of all three aircrew.

Pickering recorded:

> "Three more Plt. Off.s, Taylor, Kealsey and Langdon, were killed."

Another one of the Hurricanes was so badly shot-up that its pilot had to crash land.

Due to the mauling it had received 261 Squadron had few fighters left to intercept the number of Bf109s that appeared two days later, harassing military installations. Plots of large formations of enemy aircraft appeared, then faded. Me109s flew around freely, hunting for patrolling RAF fighters whose pilots were foolish enough to get caught napping. However, "... there were few interceptions towards late February and early March ..." recorded Les Davies flying in Hurricane V7102. "... but lots of twitch."

On 2 March, an attempt to substitute the Hurricanes with the Fulmars of 806 Squadron proved nearly disastrous. The FAA fighters were so badly shot up by the 109s that they were forbidden from further daytime flying, and were shortly afterwards withdrawn to Egypt for embarkation on board HMS Formidable.

Plt. Off. Knoble recorded:

> 4 March – "Intercepted 9 + – Shot at 2 Ju88s – both damaged. Bullet through air-screw and tail-plane from return fire."

The next day eight Hurricanes of 261 Squadron were available to intercept a sizeable force of Luftwaffe Ju87s and Ju88s, escorted by Me109s and Bf.110s. Five enemy aircraft were claimed to have been shot down, shared with the ground defences, but two of the Hurricanes were lost in the encounter.

On 6 March, however, a few more Hurricanes arrived from the Middle East, led by two of 148 Squadron's Wellingtons, in which were two extra pilots.

To assist in softening up Wavell's 8th Army in the desert, in preparation for Rommel's first offensive against them in North Africa, Luftwaffe bomber units were at this time withdrawn from Sicily, leading to a decrease in bomber attacks over Malta. Fighters, however, still came in considerable numbers harassing airfields and other military installations on the island. These enemy tactics more than doubled the pressure under which 261 Squadron's Hurricanes were daily straining.

Plt. Off. C. Laubscher, who arrived in Malta on 29 January 1941, flying one of the first flight of six Hurricane reinforcements from Egypt, wrote about these experiences in his diary:

> "Our losses were heavy, and our successes few, as a Hurricane I was no match for an enemy who always had the advantage of height."
>
> "Violent death to Malta's fighter pilots came under numerous guises. On one occasion a pilot had his parachute caught on his aircraft's rudder, and was dragged to his death as the machine dived into the sea. Another parachuted safely in the sea, only to drown before the crash-boat could get to him."

According to Plt. Off. Laubscher neither were all RAF pilots always lost due to enemy action:

> "Pilots were even lost during test flights, their aircraft going into sudden almost vertical dives from which they never pulled out. We could only assume that these men had not used oxygen, and lost consciousness at altitude."

The Mel09s flew practically unchallenged over Malta. Their strafing attacks proved devastating. Parked aircraft were at their mercy, as well as military installations and any single moving object in sight. Harbours were no exception. Private buses driving along public roads were also at risk.

Me110s, however, were organized to mount attacks in the early morning hours, approaching low over the sea to avoid radar detection. Neither did they ever come from the same direction twice. One such attack was executed on 9 March, a Sunday, at about 07.00 hours.

Undetected, five of the twin-engined fighters approached the island from a northerly direction, a bearing which brought them over across the island of Gozo where, due to obscure reasons, one of the aircraft flew right into the ground, bursting into flames on impact. The remaining four aircraft flew on unchecked at minimum elevation across the Gozo-Malta channel, over Comino, in direct line with St Paul's Bay.

On Ta' Qali airfield everyone was taken by surprise. No one was expecting that early a visit by the enemy. Some mistook the aircraft for RAF bombers returning from a night strike, which was understandable for no warning alarms were sounded.

Encountering no opposition the enemy aircraft swept over the airfield in a loose finger-four formation, guns firing. Hurricanes parked on the grass were caught in the line of fire and burst into flames. Luckily only one fighter was destroyed, although considerable damage was inflicted on others. Passengers in a Rabat route bus escaped being massacred by a hair's breadth. Lasting only seconds there was only that one pass and the Bf.110s disappeared, flying in a wide curving turn northward, Sicily-bound.

The result of a Luftwaffe attack on the Hurricanes of 249 Squadron at Ta' Qali on 23 May 1941.

The next day Me109s executed more strafing sweeps inside St Paul's Bay.

Plt. Off. Knoble had this entered in his logbook:

10 March
"Dogfight with two 109s. 1 probably damaged."
11 March
"Jumped by 109s. Fired cannons from 500 yards at 109 that fired at me, no hits."

On 15 March, flying in Hurricane V7472, Les Davies recorded:

"With Me109s constantly on patrol major engagements were evaded. Hurricane pilots, with occasional flashes of courage, resorted to dive and zoom tactics."

Knoble was involved in more action:

17 March
"Intercepted 5 Ju88s with escort. Fired head on at leading bomber – pod engine smoked – damaged."

The next day CR42s, which had for some time disappeared from the skies over Malta, reappeared. Hurricanes were immediately on the defensive, intercepting the Italian biplanes of which they shot down two.

That same day 261 Squadron received a few more reinforcements from the Middle East. Six Hurricanes, equipped with long-range fuel tanks, and led by two navigating Wellingtons, in which were a further eight fighter pilots, reached the island.

Plt. Off. Knoble recorded:

18 March
"Plt. Off. Chuck Lester shot down by four 109s and rescued from sea wounded."

Four days later, however, the squadron experienced its greatest setback since the arrival of the Luftwaffe in the Mediterranean. In an attack by Ju88s, escorting Bf109s shot down five out of the eight Hurricanes which went up to intercept them:

P2653 – V7493 -V7799 – V7358 – V7872. All five pilots were reported missing.

A 261 Squadron officer had this noted down in his diary related to that disastrous of days: "This was the one-day when we all thought we had the edge".

Malta's location in the Central Mediterranean commanded the crossing between Italy and North Africa. The island was a vital military base related to Britain's North Africa campaign, both as a staging post between Gibraltar and Alexandria and a landing ground from where

Hurricane II, Z3757, at Ta' Qali, August 1941.
On arrival during a ferry operation. Another in the background seems to have been in a similar mishap.

strike forces could be flown against enemy shipping traversing the Central Mediterranean. The Axis were well aware of this and realized that unless they succeeded in disabling it, a victory in the desert for them would remain doubtful.

On 23 March the enemy returned with his Ju87Bs, and surprisingly the bombers had a score of Italian MC200s escorting them.

No less than fourteen Hurricanes were scrambled to intercept this attack and in the ensuing battle the German Stuka aircrews faired badly with the Macchis protecting them.

Twelve Ju87s were by sunset claimed as having been shot down, but in later years Luftwaffe records proved that only three failed to return to their base from that day's raid.

This was for the price of Hurricane V7495, flown by Sgt. F. Robertson, whose luck still held out for he baled out safely. He later reported that:

> "I had just shot down one Ju87 when I was attacked by another from ahead and got a bullet in my port main petrol tank. I followed

the enemy aircraft around in a very steep turn and finally shot it down in the sea: next I found that my aircraft was burning fiercely and so I climbed from 700 feet over the sea to a position about a mile South of Rabat and baled out."

Plt. Off. Knoble's logbook entry claims:

23 March – "Convoy Patrol. Used all ammo on Ju88 – damaged. Chased another away by feint attack when out of ammo – he jettisoned."

The next two days were repeat performances of 23 March with H.111s instead of Ju87s. The Hurricanes failed to make contact with the bombers on this occasion, then on the 28th a surprise sweep by Bf109s cost 261 Squadron a further two fighters.

Maynard was at this time promoted to Air Vice Marshall, a post which gave him more authority. He wielded it to try gaining further fighter aircraft reinforcements for the island.

His request gave rise to heated debates amongst the combined Chiefs of Staff in London with the Admiralty arguing that the risk to the carriers involved was not being considered. Neither were their Commanders appreciating what was being done elsewhere.

The first signs of an improvement to the island's situation became apparent shortly after the arrival of a much-needed convoy on 23 March. This was further improved on 3 April with the arrival of twelve Hurricane IIAs, which were ferried via HMS Ark Royal on operation Code-named 'WINCH', but these actions were partly motivated because of Germany's direct involvement in the Mediterranean.

In the first week of February Wavell's headlong advance in Cyrenaica petered out at El Agheila. Then, on 24 March, Rommel's Africa Korps went on the offensive, and in the ensuing weeks pushed the British 8th Army back to the borders of Egypt, so that by mid-April the 'Desert Fox was besieging Tobruk.

At this stage, Hitler had also decided to invade Greece and Yugoslavia. His involvement in the Balkans on 6 April entailed the transfer of the majority of Luftwaffe fighters from Sicily. These included the handful of Me109s of 7/JG.26, so that they would be within striking distance of Yugoslavia, consequently relieving Malta of the 109 scourge, albeit briefly, for these enemy fighters returned to Sicily three days later.

Plt. Off. A. Anderson's painting of a dogfight between Hurricane and Me109.

On 11 April, the Hurricanes had a harrowing time fighting off gaggles of Axis fighters, from Italian CR42s and MC200s to Bf109s, that come escorting large formations of Ju88s. Although the RAF fighters succeeded in shooting down one Ju88 and an Me109, 261 Squadron had by the end of the day lost two Hurricanes, two pilots, and suffered two crash landings.

Sgt. Plt. A.H. Deacon, a 261 Sqdn. pilot, flying in Hurricane V7978, recorded that on 11 April he was attacked by a strong formation of Mel09s and MC200s. He succeeded in fighting back to report shooting one 109 into the sea and another was last seen loosing height and smoking. However two others jumped him from astern and he had to make a forced landing on Hal Far airfield, where the undercarriage of his aircraft collapsed.

On 13 April, flying in Hurricane V7472, Davies recorded:

> "Me109s raised their patrolling height. 'Imshi' Mason was shot up by some of these fighters but came out of the encounter OK."

During the next few days, another Hurricane fell to the guns of the 109s and another was badly shot up. However, a Luftwaffe fighter was shot down in an encounter.

On 19 April, flying in Hurricane Z2904, Deacon intercepted a Ju88 on a reconnaissance sortie but was pounced by some Me109s. He fired at one but the enemy suddenly scattered and disappeared.

The next day three SM79s, escorted by more than a score of Italian fighters, approached the island. These were immediately intercepted by patrolling Hurricanes who had a field day, shooting down three CR42s.

"Round about mid-April we received our first six Hurricane llAs". Wrote down Plt. Off. Laubscher in his diary:

> "... and on the 20th, detailed to give top cover to the squadron who were on an interception scramble, we were allotted two of the new machines and I flew in one of them. Soon after taking off from Ta' Qali towards Rabat hill, although laterally we were little more than abreast of the squadron, it was immediately evident how well the Mk.IIA climbed as we wheeled to the Southwest, already six or seven hundred feet above the rest."

Plt. Off. John 'Tiger' Pain, an Australian, who was flying in the second Hurricane IIA, reported that they attacked three SM79s, nine CR42s and fifteen MC200s over Valletta, and destroyed one, possibly two, CR42s.

On 23 April Me109s suddenly jumped Les Davies, who was patrolling at 30,000 feet in Hurricane Z2901 but he evaded the attack in the usual manner. He also recorded that on the 27th the Hun was using booby-traps, with large enemy fighter escorts, but the RAF pilots refused to take the bait. That same day 23 Hurricane reinforcements, which were to form the strength of 185 Squadron, were ferried to Malta via HMS Ark Royal on Operation Codenamed "DUNLOP".

On 3 May, Ta' Qali was heavily bombed, and the next day, six Blenheims of 21 Squadron, under the command of Sqdn. Ldr. L.V.E. Atkinson, landed at Luqa via Gibraltar from the UK.

Meanwhile Rear Admiral (AIR) R.A. Boyd was sent by Admiral Cunningham himself to press his case for bigger consignments of fighter aircraft reinforcements. Hurricanes were at this time still being shipped

Ta' Qali under attack as seen from the battlements of Mdina.

to Gibraltar in wooden crates where, assembled before delivery, led to delays in ferrying. Due to the pressure being put on by the Admiral of the Mediterranean Fleet, however, to save valuable time, 21 of the crated fighters were embarked on the SS. Paracombe, a cargo steamer, and dispatched Malta-bound unescorted on 1 May. On this date Oblt. Joachim Muncheberg, in command of 7/JG26, scored his 39th and 40th victory over Malta.

Thirteen Beaufighters of 252 Squadron, for which a maintenance crew was flown to the island on 27 April in Sunderland P9600 of No. 10 R. Australian AF Squadron also reached Malta on 1 May. These were to provide the Paracombe with an air cover, but, unfortunately, the steamer struck a mine en route and sank.

Shortly after arriving at M'Xlokk Bay the Sunderland was attacked by Oblt. Muncheberg and his wingman at its moorings, and the aircraft was set ablaze in a single pass.

Beaufighter T3237 of 252 Squadron, mistaken for a Ju88, was on 3 May shot up by a patrolling Hurricane. The pilot was forced to crash land, and became the Unit's first casualty on the island.

On 6 May four more Hurricanes were shot down during an encounter with a gaggle of Bf109s and MC200s that came in escorting some He.111s. Two of the Italian fighters, however, fell to the guns of the RAF Hurricanes.

That same day, having been promoted to Air Vice-Marshall, Group Capt. h.p. Lloyd arrived from Britain to take over command of the island from Maynard.

As if the sinking of the 'Paracombe' was not a severe enough blow to the RAF, that same day 261 Squadron lost four more Hurricanes to marauding Bf.l09s.

Oblt Muncheberg Bf109Es reigned supreme over Malta, ruling the progress of air fighting. They flew high altitude sweeps, disabling the RAF Hurricanes, which they then found easy to shoot down.

Davies recalls that on 7 May two RAF Hurricanes collided in midair, killing Sgt. Jennings. Shortly afterwards he was airborne searching for signs of the other pilot who baled out before his stricken aircraft crashed off the coast.

The Blenheims of 21 Squadron were meanwhile out on their first experimental anti-shipping operation from Luqa.

Shortly after a survey of the situation in Malta, the new AVM realized that, before an effective operation of any magnitude could be brought to bear against the enemy, a re-organization Program had to be planned.

Sir Dudley Pound received a severe tongue lashing for his efforts and a few days later Chief Marshall Tedder visited Malta.

Then shortly afterwards, following Churchill's statement of 10 May 1941:

> "... the Island, along with Egypt and Gibraltar, ... will be defended with the full strength of the Empire" ... the island's RAF fighter strength was increasing.

Chapter VII

The Hurricane

(Part 2)

AVM H.P. Lloyd – Again the Regia Aeronautica – 'Splice' 'Rocket' – 'Tracer' – 'Railway I' & 'II' – E-Boat Assault – 'Status I' & 'II' – Hurri-bombers – Fuel problem – 'Perpetual' – Again the 'Luftwaffe' – List of Ferry operations

Proposals by enemy officials to occupy the battered island went unheeded by the Axis High Command. The latter felt confident that, by way of the Balkans, their supply convoys could easily navigate their way to Tripoli out of range of Malta's anti-shipping strike forces, a theory upon which General Geisler could do nothing else but proceed by moving his Fleigerkorps to bases in Greece, Rhodes, and later in Crete.

This unforeseen withdrawal of the Luftwaffe from Sicily gave the British the opportunity to strengthen their RAF defences in Malta, and A.V.M. Lloyd the chance to reorganize his striking forces there.

Air Vice Marshall H. P. Lloyd being sworn in as the island's new AOC.

Long before his inspection duties were over Lloyd was horrified at the state of the Island's RAF establishments. He did not blame his predecessor for, compared to him, he knew he was better off by far for what AVM Maynard had succeeded in building had been done from scratch.

As a peacetime establishment, Kalafrana was ideal. The flying boat base and air-sea rescue headquarters stocked the majority of spares and equipment used by the RAF, while a proportion of all technical work was done in a big hangar. Close to it was the only engine repair shop, and next to the latter, out in the open, was an engine test-rig. Miraculously, while all this had been so vulnerably exposed to air attacks, no bombs had dropped on this establishment.

The result, had this happened, would have been disastrous for the Air Ministry would have been unable to operate an air force from Malta without it.

Dispersal on airfields was limited to a few solid stone blast pens erected on their perimeters, right where a few well-aimed bombs would have demolished them. Fuel was kept in five-gallon jerry cans, stored in small dumps, mainly exposed to the elements and air attacks.

Serviceable aircraft numbered 59, of which only 29 were Hurricanes. The others consisted of an array of Swordfish, Marylands and a few other types.

Engines and airframes had to be overhauled and repaired, but worst of all was the fact that numerous aircraft parts, if found unserviceable, had to be made to work for no replacement parts were available on the island.

Meanwhile Axis shipping traversed the Central Mediterranean unmolested. That narrow strip of water separating Europe from North Africa at that stage in the war belonged to the enemy.

This was early in June 1941, shortly after the fall of Crete, given greater importance. The Germans, possessing in air power what they lacked at sea, could not have made better use of occupied aerodromes. This led the British naval forces involved in the campaign to confirm what had already been foretold, that air power would be the deciding factor in the control of the Mediterranean.

In the grip of this crisis, another buildup of RAF fighters for Malta was underway. For this purpose, more aircraft protection was needed on the ground, and the new AVM was determined to provide this by expanding on dispersal. It was a hard task indeed for manual labour was the only means available, the pick and the shovel the main tools at hand.

Malta, a military objective, surrounded by enemy bases,
isolated from Gibraltar by nearly 1,000 miles and almost just as farther
from Alexandria, with minefields harassing the Sicilian narrows,
literally imprisoned the inhabitants.

Construction of more re-enforced stone blast pens.

To shift building material along short hauls the wheelbarrow was used while horse-drawn carts were provided for longer hauls. A slow, primitive, time consuming process where so much was needed to be done as in as short a time as was humanly possible. However, signs of the radical change related to the re-organization of the RAF in Malta began to show.

Earlier in the year, with Germany involved in the Middle East, Britain was aware that loosing Malta at that stage of the war would prove disastrous to the Allied cause in North Africa. British naval forces in the Eastern Mediterranean would find themselves in a hazardous position, and Britain would be deprived of the 'springboard' needed to keep reinforcements flowing towards the Middle East, as well as a base from where to strike at Tripoli-bound enemy supply convoys steaming out of Southern Italy.

This situation in the Central Mediterranean was the cause of great concern to Britain. In a dispatch dated 14 April 1941, regarding the war in the region, sent to the C-in-C Malta, under item 5 in a list of directives, Sir Winston Churchill wrote:

> "In order to control the sea communication across the Mediterranean sufficient suitable naval forces must be based on Malta. Protection must be afforded to these naval forces by the Air Forces at Malta, which must be kept at the highest strength in fighters of the latest and best quality that the Malta aerodromes can contain. The duty of affording fighter protection to the naval forces holding Malta should have priority over the use of the aerodromes by bombers engaged in attacking Tripoli."

During April two Army Cooperation Units, Nos 250 and 251 Squadrons, were being formed in Palestine in preparation for a move to Greece. On 2 May, however, the personnel of 251 Squadron were instead posted to RAF Amyria in Egypt where they were joined by part of the ex-members of 1430 Flight.

Four days later this group was heading towards Malta on board HMS Breconshire, arriving on the island on 9 May.

On 12 May, by amalgamating the Army Cooperation Unit from Palestine, 1430 Flight and 'C' Flight of 261 Squadron, 185 Squadron, equipped with Hurricane IIs, was formed at Hal Far under the command of Sqdn. Ldr. P W 'Boy' Mould DFC.

Original 185 Squadron insignia that was sketched by a squadron pilot shortly after the unit was formed. Though unofficially approved until 1945, after some alterations were made to it, 185 Squadron kept it on display during the war years.

The squadron's insignia was first sketched by one of the unit's own pilots shortly after it was formed in Malta. Although, as it later developed, this was not officially approved until February, 1945, after slight alteration were made to the original, the badge was kept on display by 185 Squadron throughout the war years.

On 13 May, the day following its forming, 185 Squadron was for the first time blooded when its Hurricanes were jumped from above cloud by a formation of Bf109s. Instant evasive action was taken, saving the RAF fighters from getting slaughtered. Immediately afterwards orders to reform over Ta' Qali were relayed to the dispersed squadron, but Fly. Off. Westmacott, mistaking two enemy fighters with red spinners for reforming Hurricanes, was shot at by the l09s. His aircraft was damaged, and but the wounded Westmacott managed to bale out and parachute to safety.

In a span of four days 185 Squadron suffered the loss of three Hurricanes and two pilots to the guns of the Mel09s.

Based in Sicily 7/JG26 were at this time joined by another Bf109E equipped unit, III/JG27, remaining on the island until late May, when they were both withdrawn to the Eastern Front.

Davies, who was in May impressed with a newly formed MNFU, recorded that the Mel09s were at this time operating in the fighter/ bomber role.

A relief squadron was expected to arrive from the UK on 20 May, and a large plot of Mel09s was spotted close to the island.

On the 21st, in Operation code-named 'SPLICE', the carriers HMS Ark Royal and Furious ferried 41 Hurricanes to Malta, the first time in which established units, 213, 229 and 249 Squadrons, were sent abroad. Of this lot 14 aircraft were diverted to Hal Far while the rest were dispersed between Luqa and Ta' Qali where 249 Squadron was given permanent headquarters.

Meanwhile the Hurricanes of 213 and 229 Squadrons, led by four Beaufighters of 252 Squadron, moved on to the Middle East.

En route, however, some of 213 Squadron's fighters, losing sight of the leading aircraft, returned to the island.

The late Kenneth Cox, an ex-L.A.C. with 185 Squadron, recalls the incident:

> "The fourteen Hurricanes that landed at Hal Far on 21 May were serviced during the day. Early the next morning they were again airborne, on their way to the Middle East. Four of them, however, returned to the airfield some hours later. Two had developed technical problems and the other two had lost sight of the navigational leader."

That same day the ten Hurricane Mk.ls of 185 Squadron moved to Ta' Qali with 249 Squadron. On 23 May Flt. Lt. Hancock and Plt. Off. Gray took off from Hal Far in the squadron's remaining Mk.IIs, and flew them to Ta' Qali, bringing the unit up to full strength.

Cox continued:

> "On 25 May the long range fuel tanks fitted to the four Hurricanes that had turned back from their flight eastward were removed, and the fighters kept at Hal Far."

On that date 261 Squadron was disbanded and 249 Squadron took over its duties at Ta' Qali.

Flt. Lt. T.F. Neil, arriving from Luqa by bus, decided to pick one of the Hurricanes at Ta' Qali, after having been relieved of the new one which he had ferried off HMS Ark Royal. He had this written in relation to the state of the fighters available on the airfield:

> "I was not encouraged. God, what a rag-bag set!"

Later in the day seven Bf.l09s, with Muncheberg leading them, made a low level strafing attack on Ta' Qali airfield and the Hurricane Is of 249 Squadron parked there, leaving behind them two burnt-out Hurricanes, a badly damaged two, several wounded airmen, and a pilot. This fighter aircraft sweep severely undermined the defenders' morale as they were shocked by the unexpectedness of the attack. Miraculously, however, no one was killed.

The next day, 26 May, pilots from 249 Squadron, having been left with few serviceable aircraft, were driven over to Hal Far to fly whatever Hurricanes were available on the airfield.

Arriving at Gibraltar on board HMS Argus 46 Squadron's pilots and their aircraft were on 29 May transferred to the decks of the carriers 'Furious' and 'Ark Royal', where they joined the remaining element of 229 Squadron preparatory to their departure for Malta. Code-named 'ROCKET' this operation saw to the ferrying of 43 more Hurricanes to the island, of which none went missing. These were led by nine Blenheims of 82 Squadron who were also due to join the rest of their unit on Malta.

The Hurricane Mk.IIs of 46 Squadron were on arrival diverted to Hal Far, and remained there till the end of June.

To L.A.C. Cox these fighters, which landed on the airfield on 6 June, were to all intents and purposes reinforcements for 185 Squadron.

Flt. Lt. P.W. LeFevre, DFC, landed at Luqa in Hurricane II Z2491, but moved on to Hal Far later in the day.

Night attacks had meanwhile been on the increase. Made by only a few aircraft at a time, bombs were more often than not dropped at random, as if more to demoralize the defenders than to inflict damage anywhere in particular. Air Headquarters, Malta, however, decided to organize a proper front to counter these enemy activities.

Desultory night attacks had been going on and off since late 1940. An entry for 5.

May in L. Davies flying logbook, a 261 Squadron's fighter pilot recalls a Night Flight. However, it was not until 1 June 1941 that four Hurricanes, all from 185 Squadron, were assigned to standby for night flying duties as of 20.45 hours.

The pilots that first night were Flt. Lts. Hancock and Elliot, and Sgts. Bamberger and Branson. The following night the number of aircraft detailed was reduced to two, of which one was scrambled at 22.20 hours.

On 3 June Sqdn. Ldr. Barton of 249 Squadron shot down an SM79 and claimed his unit's first night victory.

Three days later, due to a shortage of Hurricanes, some pilots from 185 Squadron went over to 249, and on the 8th the squadron had fighters intercepting night intruding BR20Ms.

Sqdn. Ldr. Barton
of 249 Squadron.

Meanwhile, early in the morning of 6 June, circa. 00.55 hours, Flt. Lt. Hancock intercepted a Heinkel He.111, and was credited with 185 Squadron's first nighttime, probably destroyed, enemy aircraft.

As of late evening of that day 185 Squadron's role became that of a night fighter unit, the first Malta-based RAF squadron to be given those duties on a full time basis. But except for one isolated incident on the night of 11 June the month proved to be uneventful for the squadron. At 21.30 hours, Sgt. Burton, returning from an airborne searchlight cooperation exercise, landed downwind, overshot the runway, and was injured when he crashed into a hangar.

Meanwhile, exchanging their Hurricane Mk.IIs with the island's battered Mk.ls, 229 Squadron, led by two Blenhiems, moved on to the Middle east.

Action for 46 Squadron was not long in coming as aircraft of the Regia Aeronautica were at this lime appearing in larger numbers. Seven of its Hurricanes were scrambled for the first time on 11 June, and succeeded in shooting down a lone reconnaissance SM79. However escorting MC200s blooded the squadron when they shot down Hurricane Z2480. The pilot was also reported missing.

On 12 June, accompanied by Hurricanes from 249 Squadron, the pilots of 46 Squadron were kept busy fighting off gaggles of Italian fighters.

That same day, airborne on dawn patrol in Hurricane Z2491, LeFevre encountered some CR42s and succeeded in shooting his first enemy aircraft and damaging another over Malta.

In these clashes, the RAF units lost two pilots and their aircraft, including damages to some of their other fighters. However the enemy, probably doubtful about the outcome of these encounters, even with the odds in his favour, kept his distance from the island during the next few days.

"The squadron's done pretty well, ten Italians down for two of ours" wrote Plt.Off. Anderson to his family.

"If we go on at this rate I'm afraid they'll fetch the Jerries back down to help them again, and then it won't be nearly as pleasant."

Plt. Off. Bowerman and another pilot on standby playing a game of chess.

Originally a Spitfire pilot, Anderson did not dislike flying the Hurricane, in spite of its drawbacks, as he himself wrote in one of his letters:

> "I'm quite used to the Hurricane now and like it the more I fly it."

However,

> "... to date it's proved superior to the Italian fighters in performance. We only hope, and pray, they don't send anymore Messerschmitts down this way ...".

On operation Code-named 'TRACER', in which HMS Ark Royal and Victorious ferried 47 Hurricanes to Malta on 14 June, only 43 reached the island.

In May, newly commissioned HMS Victorious embarked the crated Hurricanes of 238 and 260 Squadrons, destined for service in the Middle East. Setting off from Greenock the carrier was shortly afterwards diverted to the Home Fleet, which was then out at sea hunting for the Bismark. By the time the carrier reached Gibraltar all the Hurricanes had been assembled below decks, so on arrival their transfer to HMS Ark Royal was immediately effected.

Robert McInnes Wilson, a Scotsman, who was ferrying one of the Hurricanes, recalled what actually ensued during this stage of the ferrying phase:

> "While the carrier approached south of the Balearic Islands the fighters were brought on deck, preparatory to the flight to Malta en route to Egypt, fitted with long-range fuel tanks."

Of the four navigational Hudsons of 200 Squadron one flew astray, and by the time Malta was sighted the fuel gauges in each Hurricane, including McInnes's, were at their lowest mark.

"Soon one of the Hurricanes was abandoned and Saunders parachuted into the sea, from where he was later picked up." continued McInnes.

"Debriefed to land of Hal Far we used the airfield nearest to our approach – Luqa."

Tanks now dry Sgt. Robert MacPherson undershot the runway and crashed killing himself and writing off a fighter. McInnes Wilson, contrary to his squadron companion, when the engine of his Hurricane cut out, he made a glided landing. Touching down at high speed nearly halfway down the runway, he was soon running off its end where:

> "... over shooting a slit trench I came to a stop against a rubble wall." ... breaking up a third valuable fighter, but coming away from the wreck without injury.

During this mishap Hurricanes of 249 Squadron were scrambled and directed to fly on diverse bearings in an effort to intercept this lost flight and lead them to the island, but the attempt failed.

Of this consignment, however, consisting of two units, 238 and 260 Squadrons, few of the fighters, if any, remained in Malta as these were all earmarked for the Middle East.

On 15 June nearly half moved on eastwards.

A further eight followed them the next day and another five departed on 17 June.

The next day, having got their forces re-organized, the Regia Aeronautica launched a new offensive against Malta. Hurricanes of 249 Squadron were scrambled to intercept an all fighter strike force formed of MC200s.

Sgt. F. Sheppard, an Australian, on loan from 185 Sqdn, owing to its shortage of aircraft, shared the destruction of an MC200 with another pilot and claimed a second as a probably, in this encounter.

At the break of dawn of 23 June Hurricanes of 46 Squadron struck at a seaplane base in Syracuse, wreaking havoc with their 20mm cannon-armed fighters.

Flt. Lt. LeFevre recorded this attack, that ensued at 04.45 hours, as he took part in it flying in Hurricane Z3058.

Two days later, in a joint scramble with aircraft of 249 Squadron, the Hurricanes of 46 Squadron came to grips with a gaggle of escorting MC200s, an encounter in which they were credited with the destruction of three enemy fighters.

That day Plt. Off. Anderson drew his first blood.

As the squadron charged the enemy formation, led by Sqdn. Ldr. Rabagliati, to whom Anderson was wingman, the latter fired on one enemy fighter. Shortly afterwards he was hotly in pursuit of two others. Diving after them from 18,000 feet to sea level he shot down one of the two MC200s into the sea. On 27 June 46 Sqdn. succeeded in breaking

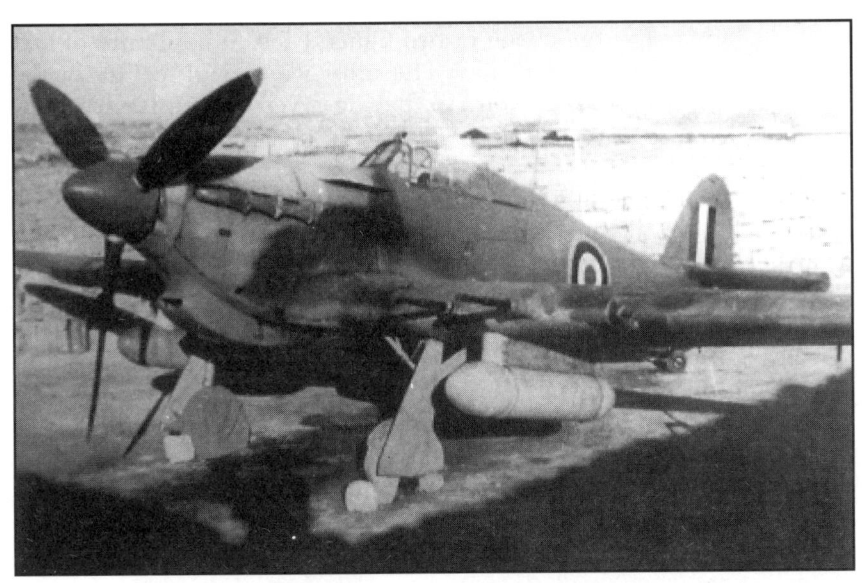

A newly arrived Hurricane IIC from a batch ferried to Malta on 27 June 1941 on operation 'Railway I'. These were armed with four 20mm Hispano cannons.

this record, in two separate encounters, by shooting down six enemy aircraft without suffering any self losses.

That day HMS Ark Royal, engaged on operation Code named 'RAILWAY – I', ferried 22 new Hurricanes to Malta. Unfortunately, however, one fighter crashed on arrival, and another was reported missing en route. These Hurricanes, armed with four 20mm cannons, were the first of type to appear in Malta.

On 28 June 126 Squadron was formed at Hal Far by renumbering 46 Squadron, and at the end of the month, the day the unit moved to Ta' Qali, the new squadron was for the first time airborne engaging MC200s, of which two were reported shot down and another damaged. Two days later LeFevre took off from Hal Far in Hurricane L2481 and landed at TaQali to join newly formed 126 Sqdn.

Anderson, in another of his family letters, described his feelings regarding his involvement in the air-fighting going on over the island:

> "We get air raids with monotonous regularity. We get used to them and I always stay in bed ...".

"So far I've only been in two fights. I felt ... a mixture of fear and wonderful exhilaration. The most wonderful feeling in the world; only trouble is, you risk paying a very expensive price for the pleasure."

Meanwhile operation Code named 'RAILWAY – II', executed by the carriers 'Ark Royal' and 'Furious' on 30 June, provided the island with a further 35 Hurricanes.

On 1 July 185 Squadron returned to Hal Far where it gained more equipment to its two flights, by the addition of the 14 Hurricane IIAs already on the airfield.

Flying this type against the MC200 for the first time on 4 July the pilots of 185 Squadron found the cannon-armed fighter more effective in air combat than the poorly armed Mk.l, and succeeded in shooting down two enemy fighters and damaging three others.

Hurricanes of 126 Sqdn. also came to grips with the MC200 at dawn, and lost Sgt. Thomas Hackston in Z3055 who was reported missing.

(In mid 1995 scuba divers recovered the wreck of a Hurricane from a depth of 42 metres off Malta's south coast, and the Malta Aviation Museum Foundation provided the information that solved the mysterious circumstances of Hackston's death.

Identified as Hurricane II, Z3055, the probable cause of the crash was engine failure due to overheating. The pilot is presumed to have drowned in rough seas shortly after ditching. Hackston's body was never found.

Hurricane Z3055, currently under restoration at Ta' Qali's Aviation Museum is, at the time of writing, nearing completion. This aircraft, which is to be provided with a serviceable engine, albeit unflyable, will most certainly be seen taxing around the Museum complex for the benefit of visitors at preset times of the day. – Author.)

On 9 July, five of these Hurricane IIAs, from 185 and 126 Squadrons, attacked a Seaplane base in Syracuse. Flown by Sqdn. Ldrs Mould, Rabagliati, Flt. Lts. LeFevre, Jeffries and Flt. Sgt. MacKay, they used the cannon-armed fighters with devastating effect.

LeFevre recorded that afternoon's fighter sweep in his logbook:

"Attacked Sea plane base, hangars, railway, trains, etc. Three seaplanes were set on fire."

With the return of the Regia Aeronautica a substantial number of Italian aircraft found their way on to 185 Squadrons scoreboard. However, when on 11 July Hal Far airfield became the target of a big enemy fighter mission, and twelve of the squadron's Hurricanes were scrambled to intercept the gaggles of MC200s, there were no reports of any aircraft claims after the encounter.

The strongest force of RAF fighters that were scrambled to defend the island since the outbreak of hostilities in the Mediterranean was on 25 July 1941. Numbering 22 Hurricanes, from 185 and 249 Squadrons, they intercepted a large number of MC200s that arrived escorting a lone Z.1007bis, dispatched on a reconnaissance mission. In the ensuing battle the latter was shot down, as well as two of the enemy fighters.

At this time Italy, after two previous attempts to mount seaward assaults on Malta's Grand Harbour, that had to abandon due to unfavourable weather conditions, towards midnight of 25 July 1941 had her 10th MTB Flotilla (X-MAS), with the sloop 'Diana' in attendance en route for the third time. The radar station AMES 502 at Madliena detected this enemy approach and alerted the island's coastal defences.

After the 'Diana' launched the assault vessels, comprised of nine one-man crewed explosive-primed MTs -barchinis- about 20 miles short of Malta, and released the two MTLs (Slow Touring Motor Boats) she had on tow, each carrying an SLC, a two-men crew Slow Speed Human Torpedo, she withdrew. The two MTBs, anti-submarine torpedo boats, MAS 451 and 452, which had been provided to escort the 'Diana', remained with the assault vessels.

After midnight, as the 'Diana' steamed northwards out of radar range, Malta's coastal defences were stood down from alert.

Three diversionary air-raid bombings by BR.20Ms were supposed to be made in the morning of 26 July 1941, between 01.45 and 04.30, but the first one was abandoned. The other two attacks, which were to be on Valletta and Floriana, were erroneously made on Marsascala and St. Paul's Bay at 02.00 and 04.30 hours respectively. Air raids that were to prelude the Italian harbour assault.

At about 03.45 hours a Maggore Teseo Tesei set out towards his objective at the controls of an SLC, with which he was to blow a hole in the anti-torpedo net blocking the entrance to the main harbour under the bridge. Through this opening were to be driven the nine MTs inside the harbour to attack targets of opportunity therein.

Whatever happened to Maggore Tesei nobody knows for the explosion scheduled to take place at 04.30 hours failed to materialize.

An artist's impression of the Italian E-Boat attempted assault on the Grand Harbour on 26 July 1941.

Two MTs were then dispatched to execute the task. One was set to explode on the surface to protect the one intended to blow up the net from any attacking enemy vessel, but fate did not favour the Italians that night for the latter failed to explode as it hit the net.

At 04.48 hours, in desperation, Carabelli, the pilot, sacrificed his own life in one final effort to achieve his goal, but the vessel, designed to explode underwater, where the net was securely set up, exploded on the surface ineffectively. The concussion, unfortunately, activated his escort's bomb-primed boat simultaneously, killing Frasetto and alarming Malta's harbour defences to something about which they had been unaware until then.

Coastline anti-aircraft batteries opened fire at the dispersed enemy vessels across the harbour entrance as searchlights were brought to bear on them.

By this time the first dawn greyness was breaking over the horizon and Hurricanes from 126 and 185 Squadrons were scrambled to go into action against the four support vessels patrolling offshore.

Plt. Off. Bailey of 185 Sqdn reported sinking one of these enemy boats, undoubtedly one of the MTLs or MAS 451. Hard hit the latter was immediately abandoned by the crew, jumping overboard just as the boat blew up, killing four of the seamen.

Meanwhile MC200s, detailed to fly out at dawn from a base in Syracuse to escort their Flotilla, arrived on the scene and came to grips with the RAF Hurricanes.

Sgt. Plt. Haley of 126 Sqdn chased one of the enemy fighters and shot it down in the sea but another had moved in behind him. Plt. Off. Thompson of 185 Squadron, however, went to his rescue and between them disposed off a second MC200.

Flt. Lt. Lefevre of 126 Sqdn had opened up with his cannons on MAS 452. The crew immediately signalled surrender, but those who were still able to take action launched the small MTS they had on board, which was still intact, and escaped to Sicily in the ensuing battle.

The Hurricane of Plt. Off. Denis Winton, pounced by the enemy fighters, was so badly shot up that he had to abandon the aircraft and bale out over the sea.

After hours in his dinghy Winton spotted MAS 452 floating nearby. He swam to it and climbed on board to find out that those still on the vessel was either dead or severely wounded.

Six hours had elapsed since Winton was shot down when an Army rescue boat approached, but wary of who might still be on board the vessel remained circling around MAS 452.

Shortly afterwards a Swordfish floatplane arrived, landed alongside, picked up Winton, who had taken with him the flag MAS 452 had been flying, and flew back to Malta.

The enemy vessel was later taken in tow by the British rescue launch 'Jade' and brought into the harbour.

The Italians, despite their gallant effort, had achieved nothing. The assault had cost them fifteen dead seamen and eighteen others taken prisoners, amongst whom were three officers. Eight of the MTs were somehow or other destroyed, as well as both MTLs, MAS 451 and two MC200s while MAS 452 and one MT had been captured.

Three days later Beaufighlers of 272 Squadron, escorted by Hurricanes from Malta based units provided a distraction by attacking airfields in Sicily. This was while Force 'X' ferried men from Gibraltar to the island. Furthermore, fighter aircraft strength had increased to seventy five serviceable Hurricanes, of which only fifteen Mk.ls remained. However, until August the RAF fighters failed to encounter enemy aircraft during patrols. Still a newly formed Malta Night Fighter Unit was kept busy intercepting the enemy's intruders that had recently stepped up nighttime activities.

On 15 August, the Hurricanes again went on the offensive, striking at the Seaplane base in Syracuse. These attacks were five days later repeated by fighters of 126 Squadron, who shot up Augusta harbour, inflicting damages to seaplanes and harbour installations.

Defensively, Malta-based fighter aircraft were in action on 19 and 28 August respectively, shooting down eight MC200s and damaging others. Italian sources, however, claimed the destruction of two Hurricanes for the loss of only one of their Macchis for the 26th.

On 19 August, airborne in Hurricane Z3512, LeFevre intercepted several Macchis. He claimed shooting down one of the enemy fighters, and credited two to Burke.

The next day LeFevre's squadron was again on the offensive, strafing military installations in Augusta. He recorded flying in Hurricane Z3505, and claimed having shot up a balloon and a boat. Carpenter, his wingman, however, returned with a damaged aircraft.

At this time fuel stocks exceeded three million gallons in 4-gallon tins, distributed at fifteen sites. Sqdn. Ldr. S. F. Barnes wrote that:

> "Stacking on the field sites had its own problems, especially as none of us knew how a stock would react to being hit by a bomb."

Opinionated discussions were raised about this as a consignment of 400 tons arrived when a site had not yet been found for it, with the result that it had to be moved several times before it was finally split up into two large stacks in a field.

This was further complicated when the new CO gave orders that stacks should not contain more than 100 cases at intervals of 50 yards. These were obviously spread over a considerable area of countryside, around which had to be set up a barbed wire fence.

"I visited the site a few days later "Recalled Barnes" and found all the cases in one field, now in small dumps close together, and the field wired-in."

The Army, who was responsible for the fencing, finally had their fill of it in the end. No comments were raised about this but Barnes recalled that the movements resulted in 20% losses of fuel, proving that this was a difficult procedure to follow.

Fifty-gallon drums were then introduced. It was decided that these were to be filled at the storage site, to be later emptied on airfields at bulk installations.

For this purpose decanting troughs had to be introduced and the 'Works & Bricks' and HM Dockyard were called to assist in their planning and manufacture. This worked out perfectly both in decanting fuel on site and transporting it in bulk to airfields with the minimum of wastage. However, at wintertime, when the weather was extremely wet, tins had to be taken to the Shell Installations for decanting to filter them of water before use. This task finally led to the establishing of the Command Petrol Pool in September 1941.

Some good lorries were provided, but so were a number of crudely improvised road tank wagons. These consisted of burnt out bowsers mounted on to old bus chassis. At the outset, however, refuellers were standard 450-gallon trailers with pumps operated by hand-cranked Lister engines that were frequently strenuous to operate.

Still, up to 30,000 gallons of fuel reached airfields daily by these means. Bad weather conditions did not deter the men from their duties, and neither did the constant threat of enemy attacks, hence flying was never held up due to fuel shortage.

An old London open top double-decker bus improvised as a Hurricane refuelling bowser at Ta' Qali, 1940.

Enemy activity was noted to have decreased during the next few days, but following several offensive operations by Malta-based strike units, Air Headquarters were expecting retaliatory action from the Italians.

Finally on 4 September nine Hurricanes of 185 Squadron and twelve of 126 were scrambled to intercept a large number of enemy aircraft off the island.

Contact with these MC200s was made at 22,000 feet in the Grand Harbour area.

Sqdn. Ldr. Rabagliati, in Hurricane Z4941 attacked two of the Macchis, of which he shot down one in the sea.

Flg. Off. Carpenter, flying top cover for his companions, climbed after 4 of the enemy fighters which were there for the same purpose as he over their formation. Plt. Off. Lardner-Burke followed him and both attacked the Macchis, each later reporting having shot one down.

Plt. Off. Blackburn claimed a probable and a damaged. Flt. Lt. LeFevre, Sgts. Simpson, Russell, and MacGregor each claimed a MC200 shot down. The latter, however, flying Z3498, had to crash land on Ta' Qali due to the damages sustained in the battle.

Jeffries of 185 Sqdn. also got a probable.

Unfortunately, however, in another fierce free for all later in the day, in which were involved eight Hurricanes of 249 Squadron, two of the RAF fighters, Z3056 and Z3521, were reported missing. Their pilots, Plt. Off. G Smith and Sgt. J Kimberly, were believed killed as no sign of them was found in a search organized for the purpose, although two MC200s were claimed to have been shot down.

Sqdn. Ldr. Barton, in Hurricane Z2794, described it as the hardest fight of his career:

> "... We had the advantage but somehow the Italians reacted strongly and an unhappy dogfight ensued ... all low down close to the water. ... I ordered disengage ... I doubt if anyone heard ... and we ran for home ... a most dangerous situation, hence our losses."

Barton claimed a probable and a damaged. Sgts Owen and Carter reported having shot an enemy aircraft each. Plt. Off. Matthews one damaged.

On 9 September, fourteen Hurricanes staged through the island, via HMS Ark Royal, in another ferrying operation Cade named 'STATUS – I', on transit to the Middle East.

On 13 September, the carriers 'Ark Royal' and 'Furious' executed Operation 'STATUS – II', ferrying 46 further Hurricanes to Malta, of which 45 reached the island.

Twenty-two of the fighters were immediately posted with locally based units, while the remaining 23 were shortly afterwards dispatched eastward.

Among the pilots who arrived on the island that particular day were the first few Americans, Plt. Offs. H.M. Coffin, D.A. Tetford, E.E. Steele and E.E. Streets, who, whether incidentally or otherwise, were all posted to 126 Squadron.

During September all Malta-based fighter aircraft units were brought up to their established strength and for the first time had more Hurricanes in hand than they actually used.

"After the wrecks we had been flying over the past several months ..." wrote Sqdn. Ldr. Neil, in his book 'Onward to Malta' "... here were aircraft we could now fight in with confidence."

The British pressed on relentlessly with their anti-shipping strikes, but with the launching of a convoy operation Code-named 'HALBERD' Malta-based strike units were diverted to attack Axis airfields in Sicily in an effort to distract the enemy from harassing the Malta-bound convoy.

Meanwhile a large detachment of 272 Squadron's Beaufighters arrived on the island from North Africa and, supplemented by Blenheim IVFs from the Middle East-based 113 Squadron, provided the supply ships with an air cover.

When the convoy finally neared the island Malta-based RAF units struck out in all directions in the Mediterranean, an operation in which even Hurricanes, to which bomb racks were fitted, went into action as bombers:

> In the UK Hurricane P2989 served as the trial installation 'Hurri-bomber' in April 1941.

The following month Z2328 was flown to Bascombe Down for type trials where two 250lb bombs were carried – later two 500lbs – attached to underwing racks. Finally, on 30 October, 607 Squadron for the first time went into action with the 'Hurri-bomber' on anti-shipping strikes from Britain.

In the desert Hurricanes, fitted with racks capable of carrying eight 401b bombs first went into action on 20 November.

All this confirms that Malta was where the 'Hurri-bomber' was first

A bombed-up Hurricane IIB about to be taken over for an offensive sortie by a FAA pilot from Hal Far in the summer of 1941.

pressed into operational service, with 185 Squadron, more than a month before the sortie flown with 607 Squadron.

The late Kenneth Cox recalled:

> "The under-wing bomb-racks we fitted to these Hurricanes on 26 September were made to carry eight small bombs; four under each wing."

The first mission from Hal Far airfield was flown on 28 September at 06.40hrs, with six Hurricanes flying in two waves of three each, one led by Sqdn. Ldr. Mould and the other by Flt. Lt. Pike, carrying six 401b bombs and two 25lb incendiaries.

Six other Hurricanes, led by Fly. Off. Thompson, provided the fighter-bombers with an escort.

The raid on Comiso aerodrome was repeated three hours later, after a change of pilots, with one final attack for the day carried out at l4.00hrs. The operation was a success. Several buildings were left in ruins, and a good number of aircraft were either destroyed or extensively damaged on the ground.

Two days later the squadron had five Hurricanes airborne on another offensive operation on Comiso, escorted by six more of the fighters.

The Hurricanes of 185 Squadron were on 1 October scrambled to intercept some enemy fighters. Although the squadron pilots had already come to grips with the new Mc202 a few miles to the north of the island the previous day, and lost Hurricane Z5285 in the encounter, that was the day when the fighters of 4 Stormo first appeared directly over Malta.

The two opposing forces were numerically even, but the Macchis jumped the RAF fighters and two of the Hurricanes were shot down. The squadron lost its CO, Sqdn. Ldr. 'Boy' Mould in this encounter.

On 7 October it was 249 Squadron's turn to go on the offensive, and with a flight of its Hurricanes armed with bombs they made a night time attack on Gela Station. Comiso aerodrome was bombed the following night.

The first MC202 was shot down on 14 October when some of the fighters made an early low level attack on Luqa aerodrome. Plt. Off. Barnwell, however, a Malta Night Fighter pilot, was himself reported missing after the encounter was broken off.

At this time reports that troop carrying aircraft were spotted flying out reinforcements, supplies and equipment to Rommel's desert forces in North Africa, led to the dispatch of Malta-based fighters to patrol the airspace to the south of Lampedusa.

For this purpose, due to the long distances they had to cover, Hurricanes were fitted with external underwing long-range fuel tanks, the same ones with which the fighters had been ferried to the island.

Equipped with these 44-gallon tanks it was estimated that the Hurricane could remain airborne on 3 hour-long patrols searching for any Axis transport aircraft traversing between Sicily and North Africa.

"These tanks were designed for ferrying, ..." explained Sqdn. Ldr. Barton, and "... quite unsuitable for combat."

They could not be jettisoned when empty.

The RAF fighters flew in pairs on these missions. Contact with a lone SM81 was first made by Hurricanes of 249 Squadron on 19 October 1941. The enemy aircraft was shot down in the sea.

LeFevre recorded that during that day he was aloft practicing bombing, prior to an operational sortie on Comiso, with six 40lb and two 25lb bombs.

On 20 October the fighters detailed to patrol over Lampedusa belonged to 185 Squadron. Spotting five SM81s the Hurricanes immediately attacked. Sgt. Lillywhite, who flew close to an enemy bomber, was credited with its destruction. However his Hurricane was damaged from return fire put up by the Italian air gunners.

LeFevre was on an early morning bombing raid on the railway at Ragusa on 24 October. Just as soon as he returned his aircraft was immediately refuelled and at 08.45 hrs he was back in the air on patrol duties.

The next day he was again airborne on a 2hour 40mins afternoon patrol over Lampedusa in Hurricane LR500.

Since mid-Summer of 1941 Italy had frequently laid bare her impotency in the Mediterrnnean conflict. Her forces were unable to neutralize the British anti-shipping campaign that was so badly threatening their Axis supply lines that they had to suspend all Tripoli-bound convoys, which led them to attempt the airlift.

This campaign had cost Malta-based strike units dearly in life and equipment, but it had greatly reduced the chances of a successful conclusion for the Axis in the battle in the desert and the Middle East.

Daytime attacks on Malta by the Regia Aeronautica had waned to their lowest level, and those carried out at night began to fall short of their purpose.

Malta-based RAF Hurricane units, with a great reduction in interception duties, carried out numerous fighter-bomber missions over Sicilian targets, with the result that Malta gained in importance as a decisive strategic key-point.

On 8 November the Regia Aeronautica came out of its retreat and four Z1007bis bombers, escorted by some twenty fighters between Macchi MC200s and MC202s, approached the island. Six Hurricanes of 249 Sqdn, scrambled to intercept them, failed to make contact. Then four RAF fighters of 126 Sqdn, airborne for the same purpose, met the enemy at an elevation of some 21,000feet. But as they were climbing to attack the bombers, escorting Macchis moved in to protect them.

In the ensuing battle two enemy fighters were shot down, for the loss of an RAF Hurricane from which the pilot parachuted to safety.

That same day Sgt. Simpson recorded in his logbook that, flying in Hurricane BD826/A he was one of four fighters of 126 Squadron that intercepted 4 Cant ZlOO7bis bombers and 20 escorting MC202 fighters:

> "Carpenter, Burke and Haley one each confirmed – Haley and Worral one probable each."
>
> "Unfortunately Haley collided with a Macchi in a head-on attack

and had to bale out. Burke was wounded but flew his aircraft back to base."

Haley's combat report states:

"Dived on to top cover fighters who were diving on to P/O Carpenter and as they broke away fired from 50 yards at nearest Macchi giving him a total of six seconds. Observed first white smoke changing to black. Turned away and saw a second Macchi coming straight at me and kept firing at him at 300 yards range and my bullets were going into him the whole time until we collided. I pulled cover back and found myself in the air and after some time found ripcord and pulled it. I dropped at first to sea but eventually inland and landed on a roof top on top of a dog."

The next day fifteen fighter pilots arrived in a Sunderland flying boat of No. 10 R. Australian A.F. Squadron.

On 12 November 1941, with ferrying operation Code named PERPETUAL' underway, as 37 Hurricanes were flown off the carriers 'Argus' and 'Ark Royal', 21 Hurricanes from the island, between 'Hurri-bombers' and their escort, attacked Gela airfield.

Early in the morning of that day LeFevre was flying escort duties to the Hurri-bombers of 249 Squadron in which McGregor and Simpson bombed Gela. Simpson was shot down and taken prisoner in the attack.

Of the batch of 37 ferried Hurricanes three went astray en-route and another crashed on arrival at Hal Far airfield. These fighter reinforcements represented 266 Wing, consisting of three separate units, 242, 258 and 605 Squadrons, which were led by four Blenheims dispatched from Gibraltar for the purpose.

On 13 November, while homeward bound following operation 'Perpetual', HMS Ark Royal was torpedoed by a German U-Boat and sunk.

Despite the fact that numerous Hurricanes still remained in Gibraltar awaiting delivery, Argus, due to her vulnerability to enemy attacks, could not be risked to make runs on her own.

So, while waiting for an alternative regarding further aircraft ferrying to the Island, the breakout of hostilities in the Far East resulted in the diversion of these last Hurricanes to that direction. So "PERPETUAL" became Britain's final Hurricane ferrying operation.

Meanwhile in Malta, while the newly arrived Hurricanes were being

HMS Ark Royal – Hit by torpedoes fired from a German U-Boat, lists to port and begins to sink shortly after delivering one final batch of Hurricanes to Malta in 1941.

serviced, many of their pilots found themselves flying with 185 and 249 Squadrons. Some of 605 and 258 Squadrons' pilots, however, subsequently moved on to the Far East.

The ground party of 242 Squadron, joined by the pilots from another unit, formed a new 242 Squadron at Palembang, Sumatra. These movements resulted that, for some time, there seemed to have been, or rather were, two identically numbered units operating simultaneously in two widely separated theatres of war.

While the British land forces struggled to check the advance of Rommels Africa Korps towards Egypt during Operation 'CRUSADER', and hold on to their strategically held positions in the desert, Malta-based anti-shipping strike operations against Axis supply convoys and ports of embarkation escalated. This forced the Regia Aeronautica into taking more aggressive action on 21 November when 12 Macchis, between MC200s and MC2O2s, struck at Hal Far airfield.

Seven Hurricanes of 185 Squadron were scrambled to intercept them, and the two forces came to grips. When the two opposing forces separated there were no reports of losses from either side.

Later in the day, however, four Hurricanes from the same unit, engaged in patrolling a British supply convoy, fell foul of a score of MC2O2s and one of the RAF fighters was shot down.

On 22 November Hurricanes of 126 and 249 Squadrons were involved in violent clashes with gaggles of MC200s which came escorting ten Ju87s. Miraculously there were no reports of RAF fighter losses, and 249 Squadron claimed that they shot down three of the Macchis, a probable and damaged a fifth.

LeFevre was at 15.10 hours scrambled to join 249 Squadron as wing top cover for the Hurricanes which were clashing with 15 enemy aircraft at 27,000 feet.

In the encounter 249 Sqdn. claimed shooting down two of the enemy aircraft and 126 Sqdn. was credited with one confirmed, two probables and two damaged.

On 24 November LeFevre again participated in a fighter aircraft sweep over Comiso at 17.50 hours.

"Visibility was very poor ..." recorded LeFevre "... and Greenhalgh was lost, having been taken prisoner."

Rommel had long been demanding of his Fuhrer that all airfields in Malta should be neutralized. Hitler, however, relying on Italy's Regia Aeronautica to keep the island subdued, in the absence of his own Luftwaffe, was far too absorbed with Russia to be easily persuaded to heed his General's urgent requests. But finally convinced that his ally was again loosing his grip in the Mediterranean, the Fuhrer decided to intervene, and on 28 November Field Marshall Albert Kesselring, to whom was assigned Fleigerkorps II to open a new offensive against Malta, arrived in Rome.

Due to the heavy losses this Fleigerkorps had suffered on the Russian Front, Me109s, Ju87s and Ju88s from Russia and Western Europe gathered in Sicily and southern Italy to bring it back up to its original strength, an operation that took up till mid December to conclude.

Kesselring would have preferred to occupy Malta but his superiors refused him. This rejection probably worked in favour of Britain for had it been granted it would have probably cost her both the Mediterranean and the Middle East. But all that Kesselring was detailed to execute was the neutralization of the island.

The Regia Aeronautica mounted few attacks during the remaining days of November until mid-December. However the British pressed on relentlessly with their offensive in the Mediterranean and North Africa

May 1941. The dilapidated condition of the control tower at Luqa.

where Rommel's forces were on 7 December driven westwards from Tobruk.

LeFevre have recorded that on this date he took off in Hurricane GN-T with 249 Sqdn. at 16.05 hours in an attack on Ragusa. No. 185 Squadron provided top cover.

Five days later he was again airborne in a mid-day operation over Comiso in Hurricane GN-S.

Meanwhile the war had spread farther across the Globe. On 8 December Japan had attacked Pearl Harbour. This action may have temporarily affected Britain and her resources unfavourably, but now with the United States directly involved in the war, the British had overnight found a powerful ally fighting at their side.

The Luftwaffe returned over Malta on 19 December when a lone Ju88 flew an early morning reconnaissance sortie over the Grand Harbour. Patrolling Hurricanes moved in to intercept, but could only report damaging the intruder.

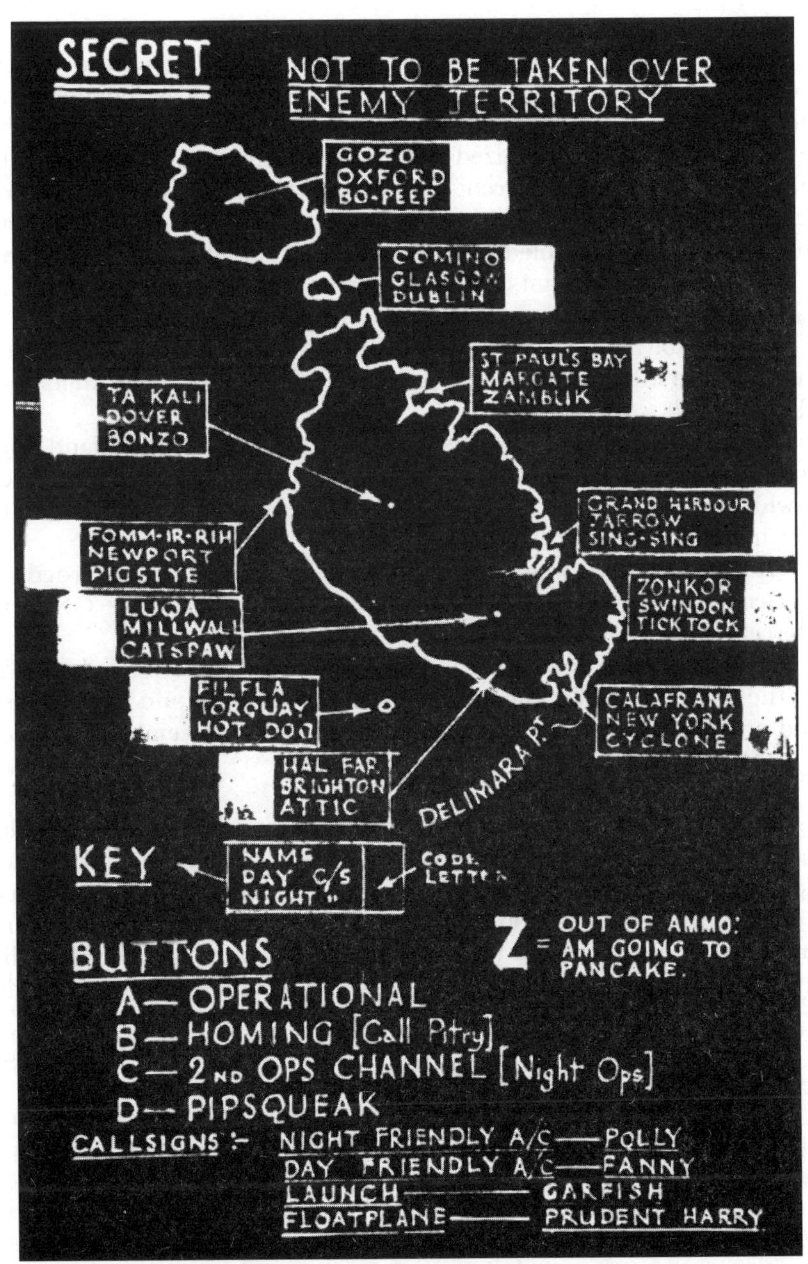

Every RAF pilot's guide card during patrols over Malta's territorial waters.

A further three of the type, however, which flew over intending to attack the supply ships berthed inside the harbour, were immediately pounced on by Hurricanes of 126 Squadron. One of the bombers was shot down and the other two damaged.

A more strongly organized third attack formed of more than a 12 Ju88s, escorted by an all Macchi fighter force, was made in the afternoon.

The weather had by then turned foul, impairing visibility. Although Hurricanes were scrambled to intercept the enemy their aircrews found it difficult to engage him, and with the exception of a Ju88 that was claimed shot down, no other reports were made.

Regrettably, however, this attack sealed the fate of Plt. Off. Ed. 'Pete' Steele, the first of the American pilots to be shot down over Malta and killed.

On 23 December the Mel09F made its debut over the island, and from that date Luftwaffe attacks on Malta became more frequent, raids in which enemy bomber aircraft, heavily escorted by fighters, came in ever increasing numbers.

In fact LeFevre's last active entry over Malta is found recorded on 23 December 1941 when he was scrambled in Hurricane GN-T to intercept some l09s.

Sqdn. Ldr. Mortimer-Rose led 126 Squadron, accompanied by 249.

LeFevre was in this encounter shot up by the 109s and had to crash land on Hal Far, with the result that he was on 26 December sent back to Britain.

By Christmas-eve the Axis had carried out their 25th raid over Malta and on 29 December the Luftwaffe organized one of their blitzes since their return to Sicily. Some 36 enemy aircraft first appeared around ten in the morning. Hurricanes from 185 and 252 Squadrons were scrambled to intercept, but just before they flew into combat two of the RAF fighters somehow collided in mid-air. One pilot was killed outright but the other managed to bale out safely.

Whatever British shipping was anchored inside the Grand Harbour became the enemy's primary objectives.

After the raid was over there were no reports of losses to enemy action, but four Hurricanes sustained extensive damages, one of which from friendly anti-aircraft fire.

Towards mid-afternoon eighteen Hurricanes were dispatched to intercept a radar plot that indicated the approach of nearly two dozen 'boogies'. Contact was made between the RAF fighters and the Bf.l09s, and one of the latter was reported shot down and others damaged by the time the encounter was over. A Hurricane, however, returning back to base, crashed on arrival, killing the pilot.

At about 4 o'clock five Mel09s flew over the Grand Harbour, strafing shipping. Four Hurricanes, which were scrambled to intercept them, immediately engaged the enemy fighters, but in the ensuing battle two of the RAF aircraft were shot down in the sea.

Air Sea rescue sorties were immediately organized but failed to spot any sign of either pilot.

The Bf.l09s had not faired well in the desert during the rest of 1941, but returning to Sicily in December their ensuing encounters with the RAF Hurricanes over the island not only boosted the individual Jagdflieger's morale, but also its score, and reduced enemy bomber losses significantly.

Hardly had the first wave withdrew when more 109s appeared, escorting a number of Ju88s that bombed Luqa aerodrome where more than twelve RAF bombers were either destroyed or extensively damaged on the ground.

In the New Year, when Anderson finally came to grips with the Luftwaffe, there had been a drastic change to the situation. He discovered that the Germans were tougher adversaries than the Italians. Despite having succeeded in fighting back effectively, on 25 January his Hurricane was so badly shot-up that he had to abandon it.

> "I got shot down the other day ...".

He later wrote.

> "... and had to make an undignified and hurried exit from my airplane."
>
> "... That's the third time I've baled out .... Things are certainly lively around here now-a-days."

Anderson's Hurricane was that day one of seven that were shot down in combat. Fortunately, of these RAF pilots only one, Plt. Off. John Russell of 126 Squadron went missing and believed killed. Of the other six, although some suffered injuries, all were back in action within days.

This situation proved advantageous to Rommel's campaign in the desert. A fleet of Ju.52s shuttled unmolested back and forth across the

Mediterranean with troops, supplies and equipment, reinforcements with which the Desert Fox had, by mid-January 1942, the British 8th Army on the run, retreating back towards Gazala, and on the 29th of the month he had taken Benghazi.

Since the Hurricane first appeared in Malta in June 1940, more than 90 of the fighters had by the early days of 1942 been destroyed in action. Several others had either been knocked out on the ground or suffered the same fate due to accidents. Pilot losses numbered 52, of whom four were taken prisoners. In comparison the number of enemy aircraft credited to them, 199 destroyed, with more than 200 between probably destroyed and damaged, seems highly favourable. However, it must be kept in mind that the majority of these aircraft belonged to the Regia Aeronautica.

The return of the Bf 109 in the Mediterranean at this time had again proved that the Hurricane was no match for its German counterpart. The RAF aircraft seemed to have reached its operational peak as a fighter, with the result that only in experienced hands could it still be effective. Under the circumstances, however, neither could anyone dispute what it was achieving, for its work-rate was extraordinary. Engines began to need more frequent changes, and by the mid-January 1941 very few spares remained. This resulted that it became extremely difficult to keep a large enough number of Hurricanes flying in defence of the Island.

These exigencies finally led the Air Ministry to have Hurricane engine overhauling and repairs organized on a bigger scale. A 'garage' on a massed output principle, was put into operation. Mamo's and Gasan's garages, both located at Gzira, away from the vicinity of local airfields, were put at the disposal of the RAF.

About half-a-kilometre apart, Mamo's garage was used for the storage of all available aircraft parts, and Gasan's spacious backyard, where protection from enemy air surveillance was provided via camouflaged nets, was cleared to accommodate Hurricanes brought there for engine overhauling and repairs. The operation proved a success, but work on all other types of aircraft suffered as many men were withdrawn from various RAF workshops on the island.

At this time a convoy was launched from Alexandria with the scope of supplying Malta with stocks of provisions and other needs. Effectively protected by Beaufighters from Nos.252 and 272 Squadrons of the Naval Cooperation Group, RAF, the two units were also instrumental in providing the convoy with air reconnaissance. Malta-based Hurricanes

Repairs to Hurricanes and other related equipment being carried out at either one of two major garages at Gzira, Gasan and Mamo.

Repairs to RAF Hurricanes at the Gzira 'workshops' of which neither is situated far from Luqa or Ta' Qali airfields.

were meanwhile to be responsible for the convoy's protection once it reached the Grand Harbour.

Before the end of January the supply ships Glengyle and Breconshire were again ran safely to Malta with essential supplies including oil fuel, however, this opening of the channel was attributed to the British 8th Army's advance in North Africa. The Allies and their enemy were during this period both using the Central Mediterranean for the same purpose, without either claiming to be in control of it. However the Luftwaffe was striking harder at Malta's airfields, with the scope of gaining the needed advantage as the British began falling back under Rommel's new offensive.

Upon the Island's survival now depended whether the Allies would be able to keep up their desperate defence of Egypt and the Suez Canal. After the success of the British naval operation to Malta the Axis had by the end of February flown more than eighteen hundred bomber missions against the island, crippling RAF strike units based there, with the result that enemy shipping losses dropped to a minimum.

From the 361 Hurricanes ferried to Malta by British naval carriers 333 had reached the island; however, many of these had been moved on to the Middle East, and of those that remained a good percentage had by February disappeared.

Although the cause of the RAF fighter losses had already been explained, a passage from the recollections of 'Laddie' Lucas, one of the few pilots who were at that time flown to Malta in a Sunderland flying-boat, gives the situation then prevailing greater emphasis:

> "... on our way to the mess for breakfast ..." (just as he came ashore) "... the sirens began to wail. In a moment or two a section of four manifestly old Hurricane passed overhead, strung out in vee formation, labouring to gain height over the island."
>
> "High above them, eight Me109s, flying fast and purposefully in pairs in line abreast, swept southwards across the brightening sky, dominant and unchallenged."

Stan Turner, another pilot whose remarkable achievement in organizing the islands fighter defences in 1942 remain unsurpassed, standing beside Lucas, watching the scene in silence and gathering apprehension, as the Hurricanes disappeared into cloud, could only utter "Good God" ... before striding on towards the mess.

Shortly before mid-day of 7 February four Ju88s, escorted by some

Sqdn. Ldr. Stan Turner.
He organised Malta's
fighter aircraft defences.

eighteen Me109s mounted a raid on Hal Far. While the bombers dropped their bombs on the airfield two 109s strafed a 69 Squadron Beaufighter while it was landing on Luqa.

The RAF aircrew of two was wounded and the aircraft set on fire. However, the observer succeeded in extinguishing the flames and salvaging the photographs they had taken over Sicily earlier in the day. L.A.C. N. Shirley was later awarded a DFM for his deed.

Plt. Off. O. Ormrod of 605 Squadron was watching the action on Hal Far from the road with another pilot when they spotted one of two low flying 109s coming straight at them. Both rushed behind a nearby building for shelter.

According to Ormrod's recollections, however, a Bofors gun on the airfield's perimeter hit the 109. The enemy fighter had slammed into a slope to the left of the Albacore dispersal where he could still see its remains smoking.

"I was rather irritated that he'd 'gone in' because it shook my faith in ground strafing a little. On the other hand he should have kept lower. Probably there is a bigger concentration of Bofors guns on Malta than I am likely to meet."

"I did not visit the remains, but I understand that there was little left of either pilot or aircraft. I've heard gruesome descriptions of an instrument panel, or rather its remains, coated with flesh and blood. Of a pulped corpse with one foot sticking out ..."

"Such are the effects on the pilot of a high speed crash. Low flying offers quick death for a mistaken judgement."

Shortly after the AVM's insistence for stronger and better aircraft reinforcements, a Secret Cypher telegram dated 1 February 1942 was received from the Air Ministry in London. This information was to let HQ RAF Malta know that a few Spitfires were to be sent to the island that month.

In a return Cypher, dated 8 February, AOC Malta took the opportunity to explain in detail the deteriorating fighter aircraft/pilot situation reigning on the island.

This resulted that AVM Lloyd, in another Cypher telegram dated 9 February, was advised that five Spitfire units and one Hurricane IIC squadron would shortly be made available. However owing to the possibility that the Spitfire might not prove successful, preparations to maintain two squadrons of Kittyhawks, which might be substituted for just as many Spitfire units, must be set up. Nevertheless it was explained that these reinforcements would be gradually infiltrated and superimposed on the existing Hurricane squadrons. As the enemy pressed on with his offensive over Malta, on 15 February the ground defences succeeded in shooting down a Ju88 during a mid-morning raid. Two of the four-men crew baled out of the burning aircraft over the sea, however, only the observer was recovered. The pilot, Lt. Waldemar Stadermann, and the other crew member perished in the wreck which fell on the outskirts of Zurrieq.

Sgt. Plt. C.E. Broad of York, who joined 185 Squadron in the early days of March 1942, also recalled some of his own experiences flying a Hurricane in defence of the island at the time. However, his first flight in one over Malta on 11 March was on practice.

"I did fly a couple of times that day, a time when the enemy operated over the island regularly, attacking in formations of four to six or eight aircraft, occasionally with as many as ten at a time. But our greatest worry were the escorting l09s, never coming over in a number less than twelve or so."

A few days later;

"I nearly drew first blood, on two separate scrambles in one day. My first opportunity came when I intercepted a Ju88, but only had

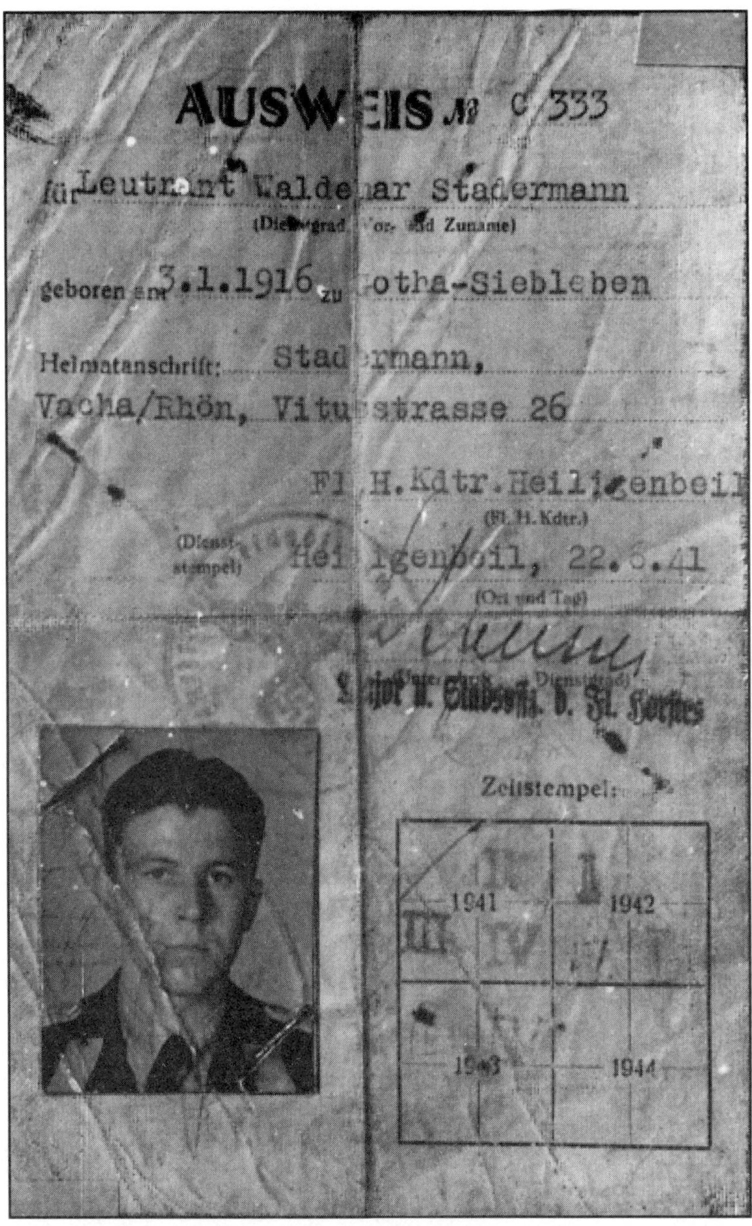

AUSWEIS № C 333

für Leutnant Waldemar Stadermann
(Dienstgrad, Vor- und Zuname)

geboren am 3.1.1916 zu Gotha-Siebleben

Heimatanschrift: Stadermann,
Vacha/Rhön, Vitusstrasse 26

Fl. H. Kdtr. Heiligenbeil
(Fl. H. Kdtr.)

(Dienst-stempel) Heiligenbeil, 22.[illegible].41
(Ort und Tag)

(Unterschrift und Dienstgrad)
Major u. Stabsoffz. d. Fl. Horstes

Zeitstempel:

1941	1942
1943	1944

I.D. Card of Ju88 pilot Waldemar Stadermann whose aircraft was shot down by a/a fire in the morning hours of 15 February 1942.

the satisfaction of seeing some of my tracer reaching him, nothing more. On my second time up I just couldn't get within range of another. The Hurricane was simply too slow. I was unable to catch up with that one Ju88."

Finally, on 23 March, Sgt. Plt. Broad was credited with his first 'kill.'

"Shortly afterwards I bagged my first enemy plane, a Heinkel III."

Broad recalled:

"I had to make five passes at it too before it went down."

For a few more of Mr Broad's experiences with the Hurricane, the following excerpts were drawn from his personal flying logbook:

24 March – Scramble.
1 Ju88 damaged – 4 Hurricanes airborne – all shot up.
26 March – Scramble.
1 Ju87 damaged and hits on another. Jumped by Me109s twice.
31 March – Scramble.
Jumped by 4 109s. – Sgt. Steele killed. – Had a short burst at last 109. But went into spin, pulling out at 100 feet.

On 1 April, amid numerous clashes, Sgt. Tony Boyd, another 185 Sqdn. pilot, claimed more than one Ju87 as a probable. Sgt. Jack Pauley of 229 Sqdn, however, had to bail out of his shot up Hurricane.

Four days later, flying in a Spitfire with 126 Sqdn, Pt Off. John Bisley shot down a Ju87 and a Ju88.

On 8 April, Tony Boyd, flying Hurricane GL-W in pursuit of a formation of Ju88s, shot one down, got a probable, and a damaged another.

The next day, flying in a Hurricane IIc, Boyd claimed a probably destroyed Ju88. Sgt. Pauley of 229 Sqdn, however, flying Hurricane Z3805, was once more shot down by a 109. Badly injured this time, he had to bale out off Grand Harbour, from where he was shortly afterwards picked up by an ASR launch.

Broad's logbook then records:

> 10 April – Scramble.
> 8 Hurricanes airborne to + 130. – Jumped by 109s when attacking Ju88s – shot up badly – baled out. – Plt. Off. Wigley baled out. – 2 others crash landed. Remaining four shot up badly.

Sgt. Plt. Broad was hospitalized in St George's Barracks, and did not fly again until 8 May and that was his last in a Hurricane, for the next day 185 Squadron received its first Spitfire Mk.Vcs.

AIRCRAFT DELIVERIES TO MALTA FROM CARRIERS

Dates	Codenames A/C	Carriers A/C	Ferried	Reached Malta
2/8/40	'Hurry'	HMS Argus	12 Hurricanes	12 Hurricanes
17/11	'White'	HMS Argus	12 "	04 "
3/4/41	'Winch'	HMS Ark Royal	12 "	12 "
27/04	'Dunlop'	HMS Ark Royal	24 "	23 "
21/05	'Splice'	HMS Ark Royal HMS Furious	48 "	46 "
6/6/41	'Rocket'	HMS Ark Royal HMS Furious	44 "	43 "
14/06	'Tracer'	HMS Ark Royal HMS Victorious	48 "	45 "
27/06	'Railway I'	HMS Ark Royal	22 "	21 "
30/06	'Railway II'	HMS Ark Royal HMS Furious	42 "	34 "
09/09	'Status I'	HMS Ark Royal	14 "	14 "
13/09	'Status II'	HMS Ark Royal HMS Furious	46 "	45 "
12/11	'Perpetual'	HMS Argus HMS Ark Royal	37 "	34 "
			361	333

In twelve operations 361 Hurricanes were ferried to the island.
Of this lot, 28 failed to reach Malta for diverse reasons.

That month another convoy had sailed from Alexandria to succour Malta. However the passage to the island was so hazardous that only three of the original number of supply ships reached the island. The Breconshire steamed directly inside M'Xlokk Bay while the Pampas and the Talabot entered the Grand Harbour.

The enemy, pressing on with his attacks on the three vessels at their anchorage, set Pampas and the Talabott on fire before the greater percentage of their cargo could be saved.

Meanwhile the Breconshire, having survived several bombing attacks, was so extensively damaged that the ship sank during the morning of 27 March after the oil fuel she had on board was salved.

After having survived the thousand-mile voyage, in which they had been constantly under attack by several Axis bombers, and reached Malta with their cargo practically intact, the three ships should not have been so negligently wasted.

An enquiry into the matter disclosed that arrangements by the authorities to have the ships unloaded, after they were securely moored, had taken twelve hours. As for the RAF fighters, these proved to have been so inadequate that they could not even control the air space over the island.

Chapter VIII

Reconnaissance

Malta, 1940/43

With whatever is at hand – 431 Flight – Warburton – Fuel control – Blenheim reinforcements – 228 & 230 Squadrons – 69 Squadron – Spitfire 1D – 'Colossus' – Cant Z501 – Hurricanes Z7101 & Z3053 – 69 on convoy attack AVM Lloyd – PR Spitfire Mk.4 – 'T' Flight Beaufighter – Maryland losses 221 Special Duties Flight – 830 Squadron – 69 Squadron's CO – 683 Squadron Advance Unit 3 USAAF – Off. to Italy – 683 Squadron's Inventory

In September 1940, while recently formed 261 Squadron was busy defending the island from the Regia Aeronautica the nucleus of what should have been properly established earlier in the year finally reached RAF Luqa, the forming of a General Reconnaissance unit.

Actually this was an undertaking difficult to accomplish at the breakout of hostilities in the Mediterranean due to the shortage of both aircraft and aircrews in Malta. The Target Towing Swordfish of No. 3 AACU (Anti-Aircraft Co-operation Unit) though only a few, might have managed the task to a limited extent, but those who were supposed to man them had opted to fly the Gladiators in defence of the island.

When the Swordfish of 767 Squadron arrived at Hal Far, only days after Italy's entry in the war, they were immediately engaged on reconnaissance duties. However, these activities were discontinued on

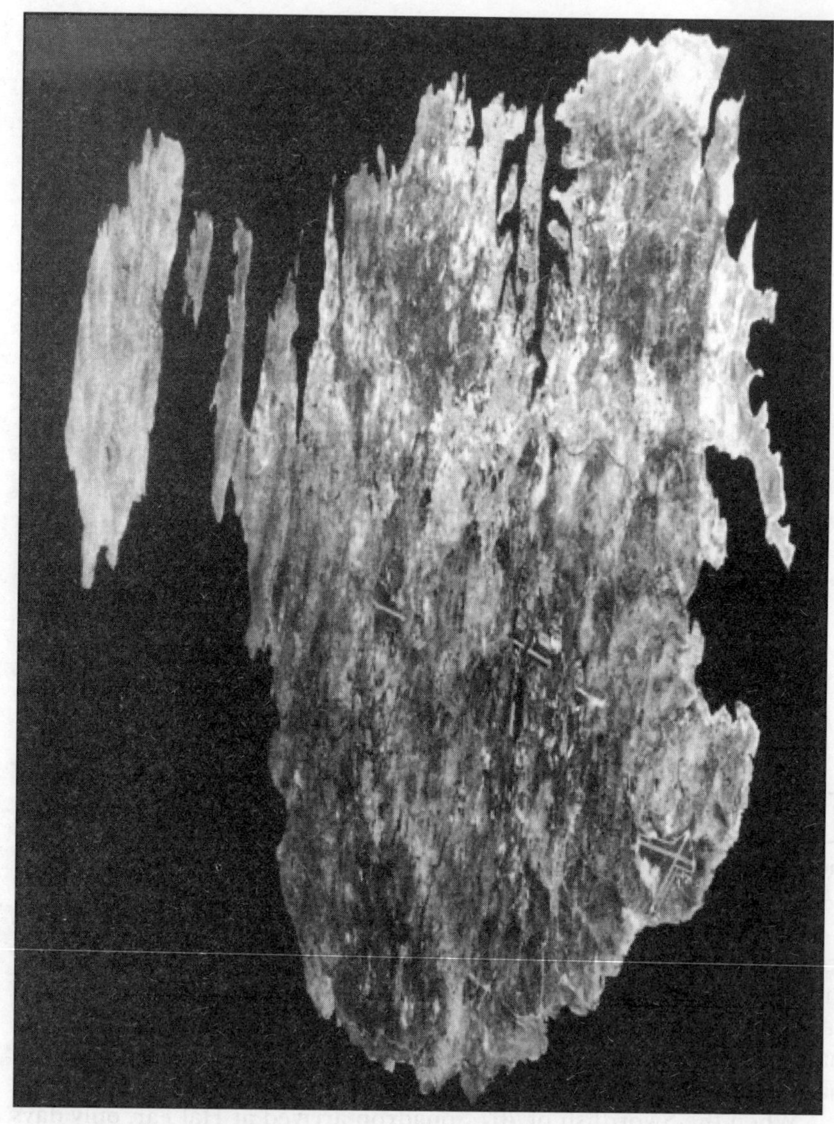

More than a bird's eye view of the Maltese Islands.

1 July 1940 due to the squadron's designation to 830, which imposed upon it the role of a strike unit, the first wartime one established in Malta.

That same day a Sunderland of 228 Squadron arrived at Marsaxlokk Bay. During the next two days it was engaged on some observation, patrol duties, but then it had to return to the Middle East.

That summer the Sunderlands were kept shuttling back and forth sporadically between Malta and Alexandria attending to diverse military duties.

Next to be given observation duties was the lone Hudson I of 233 Squadron, a task that lasted up till 2 September 1940 when, due to a case of mistaken identity, a British naval Fulmar shot down the Lockheed.

The late G.V.W. Davies, the Hudson's pilot, recalled the times he had taken a camera along to take photographs that he thought might be of use to Air Headquarters. The Admiralty, however, were at this time expecting something more lasting from the Air Ministry, preferably a permanently established observation unit based in the Central Mediterranean, from where it would be most valuable to the fleet in its struggle for control of the Mediterranean. However, with August gone, nothing seemed to have been done to improve the temporary means of reconnaissance adopted from Malta since June.

But up to the advent of the Maryland the RAF had few aircraft to spare, and the American Glenn Martin became available to the British just weeks before its arrival in Malta.

With the collapse of the Franco-British Alliance the United States banned the issue of further war armament to the French. This included even that equipment which, having already been under contract, was either awaiting shipment or at the final stages of construction. Amongst the latter was a substantial number of aircraft, of which a batch of 75 Maryland 167Fs were turned over to the British Purchasing Commission.

Eventually the majority of these aircraft found their way to the Middle East where they were rigged-up as bombers. Nonetheless, on arrival in Britain, prior to their being pressed into operational service, the Maryland was put to the test on numerous non-operational uses.

The Admiralty, who were privileged with the first few, used the twin-engine aircraft for target-towing duties, but 771 Squadron discovered the Maryland's great potential as a long-range reconnaissance aircraft.

When the RAF finally received the Maryland, the first operational unit to equip with the type was 431 Flight, which was formed in Malta in September 1940.

Early in the month three Marylands, AR705, AR707 and AR712, were diverted to North Coates. At this Coastal Command Station was based 22 Squadron, from which three aircrews were picked to man the aircraft that, earmarked for the Mediterranean, became the squadron's charges to prepare them for the flight, and on 6 September they were flown to Thorny Island preparatory to their departure to Malta.

On arrival at Luqa the Glenn Martins came under the administration of Mediterranean Command where they were joined by one of the two Blackburn Skuas, L2911, that had led the August Hurricanes to Malta, while the other, L2969, remained with 261 Squadron.

On 14 September, Maryland AR712 flew 431 Flight's first patrol, sighting and photographing enemy battleships. That same day Capt. Ford, airborne in his Skua, reported that he had spotted Italian merchant shipping berthed inside two separate harbours in Sicily.

Four days later AR707 and AR712 were both airborne at separate intervals during the day, but there were no reports of any sightings.

Martin 'Maryland' AR735 of 431 Flight on arrival at Luqa in December 1940.

On 19 September, No. 3 AACU was disbanded, and its equipment taken over by 830 Squadron. However, the personnel was absorbed into 431 Flight, which was at the same time officially formed as an RAF General Reconnaissance Unit, with Capt. Ford, RN, assuming command.

A fourth Maryland, AR709, that is recorded as having been held in reserve, was in actual fact never on Malta at any time during the duration of 431 Flight's operational existence.

Surprisingly the Flight, later 69 Squadron, with the exception of 830 FAA Squadron, was the only Malta-based RAF unit that remained operating from the island throughout the duration of the Mediterranean Air War, and was instrumental in giving birth to one of the most gallant characters of the war. He became the squadron's elite flyer, as well as a legend in his own lifetime, and around whom is woven this epic chapter of wartime reconnaissance from Malta.

In those bleak war years, like the isolated outpost that Malta actually was, surrounded by enemy occupied lands, and through which British military movements and activities were daily events, outcasts from all walks of life flourished on the island like blooms in springtime, turning it into a no man's land. Some fell in combat. Others, having gone through a baptism of fire, battle-wise, moved on elsewhere to disappear into obscurity, leaving behind them solitary figures that, surviving the rigours of a relentless war in which they fought, eventually suffered the same fate, or became aces. Men upon whose exploits can be evaluated the lives of the majority who, due to various reasons, may have failed to reach the same peak.

Adrian Warburton who, for obscure reasons, may have been indirectly or otherwise exiled from his own country, developed into a rare and extraordinary man on the same island where, in his infancy, he had been baptized.

He joined the RAF or a short service commission just before the war broke out. Due to a not too bright a record as a flyer, however, who some claim were landing and take off errors, which might have well been the cause of some of his mishaps in Malta, first served in a Botha unit. Then to mar an already complicated private life his Wg. Cdr. posted him away from his unit and Adrian found himself with 22 Squadron, and a recently formed flight which was preparing themselves for overseas posting.

Warburton's new CO, 'Tich' Whiteley, however, aware of the man's troubled past felt that, whatever Adrian's shortcomings, he deserved a chance to settle down and prove himself. Whiteley was more convinced of this when, having detailed him, and another crew member, the task

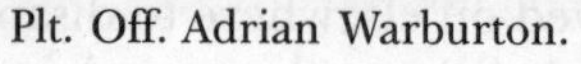

Plt. Off. Adrian Warburton.

Sqdn. Ldr. 'Titch' Whiteley of 431 Flight.

of working out a flight plan to Malta, Warburton responded with great enthusiasm, and as a result was partially responsible for the successful night flight of the Marylands across enemy occupied France.

In Malta Warburton, in some strange way, found what he seemed to have been missing in Britain. His lively personality developed an immediate attraction to the island, becoming more obvious later in the war from the way he kept turning up at Luqa, every time he was posted elsewhere in the Mediterranean.

This affinity, however, may have well been motivated by the presence of a Miss Christina Ratcliff, a female dancer he had befriended, and with whom he used to share a flat in Valletta.

No. 431 Flight lost its first Maryland, AR712, on 26 September 1940 when, en route on a reconnaissance patrol in which Warburton was for the first flying as leading pilot, due to the development of hydraulic failure, the flight had to be aborted.

Adrian had to make a 'pancake' landing on arrival at Luqa.

Although very little damage was done to the aircraft, unfortunately, the Regia Aeronautica the next day further damaged the already stricken

Maryland by incendiaries, with the result that it was shortly afterwards struck-off-charge.

As of September 1940, to conserve the stocks of fuel on the island, petrol was primarily placed under strict control. Taxis were brought to a stop and buses were committed to an alternative timetable for economical purposes.

The increase in the number of aircraft on Malta was expected to affect the stocks of aviation fuel that had been abundant at the outbreak of hostilities on the island. Shell installations at B'bugia were stocked to capacity but after that it was no longer possible to import bulk fuel. Consignments of RAF aviation fuel began to be shipped in very light 4-gallon tinplate cans.

This method of transportation was obviously to save weight in transit so that more fuel could be carried. These cans were packed in pairs in wooden crates, over which a top was nailed down, resulting in punctured cans and supposedly 'full'cans were arriving empty.

Storage space for these containers had to be found elsewhere on the island, as they could not be deposited at Shell's. This had either to be in natural caves or simply open sites. Finally, over a million of these fuel-cases were stored at Ghar Dalam.

Italy's increased interest in Greece led Britain to keep an 'eye' on these developments, and on 28 September had Maryland AR707 diverted to patrol over the area before resuming with the original sortie over Southern Italy.

Meanwhile during that same day Maryland AR705 was out on its first operational patrol from Luqa.

During September 431 Flight's reconnaissance missions ran up to a total of approximately 60 hours flying time, all attributed to the Marylands, with an additional 6 hours flown by the Skua.

Sunderlands from 228 and 230 Squadrons were appearing at Kalafrana more frequently, shuttling back and forth between, Alexandria, Aboukir and Malta, performing duties that, although diverse, were mainly long-range reconnaissance and anti-submarine patrols over the Ionian Sea.

In October, when Italy invaded Greece, the two flying boat squadrons moved to Kalafrana. From here operational flying was sometimes brought to a standstill due to the heavy and treacherous sea swell inside the bay. As a counter measure temporary quarters were provided at St Paul's Bay where a secondary flying boat base had been established years before.

With five aircraft between them, three, L5806, L5807 and N9020 were on 228 Squadron's strength, while two, L2164 and L2186, were on 230 Squadron's charge.

In October, two long-nosed Blenheims on transit to the Middle East landed at RAF Luqa. Due to the need for reinforcements, the two aircraft were temporarily kept to supplement the Marylands of 431 Flight. The first of these, T2115, arrived on the 16th, and was the next day out on its first patrol.

Blenheim T2164 that arrived at Luqa on 18 October was airborne on the afternoon of the next day, patrolling in enemy airspace.

By the end of the month the two Blenheims had between them flown 82 hours 43 minutes.

The Maryland, developed by Glenn Martin to fill the role of a strike aircraft, was fitted with defensive armament, consisting of a top gun-turret amidship and four forward firing machine guns operated by the pilot. Armament that Warburton made good use of for the first time on 30 October. This was while he was out on one of his first patrols in command of a Maryland, by attacking, and shooting down a Cant Z506.

(With the exception of Malta nowhere were the Marylands kept armed.)

On 1 November, Warburton became a full time pilot. However, although he had by this time proven himself a capable one, this would not have been possible without the unflagging faith of his CO, 'Tich' Whiteley, who was on that same date promoted to Sqdn. Ldr. The faith the rest of his aircrew, Sgts. Spires and Moran, had in him also complemented his new status.

The Skua the next day terminated its last operational patrol for 431 Flight; however, a Maryland, AR713, reached the island from the UK, filling the gap. On 4 November, it was out flying on its first patrol. Maryland AR719, which was expected to arrive shortly after the former, failed to fly the route. The aircraft was reported missing somewhere between Britain and Gibraltar where no trace of either crew or wreckage was found.

On 7 November, Warburton again succeeded in establishing his capabilities as a reconnaissance pilot by providing the British Fleet with outstanding pictures of its Italian counterpart nestling inside Taranto harbour. He had these taken in spite of a heavy concentration of anti-aircraft fire, and overcast weather conditions. According to Sgt. Spire's recollections, Warburton had told them of his intentions to fly in at zero feet all the way to their target.

"So terrible was the state of the weather ...," recalled Spires, "... that more than one pass had to be made before we returned to base." (The Star. 17/3/58.)

This material was relayed to the Mediterranean Fleet by one of HMS Illustrious own 806 Squadron Fulmars. With this information in hand Admiral Cunningham succeeded in organizing the famous attack on Taranto harbour by the Swordfish of 815 Squadron on the night between 11/12 November 1940, crippling the Italian Fleet.

While Warburton enjoyed his promotion Sunderland L5806, returning from a reconnaissance patrol, was jumped by enemy fighters off Malta. Badly shot up, and with two members of the crew wounded, the pilot coaxed the damaged flying boat to Marsaxlokk Bay. To prevent the aircraft from sinking, it had to be immediately taken charge of and beached at the Kalafrana Seaplane Base. N9020, which had also been patrolling over the Ionian Sea, failed to return, to be later confirmed that it had been shot down. So, with L5807 off to the UK, 228 Squadron found themselves without any flying-boats, with the remaining two 230 Squadron machines having to shoulder the brunt of what duties had to be performed until there was a change in the situation.

On 5 November 230 Squadron's third Sunderland, N9029, arrived from Alexandria. However, the next day, while the aircraft was tied to its mooring inside Marsaxlokk bay, CR42s shot it up. Immediately the attack was over, due to the damages sustained, the aircraft had to be taken up the nearest slipway at Kalafrana to have it repaired.

Later in the day an additional Sunderland, L5803, arrived from Britain, followed on 7 November, by the return of L5807. Later, taking over L2146 from 230 Squadron, 228 was back to full strength, leaving the former with one serviceable aircraft and the other ashore undergoing repairs.

When on 17 November new Hurricanes were being expected to arrive in Malta via the carrier HMS Argus, Sunderland L5803 was provided for navigational purposes. After the fighters lost their way, and rescue flights were organized to search for the missing Hurricane pilots, Sunderlands flew far-and-wide over the Mediterranean.

Later, after hours of fruitless flying, so rough was the sea inside Marsaxlokk Bay, that all airborne flying boats had to be diverted to St Paul's Bay.

The ferrying of mail was far more often carried out when secret information to Britain was dispatched from Malta via Gibraltar by flying boats. One particular task, however, for which 228 Squadron was picked, was code-named 'X', an operation that altered the Sunderland's original role to that of a strike aircraft.

First launched from Kalafrana on 2 December it was designed to intercept enemy shipping traversing the Mediterranean at night. Three flying boats were on duty that first night; L5803, L5806 and T9048 assisted by moonlight and ASV (Air-to-Sea-Vessel) equipment. Although armed with 4 SAP and 4AS 250lb bombs, this did not necessarily mean that once a convoy was spotted it could be attacked. This decision remained that of the flying-boat captain for he could opt to call for the special FAA force of torpedo carrying Swordfish of 830 Squadron, held in readiness for the purpose.

The Blenheims terminated their period with 431 Flight on 20 November. At the same time Skua L2882, the one which had led the surviving four Hurricanes to Malta three days earlier, joined the Flight. However, in December, the two naval Skuas with the unit took leave of the island to board HMS Eagle while it was steaming eastwards off Malta.

Reinforcements for the Flight did not arrive from UK until the 19 and 24 December respectively. These were comprised of two solitary Marylands, AR721 and AR735.

After that date deliveries ceased altogether up till the advent of 69 Squadron. Even spares would have become scarce for the Glenn Martins had not Sqdn. Ldr. Whiteley taken it upon himself to make occasional trips to Great Britain for the purpose, each time returning with a new aircraft for his unit packed to bursting with Maryland parts.

To avoid encountering patrolling Axis fighters the Marylands were briefed to keep their distance when out on reconnaissance missions over enemy airfields. They were also detailed to stay at reasonable altitudes over harbour and coastal installations to minimize exposure to anti-aircraft batteries. Engaging enemy aircraft in combat was neither encouraged, but on Christmas Eve, while out on patrol over Naples, spotting an SM79, Warburton did not hesitate to attack the bomber which he succeeded in shooting down.

On 27 December, Adrian received his first gallantry award, a merited DFC. After that he was in January promoted to a Flying Officer.

On 10 January 1941, an increase in the personnel of the observation establishment resulted in the disbanding of 431 Flight. This was formed into 69 Squadron that was to resume from where the former left off. Despite the redesignation, however, the aircraft which were expected to arrive to bring it up to squadron strength, due to equipment shortage in UK, failed to materialize. But up till the end of the month, although with the promised aircraft still missing, 69 Squadron, with the exception of Maryland AR707, which was shot down over Sicily on the 11th, suffered no other casualties.

Two of this missing Maryland crew were Flt. Sgt. Devauchelle and Sgt. S. Mehouas, both Free French pilots who had succeeded in escaping from Tunis in a Latecoere 298 in the Summer of 1940. This floatplane and a flying boat, a Loire 130 that had both reached the island the same way, had been impressed with 228 Squadron.

On 19 January, an unexpected visitor, a Spitfire 1D, P9551, unarmed but fully equipped for photographic reconnaissance, landed at Luqa. The aircraft, flown from Britain for a reconnaissance somewhere north of Italy was diverted to Malta by the pilot, Flt. Lt. P. Corbishley, after suspecting that he might not have enough fuel left to fly back to base. From the island, Corbishley flew one successful sortie filming targets in Italy, but on 1 February, while out on a second flight, he was shot down and taken prisoner.

Meanwhile Warburton seemed to have become addicted to the habit of attacking heavily defended Sicilian airfields, resulting in numerous encounters with enemy aircraft during January, and an increase to his score list when he shot down a Macchi MC200. Nothing and no one was safe from his aggressiveness, but at no time were these forays ever known to have made Adrian neglect his primary duties. The unerring skill with which he flew on reconnaissance missions soon earned him the place of 69 Squadron's number one pilot, and subject to being picked to fly on special assignments.

Late in January preparations were underway for the execution of Operation code-named 'Colossus', aimed at the destruction of an important viaduct in Italy which a picked force of soldiers were to blow up. These were to be dropped by parachute from aircraft flown from Malta. Warburton, who was assigned the task of photographing the Calitri target, had the required material available days before the arrival of the troop carriers that landed at Luqa aerodrome on 8 February.

The eight Whitley bombers of 78 Squadron, which had been converted to carry paratroops, were for the first time duty-bound from Luqa on the night of 10 February, an operation from which one of the aircraft failed to return.

While six of the aircraft carried the paratroops and their equipment the other two carried bombs to create a diversion.

The paratroops were dropped in a good pattern round the target, Monte Valture, with the man farthest away falling on the bank of the River Ofanto.

A quarter of an hour after midnight the main charges were laid on the aqueduct with an amount of spare explosive remaining, with which it was decided to blow up a small bridge spanning the Ginestra, a tributary of the Tragino.

At half past twelve the aqueduct blew up, followed by the bridge shortly afterwards.

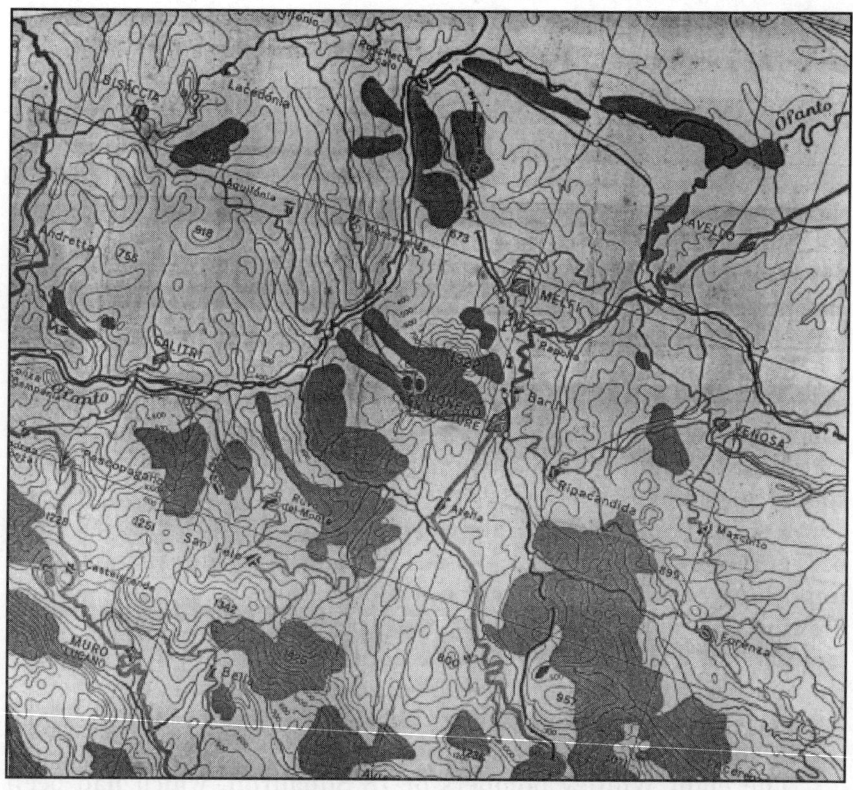

The first commando raid by the paratroops took place from Luqa Airfield on the 10th February 1941, when 8 Whitleys of 78 Squadron, flown out from East Anglia, undertook a special operation against an aqueduct in Southern Italy.

This map, used for the above operation, was donated to the National War Museum Ass. by Mr J. L. Baines of Kendal, who served with the RAF at Luqa from October 1940 to December 1942.

Warburton later returned with photographic proof of the result of the mission. This showed that the operation had not been as successful as expected, as most of the viaduct was still intact. Furthermore, it was reported that all the paratroops involved were taken prisoners and "Colossus' had to be abandoned.

Of the Whitleys six moved on to the Middle East and one remained at Luqa until 16 February when it was flown back to the UK.

The flying boat unit, contrary to 69 Squadron, flew few sorties during January, mostly due to the disturbed state of the sea inside Marsaxlokk Bay that resulted in some unexpected brisk human activity. Owing to a heavy swell and high winds, many a Sunderland had its pennant eyepiece pulled out, giving both ground and air crews a bad time, with many a flying boat having to be later taken up the slipway at Kalafrana for one repair or another. To counter this mishap Air Hdqtrs stationed two Sunderlands inside St Paul's Bay on a permanent basis, with quarters for aircrews provided in a house belonging to a Dr DePiro. Taken over by the Works Department, this building was given the name of 'Pembroke House'.

Meanwhile, on 11 January, the Loire 130 was brought down the Kalafrana slipway for the first time and air tested by Commander Nicholettes AFC. According to an entry in Group Capt. G.E. Livock's diary, who arrived in Malta in a Sunderland on the 5th to take over the post of Wg. Cdr. Michie, the following night Nicholettes was airborne on a clandestine flight, probably in the Loire.

While on the subject of foreign flying boats and floatplanes, on the night of 25 January, a Cant Z.501 of the Regia Aeronautica, with navigation lights burning, was circling over the island. A searchlight unit came into operation in the darkness and the aircraft was spotted descending in the sea close to Comino, a small island nestling between those of Malta and Gozo.

An RAF pinnace sped out of St Paul's Bay towards the spot. Taking the Italian aircrew prisoners and leaving flying boat anchored off shore, the pinnace returned to St Paul's.

Evidently, the Italian aircrew had lost their bearings while returning from a reconnaissance mission and mistaking the island of Comino for that of Pantelleria, they flew over it calling to their base to turn on a searchlight as a beacon. Actually the British 'Y' Service established at Lascaris War Rooms, intercepting these messages, decrypted them, and instructed a local searchlight unit to oblige.

On 26 January, Livock noted down in his diary that:

Cant Z501 moored inside Marsalforn Bay, Gozo. Probably after Gozitan fisherman towed it from the waters near to Comino.

"Flew with Nicholettes in Loire from Kalafrana to St Paul's, and flew over where the Cant Z.501 stood anchored at Gozo. It had mistaken Comino for Pantelleria the previous day."

Livock later flew the Loire back to Kalafrana from St Paul's.

That day a servicing party, sent to Comino to bring the Cant to Malta, discovered that some fishermen had taken the liberty of towing the aircraft to Gozo, and had it anchored inside Mgarr Harbour.

Late in the afternoon while the Z501 was under tow on its way to Malta the rough sea broke-off a wing-tip assembly. The flying boat began to take in water, and shortly afterwards it sunk.

February for 228 Squadron began with Sunderland L2164 taking off on a C111 Patrol while L5807, with Wg. Cdr. Nicholettes AFC at the controls, was dispatched on a mission of special importance.

On 2 February six new pilots joined the squadron while Sunderland L5803 was expected to arrive from the UK. The flying boats had meanwhile been detailed to patrol over Tunisian territorial waters, and attack all unescorted merchant shipping identified as belonging to the enemy.

In the afternoon of 5 February two Sunderlands of 10 R. Australian A. F Squadron landed inside M'xlokk bay.

Patrols flown during the ensuing days were few then on 11 February three Luftwaffe bombers struck inside St Paul's Bay. Luckily, however, only superficial damages were inflicted.

Meanwhile the pilot of a missing Hurricane was spotted northeast of Malta by Flg. Off. Lamond in Sundertand L2164. A RAF pinnace, dispatched to pick him up from the sea, sped to the rescue.

On 5 March, while moored inside St Paul's Bay, a 228 Squadron Sunderland, and the Loire 130 were both strafed and damaged.

Two days later two Bf.l09s strafed Sunderland L2164, damaging the flying boat and mortally wounding a guard who had fired back at them from inside the aircraft.

This was repeated on 10 March with Sunderland T9046, which drew most of the enemy's fire. L2164, however, that was still inside the bay, was hit again and caught fire.

Moored inside St Paul's Bay on 10 March 1941, Sunderland L2164, strafed by Me109s, caught fire and was destroyed before the flames could be put out.

Rescuers tried to control the flames, but the blaze, thought to have been neutralized, burst forth with renewed fury. The aircraft was labouriously beached, but it had to be abandoned, and eventually sunk.

Temporary on site repairs were carried out on T9064 which was then flown to Kalafrana. Properly attended to at the seaplane base, was withdrawn to the Middle East with the rest of 228 Squadron by the end of the month.

Constant surveillance of the Mediterranean, and braving the hazards this entailed from patrolling enemy fighters, mainly Me109s, were the duties 69 Squadron was now expected to perform. But unlike 228 Squadron the unit could not be transferred to safer grounds elsewhere without affecting its operational reconnaissance efficiency.

The squadron had to remain operating from a strategically located base and in the Central Mediterranean none other existed than in Malta.

From the 90 flying hours recorded in February 1941, by the end of March the Marylands had flown 144hrs 15mins. Reinforcements, however, when any did arrived were poor. Only one Glenn Martin, AR706, was on 25 February delivered from the UK, and this was by none other than Sqdn. Ldr. Whiteley. He brought it across enemy occupied France at night in approximately 5 hours, packed with every essential spare part he could scrape for his squadron's Marylands.

During March there was a notable increase in enemy shipping movements resulting from the Luftwaffe's air superiority in the Central Mediterranean, that gained the Axis freedom of passage to many Tripoli-bound convoys.

This eased some of the enemy's pressure on the island and fresh reinforcements for 69 Squadron began to arrive.

On 11 March Marylands AR714 and AR724 landed at Luqa. These were four days later followed by AR727 and AR741, raising the squadron's strength to eight aircraft, due to the loss of AR706 that was shot down by Bf.109s while returning from a reconnaissance patrol.

Crashing near to Dingli Cliffs, westward of the Island, all that was left of the aircraft was a blazing wreck, from which only the observer managed to parachute to safety.

An additional task had to be taken up by 69 Squadron as of 18 March that entailed keeping aircrews at standby for spotting purposes, duties for which an alteration to the establishment had to be made to include four extra corporals and twelve A.C.s so that two crews could be trained in that line of work.

On 29 March, another Maryland, AR727 was lost over Zante due to mechanical problems. Then towards the end of the month, while out on an anti-shipping patrol, Warburton spotted the Italian Fleet at sea, however, due to too much wireless interference, he was unable to relay a report back to base. Despite knowing that he would be harshly reprimanded for the offense, in desperation Adrian broke the official rules and used a high priority prefix to get his message through to headquarters.

On 14 April, Maryland AR735, mistaken for a Ju88, was shot up by a patrolling Hurricane, then ten days later a direct hit during an air attack destroyed AR705 on the ground. A Hurricane, V7101, however, had meanwhile been added to 69 Squadron's inventory.

Hurricane I, V7101, stripped down for reconnaissance purposes with 69 Squadron, although already painted bluish in colour, its tail section is still in camouflage.

Stripped of everything that could be safely removed, including its guns, two cameras were fitted to the aircraft which was then painted sky blue, but this modification left no space where extra fuel could be stored with the result that reconnaissance patrols were limited to extend no farther than Sicily.

Flg. Off. Roger-Hilton Barber, in flying boots, was given charge of Hurricane V7101 immediately it was ready for operational flying with 69 Squadron.

The Hurricane was test flown by Flt. Lt. G. Burgess, the ex-Gladiator pilot, who reported that it felt unstable when taken up to 36,888 feet.

Meanwhile, Flt. Lt. Roger H. Barber who had been in Malta flying Hurricanes since June of 1940, was on 25 April transferred from 261 Squadron to 69 with the result that he became the first pilot to fly the Hurricane on a practice reconnaissance patrol lasting one hour. Two days later Barber had V7101 out on its first official operational sortie over Sicily.

That same day, with more Hurricanes expected to be ferried to Malta, Marylands AR721 and AR741 were engaged to escort the fighters to the island, and concluded the month of April by clocking a total of 264 flying hours.

In May 69 Squadron received some additional reinforcements when on the 5th of the month two Marylands, AR725 and AR733, landed at Luqa.

The next morning a third aircraft, AR726, arrived, but AR724 was destroyed on the ground.

Meanwhile with Hurricane V7101 engaged on spotting patrol duties over territorial waters 69 Squadron had on 12 May another one, Z3053, included to its strength for long-range photo reconnaissance purposes. However, due to the modifications needed to increase to its fuel capacity, this Hurricane IIA could not be flown until June.

On 28 May another Maryland, AR733, was again provided for navigational duties when fighters were flown on to the Middle East, a task which was the next day carried out by another two, AR721 and AR726.

In June DFMs were awarded to three of 69 Squadron's officers.

With an increase to the squadron's personnel, more aircraft reinforcements were at this time being expected to arrive from the UK. However, of two Marylands due from Gibraltar, for which Fly. Off.s Warburton and Bloxam had been dispatched, only AR729 reached Luqa on the 8 June, flown by Warburton as the second aircraft had accidentally crashed on the 'Rock'.

Many of Warburton's successful photo reconnaissance missions were attributed to his low flying tactics that, despite their great risk did not in any way discourage Adrian or affect his efficiency. When in June the British forces wanted to have the entire coastal road spanning Tripoli to Benghazi photographed 69 Squadron was given the assignment. Off. handedly it was estimated that it would take at least a week, if not more, to cover the 250-mile long Via Balbia, along which supply convoys were being driven to reinforce Rommel's Korps. But while they had Warburton available, the man who was reputed to have never said 'no' to any order, the squadron felt that the job was as good as done, and dropped it in his 'lap'.

Undaunted in spite of knowing that he would be encountering patrolling enemy fighters in the area, Warburton flew sortie after sortie. Frequently chased out over the sea, to return time and again, flying back to base only when he had in his camera what he had set out to record.

On one particular flight over this objective Warburton, forced to fly farther inland than intended, to avoid some patrolling enemy aircraft he had spotted, approached Misurata airfield where he saw several SM79s parked. He did not resist the temptation and immediately went into a shallow dive, taking advantage of the opportunity. With his wing guns blazing, Warburton strafed the enemy bombers, leaving a number of them burning on the ground as he climbed and turned away northwards.

On 19 June, Maryland AR739 arrived from the UK, and the next day, with modifications concluded, Hurricane Z3053 was flight tested by R. H. Barber.

On 22 June, he was testing the aircraft against fuel consumption. He found out it was capable of remaining airborne for 2 hours 15 minutes, and the next day Barber had the Hurricane operationally flown for the first time. However, due to a minor fault in the photographic gear, the morning flight had to be abandoned but with repairs immediately effected, Z3053 was in the afternoon mission-bound over Messina, from where Barber returned with the material required.

On 24 June, with Hilton Barber now attached to Hurricane Z3053, which he remained flying until his tour of duty in Malta expired in July, Warburton for the first time had V7101 all to himself on a reconnaissance patrol over Sicily.

While out on an observation patrol on 26 June Barber reported the presence of enemy merchant shipping southeast of Malta. A Maryland was immediately dispatched to shadow the convoy, and, due to the unavailability of a daytime anti-shipping strike unit on the island, wartime exigencies that particular day temporarily altered the role of 69 Squadron's Marylands.

Four of the squadron's Marylands, AR726, AR729, AR733 and AR739, discarded their cameras, and each carrying two 500lb bombs were quickly organized to attack the enemy convoy.

In the afternoon of 27 June the aircraft made their first strike, in which they lost AR726.

The next day reports that one of the ships had escaped the attack, and was still heading for North Africa, led to the dispatch of a bomb-loaded Maryland, flown by Warburton, to finish the job.

Sgt. Spires wrote about the result of that particular sortie in the 'Star' of 17/3/58:

> "Possibly, the ship had escaped the attack so off we went to a tour of Tunisian ports to look for it. We found it in Sfax harbour."

They approached the harbour flying mast high over the ships. Spires concluded:

> "Just as I said 'bombs gone' I saw a red flag fluttering below. I shouted, 'It's a munitions ship. For God's sake get down on the water.' I shall never forget the roar as the ship went up. Neither do I know how we weren't blown to pieces."

(In actual fact none of the Italian vessels in this convoy were sunk).

That month, his tour of duty over, 'Tich' Whiteley moved away from Malta and 69 Squadron, and shortly afterwards Warburton was noted wearing whatever took his fancy. He flew in all sorts of garb, except service clothing, but his favourite was a set of thigh length sheepskin leggings, topped by an army tunic adorned with RAF stripes. Also, had barbers depended on his type for their livelihood, many would have perished from lack of enough work as Adrian was in the habit of letting his blond hair grow well down his neck.

Neither was he over companionable. He avoided messes, and only on occasion was he found playing cards with flyers in any one of the homemade huts erected at dispersal sites. But however strange his behaviour he always turned up correctly dressed when meeting someone special.

With A.V.M. H.P. Lloyd in office as A.O.C. Warburton was free to work out things his own way, just as long as he did his job well. Far cast from any normal form, Warburton amazed everyone. Lacking the aid of any meteorological services, he flew unerringly anywhere in the Mediterranean with instincts unknown to man. His daring and unusual skills as a pilot were outstanding. Despite the fact that he was frequently shot at during patrols only on one occasion was he ever shot up.

Furthermore, in whatever state of damage, he always managed to coax his aircraft back to base, himself miraculously unharmed, from operations. Even when, mistaken for a Ju88, he was shot at by a Hurricane, an error which was also made by the crew of a local anti-aircraft battery who failed to shoot down his Maryland by a hair's breadth, although still forcing him to crash land due to a damaged undercarriage.

Mysteriously even his aircraft seemed to bear a charmed existence. Warburton was in the habit of parking his machines near to the Operations Room at Luqa yet, although the spot was bombed often, his airplane was rarely damaged.

On one occasion, while flying over Sicily on a photo reconnaissance patrol, mistaken for a Ju88, he was given a landing signal.

Another strange case in Warburton's life in the Mediterranean was the excessive period of time he spent flying from Malta. Pilots in his own squadron were operationally rested after concluding their tour of duty from the island. Adrian, however, who by the summer of 1941 had flown nearly three times as many sorties as any other pilot with 69 Squadron, remained in Malta. This might well have been at Warburton's own request, and the AOC's affinity towards his ace reconnaissance pilot.

On 22 July, with, as usual, an aircrew member manning the turret guns of the Maryland, Warburton shot down a Cant Z506 over Taranto.

On 22 September 1941, prior to the launching of convoy "Halberd", surveillance of Italian fleet bases was considered so important that a Spitfire PRIV was flown to Malta.

A Photo Reconnaissance Spitfire Mk.IV.

When Flt. Lt. N.H.E. Messervy finally landed at Ta' Qali the flight had taken him exactly 4hours 30minutes from the UK.

This was as occasion that the late Mr Leslie Davies, at the time an L.A.C. with 249 Squadron, recalled:

> "... I was first posted to Ta' Qali under Station Command where my job was servicing the only Spitfire then on the island. It was a photo reconnaissance one."
>
> "When I first saw the Spitfire it was painted bluish grey, but it was later changed to pale pink so that it could blend with evening's sunset and dawn's first light. That was when the aircraft was generally flown operationally ...."

Messervy was later to fly the Spitfire on several long-range reconnaissance missions over diverse objectives in Italy.

After these duties were concluded, however, due to a set of badly worn tyres, as none were yet available on the island, both the aircraft and its pilot remained grounded for nearly three weeks waiting for the delivery of a new set to be flown from Britain.

By the end of October the Spitfire had returned to the UK.

Another Cant Z506 was added to Warburton's score list on 24 September, and five days later he bagged a Macchi MC200 by which time he had been awarded a bar to his DFC. Seven enemy aircraft destroyed was something no fighter pilot on Malta could yet boast of at that time. Had Warburton been in fighters the probability is that Beurling, Malta's highest scoring fighter ace, would have had a great contender for the top honours.

On 30 September 1941 L.A.C. B.C. Allen, a ground crew member with 148 Bomber Squadron, had this entered in his diary related to Adrian:

> "Had a chat with Warburton. Thinks he may take over a Beaufighter for reconnaissance purposes. He is a character with long hair and sheepskin knickerbockers."

Evidently Warburton was drawn to the Beaufighter despite the fact that he was at the time flight testing the Baltimore for comparison purposes with the Maryland, which it was due to replace once supplies of the latter ran out.

The Beaufighter, one of Warburton's favourite aircraft.

But on 1 October, with his first operational tour, in which he had flown 155 sorties from Malta, at an end Warburton was transferred to the Middle East, where his wish to fly in a Beaufighter was realized.

Undergoing long-range consumption tests from Benson, UK, to Malta the first DH.98 Mosquito to appear in Malta, W4055 landed at Luqa on 4 November 1941.

The next day Flt. Lt. Neil was instructed to test the performance of a Hurricane against it.

"... This visitor from Benson, lightly loaded, was by the standards of the time incredibly fast and agile," wrote Neil in his book, 'Onward to Malta'.

"... the fight thereafter developed into a chase, with me desperately, but unsuccessfully trying to remain in the same piece of sky. ... with my engine raging away at maximum boost ... I finally retired ... gracefully, I hope."

On 21 November Hurricane Z3053, attacked by enemy fighters, had to be abandoned off the island of Gozo. Meanwhile, PR Spitfire Mk.4s had at this time began arriving in Malta at intervals, from where they flew operationally for a few days at a time.

Posted to 223 Squadron, which was stationed in Cairo, Warburton returned to the island on 29 December 1941, and with him arrived 'T' Flight of No. 2 PRU, consisting of two dark blue Beaufighters, T3301 and T4705, both specially equipped for Photo Reconnaissance work.

Warburton taking notes from another squadron pilot preparatory to undertaking another reconnaissance mission.

During his second spell in Malta, which did not last more than two months or so, except for one sortie flown in a Maryland of 69 Squadron, Warburton did all his flying in Beaufighter T4705. The same aircraft in which he had flown to the island in December, a machine that in Adrian's opinion had no equal for reconnaissance work. Claiming that it could outfly any aircraft the enemy had operating out of Sicily.

Warburton's arrival in Malta occurred at a time when, with Luftflotte 2 back in Sicily gathering its strength swarms of Me109s, and lack of aircraft suitable for the tasks required, were making 69 Squadron's duties extremely difficult to perform. Furthermore, the British were concerned about plans the Axis might have of an airborne invasion of Malta. So the AOC, having no aircrew on the island familiar with the Beaufighter except Warburton's, despite rumours that neither was the aircraft supposed to be as fast as Adrian claimed, had the pilot operationally airborne the day following his arrival.

Henceforth Adrian was often out on reconnaissance patrols extending from Tripoli to every harbour and airfield in Sicily where the enemy was suspected to be preparing his invasion forces. If Britain hoped to win the Desert War, the island had to be held intact, and while Warburton flew for that sole purpose, 69 Squadron treated him, and his personal aircraft, as if both belonged to the unit.

Towards mid-January 1942 two long-range tropicalized P.R.1 DH.98 Mosquitoes, the first two of the type to be produced for operational service abroad, reached Malta via Gibraltar.

The PR Mosquito. An aircraft 69 Squadron made brief use of on Reconnaissance duties.

Intended for posting with 69 Squadron W4062 and W4063 were not destined to last long with the unit.

On 13 January, arriving at Luqa on one engine, the other having been shot up by enemy fighters en route, W4062 made a forced landing on the aerodrome that damaged it so badly that it was shortly afterwards struck-off-charge.

Four days later W4063, with Plt. Off. Walker at the controls, landed at Luqa.

By this time 69 Squadron had suffered numerous losses. On 13 January AR721 had to be ditched in the sea off Malta after an attack by Bf109s.

During that same day AR733, attacked by the Luftwaffe fighters, was so extensively damaged after a crash landing at Luqa that it was written-off.

Meanwhile Warburton's Beaufighter, jumped by Italian MC202s over Taranto, had one engine damaged; however, evading the fighters he still went on to conclude the mission.

Two days later Maryland AH288 was accidentally taxied into a bomb-loaded trolley. In the explosion that followed, the aircraft was completely destroyed and the pilot, including two ground crew members, were killed. BS772, due to technical problems, had to be force landed at Luqa, and two other Marylands, AR714 and AR725, were both shot down in the sea by patrolling Bf109s while returning to the island from diverse sorties. Regretfully no survivors were picked up from the crew of AR725.

Wellington/X of Special Duties Flight parked at Luqa, 1942.

On 28 January, flying on a Photo Reconnaissance mission over the south of Italy, Hurricane Z3173 was hit by flak and had to be abandoned by its pilot who parachuted down into the hands of the enemy and was taken prisoner. This aircraft, had recently been turned over to 69 Squadron as a replacement for Z3053. By the end of the month, however, after S. African A.F. crews delivered some Marylands from the Middle East, 69 Squadron's strength was brought up to fourteen aircraft.

On 7 February, returning from a successfully accomplished mission, Beaufighter T3301 was attacked by Bf109s. On fire and the crew wounded, the pilot managed to reach Luqa and crash-landed the RAF aircraft on the aerodrome.

On 16 February, the surviving Mosquito was damaged on the ground during an air raid. A DeHavilland representative in Egypt, notified of the mishap, arrived in Malta to supervise the repairs. However, late in March, jumped by patrolling Bf109s, the aircraft, heavily damaged, crashed while landing and burst into flames. The crew escaped unhurt but the aircraft was a total loss.

Towards the end of February, with Beaufighter T3301 written-off, two officers wounded, and a third posted to the Middle East, Warburton, Beaufighter T4750 and a two-men ground crew were all that remained of 'T' Flight of 2 PRU in Malta.

On 7 March, a Spitfire on transit to the Middle East landed at Malta to refuel.

But with Warburton expected to return to 2 PRU at Heliopolis the AOC decided to keep the aircraft, AB300, on the island for Photo Reconnaissance duties, with ferry pilot Harry Goldbeck to fly it.

This PR Mk.IV, which the pilot flew from the UK across to Gibraltar, from where he navigated the route to the Malta and landed at Ta' Qali, was the first of type to appear on the island.

On 13 March Goldbeck had it airborne operationally from the island for the first time.

The next day, had it not been for the unexpected intervention of two Spitfires, Maryland BS.762 would have fallen to the guns of patrolling enemy fighters. After this aircraft's narrow escape it was decided that 69 Squadron should suspend all flying by the Marylands while Me109s roamed the skies. They were to rely on what Spitfires they had on strength for reconnaissance duties. So, during the next two months, the Glenn Martins remained grounded until in June the Baltimore arrived on the scene.

Towards mid-March, with 43 operational sorties, all flown in the daytime in Beaufighter T4705, Warburton departed for Heliopolis. He moved away just after he was awarded a DSO. However, he was to return again on 11 August, to take over command of 69 Squadron, which was by then in a shambles despite the recent arrival of reinforcements.

On 18 March, intercepted by Bf.109s, Maryland AH294 was shot down in the sea off Malta, with the loss of all on board.

The next day Sgt. L. Colquhoun, an ex-603 Squadron pilot, arrived in Malta flying PRU Spitfire BP895, which he was instructed to get to the Middle East. Again, however, with A.V.M. Lloyd's request to retain the aircraft granted, the Spitfire, went to 69 Squadron.

By the end of the month, of the 56 missions flown by the squadron, six were attributed to the Spitfires.

During April Coldbeck flew on several missions over Sicily, of which many were flown in rotation with Sgt. Les Colquhoun, in whichever aircraft of their two was available.

Next to get "stuck" on the island was Flt. Sgt. J.O. Dalley, who was shortly afterwards followed by a fourth NCO pilot, Frank Gillians, a New Zealander. The latter also found himself "forced" into the local PR service at Luqa.

Despite the fact that he was not a formally appointed Flt. Cdr., day by day operations remained under Coldbecks control. However, when Wg. Cdr. Tennant one night disappeared, Plt. Off. Munro took over as "Acting CO of 69 Sqdn."

"The operating of the Marylands/Baltimores ...." Wrote Coldbeck in his book 'The Maltese Spitfire'. "... was an entity separate from the Spitfires attached to 69 Sqdn, and there was little or no contact between the two. The people of 69 Squadron mainly ignored the Spitfire. The groundcrews of the twin engined aircraft were aware of the location of their single engined counterparts but the latter did not enjoy the same benefit."

That summer a change in AOC resulted in the transfer of all PR Spitfires from Luqa to Safi. Park was of the opinion that only armed fighters were to remain within Luqa's airfield perimeter.

Coldbeck, recalls the evening he was nearly shot down by friendly ground fire.

> "My return from a Photo Reconnaissance patrol coincided with the tail end of an Axis bombing raid over the island in which there was a lot of fighter activity, both Axis and our own."
>
> "My approach to Luqa was signaled by red tracer coming up

to meet me. Fortunately this went past me in the failing light. My IFF was switched on so all I could do was call up Fighter Control on the VHF and tell them I was being fired on by our own guns, and request them to inform the gunners."

"This was not all. A Spitfire – obviously taking his cue from the Bofors – also made a pass at me. I turned into him, with more tracer pressing me from behind until I spoke to him on the VHF Channel which he apparently had tuned and using."

Promoted to Sqdn. Ldr. Warburton steadily moulded 69 Squadron into the strongest reconnaissance element in the Mediterranean since the breakout of hostilities with Italy, and by October 1942, the unit had expanded into three separate flights.

'A' Flight flew Baltimores, which had some weeks before replaced the remaining few worn out Marylands.

'B' Flight, with PRU Spitfires on strength, became Warburton's personal flight, having taken it upon himself to lead it, while 'C' Flight operated Wellington Mk.VIIIs, but this change to 69 Squadron's structure needs some clarification, particularly the presence of 'C' Flight's Wellingtons.

Late in summer of 1941, realizing the hazards to which his ships were being exposed while navigating along these sea lanes, the enemy, to safeguard the passage of his convoys across the Central Mediterranean, changed his tactics, and began providing fighter protection from the moment ships steamed out of harbours.

These fighters operated out of airfields in Sicily and kept up watch throughout the daylight hours until nightfall. Then, alone, the ships continued southwards during the night, and depended on Tripoli-based aircraft to provide them with an escort as they neared their destination at the break of dawn.

This manouvre doubly imperiled the Blenheims in the daytime but, they did not ease the intensity of their attacks in spite of great cost to life and equipment. Regrettably though, when the Axis convoys were most vulnerable to attack, the FAA torpedo carrying Swordfish of 830 Squadron were finding it difficult to locate the moving ships at night. Without the expertise of properly trained ASV operators, and adequate equipment, there was a notable increase to the cargo tonnage reaching Rommel's forces, which were only kilometers away from Tobruk, the land battle having settled into a temporary stalemate.

Realizing that their anti-shipping campaign was not having the desired effect on the enemy concerned the British. With the Axis occupation of Greece as well as Crete, only Malta now remained to them in the Central Mediterranean from where they hoped to severe the enemy's means of sea communication between the Italian mainland and North Africa. Hence, they immediately decided to take counter measures.

In Britain 221 Squadron, operating ASV equipped long-range Wellington Mk.VIIIs, was given instructions to have three crews ready for overseas posting, and towards the end of September Flt. Lt. Milton, Fly. Off. Watson and Fly. Off. Spooner, whose main duties were to operationally demonstrate the performance of the latest ASV (Air-to-Sea Vessel) equipment, were en route to the Mediterranean.

Navigating the final leg of their flight via Gibraltar to Malta at night, to avoid encountering patrolling enemy fighters, the aircraft landed at Luqa at first light on 1 October 1941.

On the island, with the post of CO given to a newly promoted Sqdn. Ldr., with the rest of the personnel comprising of a Capt., a Fly. Off. and the three Wellington aircrews, a Special Duties Flight was formed.

Aircraft maintenance, when this was needed, was to be carried out

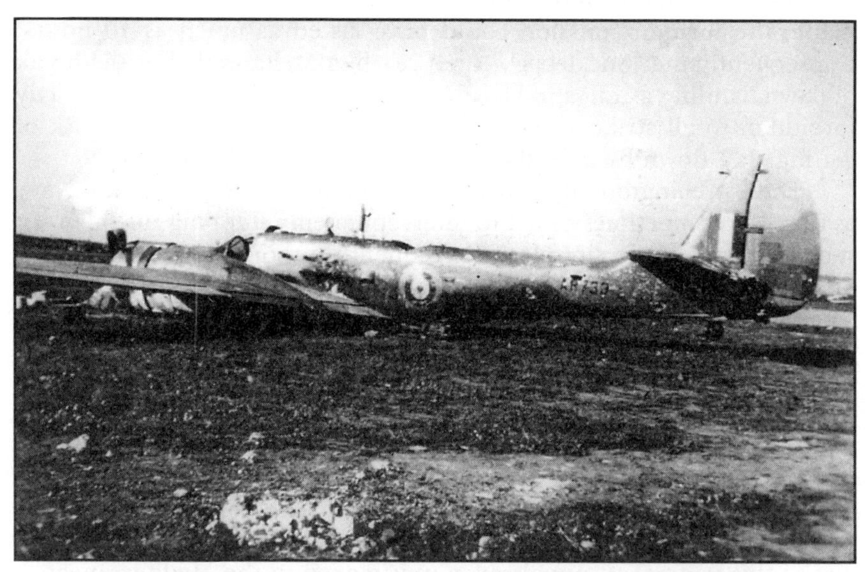

'Maryland' AR733 was so badly damaged by Luftwaffe fighters on 13 January 1942 that it was written off after crash landing.

by the same ground crews who attended to other Luqa-based Wellington units.

A feature which was most outstanding on these Wellingtons was a complex antenna required to operate the new ASV Mk.II, attached to their backs. This gained them the nicknames of "Sticklebacks", the RAF's favourite, and "Goofingtons" by the RN.

Duties for these aircraft were similar to those performed months earlier by the Sunderlands of 228 Squadron on Operation C.111. Armed with bombs the Wellingtons patrolled enemy sea-lanes at night. Spotting a solitary ship or two they generally attacked them, but when a bigger convoy was intercepted a signal was immediately relayed back to Air Control on the island, from where instructions were passed on to Hal Far airfield, where 830 Squadron had Swordfish on standby.

The torpedo carrying biplanes, formating behind the leading "Stringbag" that, equipped with an ASV Mk.I, but unarmed, homed in on the SDF Wellington's signals, and attacked their objective.

In some cases, when it was considered that the Swordfish attack had not achieved the desired effect, Wellington bomber reinforcements were called-out next.

Occasionally, when SDF Wellingtons were instructed to remain shadowing a convoy, until a further attack by 830 Squadron had been made, the formers' mission could have lasted as much as 10 hours. Consequently the "Stickleback" then reached Malta well after the break of dawn, landing at Luqa in broad daylight, a practice which was strictly forbidden to all strike aircraft on night operations due to the risk of getting shot down by patrolling enemy fighters.

These Wellingtons also proved to be an invaluable asset to the Navy as they were sometimes called to intercept enemy shipping for them. In such cases two of the aircraft were frequently airborne at the same time, one flying for Force 'K' and the other for the RAF.

By the end of the year so effective had Special Duties Flight proved to be that the enemy was forced to divert his ships to longer, but to them temporarily safer, routes, a circuitous passage skirting the Albanian and Greek coasts.

In Britain the Wellingtons of 221 Squadron were at this time being tropicalizéd and tested, in preparation for the move to the Middle East. The Air Ministry had decided that, with a detached flight already performing duties of paramount importance in Malta, it should have the rest of this general reconnaissance unit moved to the Mediterranean.

On 4 January 1942 the first of 221 Squadron's Wellingtons, on transit to the Middle East, landed at Luqa. Painted white all over these aircraft were too obvious a target to the enemy from the air, and although they were hurried through the island a few were heavily damaged during air raids. Some, however, picked to replace the ones which arrived in Malta in Autumn of 1941, and had by this time grown old and worn out, were quickly given a darker coat of paint and, along with their crews, posted to SDF.

A few of these crews flew on a mission or two, then moved on to the Middle East. Others, remaining on the island for longer periods and unaware of the existence of SDF, believed they were a detachment of 221 Squadron.

Plt. Off. Leslie arrived in Malta 16 January 1942, in Wellington Z8898, but, he did not fly operationally from the island until 15 February.

After that date he flew again on the 17, 23 and 27 of the month in aircraft Z8725 and Z8723, patrolling for enemy shipping around Tripoli, the Gulf of Gabes, Cap Bon and Marittimo.

In March he flew only once, in Wellington W5735, a patrol which he was signalled to abort three hours after take off.

On 3 April he succeeded in intercepting a small convoy off Linosa in Wellington Z8096, which he bombed as well as strafed. This was repeated on the 22 April. In early May, Plt. Off. Leslie flew one last patrol from Luqa in Wellington Z8712, one that he had to abandon after 5 hours 35mins flying due to technical difficulties.

Towards the end of May the British realized that, if they expected Malta to survive the aftermath of the Axis mauling it had taken during the past months, the island needed a supply convoy. Food, fuel and ammunition, which were being consumed at an alarming rate, were in urgent demand. Britain immediately rose to the occasion and operation code-named "JULIUS" was planned.

This entailed the launching of two simultaneous convoys, one from Gibraltar, to be code-named "HARPOON", and another from Alexandria code-named "VIGOROUS", hoping that, if not both, at least one might succeed in reaching the besieged island around mid-June.

In an effort to ensure the arrival of as many of the ships as was humanly possible, a large number of RAF aircraft were involved in the operation, including the Wellingtons of both 221 Squadron and SDF.

In the majority operating singly, some three dozen of these Wellingtons between them flew approximately 206 hours on armed anti-shipping patrols in which eighteen convoys were sighted, and attacks made on no less than ten of them, dropping a total of 10 tons of bombs. Some of these raids, however, were made in cooperation with the FAA Swordfish and Albacores of 830 and 828 Squadrons.

Operation "JULIUS' was in June also instrumental in increasing to 69 Squadron's strength by the addition of six Baltimores. Four, AG727-AG746- AG734 and AG790, complete with their crews arrived from the Middle East, intended to replace the worn out, and by now old, Marylands that still remained with the unit. Unwittingly instructed to patrol at altitudes of 5,000 feet, only after one aircraft failed to return, and their CO went missing, were aircrews briefed to fly at twice that elevation.

On 15 June, flying on a reconnaissance patrol over the Ionian Sea, Baltimore AG715 was reported missing. AG727 was later in the month destroyed on the ground from the blast of a nearby Beaufort when the torpedo it was carrying exploded, leaving 69 Squadron with only three of the aircraft.

In the early days of June, Britain, however, wanting to keep an 'eye' on the movements and dispositions of the Italian naval fleet, due to the departure of their Malta-bound convoy, had three PRU Spitfires added to 69 Squadron's strength. The scope of these three aircraft, BP908-BP945 and BP915 was to fly all photographic reconnaissance patrols concentrating on locating Tripoli-bound enemy convoys.

Flying in Spitfire BP908 Colquhoun was on 17 June watching for enemy shipping movements over Palermo. Then on the 25th, due to lack of serviceable PR Spitfires, Coldbeck had to fly in a Vc, EP140, borrowed from 249 Squadron.

By the end of the month the Spitfires and two Baltimores of 69 Squadron accumulated a total of 141 flying hours in 51 sorties. The squadron's personnel was at that time formed of four Baltimore crews and three Spitfire pilots who, after Warburton's arrival, were strengthened to become its 'A' and 'B' Flights respectively, while the disbanding of SDF provided the squadron with a third, 'C' Flight, made up of Wellingtons.

Colquhoun was in July awarded a DFM for his useful work with the squadron. Then on 11 July, while the PR Spitfire Flight still boasted of an unblooded record, another of 69 Squadron's Baltimores was reported missing, leaving the unit with only a serviceable one, AG734, as AG748 still needed an engine change.

Five days later two crews were dispatched to the Middle East to pick up two more of the type.

On 7 August, three Baltimore IIs and a Mk.I landed at Luqa from Egypt. Two joined 69 Squadron's surviving two, which were shortly afterwards augmented by two Marylands on detachment from 203 Squadron, to make up 'A' Flight.

On 11 August Warburton returned to 69 Squadron in Spitfire BP911 to assume command of his old unit.

At this time some additional Spitfires, BR662- BR663-BR665 and BR431, were included to the squadron's inventory.

On 18 August, still a Flt. Lt., Warburton flew on a reconnaissance patrol in BR663. By the end of the month he had practically flown all the PR Spitfires in 69 Squadron's 'B' Flight. These aircraft were at this time providing all reconnaissance missions over Sicily and Southern Italy while the Baltimores covered enemy sealanes preparatory to night attacks by the squadron's bomb-armed ASV Wellingtons.

On 19 September 69 Squadron lost their first PR Spitfire, AB300, when the aircraft had to be abandoned by its pilot over Agrigento due to engine problems. Sgt. F. Gillions was taken prisoner.

Since the Spitfires had first joined the unit in March they had flown nearly 400 operational missions without losses.

On 7 October 69 Squadron 's Spitfires reported a heavy build-up of enemy aircraft on Sicilian airfields. That month the unit played a major role in the shipping offensive of 1942.

With all due respect to Warburton's abilities as a Reconnaissance pilot, Coldbeck's own esteem of his CO was not high. Warburton was an individualist and, unfortunately, lack of respect towards others may have been due to this unbridled selfishness of his.

"He ran roughshod over his subordinates, and tended to boast a lot about his successes." Wrote Coldbeck in his book 'Maltese Spitfire'.

Coldbeck could never forget the time when, due for a mid-day sortie over Cagliari, he was just settling down into the cockpit when Sqdn. Ldr. Warburton hopped on to the aircraft wing and told him.

"Oh, Harry. I'm taking this trip. You're to go down to Valletta and accompany Christine, 'his girlfriend', to lunch on the Brisbane Star."

"I had by this time become tired of the long series of before first-lights and last-lights which were taking their toll."

It was while Coldbeck was on a last-light flight as a favour to one of his pilots that he was on 10 November shot down off Sicily by an enemy ship's fire and taken prisoner.

During the 8 months he was in Malta he had completed over 150 PR operational sorties with 69 Squadron.

After all had been said, while flying in Spitfire BR665 to observe the result of an attack by Beaufighters of 227 Squadron, Warburton noted one of the Beaus ditching in the sea after getting hit by enemy return fire. Spotting the crew in their dinghy Adrian risked getting shot down to attract the attention of an enemy MTB so that it could go to their rescue, which it did.

Warburton received a second Bar to his DFC for this gallant deed, then on 15 November, while out in Spitfire BR648 on a routine photo reconnaissance mission of the Axis held port of Bizerta, in Tunisia, he was jumped by a gaggle of Bf.l09s.

Only by a miracle was he missed by the hail of cannon shells that ripped into his aircraft before he could take evasive action and elude the enemy fighters by flying straight into cloud. With his Spitfire badly crippled, loosing height as it went, Adrian nursed the badly shot-up engine and coaxed the aircraft as far as Bone, where he crash-landed behind Allied lines.

Offered a lift to Algiers by a friendly naval French Admiral Warburton was two days later on his way to Gibraltar on board a Halifax, flown by a Czechoslovakian crew, in which he had literally hitch-hiked a flight.

On the 'Rock' security authorities took one look at the German pistol he carried, and a wicked-looking commando knife he had tucked in one of his flyingboots, and had him arrested as a German spy in spite of his explanations to the contrary.

Two days later, however, persuaded that he was truly an RAF Sqdn. Ldr., Warburton was set free. Lady luck seemed to favour him at every turn. A Spitfire, just arrived from Britain, lacked a ferry pilot to fly it to its destination. Turning on his charm, with a blend of his persuasive powers, Adrian succeeded in convincing the authorities to let him have the aircraft, and on 20 November he was on his way back to Malta.

Stopping to refuel in Algiers he flew on to Bone, from where he collected the camera magazine from his wrecked Spitfire before the next day resuming with the final hop to Malta.

En route Warburton spotted two Ju88s near Cap Bon, just about where only days before had nearly bought it. The fact that Spitfire ER467, a fighter version, was armed sent Adrian's adrenaline soaring, and he attacked the enemy aircraft, shooting one down in flames.

As Warburton stepped out of the Spitfire at Luqa airmen gathered around him in disbelief.

Earlier, when reports had reached them that he had been shot down by Me109s, they were shocked at the news, with Christina Ratcliff probably being the one who was affected worse of all. Hence his return, alive and well, literally out of the blue, after having been thought dead for the past seven days, astounded everyone.

During his absence Warburton, who had been promoted to Wg. Cdr., had also succeeded in increasing to his score list, as well as to his reputation as a living legend.

Just before the end of the month he had another close call, again falling foul of some Me109s, but he managed to elude them before they could damage his Spitfire.

Tirelessly Warburton flew everywhere in the Central Mediterranean, from Tripoli to Sicily, and as far north as the Italian mainland.

He tended to prefer flying in Spitfire BS364, but by the time his third tour of duty with 69 Squadron expired he had flown in no less than thirty different Spitfires and several Baltimores.

January 1943 saw the return to Malta of 221 Squadron, and a reorganization program was prepared for them. Its past role as a search and shadow aircraft was changed to that of a torpedo-carrying bomber. Only selected crews were picked for these duties, and they all underwent conversion courses at 5 M.E.T.S. before operational flying. Meanwhile, a balance of experienced crews in both roles were needed, so some of 221 Squadron's old crews were withdrawn to be replaced by others from 69 Squadron's hybrid flight of torpedo carrying Wellingtons formed from the RAF's own 38 and the Royal Australian A.F. 358 Squadrons.

When on 21 January, the operational Wellingtons departed for Malta only a selected few of 221 Squadron's original ground staff accompanied the unit. This resulted from the fact that so well supplied was the island by servicing crews at the time that very few were needed for the purpose.

The Wellingtons, however, arrived well loaded, each carrying its share of aircrew, equipment, ground crew and a brace of torpedoes.

On the night between the 23/24 January, the squadron was for the first time airborne on anti-shipping strikes off the northwest coast of Sicily, which was an immediate success.

This encouraged aircrews to go to greater lengths, and the operational system of search, illuminate and attack adopted by 221 Squadron proved to be very effective, choking Rommel's major source of supply to Tunisia. Even the enemy's use of radar jammers to shield his convoys from night attacks proved futile when Wellingtons of 179 Squadron, equipped with the latest type of radar, arrived in Malta as an additional counter measure. Unfortunately, however, spares for these aircraft, when the need arose, had to be cannibalized from scrapped Wellingtons that had been dumped in nearby quarries.

Meanwhile 69 Squadron had by this time grown stronger, boasting of twelve Baltimores and more than that number in Spitfires, Wellingtons and even a Beaufighter or two.

Warburton returned to the UK for a well-deserved rest but, as expected, he did not stay away long for shortly afterwards he returned to Malta in a brand new Spitfire

Mk.IX, EN338.

In North Africa his outstanding performance had impressed his American counterparts in the USAAF Unit 3 so much that they began to follow his directives, and obey most of his orders with great confidence.

Soon 69 Squadron, whose existence during the struggle for the Mediterranean had been an extremely hectic one, was called upon to extend themselves farther still in preparation for operation 'HUSKY', straining both men and equipment, frequently to the limit of their endurance. Finally, however, to ease the pressure under which the squadron was operating, its own 'B' Flight, flying Spitfire PR4s, was on 2 February, picked to form a separate photo reconnaissance unit, No. 683 Squadron.

Due to the continuity between flying, processing and interpretation, Allied Photographic Units, working independently, were not issuing reports earlier than 48 hours following a mission, and these were frequently needed 'immediately'. Hence it was at this time decided to amalgamate British and American units to form a Mediterranean Air Command that, would completely combine both flying and photo interpretation. This unit was jointly commanded by a Colonel, a Wing Commander and an experienced organizer of Photographic Intelligence.

To keep pace with an ever increasing demand for photographs an expansion program was set up, and by Spring of 1943 the main responsibility of the new wing was to serve as the eyes of the Allied Armies, then closing in on Tunis. The mapping of Sicily was another big undertaking, resulting in an extensive program of flights from Malta and Algiers.

Newly formed 683 Squadron's first sortie was flown on the very day the unit was officially recognized, on 8 February, with Adrian Warburton as its Commanding Officer being honoured with the flight. The number of Spitfires the squadron started with were eight: BP905 – BP932 – BR656 – BR665 BS358 – BS364 – BS496 – EN153

During March, two of the squadron's PR4s, BR656and BS364, were replaced by two others of the type EN389 and AB310 as well as a PR11, EN331.

Advance Unit 3 of the USAAF began to arrive in Malta from Maison Blanche, via Castel Benito, on 21 March, when four C.47s landed at RAF Luqa and disembarked six officers and twenty-eight enlisted men. The RAF first assisted the Americans to get located at their new station. Then on the 23 July, the first F.5A, from a detachment of six P.38 Lightnings P.4 and F.5A, amongst which were noted, 41-2266 (F.4), 42-13071, 42-13082 and 42-13089 (F.5A), landed at Luqa, with the rest following in rapid succession.

The task for which the unit was sent to Malta was to carry out the mapping and pinpointing of specific enemy military installations in Sicily and the Italian mainland.

The unit's CO, Capt. Lewis H.Richardson, was on 28 March given the honour of flying the first mission, one from which he failed to return.

A Lt. Silliman temporarily replaced Richardson until on 1April he was called back to Headquarters and Capt. Joseph D. Scalpone arrived to fill the post.

Following that loss aircraft were kept in good working order under the supervision of Warrant Officer Micketts, Engineering Officer, and operations resumed functioning without further mishaps. Lt. Haine took care of Intelligence duties while Capt. Phenning and an able crew carried out the processing of pictures.

That month a few more PR11s joined 683 Squadron, substantially increasing to the squadron's strength with the type, although it had to give up two of its original PR4s.

A further five PR11s were received in May, shortly after the unit gave up two more of their PR4s.

With the mapping of Sicily in preparation of Operation 'HUSKY' accomplished larger scale photographs of specific objectives for the 7th American and 8th British Armies, covering territory as far north as Italy, up to about the Avellino mountains, were taken up next.

Wg. Cdr. Warburton co-ordinated the assignments of the USAAF

One of the first USAAF Lightning F.5A from the 12th Photo Squadron to arrive at Luqa; on joint operations with the RAF's 683 PR Squadron.

Unit 3 with those of his own 683 Squadron, so that upon completion of the mapping the two units worked together almost as one on routine cover and new demands.

Capt. J.D. Scalpone, as CO of the USAAF 3rd Photo Group, who flew on fifteen missions from the island during that period, wrote about his own wartime experiences and impressions of photo reconnaissance from Malta:

"Fighter strength there (Sicily) was greater than that in Tunisia".

Tunisia had all but fallen to the Allies by March, forcing the majority of Axis fighter aircraft to withdraw to Sicily.

> "Interceptions were not infrequent over Sicily. But our seven pilots had 'savvy'. Ten or eleven interceptions in two months (about one hundred and twenty missions flown) netted the enemy no American PRU scalps."
>
> "Only once or twice did they prevent the pilot from getting pictures."
>
> "I flew over Palermo two or three times and was quite impressed by the flak there. Real scary stuff ... But it is a rare day when high flak knocks down a PRU ship."
>
> "On Malta our PRU boys (German – Berry – Sugg – Coughlan – Wells – Luthy – Webb) covered more and more targets each mission. We were 'getting on' in our trade since Tunisia. Time was approaching when the PRU veterans were vying with each other to cover as many as twenty-five and sometimes thirty targets at one sitting."
>
> "On Malta British radar was particularly helpful. We were warned of enemy fighters many times, though a warning does not necessarily mean that the enemy has a chance to contact us ..."
>
> "Anyway it is always a pleasant feeling to be kept informed of enemy activity in our area."
>
> "Radio homing saved our necks in bad weather when we tried to find the little island of Malta on returning from a mission. It was sweet music to hear the Malta station 'bring you in' on a bearing. As long as your radio worked ... you were sure to he safely berthed on the home field, with maybe a nice batch of pictures in your plane's belly to talk about."

> "Operating out of Malta again stressed 'navigation on your knee pad.'
>
> On sea hops, I think it imperative that the PRU pilot knows his knowledge and general experience regarding Photo Reconnaissance."

Meanwhile, on 13 May, 683 Squadron had began to operate a Mosquito Mk.II, DZ553, a PR4, on special flying duties over Sicily and southern Italy. At first Lt. Marec flew the first three sorties, but after about twenty operations 683 Squadron gave up the aircraft.

At the same time 230 Squadron operated out of Kalafrana and St Paul's Bay with six aircraft, all flying boats, of which three were Sunderlands and the rest Catalinas.

On 3 June, Warburton again proved his exceptional skill as a photo reconnaissance pilot. He succeeded in photographing the coastline of Pantelleria despite being exposed to the range of every type of ground fire. With his usual calmness and unique gallantry he flew over the island at altitudes that confused the enemy to return with the pictures he had gone after.

Finally on 7 June, the co-existence between 683 Squadron and the USAAF 3rd Photo Group was suddenly terminated when the latter was absorbed into the 12th Photo Squadron, although a flight persevered until 23 June.

In July Warburton again risked getting pounced by Me109s and newly arrived FW190s, although he was at this time being provided with Spitfires as an escort, to photograph the surrounding Sicilian coastline and its many beaches in Spitfire EP192, a specially equipped Vb. capable of taking low-level oblique photography.

Group Capt. Duncan Smith, in his book 'Spitfire into Battle', wrote about the times he escorted Warburton on some of these missions, just prior to the invasion of Sicily:

> "We flew together and once or twice I took a wing pilot along as an extra pair of eyes. We usually ran into trouble.
>
> Once 'Warby' decided to take pictures of Syracuse and without wavering I found myself following him into the harbour at zero feet, to be met by the strongest ack-ack fire. We flew up, down and out with everything shooting at us and the only reason we escaped was because the enemy could not depress their medium guns sufficiently ... we were so low."

"He was moulded in the buccaneer style, and his exploits captured the imagination. Immensely brave he delighted in taking fearful risks."

"At another time we were pounced on by four Mel09s. I told him to turn so that we could make good our escape out to sea. On the R/T he said: 'Sorry, old boy, got to finish this run – you see them off – you've got the guns.' I had a hell of a time of it ... before 'Warby' called to say he was headed out to sea and why was I not following to protect him.

I managed to get one Me109 and we damaged another, but the experience only made Warburton laugh his head off when we landed."

Warburton was that month awarded a bar to his DSO with a total score list of enemy aircraft resting at 9 confirmed, 1 probable and 2 damaged.

On 6 September 1943, Warburton flew out on his final mission from the island, terminating the longest tour of duty flown by any one pilot from Malta during the Second World War.

His unit, No. 683 Squadron, finally moved away from RAF Luqa on 20 November to join up with newly formed 336 (PR) Wg. in Tunis. However, although its CO had left in September his pilots had remained in Malta ranging over the Italian mainland in the squadron's Spitfire PR11s.

The last patrols flown in the PR4s were in July, after which all other duties were performed by a few remaining PR11s as no more of the type joined the unit until October when EB773 – EN657 – EN670 – EN678 – MB776 and MB783 were taken on.

683 SQUADRON's AIRCRAFT:

Spitfire PR4s

BS496 — 2/43		BP932 — 2/43 - 6/43
BP905 — 2/43 - 4/43		BS364 — 2/43 - 3/43
EN153 — 2/43 - 6/43		BR656 — 2/43 - 3/43
BS358 — 2/43 - 6/43		AB310 — 3/43 - 5/43
BR665 — 2/43 - 4/43		EN389 — 3/43 - 5/43

Spitfire PR11s

EN331 — 3/43 - 1/44		MB774 — 6/43
EN263 — 4/43 - 6/43		MB786 — 6/43
EN391 — 4/43 - 6/43		MB780 — 6/43

EN338 — 4/43 - 6/43	MB776 — 10/43
EN425 — 5/43 - 6/43	EN670 — 10/43
EN260 — 5/43	MB773 — 10/43
EN412 — 4/43 - 6/43	MB783 — 10/43
EN420 — 5/43 - 6/43	EN429 — 10/43
EN337 — 5/43	EN657 — 10/43
BR646 — 5/43 - 6/43	EN678 — 10/43
	EN408 — 11/43

EP192, a Mk.Vb (T A) Spitfire, was impressed with 683 Squadron on 1 June 1943.

Chapter IX

Clandestine Wings

Group Capt. Livock – Heinkel BV.185 – Lt. Haakon Offerdal Latecoere 298B – Duvachelle/Mehous – Lamb's Swordfish – Heinkel BV.187 – Dawson's Folly – 138 S.D. Whitley – Wg. Cdr. Westmacott

Militarily there were few uses Malta was not subjected to in the Second World War. Clandestine aviation operations, however, were amongst the few, but none the less important, activities. However, whatever there was undoubtedly deserve a chapter of their own in the Island's aviation history.

An entry in Group Capt. Livock's diary for 28 May 1941 mentions that he was called to see someone; 'with reference to some fantastic scheme of a semi private seaplane service of their own.'

A second entry noted down for 30 May records:

"I took Capt. Norris to M'Xlokk to see the site provided for the Heinkel."

Then, on the night of 3 June, flown by Norwegian pilot Lt. Haakon Offerdal, a Heinkel He.115A, BV.185, landed inside M'Xlokk Bay.

This German produced floatplane was one of a few that, forming part of a Norwegian Army Air Force unit, were secretly flown out of Norway during the German invasion of the country.

At the Kalafrana Seaplane base the Heinkel was immediately taken inside a hangar, where it was kept under strict security surveillance. Mechanical problems, however, then unfavourable weather conditions, prolonged the seaplane's inactivity until, on the night between 8/9 July, the enemy inflicted extensive damages to the He.115 when, in an air raid, a bomb was dropped on the hangar in which it was parked and exploded.

Although the aircraft was immediately taken in hand it was still unserviceable until the early days of September.

Group Capt. Livock again refers to the floatplane in his diary entry for 1 August.

"I went to look at the Heinkel inside the hangar at M'Xlokk."

The next entry in Livock's diary, related to his connection with the He.115, does not appear until 3 September, where he recorded that the aircraft was flown for the first time during the morning.

According to R.E.Gillman, DFC: DFM: in his book "The Shiphunters," at about this time he spotted the Heinkel being wheeled out of its hangar and towed down the slipway into the bay.

Heinkel He.115A, BV185, inside a hangar at Kalafrana.

"... Taxing out around the shoreline towards Pretty Bay the aircraft was turned around, nose pointing towards Delimara Point, the direction it finally took to take off."

"... Evidently the floatplane required long stretches of water to lift off. At least that particular evening the Heinkel was well past the 'lamphouse' before it finally became airborne."

The duties for which the Heinkel was brought to Malta were the dropping and collecting of British agents from Axis held countries in the Mediterranean, particularly the ferrying of allied agents to points along the North African coast at night.

The Heinkel's first mission, a daring, but unsuccessful operation, was attempted on 18 September. Group Capt. Livock had this event recorded in his diary:

"The Heinkel did its first show which, though unsuccessful, was a good effort."

Earlier still, and this is the first recorded clandestine operation from Malta, the Latecoere 298B impressed with 228 Squadron, on the night

A French Latecoere 298 which was occasionally used on clandestine missions.

between 10/11 September 1940, flown by Frenchmen Duvachelle and Mehous, dropped a high ranking British officer on Tunisian soil.

At BOAC's Hythe Base the He.115s were converted for top secret operations.

Most of the original cockpit glazing was removed, but its Spandau machine-gun was retained, and four 303 Brownings were fitted to each wing, of which two were rigged to fire backwards, as additional armament.

The conversion completed, the Heinkel's upper surfaces were then given a coating of matt black paint, while all under surfaces were finished in midnight blue with every military marking removed.

Mike Hendry, in his book 'Air Gunner', wrote that he had one afternoon seen such a coloured He.115 inside the Grand Harbour.

(Could the Heinkel have been moved to HM Dockyard for repairs that could not be effected at Kalafrana, or had he seen the captured Cant Z506B? – Author's note.)

In 1941, with the German offensive in North Africa progressing in their favour, Axis shipping became the focus of allied attention in the Mediterranean giving rise to intensive intelligence work.

In Tunisia two SIS agents were betrayed and had to be brought out of the country before the enemy caught them. The only way this could be managed was via a pick-up operation and, as no other unit nearer to the area could be employed, 830 Squadron, 200 miles away in Malta, was given the task.

Lt. Cdr. C. Lamb and his observer, Sub. Lt. Robertson had to prepare themselves for the long fuel consuming flight for which additional tanks were needed.

Lamb refused to have long-range tanks installed in the rear cockpit of his Swordfish, and opted to carry ten 5-gallon tins instead. These he would use to top up the main tanks on arrival at the rendezvous point, and drop them in the rear cockpit, from where Robertson would throw them overboard over open waters after puncturing them.

On the night of 28 August, after a hazardous operation, the two agents were picked up just before the break of dawn and the return flight to Malta was navigated in the daytime of the 29th.

During a second cloak and dagger operation on 17 September, in which a drop off had to be made in Tunisia, in a now modified Swordfish, Lamb landed by mistake on a muddy stretch of ground, and was unable to dislodge the aircraft to take-off again.

A Swordfish of 830 FAA Sqdn. during torpedo dropping practice inside M'Xlokk bay. It also lent its share to the dropping of spies behind enemy lines.

"Heinkel off at midnight ...". Recorded Livock in his diary for 21 September.

"... with the Frenchman and Sub Lt. Drake and is missing."

"Out looking for Heinkel." Entered the Group Cdr. for the 22nd.

"Nothing. Then wreckage spotted by Swordfish 23 miles out."

The Heinkel, dispatched to recover Lamb at a pre-arranged rendezvous, failed to contact the Commander who, along with his TAG, (Telegraphist Air Gunner) had fallen into enemy hands.

Flt. Lt. Georges Blaize, the French pilot in command of the He.115, probably suspecting what might have happened, feeded back power to his aircraft and headed back to base.

That night the weather was very bad, the seas rough. Somehow or other difficulties were encountered about twenty miles south of Malta in which it is assumed that the pilot probably lost control of the aircraft.

Several search parties were flown before a Swordfish of 830 Squadron, flown by Flt. Lt. More, finally flew over the wreckage of the Heinkel, around which could be found no signs of life.

With the loss of BV.185, BV.187, which had already been flown on secret operations from Woodhaven but was withdrawn shortly afterwards due to the risks involved in operating a typical Luftwaffe aircraft in territorial waters was sent to Malta, again flown by the Norwegian Offerdal, on 27 October 1941.

It is understood that both Offerdal and other pilots flew BV.187 on several missions to North Africa. These were later described as having been of great importance to war operations in the area.

It was also reported that after dropping agents in the Taranto area the Heinkel was pursued by an enemy aircraft which the He.115's pilot disposed of by using its backward firing Brownings.

On Christmas Eve, like its predecessor, BV.187 was damaged when enemy bombs hit the hangar it was in. Repairs on this Heinkel, however, did not take very long, and as soon as these were effected it was flown tested and moored inside Kalafrana Bay prior to its departure to the UK.

Mr George Dewey of Seaford, then serving with 828 Squadron, in a letter to the magazine 'Touchdown', described what happened to the Heinkel.

> "I was close by that morning in 1942 when two Mel09s came screaming into Kalafrana bay, and strafed the He.115 where it was tied to its mooring, leaving it blazing fiercely."
>
> "... until all that remained were a pair of floats, sitting on the water."

While British agents were being ferried in the Heinkel between Malta and enemy occupied territory in the Mediterranean, other clandestine activities were underway from the island. On 4 November two Whitleys from 138 Special Duties Squadron had arrived at Luqa for the purpose of dropping allied agents and supplies into Yugoslavia.

Two Serbian pilots, brought to Malta by Sunderland, were to guide the Whitley pilots to the dropping zone, where two agents, flown from Cairo, were to be dropped by parachute.

With the required supplies, brought to Malta by submarine, on board, Whitley Z.9159 flew out of Luqa with one Serbian as second pilot and navigator to Plt. Off. Austin.

Hugging the Adriatic coast of Albania on to Yugoslavia the aircraft, flying on a northerly course, headed inland towards the designated dropping zone where two special containers were dropped by parachute to unseen waiting partisans. Unfortunately, however, reports of severe storms, and an unserviceable Whitley, led to the discontinuation of the whole operation.

Early in the winter of 1941 one of 185 Squadron's Hurricanes, painted black all over, with the words 'Dawson's Folly' stenciled in small white letters very close to the cockpit, the only markings showing, was picked to fly on overland clandestine missions north of Malta.

Its dark finish and lack of any markings indicate this Hurricane as a Clandestine one. It is suspected to be none other than "Dawson's Folly".

The late Kenneth Cox, an L.A.C. with this squadron, who was close to the party involved in the Hurricanes servicing for these operations, recalled:

> "... Wg. Cdr. Dawson flew the aircraft on quite a number of secret trips to Sicily and Yugoslavia, although few were actually made to the latter."

"On one of these flights ..." Resumed Cox, "... the Hurricane, serviced by some of the squadron ground-crew under rigger Bill Jones, carried a long-range fuel tank to one wing and bomb-racks to the other."

"Dawson's duties over Sicily were the dropping of various aids to allied agents at pre-arranged places, packed in containers attached to the bomb-racks. This was accidentally discovered when one of the containers was dropped and burst open en route between Hal Far and Kalafrana."

"In the final weeks of 1942 Dawson failed to drop the container on his last three of four trips, to which he had the same answer every time; 'I did not see the light'."

"These dropping signals, consisting of dim lights that formed the letter 'T' for target, seems to have been what actually led to the Hurricane's withdrawal from further operations of this sort."

What Cox was unaware of, however, was the contents of classified RAF directives, of which one stated that Wg. Cdr. Dawson was the last of a number of senior RAF pilots who flew on one mission or another during 1942.

Wg. Cdr. Westmacott of 1435 flight was who originated these particular clandestine operations when, noting that since the arrival of 89 Squadron's Beaufighters his Hurricanes reaped few successes during the daylight hours, he suggested to his AOC., AVM. Lloyd, that his fighters should be fitted with long-range fuel tanks to carry out night attacks on Sicilian airfields.

The Air Vice Marshall, who had other ideas on his mind, offered Westmacott the opportunity to fly on clandestine operations, if he felt up to it, and the latter accepted.

Westmacott was put in charge for the organization of these early secret missions, and assisted by an able ground staff he devised ways by which to drop various aids to allied agents behind enemy lines.

After several practice drops Westmacott felt confident that he was ready to undertake clandestine flights.

Then in the early morning hours of 7 February, while out on his first secret mission, due to low cloud formations over the target, Westmacott had to abandon the delivery.

Flying back over the south of Toarmina he attacked a passing train.

The next night a second clandestine drop was successfully executed, after which he again strafed enemy ground traffic in Catania.

Fly. Off. Don Stones, in his book 'Operation Bograt', wrote that:

"Intelligence required our assistance to drop messages over enemy airfields in Sicily."

D. Stones recalled that further to the drops he made over Gerbini he was also briefed to drop some packages on the lower slopes of Mount Etna.

(Stones flew with the Malta Night Fighter Unit since this was first formed in 1941.)

On 10 August 1942, shortly after a Blenheim crew hijacked an Italian Cant Z.506B, the RAF used the Cant for some air sea rescue work, however, the personal belongings of the Italian aircrew, including some letters, reached their families by airmail.

Plt. Off. Coldbeck, in PRU Spitfire BP915, made the delivery in the early morning hours by dropping the package over an airfield in Catania as he flew past.

The method used however was different from the one Cox recalled.

These packets were dropped via the flare-tube, located just behind the cockpit, attached to a small parachute, but a weight had to be tied to the messages, otherwise these tended to remain inside the tube.

So the primary success of Westmacott led to a series of monthly flights that lasted for nearly a year. These were mainly flown by Wg. Cdr. Dawson, and were terminated when, caught by the enemy, the allied agent was reported shot.

Chapter X

Malta Night Fighter Unit

Enemy Night Intruding – RAF Night Fighters – 185 Sqdn's Nighttime Duties – 800X Naval Night Patrol Sqdn. – Malta-based Units' Night Fighters – Powell-Sheddon's MNFU/ "We Fight that you may sleep" – 1435 Night Fighter Flight – Heinkel He.115A. BV.185 – 830 Sqdn. Swordfish –Whitley Z9159 – Heinkel He.115A. BV.187 – Hurricane: "Dawson's Folly" – PRU Spitfire BR665

In the summer of 1942 all numbers in the 1 to 299 Series had all been allocated to regular RAF squadrons, but whether it had been intended to allocate numbers in the 500 to 699 range remains obscure. Evidently, however, it appears that when 603 Squadron was disbanded 1435 Flight was picked to fill in the gap. So on 2 August 1942, retaining its original number, 1435 Flight was expanded to squadron strength, and immediately equipped with Spitfires, to become the highest numbered unit in Royal Air Force history. Like numerous other RAF units 1435 owes its existence to wartime exigencies, and Italy's ever increasing night attacks over Malta, which were first launched in the summer of 1940. At that time no ready solution could be found to suppress nighttime enemy attacks, with the exception of anti-aircraft ground defenses registering the occasional hit.

In the early days of August 1940, shortly after the arrival of the first batch of carrier-ferried Hurricanes, to avoid encountering the RAF fighter during the daytime, the Regia Aeronautica pressed on with its night offensive.

In spite of the fact that very little damage resulted from these raids, their consistency instilled a feeling of insecurity over the island with the result that Air Headquarters, Malta, decided to take retaliatory action and a temporary night fighter section was formed.

On 13 August 1940 the first recorded wartime night interception took place over Malta, with Roger Hilton Barber, flying in Hurricane N2715, being credited with the destruction of a SM79. However, it was not till the night of 8 October that another pilot, Flg. Off. E. Taylor, scored a second victory when, aided by searchlights, destroyed one bomber and damaged another.

Still persisting in night intruding the enemy lost another of his SM79s to the guns of Hurricane P3731, flown by Sgt. F. Robertson, on 18 December.

The New Year saw the arrival of Germany's Luftwaffe in the Mediterranean who, still lacking their own fighters to escort their bombers at this time, were during the early days of February also forced to shift their offensive efforts to the hours of night to avoid encounters with the Hurricane.

Flt. Lt. MacLachlan, in Hurricane V7338, who was for the first time airborne to intercept an intruder on the night of 4 February, failed to make contact with the enemy.

On 7 February, eight Hurricanes were moved from RAF Luqa to Hal Far for night fighter duties, and the following night, aided by searchlights, a few of these were scrambled to intercept approaching intruders, but nothing developed.

Then, on the night of 9 February, led by MacLachlan, Hurricanes were again airborne at last light, splitting up just as darkness closed in around them.

Flying in Hurricane V7671 MacLachlan that night succeeded in intercepting a Ju88 at 17,000 feet and shot it down in the sea some ten miles off Malta. That same night, during a second engagement, he again succeeded in shooting down another Ju88 just off Grand Harbour.

Other pilots of 261 Squadron, although failing to shoot down any Axis aircraft, did intercept and shot at some which they reported hitting.

(Flt. Lt. MacLachlan was on 15 February so badly shot up by Bf109s that he lost an arm before parachuting to safety. After recovering he did some local flying in Magister N5428, simply for physiological reasons, then on 25 March was sent back to the UK.)

Just after midnight of 11/12 April, Plt. Off. Hamilton was scrambled to intercept an approaching intruder. Paired off with another Hurricane,

Hamilton spotted a Ju88 which he immediately attacked and claimed having shot down.

Although Luftwaffe Me109s had at this time arrived in Sicily, and were spotted escorting their bombers during daytime raids, night intruding continued over the island.

The RAF, who were expecting the arrival of a batch of Hurricane reinforcements on 27 April, the first ferry operation since the disastrous "White" was launched in November 1940, were now more determined than ever to take up the challenge.

In his entry for 5 May 1941, L.A.C. Les Davies noted down in his diary that a Night Fighter Flight had been formed, and on the night of the 6th Sqdn. Ldr. Whittingham was scrambled with another of his squadron's Hurricanes when a report of approaching intruders was received.

Spotting the enemy Whittingham attacked, and by the time the engagement was over the Sqdn. Ldr. was credited with one enemy aircraft destroyed, a second as a probable and a third as damaged.

On 1 June, four Hurricanes of 185 Squadron were picked for night flying duties, and for the first time metal plates were fitted over their manifold exhaust pipes to shield the glare from the pilots' eyes in the darkness. That night two of the aircraft were detailed to standby, and one was scrambled at 22.20 hours. However, in spite of an illuminated target, unexpected height discrepancies misled the Hurricane pilot who failed to home in on the enemy aircraft.

In the night of 6 June, at about 0055hrs, Flt. Lt. Hancock, a 185 Squadron pilot, taking advantage of a moonlit night, intercepted an enemy bomber. However, although he reported hitting the enemy several times, he could only claim a probably destroyed enemy aircraft.

Two nights later BR20Ms were intercepted by Hurricanes of 249 Squadron who succeeded in shooting down one enemy aircraft and damaged a second.

By this time 185 had ceased to exist as a daytime fighter squadron and was given the role of a night fighter unit, which lasted throughout the month of June 1941. However, except for one isolated incident, it proved to be an uneventful month for the unit.

At about 21.30 hours, on the night of 11 June, as Sgt. Plt. Burton was returning from a searchlight cooperation exercise, he landed downwind, overshot the runway, and crashed into a hangar, injuring himself.

Early in July, 185 Squadron was relieved of its night fighter duties

Despite its camouflage, Hurricane Z2827 is one of MNFUnit's fighters in a wheels up landing mishap.

and returned to Hal Far, relinquishing Ta' Qali airfield to 126 and 249 Squadrons. Night flying was then temporarily shared between the three units.

Meanwhile an independent Night Fighter Unit was on 30 June formed from recently arrived Fulmars of 800X Naval Squadron. Under the command of Lt. Manning, the Senior Observer, their main duties were to undertake night intruder sorties over enemy objectives in Sicily, armed with four 20lb bombs.

On the night of 6 July, Sub Lt.M. Tretton and Lt.Manning were on patrol over Catania. Flying at 1,500 feet the crew of the Fulmar spotted a large aircraft with its navigation lights on, in actual returning from a raid on Malta. Tretton attacked the BR20M and shot it down.

On 8 July, Hurricanes of 249 Squadron, while on night patrol duties, intercepted six SM79s but succeeded in shooting down only one of the enemy bombers.

On the night of 16 July, one of two Fulmars on night patrol duties, flown by Plt. Off. (A) Sabey and Sub. Lt. Furlong, was circling over Gerbini aerodrome with navigation lights on. At one instance, Sabey was shown a green light from the ground, a landing signal. He did not hesitate to take the hint. Sabey made a confident approach, flying low over the airfield, and released the 20lb bombs his Fulmar had attached to its wings, destroying a parked aircraft.

Three days later, on 19 July, 126 Squadron suffered the first night time casualty when one of their Hurricanes crashed during take off, killing the pilot.

On 28 July, Sqdn. Ldr. George Powell-Sheddon, an experienced Battle of Britain pilot, who arrived from the UK on the 21st, was called from Air Headquarters, Valletta, where he had had been given temporary staff duties. Flown from UK for the purpose of forming a special night fighter flight he was on that date given orders to do just that.

Fly. Off. Don Stones, who arrived in Malta on the same flight as Sheddon, was the first pilot the latter picked to assist him in forming the new unit. Between them they ensured that a high standard of cooperation existed between the island's ground defences, of which the most essential to their fighters was the assistance of searchlight units, who in turn depended on the Air Defence Room, Ground Radar and Filter Room.

By the end of July Powell-Sheddon had these elements teamed up, and with a number of aircraft at his disposal based at Ta' Qali this combined force was established as the Malta Night Fighter Unit (MNFU).

Pilots were picked from all three resident squadrons, and the Hurricanes were four Mk.IIBs and eight Mk.IICs. These were immediately taken charge of and given a coating of night-black paint.

An all black Malta Night Fighter Unit Hurricane IIB, BG727, in a wheels up landing mishap.

As Commanding Officer, and founder pioneer, of the MNFU Powell-Sheddon briefed his Hurricane pilots to always hunt in pairs, in unison with searchlights. He gave Flg. Off. D Stones command of one flight, while 'Cass' Cassidy, an ex-249 Squadron pilot, led another.

Hurricanes were generally tested at dusk, just before a night's standby, and parked on the airfield perimeter. This was close to a dispersal hut where bunks were provided for at readiness pilots to sleep in, fully clothed, waiting for the phone to ring, to send them scrambling into action.

Black painted light bulbs, from which a pale glimmer of light showed through a small-untouched area, guided Hurricane pilots during take offs and landings at night.

At dawn the aircraft were taxied away to their pens and aircrews went to the mess for a merited breakfast before a day's rest.

On the night of 5 August, Malta's newly formed NFU celebrated its first victory when, spotting eight approaching BR20Ms, the patrolling Hurricane pilots attacked the enemy bombers and shot down two of them.

Two days later another three BR20Ms made a night attack and, despite the fact that none of the bombers was intercepted, one of them mysteriously burst into flames and blew up.

Later that same night Ju87s made their first appearance over Malta during the night.

On 10th August four of MNFU'S Hurricanes, led by Powell-Sheddon, were scrambled to intercept a number of approaching enemy aircraft. The fighters attacked the bomber formations of BR20Ms, SM79s and Ju87s, however, only one aircraft was seen falling in the sea in flames.

With Sicilian airfields as their primary objectives Plt. Off. (A) Sabey and Sub Lt.Tretton, flying two separate Fulmars of 800X FAA Squadron, were on 2 September patrolling over the Gerbini-Catania area. Sub Lt.Tretton flew directly to Gerbini where he released a couple of bombs before strafing dispersal points and machine-gun posts.

From there he turned towards Comiso and relieved his aircraft of the remaining two bombs.

Plt. Off. Sabey, who was also circling over Gerbini, had other ideas. Spotting an enemy aircraft approaching the airfield with landing lights on, he tried shooting it down. However, the Italian pilot must have been more alert than Sabey thought for the aircraft disappeared as he approached.

He went after another enemy aircraft as it came in to land, but despite his attack he could see no results and it went on to land safely.

Deciding to climb up to 4,000 feet he chased a third aircraft out to sea but, spotting another to the south of Mount Etna, he turned his attention on this and finally had the satisfaction of watching the success of his fourth attempt fall in flames. However, spotting enemy fighters taking off from Comiso airfield, he released his bombs on the north side of dispersal area. Then seeing an enemy fighter prowling about he thought it best to fly back to base at Hal Far.

Just before the dawn of 6 September, three Cant.Z1007bis bombers attacked Hal Far airfield and two all black MNFU Hurricanes were scrambled to intercept them at about 05.20hrs. Flying these fighters was Plt. Off. Barnwell, who was in a MkIIB, and Flt. Lt. Stones in a MkIIC.

Turning both their attentions on one well-lit Cant they succeeded in shooting it down between them.

Two days later, sometime after 22.00hrs, Ju87s, a BR20M and a Z1007bis attacked diverse objectives on the island. On this occasion, Plt. Off. Barnes was in the company of his Sqdn. Ldr. Powell-Sheddon. Nevertheless the former, spotting a Cant that was well lit by searchlight beams, closed in on it and shot it down shortly afterwards.

Barnes later went to meet the enemy pilot, who was picked up from the sea with three other aircrew members, before he was sent to the prison camp.

That same night Plt. Off. Jopling, with Sgt. G.R.I. Parker as observer, were over Gerbini in Fulmar N4004 harassing the airfield there. Afterwards heading towards Augusta, they bombed a seaplane slipway there.

According to A.V.M. Lloyd it was suspected that few of the claims made by the Hurricane pilots were valid. He stressed that it had been disclosed that most of the explosions on these bombers were not being caused due to any RAF fighter action but by a faulty arrangement related to the bomb release mechanism, which resulted in the igniting of a newly developed incendiary immediately the trigger was activated.

The duties of the MNFU were not restricted to the defensive but also to the offensive in an attempt to discourage enemy night attacks on Malta.

Intruding patrols were flown over Sicily. For this purpose long range fuel tanks were fitted to four of the Hurricane Mk.IIBs to increase their operational range.

On the 5th and the 7th of September, taking advantage of a full moon, each Hurricane carrying eight 40lbs bombs to improvised under-wing bomb-racks, attacked numerous railroad tracks.

At first light on 14 September Macchis came in a low fighter sweep over Luqa airfield strafing everything in sight. Joined by Hurricanes from 185 and 249 Squadrons, five of MNFU's aircraft were scrambled to intercept them. In the engagement one of the night fighters, Z3512, fell foul of some of the MC202s and was shot down. Plt. Off. Barnwell had managed to relay a call that he had destroyed one of the enemy fighters just before he went missing.

In the Times of Malta of 25 October 1941, Wg. Cdr. Grant-Ferries, M.P., wrote:

This is a war of specialists. Only he who is skilled at his particular job can obtain the best results. This was realized at Home and special squadrons were formed, generally with twin-engine aircraft to deal exclusively with fighting the Night Raider. Here in Malta we have profited by this knowledge and have formed the Malta Night Flying Unit who devote the whole of their time to studying the problems of night fighting.

Their Sqdn. Ldr. maintains a very close liaison with the Searchlight Commander and there is, consequently, a very real mutual understanding of the difficulties with which the Searchlights on the one hand, and the fighters on the other, are beset. You have all seen the MNFU at work and have been able to judge their efficiency.

You have read of the exploits of Plt. Off. Barnwell, since unfortunately missing, for which he was awarded a DFC.

The Malta Night Flying Unit have chosen for their motto:

"WE FIGHT THAT YOU MAY SLEEP"

On 31 October, night attacking BR20Ms were intercepted by Hurricanes of the MNFU. One of the bombers, as is always the case, caught in the high searchlight beams was shot down after two passes. A crewmember was seen bailing out of the burning aircraft.

On the night of 9 November, while MNFU Hurricanes engaged enemy bombers in two separate attacks, one of the RAF fighters, flown by Flt. Lt. Stones, was abandoned after its engine seized, however, the pilot bailed out and parachuted to safety.

(There were no reports of enemy casualties.)

Six nights later a night patrolling Hurricane for the first time intercepted some Reggiane Re2,000s. Carrying small bombs, two of the enemy fighters reached Luqa, where they released their explosives. A third, attacked by the lone MNF Hurricane, was forced to jettison his bomb-load into the sea and abort the mission.

A second attack by more Re2,000s fighter-bombers was made on the night of 19 November. Two Hurricanes on this occasion intercepted the two formations of four enemy aircraft. The RAF fighters forced two of the Re2,000s to jettison their bombs in the sea and flee back to Sicily but the other two pressed home their attack.

A few days before receiving a promotion Powell-Sheddon was forced to make a crash-landing on the outskirts of Ta' Qali airfield when the engine of his Hurricane failed. The aircraft was extensively damaged but the pilot escaped unhurt.

Fly. Off. D. Stones was involved in a similar mishap when he was one night scrambled to intercept some intruders. The engine of his Hurricane cut out when already at an elevation above 400 feet and he had to bail out at short notice.

Promoted to Wg. Cdr., Powell-Sheddon was on 2 December 1941 relieved of his command of the MNFU, which had just been given a new title, that of 1435 (Night Fighter) Flight, by Sqdn. Ldr. I. Westmacott.

Luftwaffe units were that month returning to Sicily and with the approach of Christmas Ju88s began to reappear at last light.

On Christmas night, operating from Hal Far airfield, Hurricanes of 1435 Flight intercepted the German bombers, but failed to confirm any kills. Then on the night of the 27th a Ju88, caught in the glare of searchlight beams, was attacked by a patrolling Hurricane and shot down in the sea.

Only an enemy who was hounded by a Malta-based night fighter, and escaped to tell about it, could give a true account of the tenacity with which these RAF pilots chased their prey.

George Sattler, a highly decorated Ju88 bomber pilot who, before his untimely death in 1944, had flown more than 200 missions in less than four years active service with the Luftwaffe, did just that.

Sattler arrived in Sicily under Kesselring early in 1942, and shortly afterwards he was flying bombing sorties over Malta where one night he fell foul of a night fighter from Malta and experienced the wrath of the island's night time defences:

"Soon after releasing a 500lb bomb on Hal Far airfield," wrote Sattler in his diary "on the night between the 23/24 February, I was suddenly set upon by a night fighter. Despite a series of nerve-wracking maneuvres, which I had to keep up all the way back to Sicily, I still failed to shake the aircraft off my tail. Only when I finally reached the safety of my home base did the RAF fighter give up the chase."

Up till its disbanding in the spring of 1942 1435 Flight saw only limited action. Its night fighter duties were eventually taken over by a flight of radar-equipped Beaufighters of 89 Squadron that arrived at RAF Luqa prior to the launching of Operation 'PEDESTAL'.

Officially upgraded to as a squadron on 2 August 1942, under Sqdn. Ldr. A.D.J. Lovell, DFC., with ten victories to his credit as a veteran Battle of Britain pilot, according to surviving aircrew 1435 was operating Spitfires before that date. In fact by the end of July it had already had one probably destroyed Bf109 to its credit.

However, the first official claims credited to 1435 as a squadron are those recorded on 10 August, during an engagement between a gaggle of Me109s and a flight of Spitfires that, led by 1435's outstanding pilot, H.W. McLeod, succeeded in shooting down three of the enemy fighters. A higher toll in Axis aircraft was credited to the squadron's list three days later when some of its Spitfires again intercepted enemy bombers, destroying three Italian SM84s, a Ju88, and damaging five others.

By the close of September 1435 Squadron had accumulated a creditable number of enemy aircraft to its list.

In October, when the Luftwaffe launched one last desperate blitz on Malta, 1435 Squadron distinguished itself while the struggle lasted, raising its tally to 39 enemy aircraft destroyed by the end of the month.

Flt. Lt. McLeod, with a further ten kills to his credit, became the squadron's first pilot to get a decoration, a DFC and bar. He remained the second highest scoring pilot of the whole Malta siege with a total of thirteen victories.

The enemy, who could no longer organize a strong enough offensive at this time, reserved the last of his forces to defend himself against the Malta-based fighter units. These now hunted him down over his own ground, mercilessly hounding his troop laden transport aircraft as they attempted to fly across to Tripoli from the Italian mainland.

Spitfires of 1435 Squadron succeeded in intercepting the enemy during one of these long range patrols in mid-November 1942, and succeeded in shooting down one Italian fighter and an SM82.

On 17 December Flt. Lt. Walton shot down two Ju82s, and probably a third.

Sqdn. Ldr. Lovell, promoted to Wg. Leader, lost his post as 1435's CO to Sqdn. Ldr. W.A. Smith, DFC., in January 1943, but the latter's command of the squadron was a brief one for a few days later Sqdn. Ldr. H.F.O'Neill took over from him.

No. 1435 Squadron's rising string of successes gradually ran out. These remained static during the following months. However, in July 1943, with the launching of Operation 'HUSKY', the squadron's list soon rose by a further eight enemy aircraft as Bf109s, Fw190s and MC202s fell to the squadron guns.

But with so large a number of allied fighter units running rampant on ground support missions, airfields were shortly afterwards made available in occupied Sicily. Most of the action moved in that direction, with the result that late in October 1943, 1435 Squadron finally took leave of the island.

The Hurricane was the equipment used both by the MNFU and 1435 Flight until August 1942 when, raised to squadron strength, Spitfires replaced the former.

While the Hurricane lasted those noted with the unit were:

Z2414 – When the MNFU was dissolved this aircraft was converted to a MkIIc and taken over by 185 Squadron.

Z2418 – Went missing on 20 December 1941.

Z2680 – Struck off Charge on 26 December 1941.

Z2794 – Struck off Charge on 20 May 1942.

Z2827 – An ex-126 Sqdn. machine that saw service with the MNFU and was lost on 25 January 1942.

Z2961 – Was taken over by 249 Sqdn. from the MNFU. Later went to 185 Sqdn. and 605 Sqdn. respectively until it was finally Struck off Charge on 3 March 1943.

Z3462 – Was passed on to 1435 Flight, but what became of it remains obscure when on 6 March 1942 its undercarriage collapsed while landing at Ta' Qali.

Z3505 – Enjoyed a brief service with 1435 Flight after the MNFU, until it was destroyed in a raid on Ta' Qali on 9 April 1942.

Z3512 – Ditched off Malta on 14 October 1941.

Z3521 – Went missing on 9 September 1941.

Z3522 – On 5 March 1942 its undercarriage collapsed while landing at Ta' Qali.

Z3570 – An ex-249 Sqdn. aircraft it fell victim to Ta' Qali's rough terrain on 3 February 1942.

Z3571 – Was shot down by enemy aircraft during an air test in January 1942.

Z3580 – Struck off Charge in February 1942.
Z4941 – Was converted to a Mk.IIB and ended flying with the FRU (Fleet Requirement Unit) at Hal Far.

The Spitfires noted with 1435 Squadron were:
BS.161 – EP138 – EP203 and EP259, aircraft that seem to have been highly favoured by the squadron's elite flyers, including:
AR556 – An ex-126 Sqdn. machine, it was ditched off Sicily on 18 March 1943.
AR560 – An ex-185 Sqdn. aircraft, it was shot down by flak in June 1943.
AR551 – An ex-126 Sqdn. aircraft. Fate unknown.
AR565 – Shot down by BflW9s off Malta in March 1943.
AR595 – Another ex-126 Sqdn. aircraft. Fate unknown.

Chapter XI

'Acthung' Spitfire

(Part 1)

Middle Sea crisis – Luftwaffe blitz – Need for supply convoy – Need for a better fighter – Spitfires expected – "Spotter's" 15 – Spits in action; 10 March – Odds still great – Safety of Malta endangered – "Picket" – "Picket II" – USS Wasp – 'Wasp' again; 'Eagle' along – "L.B."

During the early months of 1942 the British War Cabinet had their attention focused on the Mediterranean, particularly the RAF's gallant, but hardly effective, struggle against the German Luftwaffe operating out of Sicily, in defense of Malta, Britain's last stronghold in the Middle Sea. During the latter half of 1941, the British strike forces had succeeded in interrupting the Axis means of sea communication between Southern Italy and North Africa from Malta.

When Kesselring first arrived in Rome in December 1941, his orders were to subdue the islands' resistance in preparation for a planned invasion, a directive which according to his estimates would take him less than two months to conclude.

It was 3 January 1942 when the 'blitz' was launched, and by the end of the month Malta experienced several heavy air raids some lasting hours during which, nearly 700 tons of bombs many aimed at the islands' three major airfields. Barracks, hangars and other buildings were razed to the ground, airfields left temporarily unserviceable, and more than fifty RAF aircraft were destroyed on the ground. Hurricanes were reduced to an impotent handful, obvious signs that Kesselring's scope was nearing fruition.. The first phase of his pre-invasion plans had gained him air superiority.

During the first half of February, low cloud formations and bad weather conditions over the island forced the enemy to limit the intensity of his attacks. Poor visibility, which obscured ground objectives, caused Kesselring unavoidable delays to his strategic campaign against Malta. However it was a heaven-sent respite to the besieged who, together with AVM Lloyd, converted a strip of countryside (SAFI) spanning Hal Far and Luqa aerodrome into a satellite airfield via which Luqa and Hal Far could be linked by means of winding taxiways. Also, since sandbag-built aircraft pens had been caving in to the bomb blasts of near misses, work on stronger ones was put on the Air Ministry's priority list as well. Jerry cans, filled with sand and earth, then lashed to one another by wire, were found to be more resistant to nearby bomb explosions. In spite of the Axis blitz, aircraft pens and revetments were constructed in large numbers along the new Safi taxiways, consisting of two 4,000 feet long grass strips, to become the Safi strip complex. However, this was a time consuming project and only the voluntary work of servicemen and civilians, who were readily available, made such a unique achievement possible. In his book 'Briefed to Attack', AVM Lloyd could not have paid them greater tribute:

> "The soldiers made by far the greater proportion of the pens. In early 1942 there were 1,500 of them working on the aerodrome, and sometimes, during the really bad periods of the continued offensive by Kesselring and the weather, there were as many as 3,000. We wanted all the help we could get in addition to that provided by the civilians. Everybody made pens. Every contribution – even for an hour a day – was gratefully acknowledged. Officers, clerks, photographers, storemen, wireless operators, aircrew, in fact everyone with a few hours to spare would arrive with their sandwiches and work hard for an hour or so, regardless of the weather or the enemy.
>
> "The interrelation between Malta and the Desert operations was never so plain as in 1942 ..." Churchill recorded in his memoirs of the Second World War. "... and the heroic defense of the island in that year formed the keystone of the prolonged struggle for the maintenance of our position in Egypt and the Middle East."

Everybody made pens. In 1942, there were 1,500 men working on them.

As early as February the British Prime Minister and the Chiefs of Staff stressed upon Auchinleck the importance of engaging Rommel into combat so that a vitally needed supply convoy could be slipped through to Malta. The defenders were threatened with starvation, while the Luftwaffe was breaking down the British means of obstructing Axis shipping to Tripoli. It was at this time that the great struggle for Malta truly began. An extract from a letter to Auchinleck on 26 February reflected Churchill's great concern for Malta due to its influence elsewhere.

> "... the supply of Malta is causing us increased anxiety, and anyone can see the magnitude of our disaster in the Far East."

On 4 March he again expressed his concern about the island in a letter to the President of the United States.

> "The danger to Malta grows constantly, and large reinforcements are reaching Rommel in Tripoli ..."

The next day Air Marshall Tedder received a signal from AVM Lloyd who stressed the urgent need of more fighter aircraft, which ended with a desperate note:

> "Delay in Spitfires annoying. Can you hasten dispatch?"

Two days later the first Spitfires reached Malta, but the ferrying of this new fighter was far more complex an operation than that of the Hurricanes due to the difference in configuration between the two aircraft.

During 1941 it was found that the most practical method by which to deliver fighter aircraft to Malta, despite the great risks and effort required for each operation, was to have them ferried by aircraft carrier from Gibraltar. This proved to be so successful that by the end of the year more than 300 Hurricanes were delivered to the beleaguered island.

In 1942, when the need to have the Spitfire in Malta was at its utmost, the same ferrying method was adopted. However, this was more difficult to execute than previous operations. Slipper type, jettisonable, 90 gallon ferry fuel tanks were developed for the purpose and produced in small quantities, while tropical filters had for the first time to be also fitted to the fighters.

At Liverpool sixteen Spitfires were packed in wooden crates and loaded on board the freighter Cape Hawk. Sixteen of 249 Squadron pilots and some 100 ground crew had already preceded them.

The Cape Hawk reached Gibraltar on 21 February. She was immediately tied up next to HMS Eagle and by the next day all the crated fighters were lined on the quayside beside the carrier. Having already taken great pains to keep this fighter aircraft movement a secret back in UK and suspecting that German paid agents might be planted amongst the many Spaniards working in Gibraltar during the day, the crates were not opened until after dark.

On 25 February the last four crated aircraft were hoisted on to Eagle's flight deck. After that assembly of the Spitfires proceeded in great haste, but, it was soon discovered that, although brand new, some of the fighters needed renewal of parts. As none were available, one of the Spitfires was sacrificed to provide the spares needed for others. The fleet left Gibraltar on 27 February to carry out operation 'Spotter' but was the next day forced to return to the 'Rock' due to the discovery of a fault in the auxiliary fuel system of the fighters.

Operation 'Spotter' was eventually executed on 7 March when 15 Spitfires were flown off HMS Eagle. 'Spotter' was an outstanding achievement for none of the Spitfires had been test flown after assembly. Neither had any of the pilots flying them ever took-off from a carrier's deck before, yet all of the fighters, led by 4 navigational Blenheims, reached the island safely.

Plt. Off. P. Brennan, an Australian, flew in one of these first Spitfires to arrive in Malta. An experience about which he later wrote:

Plt. Off. Paul Brennan.

> "The Island appeared first as a tiny speck against the horizon, standing out against the deep blueness of the Mediterranean."
>
> "... We were still ten miles out flying at 3,000 feet when we had our first experience of the ground control station, and our introduction to Group Capt. Woodhall, Senior Fighter Controller. His calm voice came to us clearly over the R/T."
>
> "'Hello, Exile boys! Keep on your present course. Watch out for a few 109s below."
>
> "Not knowing what to expect we felt nervous and apprehensive, and immediately started to weave, keeping a sharp lookout. We saw nothing of the Hun fighters. We dropped down lower, rather fearfully wondering where the 109's could be, but still seeing nothing of them ..."
>
> "From amid the patchwork of small, bright fields we picked out Ta' Qali aerodrome, and prepared to land. It bore unmistakable scars of bombing. The dispersal to which we walked was a mass of rubble, and we were told that a pilot had been killed there a few days previous."

The Spitfires' task was to cover the Hurricanes during their climb up, then keep the 109s busy while the Hurricanes dealt with the

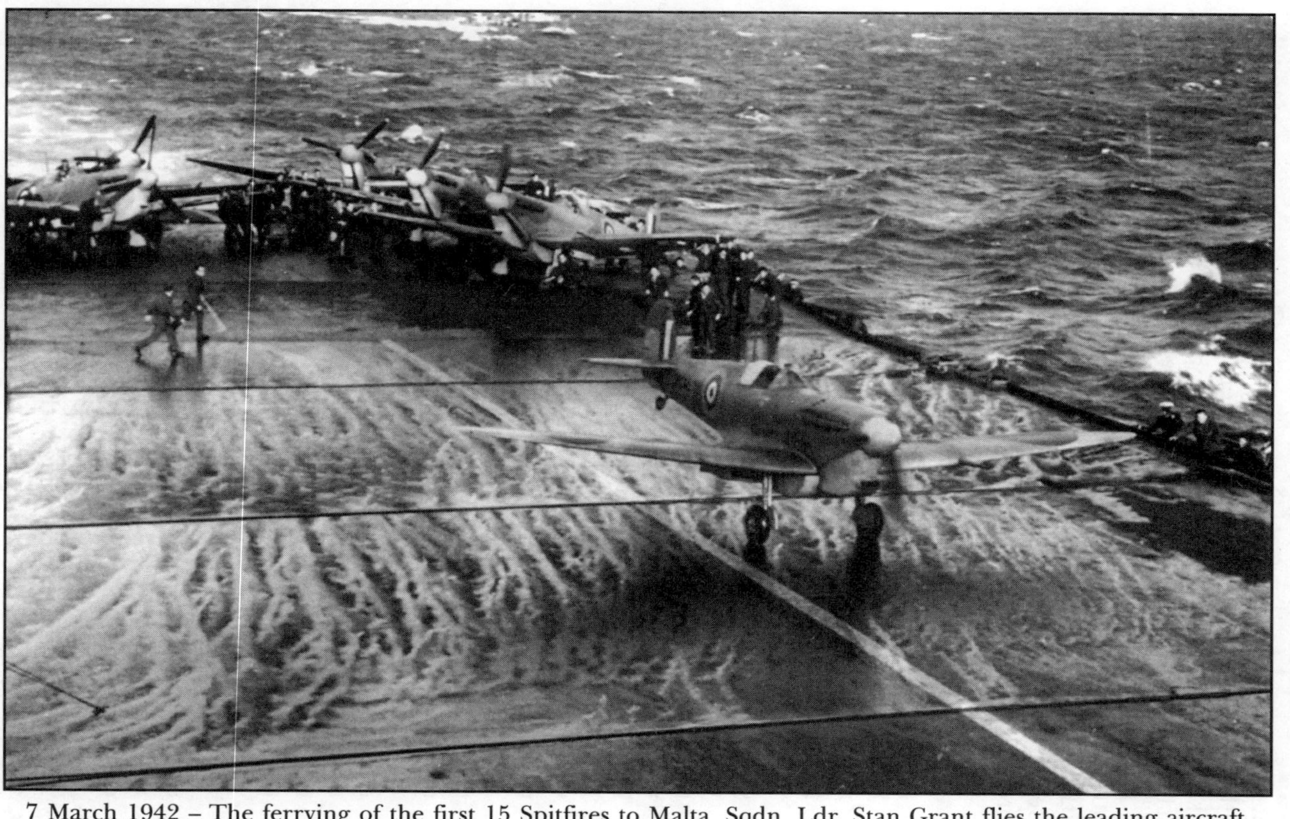

7 March 1942 – The ferrying of the first 15 Spitfires to Malta. Sqdn. Ldr. Stan Grant flies the leading aircraft, seen here taking off HMS Eagle.

bombers, but this was far easier said than done. The escorting Luftwaffe fighters were so numerous that even all the Spitfires together were not enough to be effective, despite the fact that they gave a good account of themselves. The enemy had superiority in numbers with the result that the new RAF fighters disappointedly failed to resolve the problem then prevailing on the island. In fact their arrival made the technical situation more complex because neither spares nor the maintenance equipment needed had been provided. Even the method of installing spares was different from that used in the Hurricanes. These Spitfires, led by Sqdn. Ldr. Stan Grant from the HMS Eagle, were the first of type to operate outside of Great Britain. Allotted to 249 Squadron at Ta' Qali, they came under the command of Sqdn. Ldr. Stan Turner. Excerpts from the personal diary of Mr William Metcalf, then an AC1 with this unit, give a brief but factual enough account of the grueling time these first few Spitfires and their pilots had to endure in trying to defend Malta, while the island was under siege by the Luftwaffe during the ensuing days of March:

March 7 – They arrived at last! The mere sight of the new arrivals brought the moral up 50%.

Sqdn. Ldr. S. Grant, and Flg. Off. R. Daddo-Langlois on the left.

One of the first Spitfires to arrive in Malta.

March 8 – Managed to get six Spitfires ready for action, and what a job it's been. I haven't worked so hard since I joined the RAF.

March 9 – Eight Spitfires start operations tomorrow. I hope they come up to expectations!

March 10 – The Spitfires got four plus and two probably.

Metcalf's diary entry, true as far as he believed it was at the time, was in later years proved erroneous regarding the Spitfire pilots' claims for the day. As recorded the Spitfires combat debut over Malta was on 10 March. Seven of the fighters, joined by Hurricanes from 126 and 185 Squadrons, were that day scrambled to intercept approaching Ju88s, escorted by Bf109s. Detailed to engage the enemy fighters, the Spitfires were to let the Hurricanes attend to the bombers. One Me109 was shortly afterwards shot down, but so was a Hurricane, while another, badly damaged, was forced to crash land.

Attempts to intercept two more raids around mid-day failed miserably. Later in the afternoon four Spitfires, joined by Hurricanes from 242 and 185 Squadrons, were scrambled to engage some 40 Axis aircraft plotted approaching the island. Although the RAF fighters later reported damaging a number of enemy aircraft none were claimed to have been shot down. Unfortunately, however, 249 Squadron lost Spitfire AB343 to the guns of the 109s, the first of type to be claimed by a

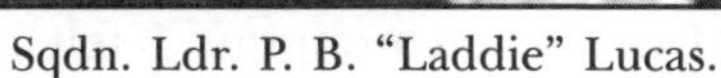

Sqdn. Ldr. P. B. "Laddie" Lucas.

Plt. Off. Peter Nash.

Luftwaffe fighter over Malta. 'Laddie' Lucas, who arrived in Malta in a Sunderland on 16 February, was that same day airborne on his first interception patrol in a Spitfire with 249 Squadron. He chased a 109, which he failed to hit. In his logbook he had this noted down:

> "Plagis gets one. Raoul damages another."

Flt. Lt. Heppell was credited with shooting down the first Bf109 over Malta in Spitfire, AB262.

Plt. Off. Peter Nash, who was also involved in that day's fighting, wrote down in his diary:

> "March 10 – Spits first day ops. I was number two to Heppell with Plagis and Leggo three and four. We scrambled about 10.30 am, got up to 21,000 feet and saw three 88's and some 109's about 4,000 feet below. A lovely pounce. Heppell got one. Plagis and I got a probable each. Leggo missed his, I think we shook them up a bit. Plagis did well to knock one off my tail. I was off this afternoon.

Murray shot down in flames. He bailed out but 109 gave him slipstream and collapsed his chute. He died in hospital. ACP tonight. I was lucky as NF cancelled. Met Sgt. W.L. 'Dusty' Miller. Fly. Off. Buchanan crash-landed on drome. Shrapnel piece in right leg. Plane badly shot up."

Metcalf continues noting down in his diary:

> March 11 – Spitfires in action again and shot down two Bf109s and a Ju88. Meanwhile Jerry's attacks had increased in ferocity, with the majority of raids concentrated on airfields day and night."

March 11 was the day in which Plt. Off. Brennan flew into combat from the island for the first time:

"Never before had I fired my guns at the enemy." he wrote. "My feelings were curious and mixed, as I suppose are those of all pilots who go into action for the first time. On the climb up I was extremely nervous and excited, but once the Hun was sighted all the nervousness and excitement left me. I was surprised to find myself cool and calm, my mind being occupied solely with the business of shooting him down and not getting shot down myself. When I first fired my guns I felt no personal animosity, no anger."

For the 14th, Lucas has this recorded:

> "Interception patrol. Damages a 109. Strikes on fuselage and tail. Raoul gets away from six. It was a busy day. Airborne escorting 'Maryland', and second interception patrol. Expended ammunition on 109. Possibly damaged. Third interception patrol. Attacked one 109, only to find three on my tail. Raoul has four on his."

"March 17 – Seven raids during the night. Ju88s bombed the camp at noon." Entered Metcalf in his diary. "All aircraft in action again and I saw one Spitfire hit the drink, but we should have a good score between us."

The Australian pilot, Brennan, that day scored his first victory, shortly after a scramble to intercept a formation of enemy aircraft. The Spitfires were vectored six miles east of Zonqor Point at an elevation of about 17,000 feet, where they shortly afterwards spotted the bomber formation, but there were too many 109s about. Pounced by some, in the confusion at the order to break up, Brennan became separated from the rest, but was soon afterwards joined by a squadron colleague.

"I felt better at having somebody with me, and started to climb with Junior right behind.

We were six miles east of Zonqor Point when, looking down, I saw six 88s, with their close fighter escort, silhouetted against the sunlit sea. I told Junior the enemy was at nine o'clock below us and we would go up sun to attack."

At that elevation the two Spitfires were engaged by two 109s and the Australian was again left to fend for himself when Junior's aircraft dived straight down due to a dislocated seat, which forced the latter forward on to the control column of the fighter. With one 109 acting as a decoy the other tried to maneuver astern of the lone Spitfire.

"I tried hard to think of all I had learned at the discussion in the mess but the paramount thought in my mind was; If I can shoot down one, or damage it, I'll be able to get home."

Brennan had just that one alternative, fight on. Had he tried to break away he would have been finished.

"I started turning with them. One was in front, the other behind. Round and round we went. Suddenly the one in front decided to go up sun. Luckily for me he was not quite certain where I was. As he straightened up I was 100 feet below and 200 yards behind him, dead astern. I pulled a bead on him at once, tracer from the other 109 whipping past my port wing as I did so. I could see my explosive cannon-shells and machine gun bullets bursting along the front 109's fuselage, behind his cockpit and on his pod wing-root. I gave him six seconds – a long burst. For a moment or two the 109 seemed to hang, then into it dived straight down. I had no time to watch it crash the sea, 2,0000 feet below. The second 109 was still firing, although his bullets were not hitting me. I glanced over my shoulder and saw that he was breaking away."

Brennan gave chase but could get no closer than 300yards, from where he fired a short burst of 303s by mistake, which made him think that he had ran out of cannon ammunition, break away and return to base.

Despite the arrival of these first few Spitfires, no immediate changes in the islands' fortunes were evident. However, although the

109's had Malta's weary defenders 'panting', the latter doggedly resisted the enemy's every attempt to defeat them during the ensuing months.

For the next three days Metcalf had this recorded in his diary:

> March 18 – Six night raids. Hal Far airfield caught a packet this morning. Luqa airfield at noon and Ta' Qali all afternoon. One Spitfire shot down, also five Hurricanes. Hurricane and Beaufighter burnt out and an 800-gallon bowser still burning, plus two more Spitfires unserviceable. Some guy says Jerry left Sicily; he has, for Malta!
>
> March 19 — Bowser, still burning after midnight. Four Ju88's on Ta' Qali; a Spitfire and another of the Beaufighters burnt out.
>
> March 20 — It is now 9.pm and I've just come through the worst blitz that's ever been in England, Germany or Malta, and all that on Ta' Qali. It is estimated that at least 250 aircraft of various makes took part and the 800 odd bombs that were dropped were made up of all shapes and sizes. I thought the end had come. Billets were blown up. Two more petrol bowsers on fire, Spitfires, Hurricanes, Beaufighters, Blenheims and the old 'Marylands' all wrecked and smoldering.

Auchinleck must have at this time given little thought about Malta's safety, but not the British Prime Minister and the Chiefs of Staff, who were in a far better position to assess the island's situation in relation to the North African campaign. In a letter dated 15 March Winston Churchill opened with:

> "Your appreciation of February 27 continues to cause deepest anxiety here, both to the Chiefs of Staff and Defense Committee. I therefore regret extremely your inability to come home for consultation. The delay you have in mind will endanger safety of Malta."

However, while the island's plight became desperate under the Luftwaffe's consistent attacks, British submarines and anti-shipping air strikes from Malta still took their toll of Axis convoys traversing the Mediterranean.

The enemy, determined to eliminate every visage of RAF resistance from the island, on 12 March bombed Ta' Qali airfield, inflicting damages

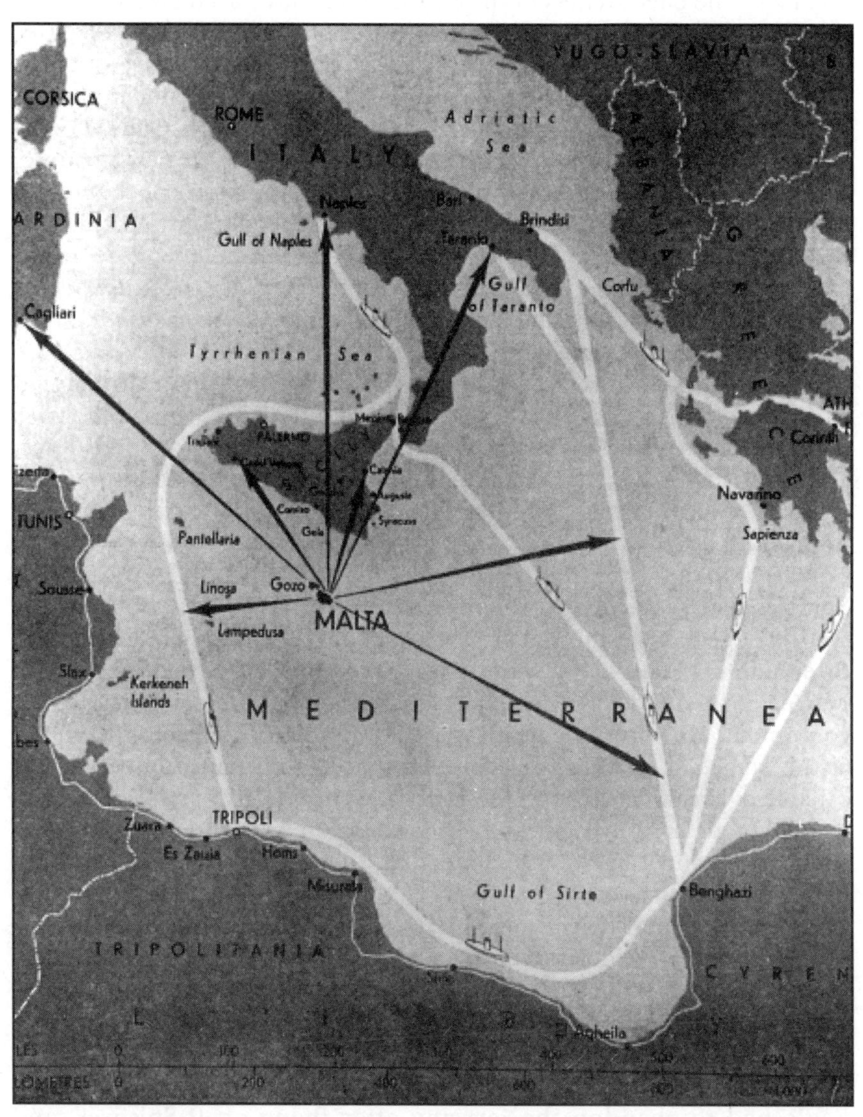

A map showing the diverse routes taken from Malta during the offensive against Rommel's North African supply lines in the two months leading up to Alamein.

to parked aircraft and buildings, and causing the death of a ground-crew member. The effectiveness of the Spitfire must have been taken seriously by the Luftwaffe. Two days later about ten of the fighters were able to be scrambled to intercept a plot traced orbiting around the coast of the island of Gozo. In the encounter a 109 was shot down. Later in the day the Luftwaffe, probably realizing that their attack on Ta' Qali two days before had been a failure, organized a stronger fighter force to counter the Spitfire threat. The RAF fighters scrambled to intercept them were involved into a running battle from which they came out miraculously unscathed. As frequent clashes took place between the Spitfires and the 109s, the Axis became gradually more unsettled by the unexpected appearance of this small, but stalwart, Spitfire force, especially when the odds were equally balanced.

On 17 March, the Axis launched the first of a chain of daily air raids that left the island exhausted by the intensity of this blitzkrieg during the ensuing days. The Spitfires were quickly whittled down, although they took their toll of enemy aircraft, and the Hurricanes were not expected to do half as much against such superior opposition.

In a span of ten days, between the 10th and 20th March, the Spitfires had succeeded in shooting down five 109's, two probably and two damaged, including hits on several Ju88's, while their losses were three fighters. This was a number that the Hurricanes had taken all of February to succeed in achieving, with a far greater loss in life and equipment. However, the garrison could not do without reinforcements at this stage. The Spitfire had proven that in sufficient numbers it was capable of breaking through the Luftwaffe superiority barrier. However, in spite of all its drawbacks, the Hurricane remained the mainstay upon which the island's air defense depended to keep the enemy at bay, until more Spitfires arrived.

During April with no Spitfires available anywhere in the Mediterranean, except for the remnants of what had been ferried to Malta during March, 15 Hurricanes, in two batches of nine and six respectively, were flown from the Middle East as reinforcements on April 6 and 19.

On 21 March, engaged in Operation code named 'Picket', HMS Eagle had to abandon the ferrying after flying off 9 Spitfires, and withdraw back to Gibraltar at full speed when only two of four navigational Blenheims failed to turn up from the 'Rock'.

Plt. Off. Peter Nash logged:

March 21 – Big blitz continues 70-80 bombers at a time knocking hell out of us. This afternoon Point de Vue Hotel, Rabat hit; killed the boys standing in the doorway – Jim Guerin, Fly. Off. John Booth, Plt. Off. Eddie 'Junior' Streets, Plt. Off. Bill Hollis Hallett, Flt. Lt. Cecil Baker and Flt. Lt. Arthur Waterfield, the information officer. I had just gone across to Mdina mess and missed it. Got there two minutes after it happened. Terrible sight, Flt. Lt. Robert 'Buck' McNair and Flt. Lt. Ronnie West badly shocked. Nine new Spits arrived.

The second phase of operation 'Picket', given the codename of 'Picket II', was executed on 29 March in which a flight of a further 7 Spitfires reached the island. After that there were no more deliveries until 20 April. Obviously, however, these few additional fighters were hardly expected to have the desired effect in the fighting. After the disastrous end of the convoy of 23 March the Chiefs of Staff had already decided that unless fighter aircraft reinforcements in greater numbers reached the island, no more ships were to be sacrificed in any attempt to get a convoy through to Malta.

Air Vice Marshall Lloyd had this written about that fateful 23rd March day in 1942:

"All that could be mustered were 14 Spitfires and 11 Hurricanes; even to achieve that figure I had been forced to restrict their use for about a week. The only occasion when all the fighters were not over them, when the ships were within range of Malta, was when they flew back to their base to be rearmed and refuelled, and pick up relief pilots. However, there were so many enemy aircraft flying about, compared to our few, that it seemed incredible that the pilots could dare to venture into a sky so full of peril. In fact they had to fight for their lives from the moment they left the ground until they were back again and safe in their pens in the dispersal areas."

Due to the Luftwaffe's numerical superiority Malta's situation was at this time desperate. So few were the RAF fighters that had they chosen to intercept the bombers they ran the risk of getting shot down by the swarms of escorting 109s. If they engaged the latter into battle the bombers would have a field day, which was frequently the case. Getting at both, had this been possible was also problematic to the RAF pilots, for fuel and ammunition would run short by the time they diverted their attention from enemy fighter to bomber, or vice-versa. The ammunition situation, which dragged on into the summer months, was further unbalanced by the intermittent arrival of more Spitfires, although RAF losses in combat were high. In the afternoon of 25 March, with the survivors Pampas, Talabot and Breconshire from Convoy MW10 anchored inside Malta's harbours, the Luftwaffe mounted a big raid. Some 50 or so bombers, between Ju87s and 88s, escorted by Me109s, were plotted approaching the island. Eight Hurricanes from 185 Squadron and six from 126 and 249 Squadrons were scrambled to intercept them.

A battle report by Plt. Off. McLeod, an American flying Spitfires with 126 Squadron describes part of his ordeal during that fateful afternoon. "Six Spitfires took off on interception" wrote McLeod.

> "While flying at 16,000 feet in vicinity of GH, several 109s were spotted below. We dived to attack; 109s were in line astern and turning left. I opened fire at about 200 yards, closing to 150, with three second burst. E/a suddenly did a violent down snap. At this time I was engaged by another 109, which opened fire on me from my right front quarter. I did a head-on attack on this e/a, finishing my ammo."

With this situation on his mind, particularly after receiving the news that HMS Eagle was to be laid up for repairs for at least a month, Winston Churchill turned to the United States for support. The British carrier 'Argus' was too small and very slow, while the lifts on HMS Victorious were too small for a Spitfire. Unless an alternative was found Malta would remain without fighter aircraft reinforcements until HMS Eagle was recommissioned. Meanwhile, with the island in this state, Rommel's needs would be shipped out to him from Sicily with very little opposition, if any.

"Air attacks on Malta are very heavy." The Prime Minister wrote in a letter to President Roosevelt, dated April 1.

> "There is now in Sicily about 400 German and 200 Italian fighters and bombers. Malta can only muster twenty or thirty serviceable fighters. We keep feeding Malta with Spitfires in packets of 16 loosed from 'Eagle' carrier from about 600 miles west of Malta."

Me109F – 1 April 1942. Force landed near to Paola almost intact.
The pilot was taken prisoner.

"This has worked a good many times quite well but 'Eagle' is now laid up for a month. Would you be willing to allow your carrier 'Wasp' to do one of the trips provided details are satisfactorily agreed between the naval staffs? With her broad lifts, capacity and length, we estimate that 'Wasp' could take fifty or more Spitfires. A powerful enough force to fight back the enemy, and possibly check his incessant onslaught on Malta."

Ju87s and Ju88s came in waves at intervals of no less than 15 minutes, frequently on raids lasting about an hour, three times a day, tactics that had by mid-April seriously exhausted Malta's fighter defence. The RAF fought for its very existence and that of the island's with the remnants of what were once squadrons, a handful of serviceable fighters, in which pilots knew that the odds against their returning from an engagement with the enemy were frightening. Ground crews toiled just as hard, servicing machines as best as they could from what was cannibalized from the wreckage of others, when

Repairs to bomb damaged airfields was a common, but a hazardous task.

such spares could be scrounged, while civilians and regimental soldiers laboured shoulder to shoulder to keep bombed airfields serviceable. The Spitfires that had been ferried to the island during March had all but disappeared. Consequently the proportion of pilots to aircraft was at this time of about three to one, and with no spares or replacements available, an increase to these figures was expected. Aircraft had, in a way, become more precious than aircrews. In an effort to minimize loss scientific fighting methods had to be adopted, although not all units were in favour of a change in tactics; indeed these new tactics failed to have the desired effect due to the superior number of escorting 109s.

Flt. Lt. Tim Johnston had this entered in his diary for March 31st:

> "Permission to scramble to intercept incoming plot forbidden due to size of the plot approaching the island."

More excerpts from Johnston's diary, spiced with combat experience, provides a moving narrative of what it was like flying a Spitfire into battle against odds which were frequently as high as ten to one at that stage in time.

April 1 – 249 bagged 10 Huns.

That was the date when Winston Churchill wrote to the President of the United States for the loan of the carrier 'Wasp', April Fools' Day, which must have left the enemy shaken by the stiff, unexpected, resistance put up by Malta's RAF defences.

The Axis High Command, now determined not simply to soften the opposition but to eliminate them, sent their aircraft from Sicily in a seemingly endless streams of Ju87s and 88s and swarms of escorting 109s, day after day bombing airfields and harbour installations.

Three Spitfires from 229 Squadron, from a batch ferried to the island via HMS Eagle three days earlier, were in mid-morning of 1 April scrambled on their first mission from Malta. However, although attacks were made on some of the Ju88s, none of these were in any way effective.

During the afternoon, with undiminished fury, the Luftwaffe organized several other air raids. By the end of the day instead of satisfied, the enemy was alarmed at the effective way its attacks were being repelled by fighters that were thought to have been neutralized. One of four Me109s engaged by six Spitfires of 249 Squadron round

A Ju88 flies over the Grand Harbour in April 1942, at the height of the Axis effort to neutralise Malta from the air.

about 13.00 hours was almost immediately shot down. Less than an hour later another four of 249's fighters were scrambled for interception purposes, followed by six Hurricanes of 185 Squadron. In this encounter even the latter claimed their share from the number of enemy aircraft destroyed or damaged. Later still, while Spitfires were expected to return from an interception mission, about 50 Ju87s were unleashed on HM Dockyard and Hal Far airfield. Two Hurricanes from 229 Squadron were immediately scrambled, their engines at maximum boost, to reach the elevation they were detailed to patrol at, 17,000 feet, from where they could provide cover for the returning Spitfires. Five more Hurricanes from 185 Squadron were shortly afterwards following the first two, but Spitfires were not released until 30 minutes later. Soon after they were airborne they were amongst the enemy bombers, shooting down three Ju87s and damaging some others, before returning back to base. The Hurricanes of 185 Squadron had, destroyed a Ju87, and damaged another. No229 Squadron had to content themselves with just probables.

Ray Hesselyn, a New Zealander, who with three others was on 1 April airborne on patrol, spotting a German Dornier Z4 flying at low level in the direction of the island, escorted by Bf109s, immediately dived down to attack. So eager was he to get to grips with the enemy that he missed one 109 on his first pass, but was soon afterwards chasing another, which he succeeded in shooting down into the sea. Then, while on his third sortie of the day, Hesselyn destroyed his second enemy aircraft, but the New Zealander was himself jumped by two 109s, from whom he succeeded to escape and was shortly afterwards safely back on Hal Far airfield.

April 2 – 4 Spitfires and 2 Hurricanes scrambled. Big raid reported.

This entry in Johnston's diary is not surprising, not after the hot reception the enemy received the day before. Towards mid-morning scores of Ju87s and 88s arrived, escorted by formations of Bf109s to protect them from patrolling RAF fighters. Although heavily outnumbered, every serviceable Spitfire and Hurricane was scrambled to intercept the enemy formations.

Ground crews, frequently by improvised methods, seemed to work miracles. It was amazingly beyond comprehension how they managed to keep these fighters going, but this they did, and pilots, in spite of the risks involved and the frightening odds against which they flew, took to the air, several times in one day.

Four of 126 Squadron's Spitfires were in the morning scrambled to intercept the enemy, followed by two Hurricanes, one each from 185 and

229 Squadrons. Flt. Lt. Tim Johnston, who was to lead the Spitfires, was unavoidably delayed when his aircraft failed to start and had to move over to another fighter. No sooner had he caught up with the other three Spitfires when Bf109s came at them with a vengeance, a terrifying experience about which Johnston himself, who survived the war, wrote in his book "Tattered Battlements".

> "... suddenly there was a 109 diving in on my port quarter, quite close and already firing. I wrenched the aircraft round as tight as it would go, kicked on full bottom rudder, called to my three companions to break up. Jimmy who was next to me, already had his nose well down, and seemed to have seen the danger, but the other two ... as I watched one of them became suddenly enveloped in smoke and flames, seemed to stall, and fell away into a spin. Quickly glanced over my left shoulder and saw what looked like ten or twelve 109s above, some diving on us, others apparently waiting their turn. It was a sinister sight. Impressions of the next few minutes are jumbled and blurred; can remember being attacked by a number of 109s, some of which fired and some didn't; remember noticing one which was trying to creep up on me from underneath, turning into him head-on and seeing him flash past ... ."
>
> "I did a half-roll and such fierce airelon turns that I was partially blacked out: Pulled out and took careful look all around, alone, thank goodness; realized then for the first time how terribly tired I was ...".

Shortly after this encounter Johnston nearly exhausted his ammunition while attacking a Ju88, but the intervention of a 109 forced him to head for cloud cover.

Back at base Johnston saw that his Spitfire had taken considerable punishment from the 109s, and frankly admitted:

> "When we'd been getting away with it we'd found the odds against us rather exhilarating, but after suffering our losses the prospect had evidently become depressing."

The 109s shot down two of Johnston's colleagues that day. One was picked up from the sea, but a Canadian was never found.

The next day, 3 April, Churchill received Roosevelt's reply regarding the loan of the USS carrier 'Wasp' to ferry Spitfires to Malta:

"Admiral King will advice Admiral Pound through Ghormly that 'Wasp' is at disposal as you request."

At this time the fighter aircraft situation on the island was in so bad a state on the island that unless these were grounded for a period of a few days no sort of definite improvement to their serviceability would ever be achieved. This decision, which resulted in giving the enemy two field days, however, would not serve to equalize the odds between the opposing fighters. Worse still was the signal received by Air Headquarters that the scores of enemy bombers coming over every day were to be the RAF fighters' primary objective, with pilots detailed to avoid all contact with the escorting 109s. This method of interception could not possibly be effective with so many patrolling 109s, to whom the RAF pilots were to be obviously sacrificed, which proved to be the case during the next few days. So badly were the RAF fighters whittled down, that the odds between them and the 109s were further increased.

Extensive damages were on 6 April inflicted inside Grand Harbour and on airfields, particularly at Luqa where five Hurricanes and two Spitfires were written-off on the ground while, albeit slightly, others were damaged on Hal Far airfield. As for Ta' Qali, L.A.C. Metcalf has this noted down in his diary related to Easter Monday:

"This Easter has been one that I'll remember. From dawn to dusk wave after wave of Ju88s, 87s and other gash kites to make weight have bombed and better bombed … ."

"What a Hellhole! And still they came, in all their might. God in heaven alone knows what's going to happen next and where this is all going to end. It's a pity we haven't some fighter protection, but we have done wonderful work and each pilot deserves a V.C. at least. To send the last few up alone would be murder in the first degree."

Johnston continues to record in his logbook:

"April 7 – No aircraft serviceable. Only 4 Spitfires and 2 Hurricanes in hand. Too, few.

April 8 – 4 Spitfires and some Hurricanes airborne to meet afternoon wave."

The garrisons' RAF defences must have had no intention of

intercepting any of the Luftwaffe's well-organized morning raids for they had no aircraft airborne at any time. But every serviceable Spitfire and Hurricane on the island was in the afternoon scrambled to do battle. This they did with great gallantry, shooting down no less than five enemy aircraft and damaging several others, all for the loss of one single Spitfire that, regretfully, fell victim to friendly ground fire. Miraculously, however, the pilot was blown clear in the explosion, and parachuted down to safety.

April 9 – "Nothing serviceable to fly." Notes down Johnston.

Contrary to this entry, however, 10 Hurricanes from 185 Squadron, joined by two of 229 Squadron's Spitfires, were scrambled to intercept nearly 100 enemy aircraft. Reports of damages to a number of Ju88s came in. However, as expected, when the odds were this size against them the majority of the Hurricanes returned with some sort of battle damage while one of the Spitfires was shot down in the sea.

April 10 – 3 raids. 4 Spitfires and 12 Hurricanes airborne to intercept enemy on last raid. Big dogfight on."

Two reports from separate pilots involved in this encounter give a clear enough account of what coming to grips with the enemy in air combat was like over Malta at this time. Sgt. Tony Boyd recorded in his diary:

> "... terrific odds. We couldn't do much about the bombers. Three Hurricanes lost, remainder shot up, but all pilots safe. Sgt. Horricks got a 109. The best flamer I've ever seen yet."

Nash, the other pilot, wrote:

> "My Ju87 gave off a lot of black smoke when I attacked from just under his tail. Then bounced by six 109s. Got strikes on wings and rear cockpit from one. Not sorry to get down again today."

Johnston's logbook entry for 11/12 April shows:

> "No aircraft but usual raids."

However, most interesting of his entries were those recorded for 15 April.

> "Rumours around that U.S. Carriers ferrying 100+ Spitfires to

Malta. ... rumours amongst the public, albeit exaggerated, and somewhat distorted, had days before got the news of the carriers nationality, when no pilots or aircrews knew anything about this highly complicated operation."

Considering the high security measures taken to keep this complex Spitfire operation a secret how, or from where, had this news filtered from amongst the public in Malta remains a mystery to this day. According to Flt. Lt. Tim Johnston when the Spitfires arrived on the island none of them could imagine were they had come from.

To ensure that the carrier would sail on schedule in this operation, minor snags found on aircraft prior to their embarkation in USS Wasp were bypassed as these were to be rectified at sea by the maintenance crews sailing with the carrier for the purpose. Unfortunately, however, for obscure reasons, these were ultimately neglected, at the expence of the Malta RAF pilots.

So rushed was the embarkation process that of the 54 Spitfires delivered to Renfrew only 50 were on board the 'Wasp' when, on 14 April, the carrier weighed anchor and sailed en route to its destination.

Spitfires on board USS Wasp during its first ferry operation to Malta, 1942.

Contrary to previous procedures, which were to bring together a number of pilots, of whom few may have ever met before, together into one group and given a designation, these consisted of two whole squadrons, No. 601 and No. 603.

"A system that had to prove favourable as it brought with it a strong number of experienced people." Approved Flt. Lt. Johnston.

'Laddie' Lucas, however, was far less discreet. He stressed that it was an act of criminal negligence for every level of authority responsible in Fighter Command to have fighter pilots with little, if any, combat experience posted to a place like Malta simply to get rid of an officer or NCO for one reason or another. It was at this time being estimated that the existence of these unfortunates seldom lasted more than two weeks. For those in possession of combat experience the chances of surviving an operational tour on the island were not that bleak, but fate, and Lady Luck, had both to bestow their favours, as Johnston wrote:

> "On that fateful April 20 day I missed lunch in my eagerness to get to Luqa where the Spitfires of 601 Squadron had been diverted to."

(Those of 603 had landed at Ta' Qali.)

These were all Mk.Vcs, the first of type armed with four cannons to be sent to the Mediterranean.

"Four cannons certainly blow hell out of an airplane!" Commented Plt. Off. McKay of 185 Squadron after shooting down a Ju88 in one of the Spitfires on 10 May.

> "... They were dispersed all over the aerodrome, but no one seemed to know which were the serviceable ones and which were not. Confusion reigned everywhere as pilots rushed about searching for something to fly."

Johnston later swore that he had never seen so many RAF fighters scrambled at any one time to intercept the enemy:

> "No sooner were we off the ground ..." He recorded. "... when I found out that the R/T on my plane was unserviceable. Sometime later my windshield began to oil up."

The Spitfire aircrews of 601 and 603 Sqdns during 'Wasp's historical ferry operation "Calendar" 20/4/42.

Johston had several encounters with the enemy that particular day. He only escaped death by a hair's breadth when, hit by a friendly anti-aircraft shell, he just managed to untangle himself out of his Spitfire cockpit and bail out to safety less than 200 feet off the ground before his plane dived into the ground.

Two other Spitfires went missing that same day and two survivors reported that both of their aircraft had developed technical defects, R/T failures, faulty oil pressure gauges and jammed cannons.

These excerpts from Johnston's and Nash's diaries, albeit brief, do much to cover the final days of April as Malta's defenders refused to admit defeat and fought on regardless of the terrible odds:

> Johnston: April 21 – Dummy attack withdraws all serviceable Spits at 4.30pm. At 5.20 real raid began and at about 6, while the Spits were about to land, 109s flew in circuit strafing.
>
> Nash: April 22 – Weather cloudy but attacks continue. By late evening, of the 50 Spitfires that were ferried to the island on Monday, only 6 serviceable ones remained.
>
> In the afternoon, Plt. Off. Frank Jemmett was killed. Things can't possibly keep on going like this. Everyone is fed up with the present situation. I think it is difficult to keep a fighter aircraft force on this island.
>
> Plt. Off. Olwer 'Sonny' Ormrod DFC, who flies Hurricanes with 185 Squadron, was yesterday shot down and killed. What's the answer to all this? Nobody knows.
>
> Johnston: April 23 – 2 Spits – 126 Squadron and 2 Hurries – 185 Squadron took off to intercept 80+.
>
> Nash: April 24 – Today bombing began by four consecutive attacks on Ta' Qali. This was followed by three or four others spread out over Ta' Qali, Luqa and the Grand Harbour. Johnston shot down a Ju88. In the afternoon we had 7 Spitfires and 4 Hurricanes airborne. We were involved in some hard fighting over Luqa until we found the opportunity to attack a number of Ju87s. Flt. Lt. P.B. 'Laddie' Lucas was forced to crash land near to Luqa. He was not hurt. So stiff is the fighting here that at present pilots like myself are considered old timers on the island and have been briefed to lead new arrivals.
>
> Four 109s strafed Ta' Qali half an hour after the last attack. One that was hit fell a short distance away from where we eat. A little bit

too close. I was airborne three times today.

Johnston: April 26 – Hurricane jumped by 109s shot down. Daddo-Langlois of 249 Squadron attacked a Bf109 head-on. The two aircraft met wing against wing. Me109's wing was sliced clean through. Spitfire was flown home and landed.

April 28 – 4 Spits and 4 Hurries – 185 Squadron, scrambled at 07.40. – 2 other Spits flew airfield's defence. Attack Ju87s on raid. As usual Bf109s interfere.

April 29 / May 3 – A decrease in air raids noted. On the 29 Italian Br.20s were seen at about 22,000 feet. High level bombing of Luqa. Next time over escorted by Italian and Luftwaffe fighters. Some on third attack. No RAF aircraft airborne, PRU Spitfire noted decrease in Luftwaffe aircraft in Sicily. Hun still busy over Malta though.

'When the war broke out, and Italy had to strengthen her position in the Mediterranean and in Africa, she should before any other action in Africa,' wrote Adolf Galland, a German Ju87 pilot, in his book 'The First and the Last', "… have made an effort to take Malta."

The need to take Malta was repeatedly impressed upon Mussolini by the Germans, but he could not make up his mind to do so. "So we tried to put Malta out of action from the air."

"With the threat of an invasion hovering over our heads …" wrote 'Laddie' Lucas in later years "… and no place anyone can escape to, with the nearest British outpost, Gibraltar, 800 miles away, leave for us was all but non-existent, except for the occasional free day. This was at the peak of Luftwaffe attacks on Malta when the odds against us pilots were no less than ten to one, daily combating the Elite of Kesselring's might."

"A combination of straight talking young men from Britain, Canada, Australia, New Zealand, America, Scotland, South Africa as well as Rhodesia. They all grumbled about the lousy existence on the island be it food, the inhabitants, foul smells, even the flies, everything that is, particularly lack of aircraft, except the job they were sent out to the island to do."

"The island was then at its worst critical phase for everything was in great demand, food, fuel and ammunition, but particularly fighter aircraft for their shortage was what was affecting the flow of the former."

Meanwhile, according to Kesselring, at that stage in the battle for North Africa, upon the capture of Malta depended the Axis guaranteed passage of supply convoys to Rommel's Africa Korps.

(The invasion of Malta by the enemy, which was planned to be launched in the summer of 1942, had finally to be abandoned. Kesselring, in his book 'The War in the Mediterranean', called this decision as: "... Strategically the one fatal blunder ... When this happened, the subsequent course of events was almost inevitable.")

In later years, in his encyclopaedia 'History of the Second World War', Churchill had this written down:

> "In March and April (1942) all the heat was turned on Malta and remorseless air attacks by day and night wore the island down and pressed it to the last gasp

Then this extract was taken from a Draft Narrative (Malta) written by the Air Historical Branch (RAF):

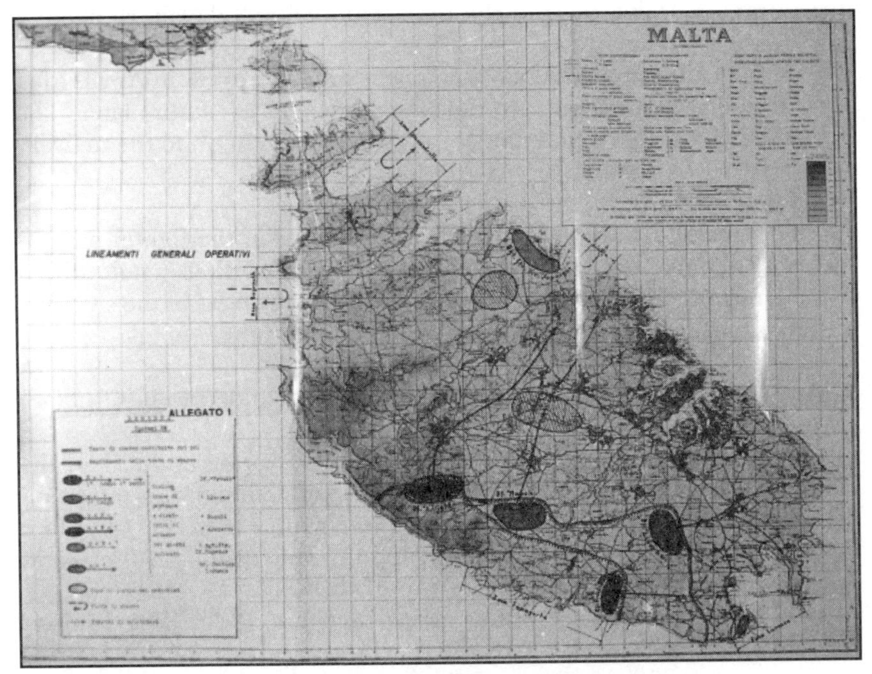

German 1942 invasion plan map of Malta.

> "After the enemy had called off the Spring 'blitz' in April 1942, and Rommel became deeply committed to his offensive (in Libya), the existence of Malta as an air and naval base was never seriously threatened by concentrated air attacks."

The enemy seemed to have been expecting the arrival of the 47 Spitfires ferried via 'Wasp' for he was bombing them within minutes of their landing. Then during the next few days those which had escaped getting destroyed on the ground were found to have become unserviceable, leaving the island as defenceless as it had previously been.

Partly responsible for this disastrous waste, however, was the poor condition in which the fighters had arrived. Defective guns caused by clogged dirt in their mechanism, and lack of synchronization as well as faulty radios. To an already grave situation the island suffered from a chronic shortage of all types of aircraft spares and skilled maintenance crews. More than 40 fighters were lost, while twice that number needed from minor to extensive repairs.

The late Lesley Davies, an ex-RAF ground-crew member who spent three years in Malta, most of the time stationed at Ta' Qali, recalled:

> "I cannot quite recall how many Spitfires came in April. All I can tell is that there were not many of them left hours later. The enemy hit us hard that day. He must have caught on to the delivery early."

Sir Winston Churchill, gravely concerned about the fighter aircraft situation in Malta, particularly after the mishap of April 20, again turned to the United States for further aid. To give the graveness of the situation on the island greater emphasis he wrote, among other things:

> "Without this aid I fear Malta will be pounded to bits."

Meanwhile in Malta A.V.M. Lloyd was of the opinion that had the maintenance crews on board Wasp attended to the numerous defects on the new Spitfires as they were supposed to en route, the effort put into Operation 'Calendar' might have turned out differently on the island during the ensuing days of April.

To avoid a recurrence of this act of negligence, Wg. Cdr. 'Jumbo.' Gracie was dispatched to UK by the AOC with instructions to supervise the testing of the fighters before delivery. Reprimanded about the diverse snags encountered on the first batch of Spitfires delivered, each fighter in this second operation was fully tested on arrival at Renfrew in Glasgow. Immediately each Spitfire landed on this small grass airfield, and propellors stopped turning, an inspection followed while ferry pilots were still in their cockpits.

There was no other practical way by which the British could have ferried so large a number of Spitfires in one single operation, in which only one carrier was involved, except by US Wasp, which was capable of accommodating 48 of the fighters. Operation 'Calendar', due to human negligence, may have to some extent been a failure, however, the lesson learned from it served to make 'Bowery', in which two aircraft carriers were involved, that much more effective.

The British carrier 'Eagle', that had just been recommissioned, took part in this operation by ferrying 17 additional Spitfires from Gibraltar while 'Wasp' flew off 47. This large consignment of Spitfires, of which 60 arrived in Malta, succeeded in arresting the enemy from putting the island into a state from where it would have offered little resistance once the planned summer invasion was launched.

During this period, with the Luftwaffe set on hammering the island into submission, fuel stocks were being consumed at an

Fuel shortage was further affected by lack of proper distribution bowsers.

alarming rate. Furthermore, due to the decision to have 'Wasp's' second Spitfire delivery turned around and prepared for immediate flying, tinned fuel, which had locally been discarded for better means of distribution, was again in demand. These were needed to be stored in pens where each arriving Spitfire could have its own supply ready. The result of so many aircraft operating from the island was that, by June, aviation fuel stocks were severely low. The first week during which local aircraft flew to provide an incoming convoy with an air cover, to safeguard the few surviving ships to reach the Grand Harbour, no less than 500 tons of fuel were used. Ironically it was later discovered that this was the same quantity of fuel with which the ships had won through.

One of the means aimed at conserving fuel on airfields was the mule driven cart.

Provided that the Spitfires on this delivery arrived in an acceptable serviceable condition, and in broad daylight, it was estimated that these could be back in the air within minutes after landing. To achieve this it was planned to place five men in each pen with a pilot experienced in flying over Malta. The latter's duty would be to first ensure that each individual knew what was required of him, then climb into the cockpit, to replace the ferry pilot, and remain at immediate readiness for take off.

Petrol, kept in five-gallon tins, was protected with sandbags outside each pen. Time was too short to use bowsers, even had there been enough available. Each pen was provided with all that was to re-arm, re-fuel and service the expected Spitfires. The under belly long-range fuel tanks were to pose no problem as these were to be jettisonable but various parts would need testing. Should any of these be found defective three special tradesmen were allocated to each group of five pens to replace them.

To ensure the minimum of delay between the landing of each Spitfire and its arrival in its allotted pen individual representatives had also been provided. Each was given a pen number which, when shouted by the aerodrome control officer, it was his duty was to run up to the taxing fighter, jump up on to its wing beside the pilot and give him directions. Once the engine was stopped the men would take hold of the aircraft and push it into the pen until its tail came against the rear wall, after which they were to work as fast as they could.

Army despatch-riders and Signalmen working together with the RAF, maintain communication between dispersal pens.

Army co-operation during this turn about exercise on 9 May 1942.

Everything was ready, down to the nearest detail.

On 8 May there were some raids during which Ju87s and 88s bombed out Luqa. The Wellingtons' dispersal was their objective.

The Italian Cants dropped their bombs right down the middle of the runway. Most unfortunately of all were the hits to a small reservoir on the aerodrome's perimeter, flooding that part of the aerodrome, and causing further damage.

Surprisingly, despite a crystal clear night, there were no sign of a single enemy intruder.

Re-enforcement traffic was the arrival of some Hudsons from UK and a solitary 'Lodestar' loaded with vital spares from the Middle East. Unloaded and refuelled these aircraft were duly returning to their dispatch points.

Suddenly all was ominously quiet ... the calm before the storm.

So great was the concern gripping those who were expecting the arrival of so large a number of Spitfires that that morning's first alert after 0300 hrs hardly registered on their minds.

At 10.30am Sqdn. Ldr. Stan Grant, who was sent to Gibraltar to lead in this ferry re-enforcement, dived out of the sky over Ta' Qali with the first sixteen of the expected sixty Spitfires.

One of the new arrivals in this group, Flg. Off. Richard Mitchell,

> "Took off from Wasp at 0645 hrs. Landed at Ta' Qali at 1030 hrs. The navigation leader flew too fast and got his navigation all to hell, so I left them 40 miles west of Bizerta, five miles off the African coast, and set course for Malta, avoiding Pantelleria and Bizerta owing to fighters and flak being there. Jettisoned the long-range tank 20 miles west of Bizerta with 20 gallons to spare in main tank. On landing at Ta' Qali, I immediately removed my kit, and the machine was re-armed and refuelled. I landed during a raid and four 109s tried to shoot me up. Soon after landing the airfield was bombed but without much damage being done."

Some of these fighters were ready for combat in four minutes, others did not take longer than seven.

The enemy was bound to follow the arrival of this re-enforcement and sometime after 11 o'clock another alert was sounded. Everyone expected the Luftwaffe to catch the Spitfires at the re-fuelling stage, before they were ready for combat. This was positively not, due to the enemy's lack of trying, but because of a mixed batch of fifteen RAF fighters between Hurricanes and Spitfires which had been scrambled to protect the new arrivals.

Plt. Off. Broad, finding himself in Spitfire BR294, was with this group. He flew in this particular fighter during two of the most decisive days in the air battle for Malta, which he had recorded in his flying logbook:

> May 9
>
> 11.45am. – Scramble – Cover to Spits landing on Ta' Qali. Ron Noble got shot up and crash-landed. Plt. Off. Milburn – killed.
>
> 12.10pm. – Sgt. Tweedale – killed. Ta' Qali to Hal Far.
>
> 12.50pm. – Scramble – Intercepted Ju87s coming out of dive on Luqa. One Ju87 probably destroyed and one Ju87 damaged.
>
> (Day's score – 27 Destroyed or Damaged.)

Half the Spitfire delivery was roaring off the airfields in record time although Axis fighters were still arriving at timed intervals.

The first eleven of the new Spitfires, all flown by 249 Sqdn. pilots and led by Sqdn. Ldr. Stan Grant, took off from Ta' Qali at 1055 hrs.

Plt. Off. Nash who was with these recorded:

> "I was leading D'Arcy, (Milburn), Almos and Linton. Sent to Hal Far to deal with 109 trouble. I got one and a probable. Milburn killed. He spun in near Safi, also Flt. Lt. John Buckstone. Second scramble for 25+ raid on Ta' Qali. Scrambled late but managed to damage 109 with one cannon. Dogfight ensued.
>
> Scrambled in afternoon for recce, no good. Stuck around at 27,000 feet for big raid. Got stuck in 87s and got probable. Battle definitely on but fighters only accounted for seven today. More, tomorrow. New E/A casualty assessment comes into force."

Meanwhile, twenty-eight more Spitfires were still airborne, either flying around the aerodromes or approaching the island just as anti-aircraft bursts pointed out the approach of another large batch of German fighters at an elevation of some 12,000 feet.

This placed the incoming Spitfires at greater risk due to the larger number of enemy aircraft about, ready to attempt catching them as they came in to land.

The enemy, however, reserved that mid-day raid for Hal Far and blundered by failing to immediately mount another but waited until after 1.30pm, by which time local RAF defences were in a strong position and improving as time went on.

Another alert was sounded at about 3 o'clock but this, like the previous one, consisted of about a score fighters.

These tactics alarmed the AOC and a large number of Spitfires were ordered to remain at alert inside dispersal. This circus of some twenty Me109s circling the island was suspected to be nothing else but a trap to involve the RAF fighters into a chase, to be later caught on the ground re-fuelling by a massed bomber raid.

At the first signs of enemy bomber movements over Sicily 58 Spitfires took off. This was some time before 5 o'clock and Ta' Qali was the Luftwaffe's objective.

The authorities considered 10 May as important a day as the 9th. The 'Welshman', a fast minelayer, having made the run from Gibraltar alone and unescorted was due to steam inside Grand Harbour at 0600. The cargo she had on board, consisting of powdered milk, canned meat, dehydrated food-stuffs, ammunition, Spitfire spares, etc, was undoubtedly as precious as the Spitfires.

Enemy attacks on the valiant vessel were certain however, despite the two score enemy fighters that came into view shortly before six o'clock, the Welshman arrived inside the Grand Harbour dead on time.

However, enemy movements and activities in the region were not only visual. At times like this, Lascaris War Rooms was one big hive of human activity, and 10 May was a particularly busy one. As instructions reached the Operations Room from the Filter Room plotters moved like animated robots at every word uttered by the controller. That amount of traffic shuffling around on the plotting table down inside the underground caves on that fateful May day morning had never before been parallelled, and perhaps neither were they at a later date, with the exception perhaps of those plotted during the invasion of Sicily.

The early morning enemy fighters kept their height, flying over open waters. Then sometime round 0830 their number was nearly doubled but the RAF fighters, familiar with these tactics, were not drawn into giving chase.

Lascaris War Rooms, wartime air traffic control room.

Signs of a bomber gathering over Sicily came through sometime round ten in the morning and shortly afterwards more than fifty enemy fighters were circuiting over the island.

Behind them followed formations of Ju87s and Ju88s that came straight down at the Welshman, which was enveloped in huge clouds of smoke screen, brought along in canisters with the minelayer's freight. So smoke screen both appeared, and was operated, in Malta for the first time on the same date. This heavy pall of white smoke over the Welshman must have blinded the enemy bombers for they missed the minelayer, although the large number of Spitfires flashing amongst them must have increased their nervous confusion.

Plt. Off. Broad was scrambled three times in the afternoon, logging these notes in his logbook:

> May10
>
> 13.15 pm. Scramble – Patrol over Grand Harbour – no interceptions.
>
> Scramble – Intercepted Ju87s and Ju88s coming out of dive on Grand Harbour.
>
> 1 Ju88 destroyed. Fired on Ju87 – saw no results.
>
> Scramble – Did not intercept bombers. Had dogfight with six Me109 alone. After a time it got too hot so I got out of it. Later chased two 109s off Grand Harbour. Damaged one of them.

Finding a suitable target was initially difficult for Plt. Off. Johnny Plagis, who was involved in the free for all, as he left recorded:

> "Flew seven miles out to sea to find Ju87 which didn't have a Spit on its tail."

Peter Nash was also having 'fun':

> "Terrific party over Grand Harbour. All the87s missed the target. Everyone got something. The Stukas stuck! Starboard wing disappeared into smoke screen at 200 feet!"

During the ensuing days the enemy was determined to wipe out the RAF's fighter aircraft defences on Malta, who were just as determined to keep up to their gallant effort to either tip the scales of this air war in their favour or die trying.

Flg. Off. Peter Nash have this daily 'bird's eye view' anecdotes of his next three consecutive days flying recorded in his diary:

> May 11 – On this morning. Plagis, Brennan and two new boys tried to hop over to Sicily this morning about 9 o'clock. Intercepted. Plagis did head on with Macchi 202 at sea level and frightened him into sea without firing. Dogfight ensued. Macchis very good, maneuverable. Brennan's engine running weak. Nearly bailed out when engine cut out 15 miles out. He made it OK. Scrambled later for 15+ 88s and 40+ 109s. Only four 88s came in and bombed Hal Far. Flt. Sgt. John Williams got 1 probable. I got a 109 over Grand Harbour when White was pounced. Brennan also closed out and got him. Off. this afternoon.
>
> May 12 – Afternoon duty. Scrambled as Eytie bombs fell on Ta' Qali. Rudder has jammed very awkwardly, could not get position for a pounce. Chased a few 109s. Williams damaged 88. Plt. Off. Mike Graves bailed out, OK. Sgt. Charles Graymark bailed, shot at in dinghy and killed. Woody broadcast – 'no mercy' – order to Sicily this evening. Lee again shot up in port wing.
>
> May 13 – on this morning. No scramble until two minutes after Grant's boys had taken over. They took off with 109s at 400 feet over circuit. Had a hell of a fight up to 6,000. Hesselyn got two 109s one of which was confirmed by Ron West. Linton attacked formation of Stukas but was himself shot up by an 87 that attacked with front guns. Williams also shot up. Reccos, later – not much doing.

The next day Nash and Plagis were both sent for a 48hr rest to St Paul's Bay.

To assist in leading ferry flights to Malta in operation 'L. B', due to be launched off the carriers 'Eagle' with 'Argus' in attendance for escort duties, Flt. Lt. 'Laddie' Lucas and Flg. Off. Daddo-Lanlois were sent to Gibraltar in a 24 Squadron 'Lodestar'.

When they eventually returned to the island at the head of the new Spitfire consignment on 18 May, they were flying in BR115 and BR117 respectively.

Plt. Off. Jerrold Smith, who was ferried off HMS Eagle in this same operation, reached Malta in Spitfire BR126/3-X, the same aircraft in which he was supposed to have reached the island on 9 May off the USS Wasp in operation 'Bowery'; but … .

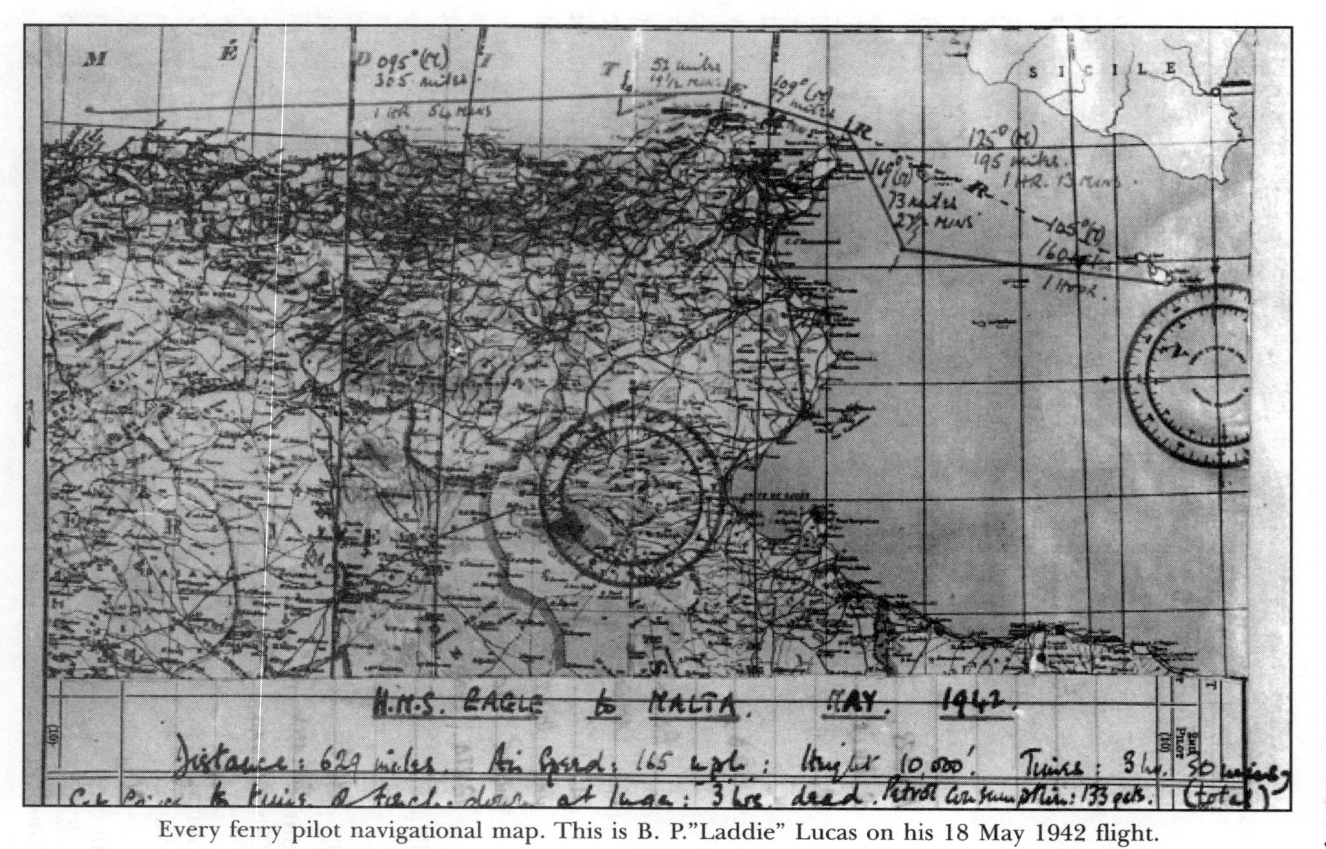

Every ferry pilot navigational map. This is B. P."Laddie" Lucas on his 18 May 1942 flight.

INFORMATION CARD

PILOTS NAME F/LT. LUCAS.

AIRCRAFT NUMBER AND LETTER B.R. 115.

ORDER OF TAKEOFF 2ND GROUP.

TAKEOFF

- As normal except:-
(a) Throttle fully open.
(b) Tail trim in central position.

AIRBORNE

Wireless -Switch on to receive on Button (B)
Undercarriage -Retract as soon as possible
Climb -Straight ahead up to 400 feet. Then reduce revs. to 2400 at +2 lbs.Boost at 170 M.P.H.
Trim -Close hood, trim for hands and feet off, then climb to rendezvous height.
Petrol -At 2000 feet switch on overload tanks and then switch off main tanks.

FORMATION

-Join up as soon as possible in predetermined positions. WIDE FORMATION.

CRUISING

Revs and petrol -Once in formation reduce to ~~2050~~ 2000. revs. Adjust throttle to get 165 M.P.H. at 10000 height. Fly on overload tank until it runs dry. Then switch on main tanks and switch off overload tank.
Note -Jettison overload tank if necessary when EMPTY -Gives extra 50 miles endurance.
Compass -Check on deviation card. Swung very recently. Also coast line.
Wireless V.H.F. -Maintain strict R/T silence after leaving carrier. Only transmit in emergency. Following are buttons and call signs.

AIRCRAFT CALLSIGN BALSAM. RED. ONE.
BUTTON "A" GONDAR.
BUTTON "B" PITRY.
BUTTON "C" GONDAR.
BUTTON "D" Fixer Wavelength

Note -For HOMING press Button B. and call PITRY
Note -Take normal air/sea rescue drill if pilot has to abandon aircraft near base. BUTTON "B".
I.F.F. -On at E.T.A. minus 30 minutes (approximately 90 miles from destination).

Tracks

Leg	Track(Mag.)	Distance	Time
1st.	095.	305.	1-04.
2nd.	095.	52.	19½.
3rd.	109.	44.	29.
4th.	169.	73.	27½.
Last Leg — 5th.	105.	160.	1 42.

Carrier Call Sign DONGA. !!! 667 29

If separated or lost -On last leg head North. Turn East on reaching land (Sicily) and follow coast to easternmost point, then set compass to 222 degrees (M) for destination. Don't Flap or Worry. 2 9

Another ferry pilot's necessity is an Information Card. ("Laddie" Lucas).

(A Canadian, Jerrold Smith's active duty from the island was tragically cut short on 10 August 1942. On that date he was reported missing over the sea somewhere halfway between Malta and Sicily and was never seen again. However, the dog-eared pages of his pocket-sized diary, in which he recorded his personal experiences, will forever remain as a tribute to his memory. – The Author.)

Drawn directly from Smith's own diary, the following is his personal entries as the carrier he was on 'Wasp', approached the Mediterranean:

> "On May 6, as we approached Gibraltar, where we were supposed to join HMS Eagle, the ship failed to turn up at rendezvous.
>
> "There was flying again today and enemy plane reported in vicinity, but not sighted.
>
> "The next day aircraft operated from 'Wasp' most of the time. About midnight we passed through the Straights of Gibraltar on our own, but later several destroyers and 'Renown' joined us.
>
> "We steamed through the Mediterranean all day long on May 8th, with 'Eagle' now in our wake."

(It was during the night, just off Europa Point, when HMS Eagle, on which were a further seventeen Spitfires, embarked at Gibraltar, joined up with 'Wasp' and the rest of Force 'W'.)

> " 'Renown' led the way, but fear of enemy submarines made us all glad that we will be off the ship soon.
>
> "During the night the aircraft were all ran up, and jettisonable tanks tested.

When the carriers reached the maximum range from where the Spitfires were to be launched, Wildcats (F4F-4s) of 'Wasps' own VF-71 commenced taking off at 06.30 hrs. Meanwhile the Spitfires were being warmed up in the hangar decks. Finally, with 'Wasp's own F4Fs providing the task force with air cover, each Spitfire was brought up by elevator to the carrier's cleared flight deck in seconds, engine running.

With the take off flag fluttering wildly, fighters took-off immediately the elevator platform drew level with the flight deck. The first Spitfire, with Sgt. Plt. Herrington at the controls, roared down the deck at 06.43 hours.

Sgt. Plt. Eric Mahar, an Australian, who was on the same ferrying trip as Smith, expressed his own feelings about this experience:

"It was disconcerting to discover that we would be flying the Spitfires off the carrier, as none of us had ever attempted this before. It had a profound effect on most of us.

"We took off to-day, May 9th, some 580 miles from Malta." Continued Plt. Off. Smith

"The first Spit went off into the sea, off the ship's end. 'Wasp' steamed right over poor Herrington, breaking his aircraft in two.

"I took off and soon found out that my wing tanks were unserviceable. After this I had to remain airborne till all the others had taken off before I could land back on 'Wasp'.

E. Mahar in later years recalled these same two incidents:

"One pilot failed to select fine pitch in his airscrew and he and the plane dropped into the sea and disappeared. Another could not get his long-range tank to work. He did something the 'Wasp's crew had never before witnessed."

No Spitfire had ever landed on a carrier before, and with no arrestor hook available it was extremely risky, but Plt. Off. Smith did it, "... with only feet to spare from the ship's forward end." Wrote down the Canadian in his diary.

"The ship's crew made a lot of fuss. They presented me with a set of naval wings. And a cake too. But they just wouldn't let me take-off when my aircraft was repaired."

Posted to 185 Squadron E. Mahar, who had never before flown operationally, was nearly shot down three times before he learned that in the sky you have to be constantly alert.

"It wasn't till we had settled into the squadron, and observed the nature of the task that we really began to understand the extremely serious nature of it."

"On two occasions I landed with a dead engine." He recalled "... and once so much damage had been caused to one of the

Jerrold Smith is refused permission to fly off again following repairs to his Spitfire.

wings that there was the real possibility that too many 'G's could have torn it off."

> "When I thought about it later I realized that I hadn't been frightened; there hadn't been time to, actually."
>
> "Many years later I met a Luftwaffe pilot and asked him if he had ever flown over Malta. He replied, 'Yes, but I did not like it.' I responded that neither did I."

Chapter XII

'Achtung' Spitfire

(Part 2)

A thorn in Rommel's side – Malta must be neutralized – A threat to desert campaign – Malta; under threat of an Invasion – Bitter struggle goes on – Odds still heavy against garrison – Need for frequent Spitfire reinforcements – "Style" – "Salient" – "Pinpoint" – "Insect" – "Bellows" costs 'Eagle' – "Baritone"

Malta was disturbing Rommel's supply route to North Africa and the Axis were determined to neutralize it permanently, but the island garrison refused to admit defeat.

On 11 May, the Governor of Malta had this message to the fighting services:

> "I congratulate all the Fighting Services on their magnificent team work over the weekend, particularly the RAF and the A/A defences on their notable success. The Luftwaffe has seen that wounded Malta can hit back gamely."

William Metcalf recorded in his diary:

> May 12 – "... Jerry is getting fed up of the T.K. Spitfires and has been trying to liquidate them all today.'

Plt. Off. Broad had that day recorded in his logbook the loss of two of his squadron pilots; Sgt. Finley and Sgt. Boyd DFM.

> Nash – May 16 – Returned from St Paul's Bay this morning. Me109s and Italians had just bombed Ta' Qali. Got two Spits on fire in dispersal pens and killed two RAF corporals. Wounded two airmen and a soldier. 109 tried to shoot up Doug Hamilton landing. Ron West and Linton dropped on ground and cannon shell burst between them. Flying this morning. We needed two more for 249's century. Buchanan got a Macchi for the 99th. Plagis and I shared a 109 for the 100th.
>
> We were attacked off Kalafrana Bay by a series of pairs and got one of them. Plagis had a squirt from 300yds and I followed up from the same range, knocking his starboard wingtip off and sent him plunging in.
>
> Party tonight, but on at dawn. Wait till to-morrow night.

May 17 – We lost three more Spitfires today, logged down Metcalf in his diary and only shot down five Mes.'

(Plt. Off. Peter Nash was one of the three unfortunates. He had just gone over his teens at 20 years of age.)

The next day Plt. Off. Jerrold Smith reached Malta in the middle of an air raid but landed on Luqa without mishap. Driven to Naxxar at dusk where he was amongst others billeted in the Palace, he was in the morning of 19 May returned to the aerodrome to join 601 Squadron.

Metcalf continues with his logging:

> May 20 – Had two bombing raids, and dozens of others today.

Jerrold Smith was on 22 May on readiness at 5 o'clock in the morning.

He was airborne on practice flying with six others an hour later and at 1030hrs he was on his first operational scramble. He failed to get involved in any action then, but in the evening he was hospitalized suffering from 'Malta Dog' (Dysentery).

Metcalf again:

> May 25 – Had a plot of 63 on the board this afternoon, and what a mix-up it was. The last I saw was just one solid mass of kites knocking hell's bells out of each other.

The Luftwaffe High Command was aware of Britain's scope behind the relentless challenge being put up by this new RAF fighter. After the arrival of the Luftwaffe in the Mediterranean, in January 1941, the RAF Hurricane failed to keep in command of the situation over Malta each time the Germans returned to Sicily. Consequently, during 1941, this went against the British and their allies in the battle for North Africa. Unable to break up the Axis means of communication between Naples and Tripoli, by mounting anti-shipping strikes from Malta, convoys were constantly reaching Rommel in the desert, supplying his Africa Korps with troops, armaments and provisions. Hence, with his forces kept up to strength, he was in a position to raise strong offensives that was forcing the British 8th Army to retreat towards Egypt.

Malta was the key, but, the Hurricane was constantly failing to provide the ultimate protection that was so vitally needed by the other forces on the island.

By early spring of 1942 the British realized that unless an immediate solution was found to neutralize this situation Rommel would eventually drive them out of Egypt. The British knew that they had to stop this from happening. They needed a victory in the desert if they expected to start moving their forces over Sicily and on to Italy and northwards into Europe where they intended to bring the war to an end. This led to the arrival of the Spitfire in Malta, an aircraft that the Luftwaffe fighter pilots began to realize was superior to their own Me109s.

Hence, the battle was now between two equal contenders, of whom one was challenging the other for air superiority over Malta at whatever cost. On the other hand the Luftwaffe fought a desperate battle to keep on top yet, despite this advantage of numerical superiority, were sensing that they were losing their grip with each passing day.

The implacable gallantry with which the RAF pilots fought back disconcerted the enemy, and Kesselring was deeply concerned about the possibility of this failure in the battle for Malta. He always knew that his Fuhrer had opened one front too many, and with the approach of summer Kesselring was aware that his Luftwaffe forces would shortly be withdrawn, partly in support of Rommel's Desert campaign and partly to the Russian Front. This would transfer the responsibility of keeping up the pressure against Malta on to the Italian Regia Aeronautica, about whom Kesselring had little faith.

A war was at stake and the island defenders were ready to sacrifice themselves to win it. They knew that upon the result of the battle in which they were involved ultimately rested the fortunes, for better or for worse, of the battle for North Africa.

Plt. Off. Broad kept recorded some of June's hectic fighting in his logbook:

> June 1 – Spitfire Vc BR249 – Scramble – Leading section of 4 a/c – intercepted 6 Me109s at 12,000 feet east of Zonqor – used all my ammo – damaged 109. Slim destroyed one. Andy (P/O McNaughton) shot down into sea and was killed.

'Style ' was the one ferrying operation in which out of the 32 Spitfires ferried off HMS Eagle four fell to the guns of Bf109s and one crashed. Launched on 3 June Robert Middlemiss recalls that eventful day:

> "My posting to 249 Squadron was perhaps the most memorable, commencing with the trip out to the island of Malta. We went part way on the a/c carrier, HMS Eagle, and when we left the carrier it was amid heavy fire from our escort ship firing at Ju88s overhead. Before we could land on Malta Me109s engaged us and in the resultant heavy fighting we lost four of our pilots and aircraft; with little gas to spare we limped into Ta' Qali airfield on the island."

By 2 July Middlemiss had shot down his third enemy aircraft and damaged a fourth, then on the 7th he was shot down in the sea from where he was picked up so badly wounded that he had to be sent back to the UK.

Operation code-named 'Salient', in which HMS Eagle ferried a further 32 Spitfires to Malta, was launched on 9 June, six days following operation 'Style'.

Plt. Off. G. F. Beurling, another Canadian, who was destined to become the island's highest scoring fighter pilot with

Canadian Spitfire Ace
Plt. Off. George F. Beurling increases to his string of victory crosses, of which he had by 25 September 1942 claimed 18.

249 Squadron, arrived with this batch. As he landed two soldiers, from a group gathered at the end of a rough track, approached his aircraft and grabbed hold of his aircraft's wing tips. A third, jumping on a wing, stepped up to the cockpit put a hand on the pilot's shoulder, and yelled instructions in his ear. Beurling spotted the remains of burnt-out aircraft pads scattered all over the place. Meanwhile his Spitfire was guided into a blast-pen where it was rushed upon by a crowd of bearded, grimy individuals dressed in relics of what had once been uniforms.

A Spitfire is taken control of as it taxies at Ta' Qali, and guided to a pre-set dispersal pen.

So successful was the scheme used during operation 'Bowery' that A.V.M. Lloyd had decided to adopt it in all subsequent Spitfire deliveries, and the Canadian was experiencing the ritual of this procedure.

As three brawny types grabbed the tail of the Spitfire its engine was switched-off for Beurling, then the fighter was swung round ready to roll out of the enclosure.

Other attendants staggered up in line with cans of petrol, while a local pilot, appearing as if from nowhere, was dragging the Canadian out of the cockpit where he still sat, overwhelmed by what was going on all around him.

Spring, 1942. A Spitfire is immediately taken in hand for refuelling and rearming during a turn-about operation.

Out of the Spitfire Beurling saw his few belongings being sent flying in every direction by the armourers who, festooned with belts of shells and cartridges, proceeded to arm the fighter for combat. The Canadian was still trying to gather his wits about him when the distant sound of anti-aircraft guns in action brought him partly to his senses.

"OK? Contact". Someone shouted in the melee. The roar of Merlin engines bursting into life could be heard echoing from every part of the airfield. The backwash of air from Beurling's Spitfire, as its propeller disappeared into a spinning blur, caught his already scattered clothing and flinging them into the air, as it suddenly moved out of the bay by a savage burst of throttle.

Walking out into the open the Canadian ran into some other pilots from the 'Eagle', who were still as dazed as he was. Beurling, looking over a shoulder, had his first view of the Bf109F as six of the fighters streaked across the airfield, strafing everything in their path.

Someone shoved him head first into a nearby slit trench.

The new arrivals, covered from head to foot with dust and rubble, were shaken by the intensity of the battle they had just witnessed, immediately realizing that here, on this small 316 Sq. Km island in the Central Mediterranean, a very real air war was going on.

Beurling went to look for his belongings inside the blast-pen but, discovering that some were missing, waited for the return of his Spitfire. He saw two RAF fighters make crash landings as others circuited in to land. A third, badly shot up, was seen making a ground somersault. A pilot exhausted from the recent battle, parachute pack slung over a humped shoulder, walked past, and looking at the Canadian from bloodshot eyes called out to him.

"No point waiting for your Spitfire. Norman Lee was flying it and he got the chop. Get weaving or you'll miss the mess bus, and it's a five mile walk!"

The other Canadian, J. Smith, after a long 'Malta Dog' relapse, was on 9 June airborne chasing 109s. He was for the first time involved in a dogfight, but nothing came out of it.

Described as the epitome of the dedicated lone-wolf in Christopher Shore's "Aces High', first impressions of the Canadian Beurling, on arrival in Malta, were not good. This was partly due to his untidy appearance and the bad reputation given by his superiors' back in Britain. Neither did the wagging tongue of some replacement pilots for 249 Squadron keep this a secret inside the camp.

"... flew with us back in England ..." A Flight Commander in the squadron explained to Wg. Cdr. 'Laddie' Lucas.

> "... sergeant pilot, Canadian, good eyes, quick, aggressive. Not much discipline in the air, tends to get separated from the squadron. Very individualistic; but he's got flair!"

Lucas, a journalist, was intrigued by the description. The Wg. Cdr. silently studied the tall, lean, 21 year old Beurling, ice-blue eyes topped by a shock of untidy fair hair. Lucas then talked to Beurling as an equal, without belittling his own authority, for he had decided to accept him in his wing. Lucas seemed to have in some strange way affected the Canadian's behaviour for he gained his trust where others had failed.

Earlier in the month two supply convoys sailed simultaneously; in an attempt to succour the beleaguered island: one from Alexandria and another from Gibraltar.

Codenamed "Vigorous" and "Harpoon" respectively, in relation to their points of departure, the former, which did not get farther than 'bomb alley', as the passage between Crete and Tobruk became known, was badly mauled by the enemy, and it was forced to turn back to Egypt.

"Harpoon" which regretfully happened to be the smaller of the two convoys, arrived within range of the Beaufighters and Beauforts, brought to Malta to provide the merchantmen with air cover. But it was when they were within range of a number of Spitfires, fitted with long-range fuel tanks, that they faired better. However, this convoy remained subject to a concentration of heavy enemy attacks as it came within range of enemy airfields in Sardinia and western Sicily.

William Metcalf's dairy records this in relation to the food supply situation then prevailing in Malta:

> June 5 – "Rained all day and Cpl. Ingham and I had big eats at the Prince of Wales then managed half a loaf of bread, ate that and two eggs, and we're still starving!"
>
> June 8 – "Started work at 03.00 hours on a breakfast of one slice bread, one spoon of mashed potatoes and a mug of tea without sugar. Our next bite was at 2.35 pm, no wonder half of the chaps are on their knees."

Spitfires undergoing servicing in a hangar in 1942.

On 11 June, Beurling, forming part of a four men scramble, for the first time flew in defence of the island but a simple routine patrol was all that this action developed into.

The next day, however, with three other Spitfires, Beurling was scrambled in Red Section which, as an old Air Force custom, was first off the ground. Shortly afterwards the four RAF fighters were involved in a dogfight with 15 Bf109s.

Although the Canadian reported shooting off the tail of one of the enemy fighters he was only credited with a damaged. After that one encounter, their aircraft found to be in need of servicing, 249 Squadron was grounded for some days.

Later in the day 185 Squadron was back in action, about which Plt. Off. Broad entered these jottings in his logbook:

> June 12 – Spitfire Vc. BR387.
> Scramble – 2 Ju88s with heavy Me109 escort bombed Luqa. – Scrambled late. ... when at 5,000 feet saw Ju88s and turned in towards them but 4 Me109s jumped us ... I turned into them but did not get a sight on them so did not fire.

Metcalf's diary:

> June 13 – "Convoy now not arriving until Monday, and one from Alex on Tuesday. ... if this convoy fails to arrive we may as well shut up shop in Malta. The grub isn't fit for pigswill and very scarce!"

Plt. Off. E. Broad was airborne protecting 'Harpoon', the lesser of the two convoys:

> June 15 – Spitfire Vc BR380.
> Convoy patrol – Leading section of 4 A/C on convoy patrol 50 miles west of Malta. At commencement of patrol saw 20 Ju88s approaching from rear port quarter above us. Turned to attack them as they dived but saw 10 Mel09s coming down on us. I slipped out and got behind one and destroyed 109F. Had few more bursts at other 109s but no result ... . Spit fired at me.
> Plt. Off. Basil bailed out and was picked up by destroyer.

J. Smith was on that same day also flying on convoy patrol. Just off

Pantelleria he had to lead the section he was with when his leader's wireless packed up:

> "Patrolled for fifteen minutes, then Junker 87s and 109s arrived. I went through flak after an 87 and saw a huge piece break off. Had a dogfight with a 109 and it left trailing smoke heading for Pantelleria. Was hit by flak on first trip but got back a few minutes before engine packed in."
>
> "One of ours missing."
>
> "Went out again about 3.20 p.m. Over convoy for an hour when 88s and 109s bombed it.
>
> Damaged an 88, shot at a 109 and shot down another 88. Its rear gunner shot me up and as I headed back for convoy I caught fire."

Smith had to abandon his aircraft after that and was 15 minutes later picked up from the sea by a friendly destroyer.

Two of the six merchantmen in the convoy that had set out of Britain finally succeeded in reaching the Grand Harbour with 25,000 tons of supplies, enough, it was estimated, to save the island from starvation for a further two months.

Broad continues:

> June 16 – Spitfire Vc BR380.
>
> Scramble – When at 17,000 feet saw 2 Me109s coming up behind so turned and Mitch and I chased them back to Sicily. Did not get within range to fire. Slim's 4 A/C jumped by 12 Me109s. Tex

Spitfire duty bound escorting an HSL during a rescue operation.

and McNamara bailed out into sea ... helped in search and escort of rescue launch that picked both up.

Meanwhile, a pernicious enemy had been undermining Malta's defenders, malnutrition. This detestable sickness disabled numerous islanders. Regretfully, RAF pilots were no exception, of whom some had to be grounded for days, suffering from dysentery which they called 'Malta Dog'.

On 22 June, the 'Malta Dog' had once again hit Jerrold Smith, right when his squadron was preparing to move on to the Middle East.

At this time, however, there was a noticeable lull in overall enemy activity over Malta, which it later developed to be the result of a difference in opinions between the German and Italian High Commands. The former, Kesselring, preferred to have the island invaded, but lacked enough paratroops for the purpose, due to the heavy losses suffered during the invasion of Crete, while the Italians did not want to shoulder the burden. Furthermore, following the shock of 10 May, and the stiff RAF fighter resistance they had encountered, the Luftwaffe were undecided whether to support their allies or not regarding the invasion of Malta.

Tobruk finally fell to the enemy, but this desert victory tended to confuse, rather than settle, the Axis High Command for now they had to decide which was most strategically important to their North African campaign, victory over the British in the Nile Delta, or the occupation of Malta. Resources to execute both were not available. Hence with Goering in command of the Luftwaffe supporting Rommel, who was seeking permission from his Fuhrer to continue his advance into Egypt, it was decided to concentrate their forces in the desert. This conclusion was reached after Rommel pointed out that after the capture of Suez, Malta could be taken with just a fraction of the Armed forces his superiors imagined were needed for the invasion, with the result that the plans for the venture were shelved for a more opportune time.

With Rommel's Army's advance towards Egypt, a steady flow of Tripoli-bound supply convoys were soon steaming out of Italian ports. Anti-shipping strike forces struck by day and at night from Malta with telling effect. This RAF activity led the Axis to launch another retaliatory 'blitz' by the Luftwaffe during the early days of July that again resulted in placing the island's very existence in jeopardy. Hard pressed by overwhelming odds, however, Malta's defenders fought back with unflagging gallantry despite all these hardships.

Due to the mishap to the Spitfires ferried in operation 'Calendar', armament was henceforth cleaned and checked manually one by one.

Luftwaffe fighter sweeps became daily occurrences over the island and although there was a noticeable drop in Italian daytime bomber activity, night intruding escalated.

Prior to the Axis decision to abandon the invasion of Malta in favour of an advance towards Egypt, the Regia Aeronautica mounted their own raids on the island, hence Plt. Off. Broad's logbook entry:

> June 23: Scramble in Spitfire Vc. BR305.
>
> '3 Cants with Macchi escort ... sighted them coming in over St Paul's Bay, turned in to attack them but broke into 4 a/c, which turned out to be Spits. Could not find the Cants again as they had dived away ... Jumped Macchi Mc202 giving it two long bursts, but could not finish it as my engine cut ...'

The entry in W. E. Metcalf's diary for 25 June, however, discloses the expected return of the Luftwaffe's Bf.109:

> "Only one raid up to 6pm, and then we had an evening fighter sweep by Mes and Macchi 202s. 249 shot down two and got a Spitfire very badly shot up. Flt. Sgt. Tomlinson was the pilot, he tried very hard to bring his kite in with a very bad glycol leak. As soon as he lowered his flaps he nose-dived into the deck and burst into flames. We'd no chance to get him out at all."

The Germans were at this time taking steps in support of their ally by dispatching detachments of Fleigerkorps II to Sicily from North Africa, where in the early days of May a large number already had been withdrawn to.

In Malta the 13,552 tons of supplies delivered by the survivors of 'Harpoon' did not seem to have had much effect on the islands logistics situation. Pilots, tired and weak from lack of enough nourishment, were ending up ill, and many of the long surviving ones more then deserved to be relieved. Meanwhile the majority of the Spitfires that were ferried to Malta during May and June had disappeared. Despite all that the Air Ministry had done to keep ferrying batches of fighter aircraft re-enforcement the rate at which they were being exhausted resulted that the remaining number of Spitfires was no longer adequate to keep locally based fighter units up to strength.

The Axis launched their new offensive on 1 July, albeit tentatively. A lone Ju88 approached the island about mid-afternoon which, although merely on a reconaissance mission, was heavily escorted by Mc202s and a flight of Bf109s. Twelve Spitfires of 185 Squadron were scrambled to intercept the enemy, an encounter from which the RAF fighters did not come out unscathed and ended with very little to show for it.

In the evening a radar plot of 30 plus bogies approaching the island led to the scrambling of twelve Spitfires of 603 Squadron. Two Italian S.84bis bombers briefed to bomb Ta' Qali came escorted by no less than 22 Macchis. Farther to the rear of this force were three more S.84s, with a stunning 48 escorting fighters, of which 15 were Reggiane Re.2001s. The rest consisted of Macchis Mc202s.

In this engagement a Spitfire was shot down and another damaged, while no RAF pilots reported any enemy aircraft casualties.

No sooner had the Italians departed, and the aircraft of 603 Squadron landed, that five Spitfires of 126 Squadron were being scrambled to intercept a plot of small jobs.

Although reporting that they had encountered six Me109s all the RAF pilots could put claim to was one probably destroyed enemy fighter.

On 2 July the fighting escalated, resulting in casualties on both sides. Plt. Off. Ogilvie, who climbed tiredly out of the cockpit of his shot up crash-landed Spitfire, recalls what happened:

> "The radio in my Spitfire had given up, so I didn't hear the call to break formation. And as a result I found myself alone, engaged with six enemy fighters, each trying to do me in."

This had began at about eight or so in the morning when 16 Spitfires, eight each from 185 and 603 Squadrons, were scrambled to intercept approaching 109s. One of the enemy fighters was shortly afterwards shot down, but a Spitfire had disappeared. This was a 603 Squadron aircraft, and two of 185 Squadron's were both shot up; one of them Ogilvie's. The pilot's attempts to evade the enemy pack hounding him failed, and only by a miracle did his Spitfire remain intact as cannon shells and machine-gun fire tore into the aircraft from all sides.

> "... machine gun bullets, penetrating the engine, spewed oil and glycol all over myself and my aircraft. The Spitfire shuddered and stalled, then plunged into a dive streaming black smoke and white vapourized glycol."

Plt. Off. J. Smith, who was transferred to 126 Squadron with another two pilots from 601 Squadron, did not fly again until:

> July 4 – "Eyties came over at about 10am. Four bombers, one turned back, the others were all shot down. One came down in flames near the drome. About 7pm five BR20s came over with large Macchi fighter escort. I had squirts at three Macchis, one of which was firing at a Spit. Was fired at several times, once by bombers, when I raked across them with only one cannon firing. All of our chaps got down safely but only one bomber was probably shot down and one damaged. Pretty poor show, but fun while it lasted. Felt a bit ill. To bed without supper."

During this period the 'blitz' was fast gathering momentum, though enemy bombers were still coming over in numbers not exceeding five or six in any one raid. But for obscure reasons escorting fighters came in mixed formations, grossly outnumbering any modest quantity the RAF could manage to send up to intercept them. However, it was by this time becoming obvious that this battle had turned into a fighter's war. The enemy seemed determined to exterminate the Spitfire to retain his air superiority over the Central Mediterranean before committing any further bombers. However, the RAF pilots undauntedly remained taking to the air gallantly, getting into battle despite the great disparity in their odds.

On 6 July the Axis began to increase to the tempo of their offensive. At about eight in the morning they mounted the first raid of the day.

A dozen Spitfires of 603 Squadron were scrambled to intercept this formation which was escorted by no less than a score of Me109s. Surprisingly, however, contact between the opposing forces was ineffective and the bombers reached Ta' Qali, obviously their intended objective, badly damaging a parked Spitfire.

J. Smith was scrambled sometime after 2pm but had to return to base due to a stuck undercart.

A second raid followed shortly after the first, catching the Spitfires of 603 Squadron still taxing towards dispersal. Eleven others from 249 Squadron were however scrambled to intercept this incoming all Italian formation. This consisted of 38 escorting fighters between Mc202s and Re200ls to watch over three Zl007bis bombers. Only minutes prior to the arrival of these Cants more Macchis flew advance sweeps over the island, obviously to clear the way for the bombers.

When, towards mid-June, Beurling was notified that his unit was to be temporarily grounded due to the servicing of all its aircraft, he impatiently yearned to fly into battle, hardly believing that he would ever get the chance.

Bob Middlemiss, another Spitfire pilot who survived the war, recalls hearing the Canadian grumbling to himself about his bad luck and telling the youngster:

> "Hold your fire, big boy. You'll get your chance, don't worry. Everybody gets it here, automatically. You don't have to go looking for it!"

From 23 June, up till the end of the month, although frequently airborne, Beurling failed to see any action since his last brief encounter on the 12th. But on 6 July, he was again scrambled with his squadron's section of Spitfires, and had his first real brush with the Regia Aeronautica.

He attacked the enemy formation, nosing down straight on a bomber, squirting a burst of cannon fire at it. Once past he gunned his Spitfire into a fast climb and went after a Macchi 202, shooting it down with a short burst from his guns to score his first victory over Malta. Without loosing his speed advantage the Canadian dipped a wing as he went and spotting a Macchi in pursuit of a Spitfire gave chase without a second's thought. The Italian broke the attack, diving away with Beurling on his tail. Suddenly the Italian pulled out of the dive to evade the Canadian and flew right into the path of a stream of 20mm cannon shells.

"Laddie' Lucas recalled when, as a Sqdn. Ldr., he first saw Beurling fly into combat and realized that here was one of a rare breed of fighter pilots.

"Leading eight aircraft of 249 Squadron, split into two sections of four, 'Screwball'," a nickname his squadron-colleagues dabbed Beurling with shortly after he joined 249, "was flying way-off to my right, 400 yards away in line abreast. Woodhall, who was in control of interception, got us perfectly placed, up sun of the incoming raid. Then his voice came over the R/T:

> 'Little jobs approaching St Paul's Bay angels 20. There are fourty plus ...'
>
> "And there they were. It was the ideal pounce. They never saw us. Having dealt with an unsuspecting 109 myself, I was just in time to see 'Screwball', with plenty of speed, way off to the right, pulling up fast under another 109, closing to what looked like his usual 150 yards. A two or three seconds burst from a quarter-into-an-astern attack and the German aircraft flicked on to its back before starting to spin earthwards."
>
> "I saw no more of Beurling in the general melee that followed. Having dispatched his 109 he had then caught a Macchi 202 and sent that plummeting down."

Beurling's score rose rapidly after that sizzling 6 July encounter with the enemy and five days later he received his first medal, a DFM.

Dysentery dogged Smith during the next few days, then:

> July 10 – "Rip Jones and I jumped seven 88s and shot down one each. Rip was being fired at by a 109 as he was firing at a bomber. I wonder he didn't 'buy it'. Larger raids coming in these days and far too many fighters. Had great dogfight with 109s and Macchis off Gozo. Was shot up thrice. Once in head-on attacks at fighters, once by bombers, and once I was hit in the oil tank by 88 I got and force landed at Hal Far while Luqa was being bombed."
>
> July 12 – "Had pot at 109 which I claimed as damaged. Later one was confirmed as destroyed."

Beurling, while he was on that day returning from a sortie with his section leader, picked up a report of two missing colleagues, and both immediately volunteered to go searching for them.

Shortly afterwards they came upon two Re2002s. As Beurling moved in to the attack, his leader provided him with top cover. The tail ender was the Canadian's first victim.

> "The boys must have been intent on the search for their missing sidekick ..." Wrote down Beurling in his battle report. "... for I swear neither had seen me as yet. I simply sneaked up behind the tail-ender and gave him a one-second squirt. He burst into flames and went down. Without further ado I whipped around on the other lad ... I came right underneath his tail. I was going faster than he

Camouflaged netting. Its either there to safeguard an aircraft, or fool the enemy into wasting bombs.

was; about 50 yards behind. I was tending to overshoot ... I closed up to about 30 yards, and I was on his portside coming in at about 15-degree angle. I could see all the details in his face because he turned and looked at me just as I had a bead on him."

The Canadian shot down both aircraft into the sea.

Jerrold Smith on 14 July exchanged some shooting with a 109 that he reported having damaged. He later learned that two of the fighters went into the sea, so he felt that he should claim a confirmed.

Meanwhile Air Vice Marshall Lloyd was that day relieved of his command when, out of a Sunderland that had arrived from Egypt, alighted the new Air Officer Commanding designate, AVM Keith Park M.C., DFC., a New Zealander.

The next day, 15 July, another 32 Spitfire re-enforcement was ferried by HMS Eagle in operation codenamed "Pinpoint" of which one crashed on take-off.

The only Spitfires delivered to the island fully assembled from Britain were the ones ferried by US Wasp. Then following that final

Air Vice Marshall Lloyd, and Air Vice Marshall Keith Park whose attention always tends to be skywards.

excellent operation, 'Bowery', Spitfires were again arriving at Gibraltar in crates where, after assembly, 'Eagle' saw to their ferrying delivery to Malta. Flt. Sgt. I.R. MacLennan recalls such an operation, one in which he finally flew a Spitfire to Malta in mid-July.

When the SS Empire Darwin sailed out of Milford Haven MacLennan marveled at the crude method by which his country still shipped out fighters to Gibraltar, remembering the freighter as he came on board, its deck torn open so that half-a-dozen dismantled Spitfires could be accommodated in its hold. Posted away from his unit on 28 June he was on 14 July en route to the Central Mediterranean on board HMS Eagle.

Early in the morning of the next day MacLennan prepared himself to take off from the deck of the carrier, a task which, like the majority of all ferry pilots, he was untrained for:

> "The Eagle had to show eight or ten knots on the wind indicator before they let us take off with our big overload tanks. It was nerve-wracking, but very easy to do once you've done it. Yet until you've done it, you're not sure; it looked agonizing. I was about fifth off."

In this operation, flying in Spitfire BR140, was a Canadian, Rod Smith, Jerrold's brother.

The latter recorded in his diary:

> "... was amazed to find that Rod landed here. He was in AOC's car when I saw him and we had a short chat before he left for the mess."

Spitfires gather in strength as the summer of 1942 approaches.

July 16 – "On readiness with Rod at first operational trip together. Saw nothing."

July 18 – "Swam in morning. Early lunch and on readiness at 1pm. Rod and I found an unescorted Ju88 about 10 miles west and left it with engine pouring white smoke going very slowly with tail down at sea level. Very bad shooting on my part."

A further Spitfire ferrying re-enforcement operation under the Codename of "Insect" was launched off HMS Eagle on 21 July in which only 29 of the 30 fighters flown off the carrier reached Malta.

The Smiths were unable to get into some real action during the next few days then:

July 24 – " Got off late on a scramble. Joined the others just as they attacked the bombers. Started to aim at port Ju88 when Rod opened fire. It went down in flames. Moved over to next one and opened fire, putting port engine aflame. Was hit in glycol and force landed on Luqa (third time this month). A sergeant saw my Ju88 go into the sea."

On 27 July, Beurling shot down a further four enemy aircraft, two 109s and two Italian fighters, his highest score in a single day. By the end of the month his score had risen to 15 destroyed. The Canadian's deadly marksmanship was unparalleled, and in later years there were some that claimed he was a ruthless, cold-blooded killer. But this may have risen from the fact, as Clayton Knight wrote in 'Malta Spitfire', that "he has schooled himself to be technically perfect." Particularly flying in which he excelled.

The planning of another convoy to strengthen Rommel's Africa Korps led to the decline of the Regia Aeronautica's second offensive against Malta. Meanwhile the Luftwaffe in Sicily had to have a large number of its units transferred to North Africa and Russia, to provide additional air support to their ground forces on these two fronts. This resulted in the Axis having their airforces so thinly spread out that they were unable to keep the pressure needed to keep Malta subdued as planned. Battle free periods at this time gave the exhausted garrison defenders breathing intervals, but the final days of July was when the enemy was at his most unpredictable as the few excerpts from MacLennan's logbook reveal:

July23 – Scramble – 45 minutes – Bounce 4 Me109s, bounced by 2 Regis, no score.

July 26 – Scramble – 1:25 – 1 "88" damaged, squadron in shambles.

July 29 – Scramble – 1:00 – cover for Beauboys in captured "Iti" floatplane, complete with "Iti" general and Station CO

July31 – Scramble – 1:05 – Bounced by 109s – no luck.

Jerrold Smith was on the 31st airborne as recorded in his diary:

> "Intercepted two squadrons of 109s twenty miles west but couldn't get near them. While flying with Rip one intrepid beggar came up behind us firing at Rip. I turned into him but he dived quickly and fired from well out of range. When fifteen miles off Sicily a squadron of 109s passed us going back; turned to chase them, but they stooged home."

It had meanwhile also been decided to take stock of fighter aircraft losses in Malta, an assessment that was to cover the first fortnight of July. When this was concluded it was found that 36 Spitfires had either been destroyed or badly damaged in action and a further three written-off in accidents, a number that represented nearly 65 percent of all available fighters on the island during that period.

Axis convoys, needed in greater numbers than ever before, again traversed Mediterranean routes east and west of Malta to diverse destinations, Tripoli, Benghazi and Tobruk, and they fell prey to British anti-shipping strike units operating from the island and Alexandria. The past severe losses sustained by the enemy made the island the most talked about topic at Axis High Command Headquarters, raising some very alarming comments. Count Ciano, Mussolini's Foreign Minister had this entered in his personal diary:

> "This Rommel campaign is becoming sheer madness. Our merchant fleet will not last a year at this rate."

Admiral Donitz's comment, albeit more constructive, agreed with Ciano's:

> "Even with all the Spanish tonnage and ships we could seize if we invaded southern France, even by increasing construction tenfold

in Italian shipyards, we could not keep up another Rommel campaign. Malta must be destroyed."

Rommel who had planned the North African campaign clearly agreed that something had to be done to resolve the convoy situation. What he wrote weighed down heavily with blame across the shoulders of a colleague:

> "With Malta in our hands, the British would have had little chance of exercising any further control over convoy traffic in the Central Mediterranean. I have personally warned Marshall Kesselring of the consequences for my lines of Communication between Italy and Africa if he does not succeed in establishing air superiority over Malta."

The British needed to have these Axis means of supplies broken. Although their Malta anti-shipping strike forces served that purpose admirably, and the island defenders fought off the enemy with unabated determination, hunger, overwork and dysentery were fast draining them of their last reserves of energy with which to resist the onslaught. Furthermore, due to lack of diverse aircraft spares, unserviceable Spitfires remained grounded. Whatever was flyable soon joined the former due to the shortage of fuel and ammunition. Consequently, with the gravity of this situation threatening to rob them of their mounting advantage over the Axis, the allied Chiefs of Staff contemplated the passage of a supply convoy to Malta. One was organized under the codename of 'Pedestal".

Consisting of 13 fast modern freighters, carrying a mixed cargo weighing 85,000 tons, and a single tanker loaded with 11,500 tons of kerosene and diesel fuel oils, this departed the Clyde on 2 August.

At this time the fuel supply situation on the island was at bottom level. Only three weeks remained on the island. Fortunately, the success of operation 'Pedestal' was to raise this stock of aviation fuel enough to keep the RAF fighters flying until the end of the year. By then the enemy was in full retreat in the desert with the result that allied shipping was able to navigate from Alexandria to Malta with very little risk.

During the year limited amounts were brought to the island in submarines, making hazardous runs that imperilled life and equipment.

Despite these heroic deeds, however, a submarine's delivery, considering the week it took to navigate its way to the island, hardly lasted the RAF fighters a day.

After ferry operation 'Bowery' empty tins accumulated in piles so large that they became a problem, even after HM Dockyard volunteered to dispose of them by a manually operated crusher.

Fortunately, however, material with which to build aircraft blast pens was shortly to be in great demand, and the tin can problem was solved.

The huge piles of empty 5-gallon fuel tins are disposed of by filling with rubble; and build aircraft pens with.

Despite that year's frequent enemy action and the fact that the Command Ferry Pool was that year forced to break several fuel regulations, never did a fire break out. This would of course have been disastrous to the Pool's hard working group of British officers and Maltese labourers who had succeeded in keeping fuel supplies flowing to airfields with the minimum of wastage throughout the war years.

Plt. Off. Jerrold Smith's diary records:

> August 5 – "Rod and I on deck level sweep along Sicilian coast at dusk looking for E-Boats to shoot up. Saw none but shot at what I thought to be one, which I saw after was a rock. Got back in dark OK. 'Jerry' blood-wagon picked up one of the hated Huns fifteen miles out. We didn't reach it in time and they got off scot-free."

On 10 August, the convoy reached the Straights of Gibraltar. Shortly afterwards the enemy was informed of this with the result that he began to amass his forces in Sicily to destroy it.

That same day Jerrold Smith, with three enemy aircraft destroyed to his credit, including one-and-a-half probables and four damaged went missing while on a routine minesweeping patrol. Reports arrived that he was last seen chasing some Ju88s in the direction of Sicily before he disappeared. At the same time Sgt. Plt. I.R. MacLennan celebrated his first confirmed victory over Malta by shooting down a Bf109, a score that he was to succeed in raising to seven enemy aircraft destroyed to his credit by the time his tour of duty expired on 13 December.

Enemy activity during the early days of August remained consistent. By the 5th of the month the RAF lost four of their Spitfires to the guns of the Me109s, regretfully for the destruction of only one enemy fighter. This was followed by a notable lull during the next two days but on the 8th the Luftwaffe fighters returned with their usual numerical superiority, and immediately shot down a Spitfire. Beurling, however, who had only just been promoted to Fly. Off., managed to square things up by destroying a 109, but he ran foul of another three that badly damaged his aircraft. Deciding not to abandon his Spitfire the Canadian ended in a ploughed field, and later recalled the risky belly landing he had to make:

> "As I came close in over the near wall I put the left wing down to take up the bump and bellied down onto the ground. The wing absorbed the wallop and stopped me cold. I climbed out, unhurt except for a superficial cut in one arm."

"Bellows", a codename for a further Spitfire ferry operation, was executed by the carrier 'Furious' on 11 August during convoy operation 'Pedestal'. In this convoy, apart from Furious', HMS Eagle, HMS Victorious and HMS Indomitable were in attendance.

11 August 1942. HMS Eagle, hit by four torpedoes fired by U-73, is sunk.

Of the 38 Spitfire re-enforcement flown to Malta one, due to some problem or another, landed on 'Indomitable'.

Flying off HMS Furious Plt. Off. W.T. Rolls DFC was given the task of navigating a flight of Spitfires to the island. With fuel gauges nearing the danger mark after three hours tense flying Rolls took a deep breath and broke radio silence, calling Malta. A calm voice shortly afterwards came on the air, instructing him to vector N.E. for eight miles and land at Luqa.

"I will never forget the first sight I had of Malta." Wrote Rolls. "It was through a hole in cloud, and it was as though it was saying welcome. I had been praying enough during my flight, but on seeing Malta perhaps its religious aura that came up into the clouds – I said one big prayer on behalf of all my flight. The cloud seemed to disappear as we went down and made easy landings. It looked as though God had opened up the sky in order to let us land safely."

Posted to 126 Squadron Rolls first flew on 13 August when, with the tanker "Ohio" limping towards Malta, the squadron's Spitfires, fitted with long-range fuel tanks, were detailed to provide the tanker with protection till it reached the island. Relays of Spitfires watched over the tanker part of the way to Grand Harbour for, had it been sunk, Malta would surely have 'gone down' with it in a matter of days.

At 1800hrs on that date four Spitfires of 126 Squadron were patrolling over the convoy at an elevation of 9,000ft when some miles away three Ju88s were spotted at the start of their dive on the 'Ohio' out of the sun. Sqdn. Ldr. Wicks was immediately charging to intercept but by the time he arrived on the scene the first bomber had already released its bombs and disappeared. For some reason the second failed to drop its bomb-load and climbed away. However, Wicks was in time to engage the third 88:

"I closed in with it. Opened fire from 200yds, closing to 100 expending all my ammunition. I saw strikes on the starboard mainplane. A piece dropped off. I then broke away."

Plt. Off. Bill Rolls, who had just been posted to the squadron, recalled:

> "The CO dived down and fired at one of them. I saw smoke coming from it so I went in and fired a two-seconds burst. Another Spitfire dived in front of me so I broke away ...".

Two 88s was reported destroyed in that encounter as the second was chased by Sgt. Tiddy who confirmed it, just as Rolls had confirmed the one he attacked.

Meanwhile a counter offensive was in progress from Malta in an effort to divert the attention of enemy's Sicily-based airforce units from 'Pedestal'. Furthermore Malta-based anti-shipping strike forces were hard-pressed harassing North Africa-bound Axis convoys.

"Pedestal" turned out to be one of the most savagely fought battles in the war for the Mediterranean. This was one convoy upon which success was vital. Should it fail the outcome of the North African campaign would prove disastrous to the allies.

In spite of all the British naval screening and air protection of 'Pedestal', however, the enemy's action proved so intense that his airforce caused it considerable damage. Furthermore, German U-Boats also succeeded in breaking through. This resulted in the loss of a destroyers and 5 cargoships from air attacks. A cruiser and 4 cargoshpis by MTBs and submarines sunk a cruiser and the aircraft carrier HMS Ark Royal.

Plt. Off. Leo Nomis, an American, who arrived at Ta' Qali on 10 August, where he was assigned to 229 Squadron, had this recorded in his logbook:

> "During heavy enemy activity we were scrambled six times a

day, sitting in cockpits on standby, taking off when a red flare was fired from the duty hut."

As to his comments regarding weather conditions during flying:

> "The haze seemed to exaggerate the blistering rays of the Mediterranean sun. Because of its glare and the dust many pilots discarded cockpit canopies for the sake of the all important visibility, although the cold at 30,000 feet was uncomfortable it was preferable to an attack by an unseen enemy."

With the survivors of 'Pedestal' inside Grand Harbour, from which 32,000 tons of assorted provisions were unloaded, enemy activity from Sicily suddenly abated. The Axis, erroneously overestimating the number of ships they had sunk, thought they had achieved a great victory over the British. Tactically, in fact, they had, but strategically they soon realized that they had failed for Malta had been supplied with enough food, ammunition, fuel and Spitfires for its defenders to keep them fighting until the autumn.

Despite Rommel's increased need for more convoys, particularly fuel-laden tankers for his Panzer Divisions, what was reaching Tripoli was to help him win no battles.

These were now being preyed on more often by Malta-based anti-shipping strike forces. The strong enemy formations of bomber aircraft, escorted by swarms of fighters, which used to mount 'blitz' upon 'blitz' on the island, had become small scale fighter sweeps during the ensuing weeks of August and September. When A.V.M. Park assumed command of RAF Malta the worst of the 'blitz' was past and enough Spitfires were in hand to resist these desultory enemy attacks.

Contrary to A.V.M. Lloyd's defensive tactics Park was more aggressive with the result that on 25 July he introduced a 'Fighter Interception Plan'. No longer would pilots be provided with a running commentary about approaching enemy formations by the sector controller, but could freely plan their own line of attack, once the enemy was intercepted north of Malta over open waters miles away from the coast. Park felt confident his fighters were a match for whatever the enemy flew across from Sicily. With a squadron patrolling high up sun, from where they could intercept any enemy fighter cover flying at that altitude, a second was instructed to engage the bombers' close escort, or the bombers themselves, should they be on their own. A third squadron was directed to deal with the bombers about ten miles north of the coastline while a fourth unit, should this be available, would be required to intercept those bombers which might succeed in breaking through the forward fighter screen. Reliable radar warning, however, and alert pilots were needed for the success of this operation.

A fortnight after the introduction of this plan the Air Vice Marshall expressed his satisfaction at the results achieved. There was a substantial drop in the percentage of aircraft destroyed on the ground. However, enemy fighter sweeps had escalated shortly after mid-September.

Meanwhile, "Very quiet today, all convoy is safe in harbour and our patrols have finished.", recorded L.A.C. Metcalf in his diary for 15 August.

Neither were there reports of any changes the next day, but on the 17th, with the arrival of more reinforcement Spitfires via HMS Furious in Operation code-named 'Baritone', Luftwaffe fighters flocked in on a sweep that resulted in the scrambling of Spitfires of 126 and 185 Squadrons. Of the 14 RAF fighters a section of four at first intercepted six 109s, while, others soon joined the fray.

Three enemy aircraft were shot down, at the cost of a RAF fighter that the pilot, Al Stead, had to abandon after it was badly shot up. He recorded this battle report:

A direct hit destroys this Swordfish, regardless of the blast pen protection.

"I was with an American sergeant flying at 31,000 feet. He saw Messerschmits that I could not, so I told him to attack and I would follow, but as he went down for six Huns, three more followed him up."

"I shot one down from his tail at pointblank range, but the next minute a great chunk flew off my starboard wing. I heard explosions and the plane shook everywhere and black smoke poured into the cockpit. I began diving out of control at 27,000 feet."

"I tried to get the hood off, but it would not budge. I tried all ways, while the Spitfire fell 14,000 feet at over 400 miles per hour the cockpit filled with smoke. I thought I had had it. It was a horrible feeling; I was expecting the plane to blow up at any moment. But fortunately the hood came off, and I suddenly found myself thrown out."

"I had seen a German pilot open his parachute at that speed and the force of the sheer speed had ripped off his harness. So I waited for a while before pulling the ripcord in order to stow up, and then I pulled the cord and landed in the sea. I spent five minutes tying to get free from the parachute and get the dinghy working. That trip shook me to the teeth."

At this time Spitfires, fitted with long-range fuel tanks, were escorting Beauforts and Beaufighters on anti-shipping operations.

'Baritone' was the Codename of the second Spitfire ferry operation HMS Furious executed for Malta. Of the 31 fighter aircraft re-enforcement flown off, one crashed on take-off, two were lost en route and 28 arrived safely.

Shortly after this ferry operation A.V.M. Park received a signal from the Air Ministry in London explaining:

"Now that 'Baritone' is completed it is intended to dispense with further carrier operations for these re-enforcements, and to make deliveries of Spitfires from Gibraltar to Malta by air carrying 170 gallon jettisonable tanks ... ."

"... Commencement of these delivery flights from Gibraltar to Malta is to await instructions from Air Ministry."

A.V.M. Park advised that for this purpose Spitfires should have their cannons removed, and carry only two brownings and 350 rounds of ammunition per gun, and that they should always proceed in pairs. But following a period of relative quite during September, and the early days of October, a run of anti-shipping successes by Malta-based RAF units resulted in the Luftwaffe's return in force.

Meanwhile AHQ Malta, taking advantage of the sporadic enemy fighter forays over the island, on 19 August twelve Spitfires of 1435 Squadron were organized on two separate fighter sweeps off the southeast coast of Sicily, raids, that provided the pattern for more of the same.

The next day there were repeat performances that were kept up during the ensuing days of August. On the other hand the anti-shipping campaign, despite the heavy casualties being suffered in life and equipment, also continued unabated.

At Hal Far a few FAA pilots, bored by the long hours of inactivity spent on the ground, requested permission to borrow some of the redundant Hurricanes dispersed on the airfield.

Following the AOC's approval the pilots were given a short conversion course on the fighters, practicing night flying as well as dive bombing; however, when the naval aircrew were ready to go into action, the AVM disappointed them no end when he ordered them to fly on daytime sorties.

On 23 August, three Hurricanes, escorted by a dozen Spitfires, attacked Gela, but the final result could not be observed due to low cloud formations.

August 25 – " Enemy action a bit more pronounced to-day". Metcalf entered in his diary.

Me109s were back again and one of the intercepting Spitfires was shot down. The day was evidently an unlucky one for, with an escort provided to cover the three naval piloted Hurricanes on a sortie over Piscari, one Spitfire blew a tyre during take off, and the fighter coming up behind rammed into it. Both aircraft burst into flames on impact; however, there were no casualties and Sgt. Plt. N. Pashen who was in the leading Spitfire recorded in his logbook:

> "On take-off, my port tyre blew and I nearly collected the flight commander. Then when stopped on the runway another kite took off straight through me ... God knows how I got away with it. Result two aircraft written off, pilots unhurt."

The next day a radar plot sent 20 Spitfires scrambling, however, although there were no reports of encounters, two of the RAF fighters went missing over the sea.

All signs of enemy activity following that one fighter plot came to stop; suddenly about twelve Ju88s crossed the coastline bombing Luqa and the surrounding villages without encountering any RAF opposition.

On 28 August Nomis, bored by his own inactivity, stole a Spitfire, and taking advantage of a moonlit night, flew on a one man sortie to Sicily. However, his adventure which was picked up by Fighter Control and Air HQ Mediterranean, who considered this unauthorized action as a grave offense due to an unnecessary expenditure of both fuel and ammunition, shortly afterward posted him to North Africa.

Enemy activity fluctuated in intensity during the ensuing days.

August 29 – " Enemy action down to nil now" wrote down Metcalf in his diary.

The next day, however, there was an enemy fighter sweep of Bf109s. A Spitfire was lost, but two 109s, of which one was of the latest type, a G-2, were shot down.

Pilot reinforcements were not all reaching the island by ferrying-in fighters.

Sqdn. Ldr. Sandy Johnstone landed at Luqa inside a Liberator in September to take over command of a Spitfire Wing. However, through no fault of his own, he reached the island nearly two weeks later than expected with the result that A.V.M. Park had given his post to another officer, so Johnstone was sent to Luqa as deputy Station Commander.

Sqdn. Ldr. Johnstone.

His duties were to run a count of bombs dropped on the airfield, and plot them as they fell from atop the remains of a small stone tower at one end of the runway.

Immediately the bombing ceased a red flag was driven in the ground at every bomb crater on the runway. Lorries on standby, loaded with clinker and gravel, raced towards these markers dumping their loads in these holes over which an old steam roller trundled back and forth, flattening them out.

"The longest it ever took to put airfields into serviceable condition was twenty minutes" wrote Johnstone.

"A final check was made to ensure that the waiting fighters, circling and sweeping around high overhead, waiting for our signal, could be called in to land."

Safi, still a crude satellite landing strip, had by this time picked up a nickname, the 'Graveyard'. Wrecks of both Allied and Axis aircraft had piled up into large heaps around its perimeter, from where unobtainable spares were salvaged by the RAF when needed.

The fact that the first few days of September were quiet did not relieve the defenders of their apprehension. These lulls in enemy activity reminded them of approaching 'storms', making them suspect that the enemy might well be up to something nasty in Sicily and did not slacken their vigil. Attacks from the island's anti-shipping strike forces on Axis convoys were disturbing Rommel's campaign in North Africa, and he was clamouring for more convoys, which Malta's defenders suspected would result in forcing the enemy into taking retaliatory action any day.

On 5 September, Bf.109s appeared sporadically in dispersed flights during the day. Only one enemy fighter was reported shot down and two others damaged from this activity.

Meanwhile orders from London, due to the shortage of fuel and ammunition on the island that was feared would not last throughout the month, put a stop to all freelance operations from Malta.

Air Headquarters explained that:

> "In order to conserve Malta's stock of aviation petrol, the Air Ministry has ordered that offensive sweeps and attacks on enemy land objectives should not be undertaken except when they contribute to the success of attacks on shipping and their escorting aircraft. Air Ministry has, however, given instructions for operational training to be re-introduced at Malta so long as it contributes to the success of offensive operations."

Wg. Cdr. Donaldson, completely disregarding the Air Ministry ruling, led nearly a score Spitfires of 229 and 249 Squadrons on a wing sweep over Sicily that same day, and received a mild rebuke for his disobedience.

Aerial photograph of RAF Safi's Ipsylon-shaped satellite airstrip; taxiways, winding out at either end, reach out to Luqa and Hal Far aerodromes.

Sept. 9 – During an early morning fighter sweep over southern Sicily by Spitfires of 185 Squadron encountering seven enemy fighters, of which six were 109s, the aircraft came to grips. Sgt. Claude Weaver radioed that he shot down a 109, however, his aircraft was in trouble, and eventually he made a belly landing on a stretch of sand on the coast of Sicily.

Little did Weaver know that Colin Parkinson a 185 Squadron companion had this recorded in his diary:

> "Claude Weaver, DFM, was shot down by Macchis, mainly through disobedience and over confidence. Dived after a Macchi but was pounced by another two and shot down. Crash landed in flames. He may be alright but I doubt it – kept firing his guns as he went down."

L.A.C. Ken Cox, a 185 Squadron airman, who was more informed about the incident, wrote:

> "Weaver was hit in the cooling system as he reported to his CO over the R/T. He was told to fly as low as possible towards Malta, and land in the sea where the HSL would be sent out to pick him up. His reply went something like this; 'You go to hell, they might not find me!' By this time he was over the sea; he turned back and landed on the beach, from where he waved to some of the aircraft that had escorted him in."

Johnston recorded that shortage of fuel severely limited operational flying:

> "Squadrons that, due to frequent air raids, used up their day's quota of fuel were forced to ground their aircraft. But enough of it was kept in reserve to provide adequate aerial cover for any convoy that might be organized next."
>
> "This endangered normal safety standards as no one was allowed to taxi aircraft, except to clear them from the duty runways. Neither was running-up engines prior to take-off permitted as they ultimately caused numerous engine failures."
>
> "Private cars could not be run on roads anywhere, with the result that bicycles became the sole means by which numerous people traveled."

Enemy activity declined over the island during the next few days, and Metcalf had this entry noted in his diary:

> Sept. 15 – There's something in the wind somewhere, whether it's Jerry or us I don't know. We've had six raids today and lost three kites. That's more activity than four weeks past."

Pounced by two Me109s four of nine Spitfires of 249 Squadron on patrol were that day claimed by the Luftwaffe pilots.

The next day an early evening visit by eight more of the enemy fighters developed into a series of dogfights that lasted nearly an hour when nine Spitfires of 249 Squadron were scrambled to intercept them. During this engagement Hetherington claimed damaging an enemy fighter but Beurling's Spitfire landed with damages to tail and starboard wing.

On 17 September Metcalf recorded that they have had four squadron scrambles during the day. Enemy activity over the island suddenly exploded into several offensive sweeps by gaggles of Mel09s and Re2001s, but the day ended with an even score of one to one.

Chapter XIII

'Achtung' Spitfire

(Part 3)

Battle still in the balance – Odds decrease – Garrison still under pressure – Spitfire bombers – Delay in Spitfires from Gibraltar – Spitfire losses need replacements – "Train" ferry saves the day – Desert advance replenishes Malta

In the morning of 19 September, Flt. Lt.Bill Rolls of 126 Squadron was airborne accompanied by his No. 2, Sgt. J.E. Mortimer on an anti E-boat patrol off Sicily. While flying along the coast between Cape Passero and Syracuse they encountered what they at first thought to be E-boats and moved in to attack, as Rolls recalled:

> "I was coming in at about 1,500yds when I saw the wake of one stop, and saw that it was a Do24 flying boat about 15 feet above the water. I opened fire with cannons and machine gun, and my No. 2 at the same time opened up on the other, which was a Do18."
>
> "A momentary orange glow appeared inside the Do24 seconds before it exploded into a splash of intense white. Climbed to avoid column of water then turned to attack second aircraft."
>
> "The Do18 had reversed direction, taxing fast landward. Fired short burst at this then Mortimer attacked. Saw more strikes and pieces flying off."
>
> "We flew round diving to look for survivors. Except for two white disturbed patches of water nothing else was visible."

Both aircraft were claimed as destroyed.

Axis aircraft were the next day noted patrolling the area in force and launches were seen searching the vicinity. The unprecedented attack on the flying boats seemed to have caused quite a stir amongst the enemy. Although nothing had ever been established regarding this unusual disturbance, radio intercepts by the 'Y' Service lead them to suspect that German Staff officers might have possibly been on board heading for some kind of conference in North Africa.

During the next few days there was an unexpected drop in enemy activity despite Britain's relentless anti-shipping strikes on Axis convoys. Then on 25 September reports of a plot N.E. of Grand Harbour sent some Spitfires of 249 Squadron scrambling to intercept.

In the ensuing battle only Beurling made contact with some Mel09s. An encounter that he recorded in his battle report:

> "As Tiger White 2, attacked two BflO9s of a formation of 12, from starboard quarter above. Fired one-and-a-half-second burst from 300 yards. Enemy aircraft disintegrated.
>
> Attacked No. 2 aircraft from astern. Two-second burst, 350 yards. E/a emitted black smoke from engine with pieces coming off cowling, then glycol followed afterwards.
>
> Attacking third e/a five minutes later, six miles east of previous position, from port quarter, slightly above, 250-300 yards. Fired two-second burst. E/a enveloped in flames, dived vertically, striking the sea. Enemy pilot was seen going down by parachute, and was fired upon by Mel09, causing parachute to stream."

(Ironically it was a case of mistaken identity – but it was an inhuman practice, whatever quarter it came from.)

One Spitfire, damaged in the encounter, had to be crash-landed at Ta' Qali.

The island's fighter aircraft situation was so unstable that whatever was available was often shared between locally based units. Servicing was attended to by whatever ground crew was most handy, irrespective of the unit it belonged to. Enemy activity over the island was again escalating alarmingly.

With the passage of each successive day anti-shipping operations proved their worth, however, it was noted that a substantial number of supply ships still reached Tripoli. Yet these attacks were the cause of raising great concern to the Axis as it was threatening their convoys' stability, for upon these depended Rommel's campaign in North Africa.

Angry, frustrated, and partly demoralized, Kesselring stressed that nothing short of a large scale air operation against Malta would relieve their convoys from the island's effective ant-shipping strike forces.

"I knew the difficulties well enough," Kesselring later wrote; "the island was fully capable of defending herself and had a substantially strengthened fighter force on hand. The transfer of British fighter aircraft, taking off from aircraft carriers, was going on apace without our being able to do anything about it. Even though we were able to spot their approach by radar, our fighters always arrived on the scene too late; we just could not overcome the difficulties of getting fast aircraft into the area."

"It followed that as regards comparative strength, the scales had tipped against us, German-Italian formations being so much in demand to shield our convoys. Finally, the British had learnt the lesson of the first air battle of Malta; they had widened their base and achieved the highest degree of protection from bomber attacks."

Kesselring, however, despite this air of hopelessness, remained optimistic and confident that his men would come out victorious in the forthcoming battle.

"The C-in-C Luftwaffe gave extensive support to the proposed operation; but still every requirement could not be fulfilled. The quality of the formations, however, made up for this to some extent. The fighter wings were old hands at taking on the British, and the bomber formations had years of operational experience. It was hardly possible, however, to place much reliance on the Italian bombers and fighters because their aircraft were obsolescent and the bomber crews had insufficient night operational training."

The RAF fighter units then based on Malta numbered five:

Ta' Qali Wing – 229 and 249 Squadrons under the command of Wg. Cdr. A. Donaldson.

Luqa Wing – 126 and 1435 Squadrons under the command of Wg. Cdr. Peter Prosser Hanks.

Hal Far Wing – 185 Squadron under the command of Wg. Cdr. U. Thompson.

The build-up of Axis air forces in Sicily, in preparation for another full-scale assault on Malta, awarded the island with nearly a forthnight of relative inactivity before the 'blitz' was launched. Consequently during this quiet period, under the instructions of AVM Park, Wg. Cdr. PP. Hanks experimented with a bomb loaded Spitfire.

Armed with a 250lb bomb under each wing, to which had been fitted a Beaufighter's bomb racks, dive-bombing practice sessions were carried out by the fighters.

A 249 Squadron Spitfire armed with a pair of 250lbs waiting to be flown on an offensive sortie.

Test flights were also carried out to experiment how much would the additional 500lb overweight affect the aircraft's overall flying performance.

Over the target bombs had to be manually released by the crudest of methods. The pilot had to pull the two pins holding the bombs in the racks from inside the cockpit via a piece of string, or wire. The first Spitfire modified for the purpose was EP201, which was flown by Wg. Cdr. PP Hanks. Wg. Cdr. Donaldson tried it next and reported that it had gone through every trial successfully.

Encouraged by these results other Spitfires were soon modified and pilots given the opportunity to fly them on dive-bombing practice.

"I went up with a 250lb bomb under each wing and performed various maneuvers before returning to base." Recalled Sgt. Plt. Mahar.

"I found landing was different, and the approach steeper with the extra load, but otherwise there were no problems."

Flt. Lt. Rolls comments were:

> "The danger was if the bomb got caught hooked up on one pin only because the bomb was likely to hit the ground when you landed."

A case in point was that of Flt. Cdr. P.W.E. Heppell. In February 1943, returning from Egypt, where he was evacuated to after being accidentally shot down by friendly anti-aircraft fire while attacking a Ju88 over Grand Harbour in April of 1942, he was returning from a fighter bomber raid on Lampedusa, with a 500lb bomb still attached to its rack.

"The forward attachment released itself after a time, but the back fastening remained firmly in place." Recounted Wg. Cdr. Johnstone who flew alongside Heppell in another Spitfire.

> "This left the bomb hanging nose downwards with its two feet of rod protruding below the level of the undercarriage when it was lowered."

Heppell knew the situation was hopeless. Both he and his Spitfire would be blown to bits inches off the ground should he try to land.

Further repeated attempts to jettison the bomb proved fruitless, then Heppell received orders to fly out over the sea and bale out at a rendezvous point with an air-sea-rescue launch.

Heppell jumped over the side of his aircraft, gathering speed as he fell. Shortly afterwards he released his chute and looked up to discover, with a chilly spasm of fear, that his Spitfire was spiraling down around him, as if reluctant to part with his company.

Just as horrified was the crew of the HSL who were trying to judge approximately where Heppell would fall, at the same time swinging back and forth, unable to avoid the fast falling aircraft which seemed to be coming straight at them whichever direction they took.

When collision seemed certain the launch made a frantic dash for safety, with the omnious shadow of the Spitfire passing over it before crashing into the sea with a tremendous explosion.

Water drenched those on deck, and the launch was violently rocked by the blast.

A few minutes later Heppell was safely on board the vessel speeding back to the island.

Fly. Off. Ph. Dixon, despite the fact that he agreed there were no reports of any accidents, recalled that:

> " ... The extra weight of the bombs caused some spectacular dives, and at least one aircraft returned with its wings wrinkled, having reached a very high speed before releasing the bombs. Many of these bombs were fitted with a rod out of the front which caused them to explode two feet above the ground."

However, AVM Park, who had approved of the idea, later wrote:

> "The reason I introduced the Spit-bomber was that the enemy were ignoring our fighter sweeps over his aerodromes in the south of Sicily. I used Hurricane bombers at first and the enemy reacted by sending up his fighters to intercept. As a result of flying trials we found that the fitting of two 250lb bombs to the Spitfire slightly increased the take-off run, and slowed down the rate of climb by about 10%. There was practically no difference in speed at level flight."
>
> "We designed the bomb gear so that there was no loss of performance when the bombs were dropped. Unlike the Hurricane bomb gear, our Spitfire throws away all external fittings with the exception of a steel rib which protrudes less than one inch from the wing."

Sqdn. Ldr. Sandy Johnstone, who was in January 43 finally given command of a Spitfire Wg. at the newly built Krendi airstrip, comprised of 229 and 249 Squadrons, wrote that what they experimented with were 500lb bombs, one slung under each Spitfire wing with which they carried several trials without any mishap.

"The Spitfires behaved as it they were designed specifically as bombers."

Picking out a small chemical factory in Pachino to put his experiments into practice, twelve Spitfires were bombed up and another twelve were provided as an escort.

Encountering no opposition, with the exception of some anti-aircraft fire from ground positions, the raid was a complete success, demolishing the target.

The success of this one operation encouraged Johnstone to organize more of the type on isolated objectives, mainly of military importance, during the ensuing weeks.

"Whether the tactical value of these raids was great or not was difficult to say", Commented Johnstone. "... but it certainly did not fail to raise the morale of squadron pilots and the Maltese population at the feeling that the RAF was on the offensive."

Many Spitfire pilots found plenty of idle time during this short interval. However, from reports being brought in by aircrews of 69 Squadron, they might soon be left gasping before the next respite, if they were given another to enjoy. Nearly 400 German and Italian fighters, including over 200 bombers, were being prepared for the next assault on Malta. Worse still was the shortage of food and other provisions which were the cause of great concern on the island, except for a trickle which was being shipped in via an underwater supply service run by submarines.

L.A.C. Metcalf have these comments entered in his diary:

> October 7 – Having plenty air raid warnings lately, though mostly for fighters only. Grub hasn't been fit for pigs to eat all week.
>
> October 8 – The lads rioted about the grub for breakfast time.
>
> October 9 – Grub not much better and it looks like trouble very soon. 76, 53 and 36 chaps taken to hospital in 3 days, all food was poisoning.
>
> October 10 – We've had nine raids today mostly very big plots, so it looks like Kesselring is back again.

At about eight in the morning 8 Spitfires of 249 Squadron joined by 4 of 229 Squadron were airborne, patrolling off the coast. Shortly afterward reports of a plot of 24 small jobs reached them on their R/T. Two of 229's aircraft, however, had to return back to base due to technical problems. The remaining two were jumped by Mel09s, of which one was immediately shot up. Badly damaged the Spitfire returned to Ta' Qali where the pilot was forced to crash-land the aircraft.

The fourth fighter came to grips with the 109s and succeeded in damaging one just before a section of 249's Spitfires arrived on the scene, driving the enemy fighters away.

Taking advantage of this diversion two other 109s, flying at low level, got across the coast unobserved, probably searching for stragglers as targets. However, Operations plotted them circuiting over the southern end of the island and immediately sent out reports of their whereabouts to patrolling RAF fighters.

Plt. Off. Beurling, who was at the time air-testing a newly serviced Spitfire, picking up the warning on his R/T, immediately went into action. Flying out to sea in a wide arc, and sweeping back in close to Filfla, the Canadian soon spotted the two enemy fighters at an elevation of some 1,000ft, flying in line abreast:

> "I dropped in on them. I went down and down, clean under the starboard fellow, and rolled up under him, giving him a quick burst into the engine. He pancaked right smack down on his belly on the island and flipped over onto his back."
>
> "The other fellow tried to circle away, but I stayed with him. He turned out to sea, then whipped back across Filfla again. As he did I moved onto his starboard quarter and let him have it. The burst caught the gas tank and the 'ship' blew up, complete with pilot."

After that chance engagement "Screwball's" tally rose to 21 confirmed over Malta, and with another shared with two other pilots, his overall score stood at 23-and-one-third for when he arrived from Britain the Canadian already had two Fw.l90s to his credit.

The storm finally broke out early with the dawn of 11 October.

"Another tale of the blitz," entered Metcalf in his diary. "Our boys knocked hell's bells out of Jerry, and even then we got three bashings at Ta' Qali, two at Luqa, one at Hal Far."

I.R. MacLennan, whose logbook entries were written under stressed circumstances, noted down his recordings tersely, but still brought to 'life' the action of the moment:

> "Fifteen Ju88s – got pipped in rod – also hit by flak forced landing at night – O.K. – Shaky affair. Two 88s destroyed, one 88 damaged."

Canadian Flg. Off. Rod Smith recorded:

> "Got first Hun of blitz. One of nine Ju88s 18,000ft N.E. of Grand Harbour. Fired two six-seconds bursts from 250yds. Port engine and wing caught fire; e/a exploded and fell into sea. Crewman baled out – Uffz. Gunther Grams – and picked up."

The Malta garrison, of whom only 100 were Spitfire pilots, was truly hard pressed fighting off such odds in enemy fighters, without taking into consideration more than 200 bombers.

Attacks were frequent and heavy, and casualties, albeit not high, were neither few.

Bombers came in small numbers, never exceeding ten at any one time, but the number of escorting fighters was overwhelming. However, the Spitfires that day succeeded in shooting down five Ju88s, for which they received a congratulatory message from the Governor of Malta, Lord Gort:

> "Well done. The Spitfires have produced a fine opening score."

To which the Air Officer Commanding (Malta) replied:

> "All RAF ranks are grateful for your message of congratulations. Spitfires have won the toss, and will keep up their hard hitting until the match is won."

On 12 October another five raids were organized intermittently between dawn until dusk, the first of which was executed at 0620hrs by 7 and 8 Ju88s respectively, escorted by some 24 Me109s. Battle reports from RAF Spitfire pilots gave more descriptive accounts of combats in which they were involved.

Flt. Sgt. Park recorded:

> "Went into some Ju88s. Got two."

Fly. Off. McElroy of 249 Squadron, who was amongst those scrambled to intercept the enemy during the second attack, recalled:

> "I got my sights on one (109) and let him have it fair and square and then engaged another. But the Jerries had had enough and they broke off and headed for home."

The action recorded from the third attack came from a 229 Squadron pilot, Plt. Off. Parkinson. Having been greatly disappointed in previous encounters, mainly due to the jamming of his aircraft cannons when he most needed them he had the satisfaction of attacking a 38 enemy aircraft formation with another 14 Spitfires led by Wg. Cdr. Donaldson:

"Long before we were within range the bombers started to panic. I closed to within a few yards firing head-on; could see shell bursts all over him. Put front gunner out of action, Both engines were smoking. Went into a spiral dive. In the meantime I was attacked by three 109s. One overshot me so I turned into him and gave him a burst that hit the engine and pilot. The Me109 went down in a series of wide barrel rolls, burning and smoking. Crashes into sea."

The fourth raid developed towards mid-afternoon when radar scanners tracked the approach of some 45 enemy fighters from the direction of Sicily.

Twenty-three Spitfires from 126, 229 and 185 Squadrons, led by Wg. Cdr. P.P.Hanks, engaged the enemy formation; however, only one casualty was reported, that of a 109, shot down by the Wing Commander.

Shortly after this encounter a plot estimated at more than 60 enemy aircraft, of which only about five were bombers, were reported approaching the island. Patrolling Spitfires of 1435 Squadron, however, intercepted them halfway between Malta and Sicily.

Sqdn. Ldr. Lovell, who led the eight Spitfires, recalled his own attack on one of the Ju88s:

"While closing in rapidly on the starboard bomber I fired a two-second burst from a range of 300 to 50 yards. Large pieces flew off, and flames came from the starboard engine. I then broke away sharply."

A further 8 Spitfires of 229 Squadron joined the fray shortly afterwards and in the ensuing battle Flt. Lt. A. Roscoe suddenly discovered that a 109 had moved up behind him:

"The first thing I felt was a blow to my right shoulder ... no pain at all. I instinctively broke hard right, ..."

"The 20mm shell passed through me, through the lower instrument panel and out, missing the petrol tank in front of me. As the 109 was still on my tail, and I felt disinclined to engage in a prolonged dogfight, I risked a mid-air collision by pulling the throttle all the way back kicking on a 'yard' of right rudder. The sudden deceleration of my aircraft forced the 109 to detour round

> me to port. It was at this point that we exchanged glances in passing."
>
> "As the 109 went by I applied full power and left rudder, and from almost pointblank range and dead astern I let him have it. He went down immediately."

Severely wounded, and his Spitfire damaged, Roscoe headed straight for the island. En route a second 109 jumped him, inflicting more damage to his aircraft.

An attempt to bale out of the Spitfire failed, leaving Roscoe with one option, to try and coax the stricken, smoking, low flying machine into a glide all the way to Ta' Qali.

> "The last thing I remember was praying, cursing and hoping until at the edge of the field I hit the top of a blast pen."

Two medical orderlies, in spite of the risks involved, rushed towards the burning wreckage and pulled out the unconcious Roscoe, who they immediately rushed to hospital, where he eventually recovered from his injuries.

At the end of the day it was estimated that the defenders had shot down twelve Ju88s, eleven Me109s and four Italian fighters, with thirteen others between probably destroyed or damaged. Spitfire losses numbered seven shot down, six damaged and three pilots were killed.

In later years these figures, regarding Axis estimated losses, tallied favourably with the number of bomber casualties, but fighter aircraft claims by the RAF were exaggerated.

The ensuing days of October, particularly from the 13th up to the 17th, was a continuation of the 'blitz'. Luftwaffe bombers, still in numerically small formations, flew across from Sicily escorted by swarms of fighters. On the 13th contact between the two opposing forces was first made round about 08.45 hours, after Spitfires of 185 Squadron were scrambled to intercept a radar plot the scanners had picked up. Dogfights developed all over the sky around the Ju88s, which maintained their course, but neither side reported any claims in this encounter, although damages became evident as fighters returned to base.

Eight Spitfires of 249 Squadron intercepted the Ju88s a few miles north of St Paul's Bay.

The escorting 109s protective screen remained strong, but not impenetrable.

Plt. Off. Beurling broke through it and went in for the kill:

> "I attacked eight Ju88s taking a straggler 200/50 yards from slightly above to the right with a two-seconds burst of cannon and machine guns. Pieces came off the starboard wing."
>
> "I broke away to port and down and saw one Me109 closing in from port above. I broke left and then turned onto him 50 yards line astern, and fired one-and-a-half second burst of cannon and machine guns. Enemy aircraft burst into flames."
>
> "A second Me109 came down from starboard quarter above. As enemy aircraft pulled out ahead at 250/300 yards I gave him a 4-second burst, machine guns, observed no strikes but pilot baled out. At this time I saw first enemy aircraft strike the sea."

Having disposed of the two 109s, by which time the Ju88s had dropped their bombs on Luqa and the outlying villages, Beurling went after the bombers, catching up with a straggler north of Zonqor Point:

> "I attacked the Ju88 from starboard quarter above, 300 yards, with cannon and machine guns, 2-second burst, and observed strikes on roots of starboard wing. Black smoke began pouring out. I gave it the remainder of my ammunition into the fuselage. Enemy aircraft did a diving turn to the right, striking the sea."

An ever-increasing number of escorting enemy fighters arrived with each successive raid. Obviously they were not protecting their bombers from the RAF Spitfires as effectively as they used to with the result that the 88s were finding it extremely hazardous in reaching their objectives on the island. However these tactics did little to discourage the hard-hitting RAF fighters who fought with unabated fury.

During the second, mid-morning, raid of 13 October, six Ju88s arrived, protected by an escort numbering no less than 60 fighters between Italian Mc202s and German Me109. So few were the remaining Spitfires on the island that only 18 were scrambled to intercepted this enemy fighter aircraft force.

An early afternoon attack was formed of a similar number of enemy aircraft that were intercepted by no more than 20 Spitfires or so.

In this encounter Flg. Off. Rod Smith of 126 Squadron, who was credited with an Mc202, had this recorded in his logbook:

"Gave two three-second burst of slight deflection and astern over Luqa. Hit him in engine and fuselage both times. Big flash of flames. Fell smoking into mouth of Sliema bay."

In a fourth consecutive attack seven Ju88s approached with an escort of no less than 72 fighters, again consisting of Italian Mc202s and Me109s. This strong force was again intercepted by no more than a score of RAF fighters, drawn from 249, 229 and 1435 Squadrons.

A good number of Spitfires were damaged and the Ju88s succeeded in bombing Luqa, but the RAF pilots left their mark on many a Luftwaffe aircraft in the encounter, impressing upon the enemy the fact that they were still as accountably dangerous as ever despite his superiority in numbers.

The Axis High Command persisted with their offensive for several more days, albeit gradually abating, and the fact that they had by this time realized that the scope for which so many lives and equipment had been sacrificed was failing miserably.

"The assault in the middle of October ...", later wrote Kesselring. "... had not the success we hoped for; I broke it off on the third day because, especially in view of the expected landings (the Anglo-American landings in French north-west Africa) our losses were too high.

The surprise had not come off and neither had our bomber attacks against their bases. Instead the battle had to be fought against enemy fighters in the air and their bombproof shelters on the ground."

In fact the Luftwaffe had lost many of their highly trained crews, with the result that unless immediate reinforcements were provided to replace them their bomber offensive against the island could not be sustained.

In Malta, there were others worthy of praise for the successes Spitfire pilots' were enjoying. Amongst these were the fighter controllers, without whose great knowledge in tactical air warfare the former might not have achieved so valourous a victory.

Airmen are just as praise worthy, but no triumph, as has already been proven, can be gained without sacrifices. For Battle of Britain veteran fighter pilot Wg. Cdr. Donaldson, miraculously, his sacrifice was not the ultimate when, on 14 October, while leading a section of four Spitfires of 229 Squadron in a head-on attack against a formation of about eight Ju88s, an Me109 attacked him from astern. Bullets smashed his Spitfire's cockpit and disabled its engine.

There were few parts of Donaldson's body, which were not hit by flying splinters, including a shattered left hand, from which two fingers were blown-off. But fear of drowning stopped Donaldson from abandoning his stricken Spitfire over the sea. Hence with his one good hand he succeeded in manoeuvering his aircraft into a controlled glide all the way back to Ta' Qali, where he made a creditable belly landing. A fire-tender sped up alongside the shot-up Spitfire and Donaldson was immediately dragged free from a blood-splattered cockpit and rushed to hospital.

At about 1300 hours the Luftwaffe organized a third raid, one in which Plt. Off. Beurling again proved himself as a fighter ace. But unlike Wg. Cdr. Donaldson he faired far better.

Enemy bomber formations kept mounting attack after attack. There was a lot of bitter fighting in which RAF pilots pitted their lot against overwhelming odds, but for Plt. Off. G. Beurling, as he later recalled, 14th October, was an exception;

> "It was my last day in the air over Malta."
>
> "Shortly after noon the whole squadron, and another at Luqa, was on immediate readiness."
>
> "Operations scrambled the works, to intercept eight Ju88s and some fifty fighters, and Hetherington, Giddings, Bryden and I were the first four off, Hether leading. We zoomed right up to 20,000ft and spotted the sweep coming in from the East end of the island some 2,000ft below us."
>
> "We didn't wait for the rest of our fighters to get up to us, Hether led us right into the mass, head-on. He took Giddy with him to break up the bombers, while Red and I took on the fighters, to keep them away from the other pair."
>
> "I spotted five fighters pulling up high, as if preparing to dive on Hether and Giddy. I called out, 'Climb, Red! Keep those yellow-nosed bastards off Hether's tail!' and we soared up to 24,000ft, just as the five Me's got there. They promptly peeled off and dived. I yelled: 'Come on, Red! Down we go!' and away we went, right among the bombers, where a free for all was developing. We each picked a Ju. I took the one on the starboard rear side position of the 'V' (formation). I gave him a two-second burst from starboard, getting him in that side's engine and gas tank. He burst into flame and went headlong towards the sea."
>
> "As I nabbed the bomber, 'Hether' came whipping just under me, diving away from eight Me's on his tail. I went down in a hurry

with them, right past my 'Flamer', and lashed into the leading Hun, just as he was going to let 'Hether' have it. As I passed the burning bomber the rear gunner took a shot at me, peppering the port side of my fuselage and the port wing. I picked up about 30 bullet holes, I guess. Explosive bullets were snapping through the cockpit and one nicked the left middle finger of my throttle hand. Another stabbed my left forearm."

" Meanwhile I'd picked up two Me's on my tail and still had 'Hether' to worry about. I took a long shot from about 450 yards from above and to port. I got the bastard in the engine and he dove for the sea, streaming smoke and shedding pieces ... one of the Me's on my tail riddled my port wing like a sieve. A couple of bullets went through the perspex hood, right over my head, while the other 'Schmitt' blasted my starboard wing full of holes."

"With Hether in the clear, and the old crate still flying, I climbed, heading someplace from where I could survey the battlefield. I reached 24,000ft, still chasing after the two Me's that had been after Hether, and all set to take a bead on one of the gentlemen when. ..."

"A call for help came over the R/T. My own position was right above Kalafrana, so I rolled over and had a look down, to see a swell melee going on below. I went down vertically, hitting 600 mph in my riddled crate and at 14,000 feet pulled up under a Messerschmitt, just as he was all set to pot 'Willie the Kid' (Williams). I gave the Hun a two-second burst and blew his whole left wing off at the root. He flicked over, and that was that. Willie's ship, shot to ribbons, was just able to cart him home, no more."

"Just as I shot Willie's pal down, another Me nailed me from behind. He got me right in the belly of the Spit. A chunk of cannon shell smashed into my right heel. Another went between my left arm and body, nicking me in the elbow and ribs. Shrapnel spattered into my left leg. The controls were blasted to bits."

Beurling may have saved Willie's life, but he had forfeited his own. Sooner or later everyone walks into a trap of his own making, no matter how careful he becomes. Beurling knew he should have watched his back before making his attack; he had not.

"I'd been so damned intent on the guy in my sights and on

Willie's tail that I'd forgotten I had one of my own. I soon had reason to remember it."

"... I threw the hood away and tried to get out, but the spin was forcing me back into the seat. ... 'This is it,' I said to myself. 'This is what it's like when you know you're going to die.'

I didn't panic. If anything, I felt resigned to it. Then I snapped out of it and began to struggle again."

"The engine was streaming flame by this time, but somehow I managed to wriggle my way out of the cockpit and out onto the port wing, from where I could bale into the inside of the spin. ... At about 1,000 feet I managed to slip off."

"Bob Seed circled around me as I spun down, 'protecting me,' as he later said, 'from a couple of 109s hovering around like vultures,' giving Ops three 'May Days'."

Some 20mins later Beurling was hauled on board HSL 128. From what Flt. Sgt. G. Head, the boat's coxswain, later recorded:

"The Canadian became very concerned when he missed his bible. This miniature volume was immediately located and returned

Beurling's 13th victory, on 27 July 1942; a Macchi C.202 was shot down over Gozo. Serg. Magg. Faliero Gelli, the Italian pilot, was taken prisoner.

to him, after which he looked more composed. Beurling explained that it had been given to him by his mother and under no circumstances would he fly without it."

Surprisingly this exposed a hidden side to Beurling's rebellious character.

A cannon-shell fragment had penetrated Beurling's right heel, where it was deeply lodged in the flesh, resulting in bringing his participation in the defence of Malta to a sudden end.

The Canadian's last three claims in this battle raised his personal score to 27 and a third, all but one whilst flying with 249 Squadron from the island.

On 14 October five Spitfires were shot down, one crash-landed, and a further seven were damaged.

In the morning of 15 October, six Ju88s succeeded in penetrating through a 28 Spitfire force, and only after the bombers had attacked their intended target and were pulling out of their dives did the Spitfires intercept them. One was shot down, but by then escorting 109s arrived,

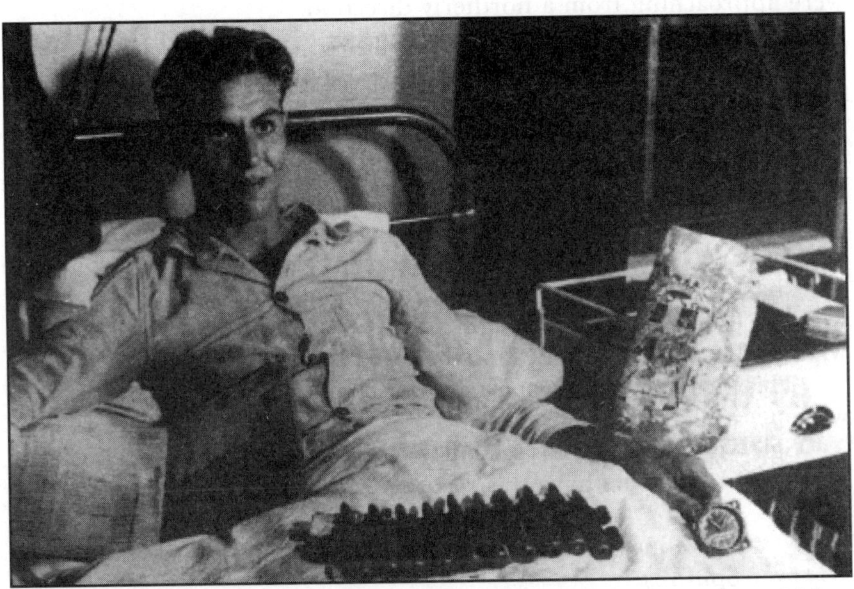

The conclusion to Beurling's final confrontation with the enemy over Malta in 1942 that netted him his 27th victory, but terminated his flying days over Malta.

attacking 8 Spitfires of 249 Squadron, which were patrolling north of Zonqor Point.

In the ensuing battle, as the bombers fled out to sea, with four Spitfires of 229 Squadron in hot pursuit, eight others of 126 Squadron had joined the fray. However, these were in turn jumped by other 109s, inflicting damages to four of the RAF fighters, of which one had to be abandoned by the pilot. Flt. Sgt. Varey, whose Spitfire was disabled in this engagement, had this recorded in his diary:

> "I was very lucky in a dogfight right over the island at 25,000 feet. Shells hit my aircraft and stopped my engine. Fortunately, I was able to glide down and land alright, only to find two cannon shells embedded in the armour plating behind my seat."

Aircraft misidentification also took some toll of RAF fighters during the war, and at times like these this is not the least surprising.

It was nearly mid-day when reports came in from Control that 'blips' appearing on their radar screens indicated that about 50 enemy fighters were approaching from a northerly direction.

Patrolling Spitfires informed Fighter Control that these were probably escorting ASR aircraft. However, some fighters of 185 Squadron came to grips with four aircraft that they identified as Mc202s.

Eight Spitfires of 229 Squadron, which were patrolling well above 4,000 feet, providing those of 185 with top cover, spotted some 109s at their own height, but they seemed to be evading a direct encounter. Suddenly an aircraft dived on the RAF fighters from above, opening fire.

Flt. Lt. Glazebrook turned immediately towards the attacker, and fired back almost instinctively, watching his bullets strike the engine of what he took for an enemy fighter before he realized it was a Spitfire whose pilot, aircraft engine smoking, had to crash-land at Hal Far.

This grave error was repeated less than 30 minutes later, fortunately without resultant casualties.

Sgt. Nigel Park and his section that were at the point attacking some Me109 dive-bombers have this recorded in his diary:

> "Were just going in on 109 bombers when we were jumped by four Spitfires."

Another case of mistaken identity was that of 16 October, when one of three Hurricanes, flown by FAA pilots, searching for missing crews about six miles north of Grand Harbour was attacked by a patrolling Spitfire, when the pilot mistook the Hurrie for a 109. Again the error was not fatal, although damages were inflicted to one of the Hurricane's wings before the Spitfire pilot realized his mistake.

(These few off hand cases makes one wonder whether any others resulted with more tragic consequences, about which none will ever be aware. – Author's Note.)

Fierce encounters were that day again experienced with casualties reported by both sides. The battle report of a Luftwaffe fighter pilot gives this description:

> "After dropping bombs the Ju88s were attacked by 8-10 Spitfires. After the attack I noticed two other Spitfires above the fighter group. I managed to go up into the sun unnoticed and placed myself behind the enemy. From a close distance I fired with all my weapons at the left plane. It went down showing a dark smoke trail, turning again and again and burned when it hit the sea 3Km south of Hal Far."

In another raid Flg. Off. McElroy was forced to crash-land shortly after his aircraft was disabled by escorting 109s; Plt. Off. Sanderson recorded in his logbook:

> "Had a scrap with some 109s. Got a squirt at one. One Me109 destroyed."

The entry in Metcalf's diary describes the day's events, including those of 17 October, as he personally saw them at the time:

> October 16 – More raids – same results. We were just sitting down to tea when a big Ju88 came diving over the billet with a Spitfire chasing it, guns firing. He hit the drink about half-a-mile out.

This eye-witnessed action was probably that of the Spitfire flown by Sgt. Charron.

October 17 – Usual 'blitz' all day. At lunchtime the HSL went out to pick up a few Jerries and we went down to the jetty to see it come in. What a job they had to keep the locals from getting hold of them. – Total kites shot down in week now 110.

During the early morning hours before the break of dawn a Hudson reached the island via Gibraltar, bringing over a number of replacement fighter pilots.

At this time AVM Park was forced to inform the Air Ministry in London that:

> "When the present battle began on 10 October we had 141 Spitfires of which 113 were serviceable. In addition to the absolute losses of 22 Spitfires in the last five days a further 20 are beyond our capacity to repair before the end of October, making a total wastage of 42. If the enemy maintains his present scale of attack for another week we shall not be in a position to put up any effective fighter defence owing to lack of serviceable Spitfires. Therefore the twelve Spitfires promised by the end of October are totally inadequate as previously reported."

With the first Spitfires still not ready to make the direct flight from Gibraltar to Malta, to make good the losses, one last carrier ferrying operation Code-named 'Train' was to be made on 24 October.

The day's first early morning encounter was between some two score enemy aircraft, amongst which were seven Ju88s and the Spitfires of 249 and 1435 Squadrons. While fighters from the two RAF units engaged the escorting fighters a section of 1435 Squadron's aircraft turned on the bombers. These were shortly afterwards joined by 8 more Spitfires of 126 Squadron, which attacked the Ju88s head-on.

Three of the bombers were shot down, and a further two probably destroyed. However, one of the Spitfire pilots, who was rapidly closing in on the leading Ju88, was either hit by return fire or, too intent on his target, due to some error of judgement, he collided head-on with the bomber. Both pilots were killed outright, but three German aircrew members baled out.

By 20 October there were clear indications that the 'blitz' was loosing its original intensity, but this did not exclude the continuation of fighter-bomber raids, as L.A.C. Metcalf recalled.

October 20 – Raids all by fighter-bombers, not much damage.

After this date, although Luftwaffe Me109s still appeared over Malta, albeit in limited numbers, these were for some days replaced by Italian Mc202s and Re2001s.

October 21 – All flying cancelled from Ta' Qali for U/S drome. 249 are off to Luqa for ops. Me,s over Island with bombs nearly all day.

October 22 – For the past five days we've averaged 12-14 raids per day and an average to five down per day.

October 23 – The grub has been cut down again and the bread ration is now down to 7 ounces per day 'biss' (only). I wonder what the hell we shall live on soon?

October 24 – Just before lunchtime some Mes bombed the drome and I was on the runway. Hungry as I was I made the 120 yards or so to the shelter and beat the bombs. I don't know what we cling to life for in this hole, but we all do!

The final Spitfire ferrying operation, 'Train', was on 29th October executed by HMS Furious on a fairly quiet day. However, tipped-off about the arrival of this new 29-Spitfire reinforcement, the enemy had a number of his Mel09s flown across from Sicily about mid-day, hoping to intercept the delivery en route. But with some 27 Spitfires on patrol the enemy fighter pilots lost most of their enthusiasm and avoided engaging their RAF counterparts in combat, as no reports were brought in at the end of the day.

October 25 – More near misses by Me bombs." Recalled Metcalf.

There were two fighter-bomber raids on the airfield during the day. Spitfires of 126 and 229 Squadrons were scrambled to intercept

HMS Furious undertakes one final ferrying operation on 29 October 1942 – "Train".

and shortly afterwards engaged the enemy. Flt. Lt. Rod Smith, who only days before had received the promotion, had this battle report recorded:

> "Pounced by 109s from 24,000 feet; 4-second burst – flash from cockpit and pieces fly off – dived into sea – confirmed rest of section and 'V' service."

Later in the day another fighter sweep was intercepted by 'B' Flight of 126 Squadron.

Returning from the engagement the Flight leader, Flt. Lt. Rolls, his aircraft damaged, soon discovered that one of his charges was missing:

> "One pilot reported he had seen Sgt. Park's aircraft hit the sea, and thought he saw a parachute opening. Another said he saw a Spitfire crash into the sea, with the pilot still inside."

"I hastily rang the Air Sea Rescue," continued Rolls. "and they told me they had the information but it would take some time to get there and it would be getting dark soon."

> "I rang Operations to ask permission to go out and search for Parky or to protect him if he was in his dinghy. – We took off to that area which we searched for almost an hour and as it was getting dark, we had to return to base and leave it to the Air Sea Rescue."

The New Zealander was never found.

The gravity of the situation on the island was again deteriorating with each passing day, as Metcalf's diary entry for 25 October shows. Food was in great demand, as were various other necessities, particularly fuel and ammunition.

> "To-day's grub has been the worst ever and most of the chaps seem to be getting a bit out of hand both as far as work and orders go – personally I'm feeling the same myself even though I got a bit of bread from my new racket. Ack-ack shot down an Me-bomber on the extension of the runway, and was that pilot a mess!"

That same day, of the long-range Spitfires expected to arrive via Gibraltar, the first two Vcs, flown by Flt. Lt. J.H. Burgess and Flt. Sgt. L.G. Pow RCAF, reached the island after a direct flight lasting 5 hours 15 minutes.

October 26 – Same as the rest of the week, it's been one succession of drips from the erks, followed by the usual fighter-bomber raids.

October 28 – Fewer raids than usual today. I'm so hungry that my stomach aches something-awful ... .

The Axis High Command, now realizing that over Malta they were fighting a loosing battle, were in desperation using whatever their Luftwaffe had at its disposal in Sicily; in one final bid to regain the air superiority they had until recently enjoyed. For days on end, as well as the nights, the fighting went on unabated. Field Marshall Kesselring, however, was also aware that he was fast running short of bomber aircraft, as well as aircrews with operational experience, who were becoming harder to replace with every passing day. But his orders remained the same and against his better judgement, had to press on with the offensive, forced to sacrifice more of his Bf109s on fruitless fighter-bomber sweeps.

This went on for several days, during which casualties were escalating to alarming heights, becoming ever clearer that the days when the island of Malta could be kept subdued were past. The Luftwaffe's air superiority in the region was fast dissolving.

Spitfires had amassed into a fighter force too highly organized for the enemy to control.

A drawback that further defeated the Axis in the Central Mediterranean was the threat of an Anglo-American invasion of Algeria and Morocco. In November whatever Luftwaffe units remained in Sicily were drained further still by the withdrawal of many of those stationed there to provide tactical air support in the North African campaign, resulting in easing the pressure under which the Malta garrison had been straining during previous weeks.

Enemy aircraft activity dried up all of a sudden and remained relatively so for more than 48 hours after that, during which time the RAF took stock of its losses.

Surprisingly, considering the high number of Spitfire casualties, pilot losses numbered far less up to 29 October. Reported claims of enemy aircraft during the month totaled 126 destroyed, 62 probables and 162 damaged, of which the highest number amongst both destroyed and damaged was, quite obviously, Me109s.

During November Axis fighter attacks began again but these were noted to be intermittent.

These were successively either driven off or intercepted over their intended objectives by patrolling Spitfires.

It was now Malta's turn to hit back at military objectives in Sicily.

The British forces, having by this time broken through at Alamein, had Rommel's Africa Korps in full retreat, while Operation 'Torch' only days away. It had by the first few days of the month been estimated that the RAF fighters, since the breakout of hostilities in the Mediterranean, up to 7 November 1942, night time victories included, were credited with 863 enemy aircraft destroyed, 316 probables and 814 damaged. However, according to Axis reports of their estimated losses over Malta, between 19 December 1941 and 7 November 1942, no more than 249 are recorded lost and 50 more damaged, of which only 26 were badly shot up.

In the period between 1 January and 7 November 1942 British Ministry of Defence records show that Hurricane losses numbered 45. Spitfire losses were 148, all lost in action, of which very few were destroyed in accidents. It has also been recorded that at least 16 Hurricanes and 66 Spitfires either force, or crash, landed, mainly due to damages sustained in combat.

Then there were those which were destroyed on the ground, totaling 84, of which only five were Spitfires. Due to the shortage of all types of spares for this aircraft on the island, a problem that was never really solved, these were all cannibalized.

Entries in L.A.C. Metcalf's diary describe some of November's activities:

> November 17 – Spits back on bombing from to-morrow at dawn.
>
> November 18 – At 6pm the convoy (15 strong) was within fifteen minutes flying time away, and was proceeding at 14 knots which should make it due off the island during the early hours of tomorrow.
>
> November 22 – Our Spitfires shot up Catania and Comiso this morning and then after lunch we loaded two 250lb H.E's to each Spit and they went again.

At the end of the month Wg. Cdr. Johnstone went to Valletta to undertake the duties of Fighter Controller in the Operations Room at Lascaris. On one occasion, while he was on duty, he noted that the enemy had two fighter squadrons airborne to meet an approaching British raid when the weather was so bad over the island that all RAF aircraft were grounded.

"The opportunity was too good to miss," wrote Johnstone.

> "I picked up the mouth.p.iece of the transmitting set and called up one of our squadrons, which I knew was securely grounded out at Ta' Qali."

Imaginative messages were sent out, keeping up the performance for 30 minutes, which must have confused the Luftwaffe pilots as they flew in circles searching the sky for signs of a non-existent squadron.

> "My orders for our squadron to 'return' to base finally sent the Axis plots to disappear singly from our table as bewildered, and positively exhausted aircrews, returned to their bases."

By the first week of December fifteen Spitfires had been dispatched Malta-bound from Gibraltar. Of these one failed to reach the island. However, with the turn of events in North Africa, and the siege over Malta expected to be lifted, it was at this time decided that there was no longer any need to keep the island supplied with Spitfires for its defence, from Gibraltar as Cyrenaica had fallen in British hands and these arrived from that direction.

Towards the middle of December some Ju88s appeared over the island, and on the night of the 19th Luqa was bombed. Seven Wellingtons were either destroyed or extensively damaged, including two Spitfires; 21 died. But on Christmas Eve an announcement was made that since 1 December the Malta Spitfires had accounted for 75 Axis aircraft, with 89 probably and 120 damaged.

By the end of the year some 400 Spitfires had been ferried to Malta in batches from the decks of British, and twice from one American, carriers.

The Hurricane had its merits but it was no match for he Me109. It was with the Spitfire that the RAF finally succeeded in breaking the Luftwaffe's air superiority over Malta during those bleak nine months of air warfare in 1942.

In January 1943 Wg. Cdr. Johnstone was given command of one of the Spitfire Wings, comprising 229 and 249 Squadrons, both based on the newly built Krendi airstrip where he returned to operational flying since the Battle of Britain, on offensive operations.

> "The enemy scarcely ventured over Malta, without even bothering to patrol their own air space over Sicily. RAF fighters flew on several fruitless missions as they encountered no opposition."

At this time with Von Armin clamouring for urgently needed stores and equipment to be flown to him across in Tunisia from nearby Italy and Sicily, Luftwaffe Ju52 transport aircraft were used for the task, flying at sea level to avoid radar detection. But in Malta, which was comparatively free from enemy attacks, the RAF had long-range fuel tanks fitted to their Spitfires and they went hunting for the big Junkers.

"But this entailed numerous hazards," recorded Johnstone. "These patrols frequently extended as far out afield as Tunisia, taking anything up to five hours or more of flying. Neither was flying at sea level, as close to the waves as it was safe to descend for several hours an exhilarating experience.

> "An engine failure at that stage meant complete disaster as the Spitfire could not be pancaked on to the sea. The aircraft simply dived straight into the water like a knife giving the pilot no chance to break free from his cramped cockpit. Several pilots are known to have been lost this way."

"Since I last flew in 1940 I began to feel old." Confessed Johnstone. "And I was only 26 then."

He noted that he no longer flew into battle with the same carefree abandon of the Battle of Britain days. Many of the new pilots arriving were much younger than he, which soon made Johnstone realize that the experience gained in the two years of air combat had matured him.

Still, worrying about what he should do if anything went wrong in the air alarmed him, particularly when he watched what many of his comrades had gone through.

Early in March of 1943, however, Johnstone contracted undulant fever and had to stop flying. Then on the 13th of the month, appearing in front of a medical board, he was shortly afterwards posted back to the UK.

So during the early months of 1943 the Spitfires were mainly engaged on fighter-bomber sweeps and bomber escort duties, which predominated with the build-up of a major offensive in preparation for operation 'Husky', the Invasion of Sicily.

After July the allies had began to overrun Sicily. The fighting faded away altogether from Malta, as did all the units that had used the island as an advance base, until by the end of the year, except for a squadron or two, all others had moved away from Malta.

When Churchill uttered the words:

> "Never in the field of human conflict was so much owed by so many to so few."

they were intended to honour those men who fought in the Battle of Britain. However, no greater words could be found by which to pay tribute to the men who flew, fought and died in the Battle for Malta. All those who served there will not readily forget it. The way they lived was indescribable for it was not unlike a daily tragedy. Oppression and hunger, like the Axis bombing, was as unforgiving.

This lack of proper nourishment was the cause of numerous illnesses, however, morale was high, maybe because craziness was beginning to affect everyone to a certain extent, but, as Wg. Cdr. 'Jumbo' Gracie recalls:

> "Nowhere was there aerial warfare to compare with this."

The carrier ferrying operation that was organized to fly off the first Spitfires to Malta was made on 7 March 1942 by two carriers, HMS Eagle and HMS Argus, flying between them fifteen of the fighters.

The pilots who flew these first fighter aircraft to the island were the following:

Sqdn. Ldr. Stan Grant

Flt. Sgts. Ferraby, and Ian Cormack.

Flg. Offs. Norman Lee, and Peter Nash.

Flt. Lts. Norman Macqueen, and Hepple.

Sgts. John Tayleur, Jack 'Slim' Yarra, Paul Brennan, Ray Hesselyn, and Bob Sim.

Plt. Offs. Ken Murray, Jim Guerin, John Plagis and Doug Leggo.

These were the Spitfires:

AB262 – 264 – 329 to 338 – 341 – 343 – 344 and 346.

Spitfire ferrying to Malta during 1942:

Dates	Codenames	Carriers	A/C Ferried	Arrived
7/3	SPOTTER	HMS EAGLE	15	15
21/3	PICKET I	HMS EAGLE	9	9
29/3	PICKET II	HMS EAGLE	7	7
20/4	CALENDAR	USS WASP	47	46
9/5	BOWERY	USS WASP		
		HMS EAGLE	64	60
19/5	L. B.	HMS EAGLE	17	17
3/6	STYLE	HMS EAGLE	32	27
9/6	SALIENT	HMS EAGLE	32	32
15/7	PINPOINT	HMS EAGLE	32	31
21/7	INSECT	HMS EAGLE	29	28
11/8	BELLOWS	HMS FURIOUS	38	37
17/8	BARITONE	HMS FURIOUS	31	29
29/10	TRAIN	HMS FURIOUS	29	28

Chapter XIV

US Air Force – Gozo

Desert battle – Plans to Invade Sicily – Gozo; USAAF choice Airfield construction – 31st Fighter Group – Invasion Operations – Advance

Never, in the annals of Malta's aviation history, have aircraft movements and activities exceeded a peak higher than that reached in 1943, when the British and their allies, having finally driven the Axis out of North Africa, prepared their combined forces for operation 'HUSKY', the invasion of Sicily in which Malta was to serve as a frontline base of operations.

For this purpose, to further increase the Island's capacity for the handling of aircraft, some airfields were expanded. A recently completed airstrip at Krendi was taken over by resident fighter squadrons to make room at the other airfields for new arrivals.

Where the RAF's recent role from the island was waging war against enemy communication and supply lines, fighter aircraft were now being prepared to provide the necessary backup and protection of the eastern invasion beaches of Sicily. However, although approval to improve existing airfields on the island was given as early as January, initially this was all on a tentative basis. A new fighter operations room, capable of controlling thirty squadrons, was built, and existing radar facilities improved, while large stocks of fuel and supplies were shipped to the island.

(The majority of these units were ultimately British, but for the first time a substantial number were from British Dominions, and the United States who had only months earlier become involved in the war. – Author.)

The Spitfire defense of Malta had by October 1942 grown so strong that Kesselring, concerned about his fast dwindling formations of Ju88s, was forced to withdraw his bombers from the majority of daytime operations over the island. Even heavy fighter cover had failed to prevent the rise in bomber losses. Hence the usual frightening Luftwaffe air raids on local airfields soon turned into sporadic forays, loosing all of their original effectiveness.

In November, from airfields won in the Desert campaign, the sea route to Malta gained the protection needed for the passage of convoys, and on the 19th four ships reached the island safely with 29,000 tons of supplies, fuel and ammunition. From that date onwards convoys to Malta began to arrive at regular intervals.

On 25 November the arrival of Tedder, Brereton and Timberlake at Luqa was an arresting occasion in itself, but this was the prelude to far more serious proceedings. A.V.M. Park himself conducted the three prominent war chiefs on a tour of the island.

The outcome in North Africa was now plainly the deciding factor on who was to have final control over Europe. In 1942 the British and their allies, aware of the stakes they were struggling for, strategically began to concentrate large numbers of aircraft units on this front during the year.

Gradually, following long strenuous battles in which the two sides at times retreated, recuperated and advanced in turn, the Allies finally gained the initiative, and kept it.

With victory then in sight their next plan was to keep putting on the pressure, and while this great land battle in North Africa raged on, operation 'HUSKY' was already being discussed.

In January 1943 the President of the United States met Britain's Premier at a conference in Casablanca to talk about the operation, but differences in opinion, prolonged discussions, and frequent changes of decisions amongst the Chiefs of Staff resulted in a six months delay to 'HUSKY's finalization of the plan of the operation.

When the outcome of the Tunisian campaign finally became clear, however, preparations for the forthcoming conflict in Sicily proceeded with great haste. All anti-shipping aircraft units that had been operating out of Malta were withdrawn from the island to make room for the expected arrival of three Desert Air Force Wings and their Advance Headquarters.

Since early in May 1943, Allied Commanders had been expecting airfields on Malta to become crammed to the limit, and space for more aircraft would eventually run out. What was being foreseen was that the three USAAF Spitfire squadron; on whose support General Patton's invasion forces depended during their landings in Sicily, would probably have to be left out. So an answer to the space problem had to be found at the earliest possible time, and the urgency for an improvised airfield stirred up the Allied High Command to go to greater lengths.

Towards the end of the month a commission led by the Governor of Malta, Lord Gort, and AVM Keith Park, accompanied by various British and American engineers, visited the island of Gozo where a site was picked out. This skirted the villages of Xewkija, Ghajnsielem, Nadur and Xaghra. However General Eisenhower explained that,

> "... so unfavourable was the rocky nature of the terrain that he had given up all hope of finishing an airfield in time for use in the Sicilian campaign."

This was due to the equipment used by British field engineers, which to a great extent consisted of hand tools and light machinery.

With the matter at its most critical phase, on 25 May, an American engineer, Major Lee Baron Colt C.E, hearing of Park's desire to have an airstrip constructed in Gozo, visited the site with the AVM. Colt informed the AOC that he could have the airstrip completed in two weeks. AVM Park asked the Major when he could start working on the project.

"As soon as my equipment can get here, which should take several days." replied Colt.

Park immediately called American General Spatz in Tunis, requesting his assistance to supply the men and equipment needed for the Gozo project, and on 27 May orders were relayed to Company 'E' 21st Engineer Aviation Regiment at Bone to move to the island of Gozo.

Operation Order No. 52, regarding the role of the Air Forces in Malta during operation 'HUSKY', dated 27 May, reached Air Headquarters Malta that month. However, its contents were not to be made known to anyone below the rank of Wg. Cdr. in RAF units until permission was granted by the Island's Air Headquarters.

Air operations from Malta were to be divided into a three phase sequence, with Phase 1 (The Preparatory Period) covering the period from the end of the Tunisian campaign until D-7, and from D-7 to D-1. At this stage the duties of the fighter units were to maintain sustained air operations to paralize and destroy the enemy air forces in the period up to D-Day.

In Phase 2 (The Assault Period) their task was to provide cover to shipping lying off the Sicilian beaches, and assist the Army to get ashore to capture landing grounds.

The attack on Catania, of which Phase 3 consisted, was considered the most critical part in operation 'HUSKY', due to the danger to which every assault craft had to be exposed from the possibility of enemy air attacks during the landings. Hence, providing off shore protection to shipping from air attacks was of major importance, while the need to keep enemy defenses under attack night and day was just as essential towards the success of the invasion.

Ultimately, when a beachhead was established, close cooperation above and behind the battlefield was to be kept up at all times. Then, once landing grounds in Sicily were captured, fighter squadrons were to move there from Malta to provide air cover over the battlefield, and fighter/bomber units from the African desert were to fly in to occupy the vacated airfields on the island. Subsequently, as more ground became available for the latter in Sicily, their northbound move will in turn provide space for the advance of light and medium bombers from bases in North Africa to Malta.

In order to exploit to the fullest the inherent flexibility of air power and assure a high degree of coordination between Strategic and Tactical, during and after the invasion, some method had to be provided. For this purpose it was agreed that aircraft units of either Air Force might be placed under the operational control of the other for specific operations according to exigencies.

Furthermore, in order to coordinate tactical operations over the Eastern and Western task forces, all squadrons based on the island were placed under the command of the AOC RAF, Malta, who in his turn was under the general direction of the Commander of NATAF (North Africa Tactical Air Force). This arrangement permitted the bulk of the air force to be shifted and concentrated according to the ground situation, and enemy air reaction.

A convoy of nine L.C.T.s reached Malta on 5 June, and the next day they were landed at Marsalforn Bay, Gozo, transferring it into a beehive of military activity.

On 7 June, tents and various other improvised shelters were erected on the airfield site, and the next day work began in earnest, engaging local labour.

The land, of which most was cultivated fields, was relinquished by the farmers after His Grace Monsignor, later Sir, Micheal Gonzi, at the time occupying the post of Bishop in Gozo, convinced them that they will be duly compensated for it all.

The following statement, relating to this arrangement, is found in Appendix 'F' of the Gozo Information Record Office, File 28:

> At the beginning of June 1943, two runways were constructed by the Americans in different plots of land falling within the limits of Xewkija, Ghajnsielem, Nadur and Xaghra. The different plots of land taken up were dominated by "Ta' Hamet", "Tal Barmil" (of the Bucket), "Ta' Gourgiori", "Ta' San Bartilmew", "Tas-Salvatur" (of the Saviour), "Tat-Torn" (of the Tower), and "Tan-Nuffara".
>
> St Bartholomew's Street, Xewkija and the road from Victoria to Nadur village bound the area on the North. On the East by a line to the West of Ghajnsielem running from Nadur road South of "It-Torri ta' Kanura", across Qala and Mgarr road to "Tal Kanal" (of the Gutter).
>
> To the South by a line running from Xewkija village and "Ta' Lambert" to road "Tal Kanal" and on the West partly by Xewkija by the lands "Tal Barmil" and "Ta' Hamet".

The area of land involved amounted to 179 tumoli; tumolo, singular for tumoli, a kind of square land's measure).

The compensation for crops cultivated in the aerodrome area, exclusive of rent paid, was £14,000.

This figure refers only to the land taken over for the actual runways, taxiways and taxi strips, but it does not include damage claims for fields which were used as gun sites. The values that formed the basis upon which compensation was calculated were:

Rent – average 39s/- per tumolo.
Vines – £100 to £110 per tumolo (about 3/6d per vine).
Wheat – £9 per tumolo (if destroyed or cut green).
Meslin – £6 per tumolo (if destroyed or cut green).
Barley – £6 per tumolo (if destroyed or cut green.)
Melons – £7 per tumolo
Tomatoes – £7 per tumolo
Potatoes – £24 per tumolo
Fruit trees – 5s/- to 8s/- each. (Equivalent to 25 and 39 cents respectively).

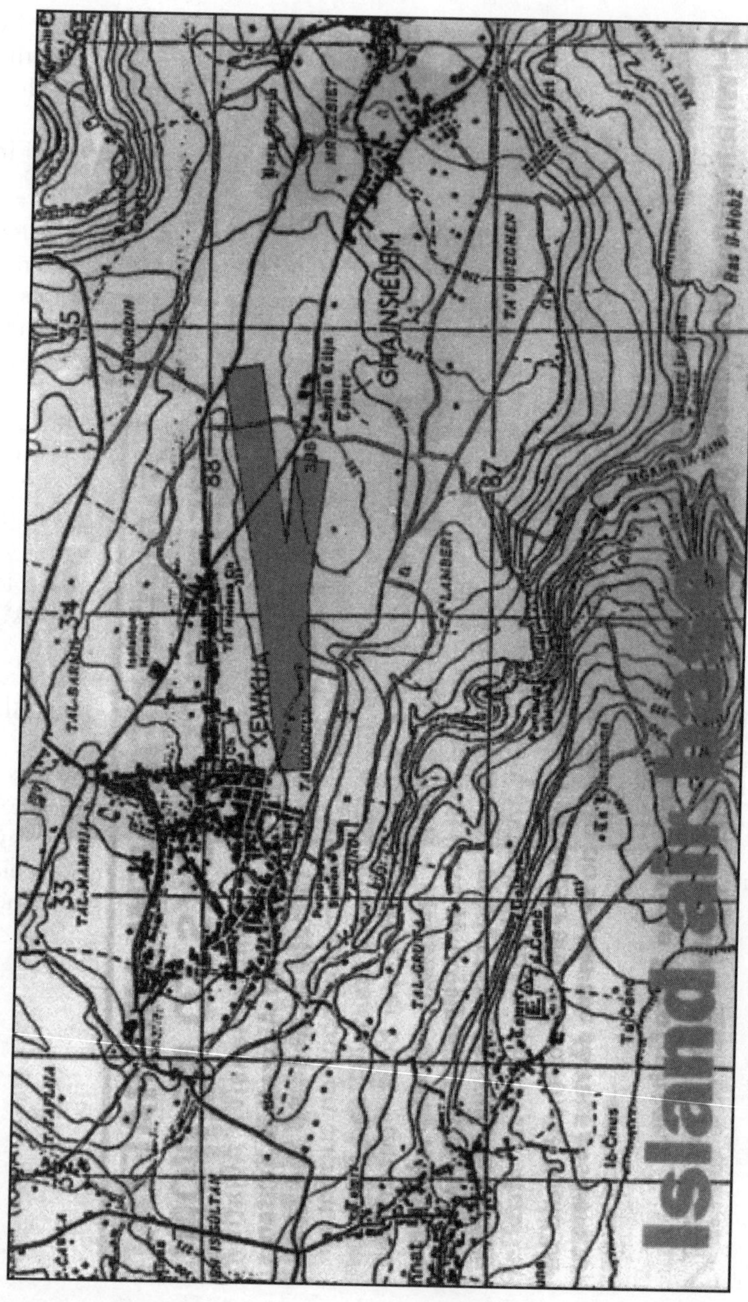

Map of area in Gozo where an Ipyslon-shaped airfield was constructed in 1943.

Cultivated fields, like everywhere else on the Maltese islands, were arranged in terraces, each section at a different level to the one next to it, and every area was enclosed by a rubble-wall three feet high.

Tractors mowed down walls, bulldozing material to the edges of the proposed runway, with dimensions approximately 4,000 feet long and 150 feet wide.

With work progressing in earnest terraces were soon leveled off and on 19 June A.V.M. Park, accompanied by Lt. Col. Dorland and Major Livingstone, engineer of the 12th Air Force, arrived in Gozo. Between them they decided to include an additional runway, as well as the erection of revetments around all hard standings.

The next day Major Livingstone was off to Algiers to arrange for the dispatch of more equipment, while the Works section of the Air Ministry in Malta supplied the American builders with 70,000 sandbags, and the loan of two tractors, a D-4 and a 0-7.

With this order work, which had been split up in two eight hourly shifts, was immediately extended to three. Using their ingenuity the Americans constructed a southeasterly branch from about 1400 feet down the length of the first East-West runway, to form an Ipsylon.

(A labour force of a further three hundred men was engaged to assist in finishing this second runway that was started on 15 June.)

On 20 June 1943 the two runways were completed, with the construction work on taxiways, hard standings and revetments, built of stone and sandbags, at an advanced stage.

Runway surfaces were of packed earth with a tendency to become waterlogged in wintertime, and extremely dusty in the summer. The airfield was calculated to become operational by 22 June with a dispersal capacity to accommodate 78 fighter aircraft.

Air Vice Marshall Park is reputed to have been the first RAF Officer to land on the Gozo airfield in his Spitfire. What is positive, however, is that on 23 June three Spitfires did land there, piloted by Group Capt. Rysley, Wg. Cdr. Thompson and Wg. Cdr. A. Warburton.

Two days later the airfield, around which was now an array of anti-aircraft batteries, was completed. Hence, as originally agreed, that the RAF should keep it maintained, it was turned over to the British 5051 (Airfield Construction) Squadron.

This USAAF Spitfire Mk.Vb, parked on the airfield at Gozo, according to the fuselage lettering, belongs to Colonel Fred M Dean of the 31st Fighter Group.

On 29 June 1943 the Spitfires of the USAAF 31st Fighter Group began arriving in Gozo from Korba North, Africa.

Tracing its origins back to the First World War's No. 1 Pursuit Group, the 31st Pursuit Group was formed on 1 February 1940, composed of three squadrons, No. 39, 40 and 41. Then on 7 December 1941 Japan bombed Pearl Harbour and the United States was brought into the war.

Shortly afterwards the 31st Pursuit Group's strength was increased. Its original squadrons, the 39th, 40th and 41st, were transferred to the 35th Pursuit Group and three others, designated the 307th, 308th and 309th, were in January 1942 newly formed at Baer Field under the command of Colonel John R. "Shorty" Hawkins.

The 31st Pursuit Group was in May of that year officially transferred from the United States Third Air Force to the Eight U.S. Army Air Force. This resulted in its designation being changed to that of the 31st Fighter Group USAAF.

Destined to move to Europe, and the Mediterranean, it was shortly to become the highest scoring group in the Mediterranean Theatre of Operations, and one of only two American Fighter Groups to fly Spitfires into combat.

Having initially been decided that the group would fly their P-39D-1 Airacobras across the Atlantic to the UK, a last minute "Reverse Lend-Lease" arrangement with Britain, to have the Americans provided with Spitfire Vs on arrival, resulted in the shelving of the former plans.

Reaching England in June of 1942 the 31st Fighter Group was in November moved to North Africa where they backed the RAF during operation Torch, by which time the group had began to equip with the Spitfire IX.

When, on 28 June 1943, preparations for the 31st to move to Gozo were underway everyone knew where they were going, a destination code-named "Banjo Field', in Gozo, Malta's sister island, reputed to have been built by the Army Air Corps of Engineers in just 12 days.

Seventy-four Spitfires, led by Colonel Fred H. Dean, had departed from Korba North. Unfortunately, however, the 31st Fighter Group began suffering casualties prior to their going into action. Lt. Stevens, in Spitfire ES182 of' 308th Squadron, went missing due to engine failure, going down some 500 yards off Gozo's north coast in 36 feet of water.

Another fighter, belonging to 309th Squadron, crashed while landing.

"Banjo Field', a 'V'-shaped affair, with a small rise in the ground in between, and one of the runways some four feet higher than the other, misled a 309th Squadron pilot who crashed on arrival.

The most basic accommodation of the day used by aircrew of the USAAF 31st Fighter Group on 'Banjo' field in Gozo in 1943.

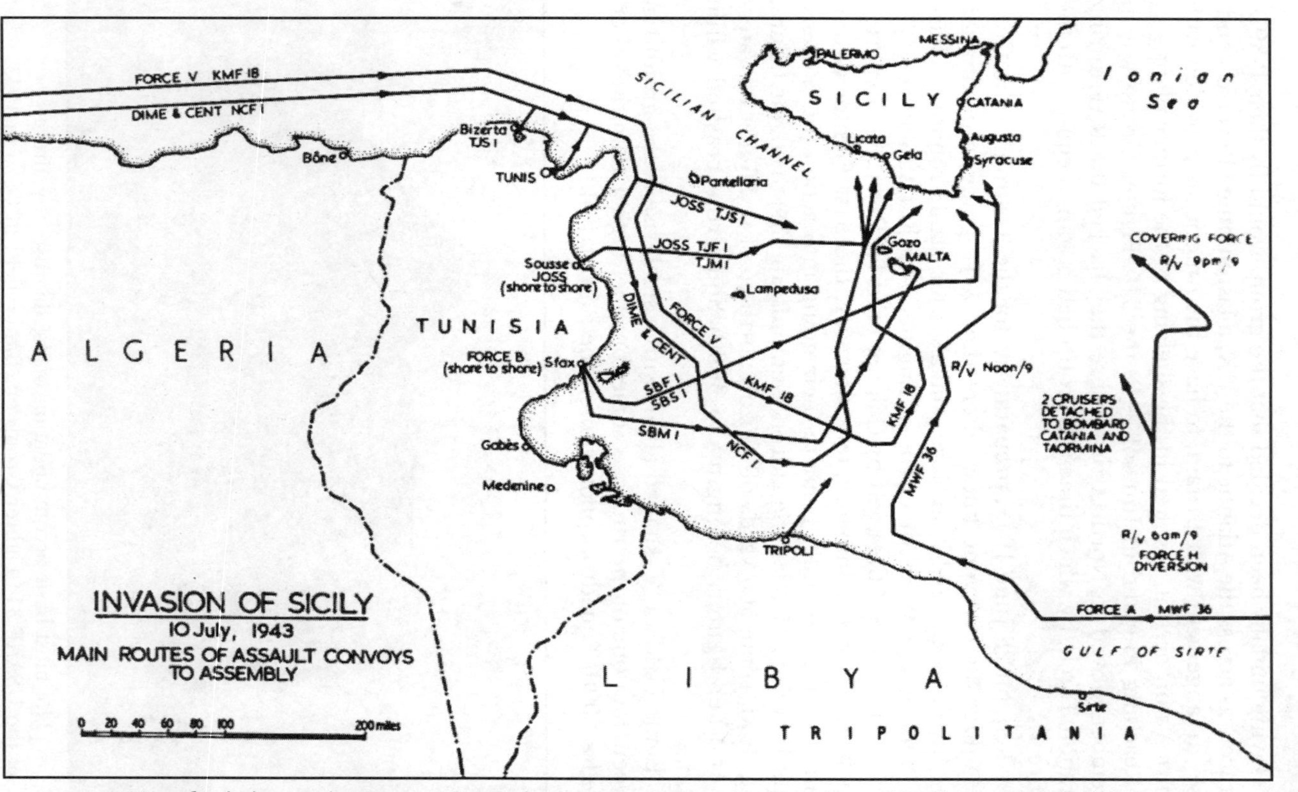

Map depicting main routes of assault convoys during the Invasion of Sicily on 10 July 1943.

Lt. Fardella also miscalculated his landing height with the result that he hit the apex of the higher runway and crashed on top of the wreckage of the Spitfire that had crashed minutes before his. Three of the four British Service commandos who were attending to the first were killed in the crash and Fardella was himself seriously injured.

Furthermore the 31st Fighter Group discovered that although the runways were as good as they could be under the circumstances they still left much to be desired.

Both strips were narrow, crooked and uneven, with either deep cuts or high fills along either side and high rock formations in between. Clouds of dust were blown about in the hot weather that kept sprinkler trucks in motion to wet it down and keep it from marring visibility.

During the first five days following their arrival at Gozo the Americans flew on numerous practice missions, preparing new pilots for the strenuous operations ahead.

Then on 6 July, the USAAF its first Spitfire operations from Gozo.

Split up in two missions 44 sorties in fighter sweeps were flown over Sicily between 11.49 – 12.59hrs and 14.48 – 15.55hrs.

In the second operation the Spitfires were pounced on by Me 109s and Macchi MC202s, an encounter in which 308th Squadron lost Capt. Fleming, its CO, and one of the new pilots, Lt. Babcock.

On 7 July, forty-eight sorties were flown in another two operations, then the next day the Spitfires were again over Comiso escorting B.25 Mitchells, flying thirty-six sorties on one mission.

Lt. Van Austell of 308th Squadron crashed violently during take-off the next day. His aircraft was ablaze within seconds but Austell miraculously escaped unharmed, albeit severely shaken by the narrow escape.

On 9 July, with the invasion vessels steaming towards Gela the Americans were in the air protecting the convoy from enemy air attacks. That day the 31st Fighter Group flew eighty-four sorties in nine operations, in two of which landing after last light.

The next day the USAAF 31st Fighter Group established a record for sorties flown in one day's operations – 193 in 17 missions.

With troops landing at Gela in progress the Americans flew continuously over Sicily between 04.35 and 22.00hrs, during which there were reports of two casualties.

At about mid day Lt. J. E. Johnston of 307th Squadron failed to return from these operations, but was later reported to have force landed on the invaded beach about two miles east of Gela, and joined the advance 31st Ground echelon there.

Lt. J.E. Conley abandoned his aircraft due to a glycol leak, parachuting in the sea, from where he was picked up by a landing craft sometime after 17.00hrs.

The 138 sorties executed in 17 missions flown on 11 July may not have exceeded those carried out on the 10th, but patrolling the Gela beachhead, where the troops were fast gaining ground, the Spitfires encountered larger formations of enemy bombers and fighters during the day.

The first interceptions were made at 06.35hrs when the Americans came up on four Ju88s about to bomb allied shipping. The enemy aircraft jettisoned their bombs in the sea and escaped.

Twenty minutes later 309th Squadron came to grips with ten Do217s, a He177, a Ju88 and two Fw190s which were attacking the convoy off Gela.

In the engagement Lt. Wright probably destroyed a Do217 and Capt. Payne damaged another. Unfortunately, however, although no one was hurt, two of the Spitfires were shot at and damaged by ground fire from allied positions.

At 08.30 four Fw.190 fighter-bombers were forced to hurriedly jettison their bombs harmlessly in the sea when Spitfires from 307th Squadron attacked them. This was when the USAAF 31st Fighter Group drew first blood since they started operating out of Gozo. Capt. Wooten shot down an enemy fighter aircraft in this encounter.

Over an hour later Major Hill and Capt. Chandler engaged a Ju88 some 15 miles northwest of Gela and shot it down between them.

About mid-day the 307th again intercepted two Fw.190s, breaking up a fighter bomber attack on allied shipping. In this engagement Capt. Winkler claimed the destruction of one of the bogies. But although the 307th was credited with the majority of kills for the day, at 15.20hrs, Lt. Goldenburg, flying in Spitfire ES.340, withdrew from the formation.

It was later discovered that he had failed to make it back to base, and was reported missing.

At 16.15hrs, while circling over Pozzello at an altitude in excess of 4,0000 feet Capt. Payne shot down a Me109.

Fourty minutes later the Spitfires of the 309th intercepted a formation of 29 Do217s over Gela. The enemy aircraft were again forced to jettison their bombs in the sea to escape retribution but they still lost

A Spitfire of the USAAF 31st Fighter Group undergoing repairs inside a pen at Qrendi, Malta.

three of their number to Capt. Paulk, Lt. Callender and Lt. Waltner, while Lt. Woodrich damaged another. This was the last battle report of the day.

On 12 July, at about 07.00hrs, while leading an eight Spitfire patrol over Ponte Olivo, Capt. J.C. Collingsworth attacked a Fw.190 and shot it down in flames, though, enemy activity that day was reported as slight during the 145 sorties flown in 17 missions.

This was destined to be the final official action report from the Gozo station.

The next day, with General Patten's ground forces firmly established on the beachhead, the USAAF 31st Fighter Group was directed to advance northwards from where it was to resume with operations.

"HUSKY" had been so well planned and executed that Sicilian defenses had started to wilt earlier than expected, to an extent that by the middle of July Sicily had all but fallen to the allied invasion forces.

The 309th was the first to take leave of Gozo on 13 July en route to Ponte Olivo, but in close support with the two other squadrons the 31st still managed to execute 145 sorties in 19 missions during the day before vacating the airfield altogether the next morning.

(In 1940 when the Maltese offered their contributions in support of the War Effort by organizing a Fighter Plane Fund, in which enough money was raised to have two Spitfires built, the presentation Mk.IIAs were named 'MALTA' and 'GHAWDEX' (GOZO).

A typical anti-aircraft defence post of which there were others at strategic positions around the airfield in Gozo.

That the fighter would eventually fly in defense of Malta was doubtful, but who would have ever foreseen the Spitfire, carrying US. Air Force markings operating out of the island of Gozo. – Author.)

Had for some reason the invasion taken longer than planned to capture Sicily more American air force units would have operated out of Gozo.

According to Appendix 'A', Page 2 of Operation Order No. 52, six units of Kittyhawks from 57 and 79 U. S. Groups should have arrived on 13 and 14 July respectively.

On 9 July, however, according to what F. Cockett wrote in his book 'The Maltese Penguin', an American Tomahawk did make an emergency landing on Gozo:

> "As it touched down an undercarriage collapsed and the aircraft keeled over on a wing, slithering to a halt in a cloud of dust right down the end of the runway."

He further claimed that on that same day, just before dusk, a Horsa, full of airsick British troops, landed on the airfield as well.

This troop carrying glider, it later developed, was under tow by an American aircraft whose pilot had lost his bearings somewhere between Sicily and North Africa, due to the latter's shortage of fuel, was released immediately land was sighted.

During the next three days two DC3s also made use of the airfield. One was packed with United States casualties, while out of the other stepped out none other than Air Vice Marshall Harry Broadhurst, AOC Desert Air Force.

By the end of July the Gozo USAAF Station was abandoned, gradually falling into disuse during the next few months.

Then it began to loose its significance as a wartime airfield, and with the passage of time it once again became part of the countryside.

When the Americans finally withdrew from Gozo the USAAF 31st Fighter Group had flown a total of 701sorties in 79 missions, totaling 998.30 combat hours over the invasion convoy, Gela and the beaches which had been code-named "DIME" for the duration of the invasion.

Claims of enemy aircraft by the American pilots, while operating out of the Gozo station, were ran up in this order:

Lt. Col. F. A. Hill	½ Do217 destroyed
Capt. J. H. Wooten	1 Fw.190 "
Capt. J. M. Winkler	1 Fw.190 "
Capt. J. D. Collinsworth	1 Fw.190 "
Capt. C. W. Payne	1 Me109 "
	1 Do217 probably destroyed
Capt. J. H. Paulk	1 Do217 "
Capt. B. Chandler	½ Do217 "
Capt. J. H. Wright	1 Do217 probably destroyed
1st Lt. J. D. Callender	1 Do217 destroyed
1st Lt. W. R. Waltner	1 Do217 "
2nd Lt. C. J. Woodrich	1 Do217 damaged
Total:	8 destroyed
	2 probably destroyed
	1 damaged

Some Spitfires noted were:

EN851/'D'	"LIMA CHALLENGER"	307TH SQDN.
EN851/'JJ'	"LADY ELLEN III"	309TH SQDN.
ES340		307TH SQDN.
ES182		308TH SQDN.
JK226/'AA'		308TH SQDN.
JK707/'P'		307TH SQDN.

Having said all that about the War in the Mediterranean it would undoubtedly prove interesting to include some facts about the Battle over Malta.

To begin with the first air raid took place on 11 June 1940, at 6.55hrs, while the last alert siren was sounded at 20.43hrs on 28 August 1944, followed with the final "all clear" at 21.00hrs.

The Battle of Malta, however, falls between 1940 and 1943 during which period there were no less than 20,000 Axis sorties against Malta.

In these raids the Axis lost 1493 aircraft, of which 1252 fell to the RAF.

Of those probably destroyed 383 are credited to the RAF and 49 to the ground defences.

Those damaged rose to 1,050 to the RAF and 161 to the ground defences.

RAF losses in the air were 547. Damaged 504.

Destroyed on the ground the RAF lost 160 aircraft and 231 damaged.

Operational hours flown by the RAF run up to a total of 112,247.

A summary of Air Raid alerts discloses that in Malta during 1940 there were a total of 211.

In 1941 these run up to 963 which were in 1942 superceded by a phenomenal 2031 alerts, reflecting the ongoing conflict in the central Mediterranean between Allies and Axis.

In 1943, with Rommel in full retreat, and the Invasion of Sicily shortly afterwards in full swing, alerts in the island dropped to 127 and finally 8 in 1944.

These add up to 3,340 alerts, totaling 2,357 hours and 6 minutes.

The civilian casualty list ran in this order – mixed:

Killed 1,190 – Died of injuries 296 – Missing 54 – Seriously injured 1,846 with 1,932 slightly injured.

Chapter XV

728 FRU

Retreat in North Africa – Need for a Fleet Requirement Unit – 728 Sqdn. at Ta' Qali – Various types of wartime aircraft – HMS Falcon – Wartime aircraft disposal – From prop to jet – The PTA – 728B Drone Sqdn. – 728C AWTU Sqdn. – 24 Years on

While in North African the Axis were scurrying in full retreat across the desert before the British Eight Army, plans for Operation 'Husky' were under discussion.

The British Fleet, with the Luftwaffe no longer a threat in the Mediterranean, returned to Malta with the result that shortly afterwards a Fleet Requirement Unit was in demand.

The Admiralty, with the heavy build up of allied air traffic on the island, had 728 Squadron formed at Gibraltar on 1 May 1943, equipped with six Defiant Target Tugs.

A detachment was shortly afterwards operating out of Tafaroui in Oran using a Swordfish. Then in June some Defiants were provided for the unit at Ouida in French Morocco, to tow for the US 80th AA Battery.

On 15 June the whole squadron moved to Dakheila where it was on 4 July 1943 absorbed into 775 Squadron.

On 14 August, 728 Squadron was reformed from 775 Squadron with the pilots flying out from Dakheila to Malta via Tripoli.

Landing at Ta' Qali the unit settled on the airfield as a resident Fleet Requirement Unit with Defiants DS128, DS129, DS132, DS134, DS147, DS156 and DS158.

The squadron was immediately engaged on towing duties,

verification runs and other tasks for Fleet and Shore establishments, as well as Army anti-aircraft batteries. These duties were in January 1944 extended to the US Fleet at Naples when four of the squadron's aircraft were detached for the purpose.

In March of 1944 some aircraft flew across to Italy where they carried out exercises from Catania.

By 25 July, of the original Defiants, only three remained as two of the five on charge carried serials DS14O and DR949. At this time more modern equipment was arriving in the form of Martinets TT1s, with EM715 and EM678 noted on strength that same month.

Prior to the Armistice, 1945. Elevated view of Ta' Qali airfield.
An array of Martinets of 728 FAA Squadron and Spitfires of 73 Squadron are parked on either side of the taxiway.

Of the three Beaufighter IIFs then on strength two examples were T3210 and T3176.

At this time, with the possible exception of 'M8-', no aircraft codes were known.

In the early days of December, with the disbanding of 727 Squadron, another FRU which had arrived at Ta' Qali on 1 November, 728 Squadron, took on charge a third Beaufighter IIF, two Hurricanes, and a Swordfish I, L2831. This inreased to the squadron's responsibilities as it was engaged to provide units of the British Pacific Fleet working up in the Mediterranean with target towing.

Seafires IIc began to arrive in 1945, with MB281, coded M8A, as an example.

Mosquito XXVs reached the squadron that same year as well, with KB.649 carrying code M8C noted among the first arrivals.

By 1 November 1945 it was estimated that 728 Squadron had carried out exercises for no less than 176 ships. And in May of that year the squadron's aircrews had flown a peak time at 715 hours.

The squadron's Mosquitoes had a task all their own. Used for pilot conversion they were also engaged on radar calibration and all other FRU commitments from 225 Squadron RAF, duties which the latter had temporarily been performing.

In the spring of 1946, with the expected RAF handover of Hal Far airfield to the Royal Navy, in January 728 Squadron moved to RAF Luqa for a spell.

Finally on 15 April Group Capt. Bates, RAF, passed on the old R.N.A. Station to the RN Capt. (AIR) Mediterranean, Capt. J.G.R. Bryant RN., in a ceremony held on the airfield on the 14th where, with the raising of the naval pennant up the ensign mast, RAF Station Hal Far was commissioned as HMS Falcon, destined to attend to numerous types of aircraft and foreign naval units.

Aerial view of Hal Far airfield shortly after the Second World War.

Despite this ceremony, however, 765 Squadron, like numerous other FAA units, had been stationed at Hal Far since October 1945. The only naval squadron to fly the Wellington Mk.X, including some Mk.XVIs, its duties was mainly to carry troops from bases around the Mediterranean to Malta for homeward embarkation. Bench seating was provided as accommodation that, albeit uncomfortable, was accepted by the majority of these passengers just as long as they were being ferried home.

In 1948, the squadron lost two of its Mk.Xs of which one, HZ470, crashed during take-off due to an engine failure 28 March.

On 5 April, HE274 failed to pull out of a dive during a fighter affiliation exercise with a 73 Squadron Spitfire IX, NH484, and crashed into the centre of Rabat. A whole block of buildings was mowed down, causing the death of all four-crew members and twenty civilians.

The squadron was on 30 April disbanded and withdrawn to the UK.

No. 728 Squadron finally moved to the old RNA Station on 5 May 1948 where it remained until it was disbanded.

The squadron arrived at Hal Far airfield with a mixed selection of aircraft, including the arrival of more Martinet TTls. Seafire XVs, of which types kept on reaching the squadron during the next two years until the following Seafires had by 1949 been taken on charge although the bulk had disappeared by the end of 1948.

Seafire MKXV:

PR391, 407, 417, 418, 423, 429, 453, 459, 476 and 495

SR465, 467, 575 and 602, SW808, 810, 855, 868, 865, 906 and 916

This was equipment that remained in squadron use until more modern types became available. However, a reduction in the size of the Mediterranean Fleet at this time affected 728 Squadron negatively with the result that it had to work at a lower strength. This resulted in the loan of two RAF Beaufighters, NT913 and SR917, between June and October 1949, remaining extremely busy with what it had on charge until spring of 1948.The disappearance of several of these aircraft from Hal Far, mainly British and American built wartime surplus, was not due to their withdrawal to the UK. So many of them had remained after 1945 that the Air Ministry had decided that it was no longer worth the expence of flying them back to Britain. Hence, stripped of all useful parts and components the remaining aircraft shells were taken charge of by disposal gangs of whom many were German prisoners of war, identified by yellow discs on the back of their overalls.

The disappearance of numerous aircrafts from Hal Far, mainly British and American built wartime surplus, was not due to their withdrawal to the UK. So many of them had remained after 1945 that the Air Ministry had decided that it was no longer worth the expence of flying them back to Britain. Hence, stripped of all useful parts and components the remaining aircraft shells were taken charge of by disposal gangs of whom many were German prisoners of war, identified by yellow discs on the back of their overalls.

Either one of two means was used to dispose of these aircraft. Any built of wood and canvas were broken up and dumped into a nearby abandoned quarry where they were put to the torch. Aluminum built ones were towed towards the cliffs where they were rolled down a ramp over the edge down the 200 feet drop to the sea.

In the spring of 1947 an offshoot of 728 Squadron was formed under the title of Hal Far Station Flight. Most probably organized to service the requirements of the Station administration the aircraft with which it began operating was the Harvard T.3, an example of which was EZ406.

Baltimore Mk.IV FA.439/801 of 728 Squadron, ex-USAAF, at Hal Far prior to its final 'flight' down Ghar Hassan's cliffs.

Two of 728 Squadron's derelicts at the bottom of the cliffs.

A Sea Otter, RD885, was also taken on charge, an amphibian which, on 14 April 1948, ran into problems as it was descending in the sea and sunk.

Harvard EZ406 was also lost later that same year. Colliding with a 73 Squadron Vampire on 25 October, it crashed some two miles west of Ta' Qali killing the pilot.

For transport purposes an Expeditor C.2 was taken on from 1950 to 1955.

A gap exists from the latter until February 1958 when a Sea Devon C.20 was taken on charge, an aircraft that, surprisingly, was disposed of the following year, and was not replaced until September 1964 when the Station Flight took on a Sea Heron C.2.

Meanwhile, despite the fact that between 1950 and 1955 Sea Furies and Fireflies also formed part of the Flight's strength, in April 1954 it took on charge a jet propelled aircraft, a Meteor T.7. This was operated until April 1957 when a Hawker Hunter T.8 eventually replaced it. A

Seahawk FB.5 was taken on charge next from August 1958 to July 1960, a period during which a Sea Vampire T.22 was also noted to have been included.

Neither were helicopters lacking from the Station Flight's inventory. Dragonfly Hr.3 was the first of type to be taken on charge in December 1952 for air-sea rescue duties. Eventually these were in 1959 replaced by the Hr.5 and some Whirlwind HAS22s.

Towards the end of 1962, the Whirlwind HAS7 replaced the Dragonflies, until 1965 when, with a Sea Heron on charge, Hal Far Station Flight was finally disbanded.

On 22 July 1947 a Martinet TT1, RG.911, was written-off due to engine failure that developed shortly after take-off from Hal Far, forcing the pilot to ditch the aircraft in the sea off Delimara point.

That year Seafires MkXVII were reaching the squadron as the older MkXVs were being gradually withdrawn from use. The former remained on squadron strength until 1952 by which date the following examples were noted:

Seafire Mk.XVII SP347 and SP327
SX126, 134, 166, 161, 166, 174, 176, 177, 185, 186, 224, 225, 226, 230, 234, 241, 266, 271, 284, 294, 302, 316, 332, 333, 338, 340, 345, 348, 351, 364, 356, 358, 359, 380, 362, 363, 365, 370 and 387

No codes are known for these aircraft.

In July 1947 was noted the arrival of further Mosquito XXVs of which the following examples were still being operated by the squadron by the end of 1949:

Mosquito XXV:
KA940, 959, 971, 974, and 967. Coded in block HF/520-529.
KA959 was coded HF/521.

In March 1948, the need for the transportation of passengers and cargo loads resulted in the arrival of two Expeditor IIs. During the ten years 728 Squadron had the type on charge these were rotationally changed with others carrying diverse serials, of which the following are examples:

Expeditor II: FT992, 994, 995, 996 and 984 – HD760, H0776 – KP110 and KP115.

All aircraft were coded HF/811 and 812 up to 1956.

KP115 carried code block HF/811.

From January 1956 the remaining aircraft were coded HF/958 i.e., FT984.

These were in May followed by more advanced equipment in the form of Mosquito PR16s and Mk.XXVs including Seafire F17s. Of the 27 Martinets which were on squadron strength, until they were finally withdrawn, the following are some examples:

Martinet TT1 – MS566 – NR492, NR382, NR665 – RG995, RG899 – RH114, RH117 and RH118.

RH114 was coded HF/513. Others displayed code blocks HF/510-519.

Meanwhile many of the old aircraft had disappeared, the majority of which having been dumped over the cliffs near Hassan's Caves into the sea, the method by which the majority of expired aircraft were disposed of at Hal Far at the time. Two examples were Baltimore FA435, a Mk.IV, and NB863 a Mk.XIV.

A Martinet of 728 Squadron comes to grief while landing.

By the end of the year target-towing duties were mostly being met by the Mosquito TT39s, as the then absolete Martinets were being withdrawn. Meanwhile the squadron's fighter exercises remained the responsibilities of the Seafires.

In autumn of that year some Beaufighter TTl0s, supplimented the Mosquito TT39s in their target-towing duties. The latter served between 1949 and 1952 during which time the following examples had been in squadron use:

Mosquito TT39: MM144, MM193.
PF482, 512, 522, 561, 662, 568, 669, 570, 676, 605 and RV295.

A glass-house nosed DH.98 Mosquito, PF.658, converted to a TT39, of 728 FAA Squadron.

On the airfield proper runways were at this time being paved over with concrete. Permanent hangars were erected. Administrative blocks and living quarters, which were destroyed by enemy action during the war, were rebuilt and expanded, an overall change which gave Hal Far airfield an important military aspect far greater than it had previously enjoyed.

On 26 March 1949, Mosquito NS531 had to be ditched into the sea off Delimara Point after an engine failure while it was returning from Algeria with mail.

A Sea Otter ASR.2, JM880, went to the rescue of the Mosquito's crew, but just as the aircraft descended in the water the heavy swell carried it on to the nearby rocky coastline, inflicting extensive damages to the amphibian.

That same year three Seafires were all written-off in crashes.

On 26 July, SX224 was the first Seafire to get smashed-up on the airfield. This was on 28 September followed by SX226. Then on 24 November, 728 Squadron lost SX241, the third Seafire, due to an engine failure. However neither were other aircraft types immune from similar mishaps, or worse.

During 1950 the Mediterranean Fleet was the squadron's main user, though, the Army increasingly took advantage ot these target towing facilities for their AA Batteries, while the RAF Regiment also became a regular customer.

By this time, with the exception of the Mk.XVII, all other Seafires had disappeared, as had the Mosquito XXV. However, 728 Squadron that year began to receive its first Sea Fury T.20. This remained on squadron strength until 1955, a period during which the following serials were noted:

> Sea Fury T.20: VX284, 288 and 303; VZ364, 370, and 371; WG656 and WG653

All aircraft carried code block HF/200- 202.

VZ364 was NF/200.

On 31 October 1960, 728 Squadron lost a Mosquito PR16, MM273, which crashed into the sea off Malta while carrying out single engine landings.

By the end of that year 728 Squadron had on charge only a limited number of aircraft, comprised of the following:

> Four Seafire XVIIs, 3 Mosquito PRl6s, 6 Mosquito TT39s and 2 Expeditor C.2s

On 24 May 1951 a Mosquito TT39, PF482 crashed off Castel Benito. The aircrew, who survived the incident, reported that severe rudder flutter had developed prior to the crash. Other pilots encountered similar problems in flight and were finding it hazardous flying the type. Henceforth the aircraft began to be avoided like the plague and was more often than not noted grounded.

More modem equipment that year updated 728 Squadron's inventory with the arrival of its first jet aircraft, the Sea Vampire F.20, that arrived at Hal Far in July. The fighter remained on squadron strength until Spring of 1955, by which time the following examples were noted:

Sea Vampire F.20:

VV136, 141, 142, 143, 146, 147, 152, and 153; carrying code block HF/580–589. – VV153 carried HF/582.

In August began to arrive the Sturgeon TT2, an aircraft that the squadron kept on charge until October 1966, by which time it had already began receiving the TT3.

A Sturgeon TT2, T5476, of 728 Squadron during an air pageant at Hal Far airfield in August 1954.

Sturgeon TT2s noted on squadron strength throughout the four-year period were:

TS476, 478; 479, 480, 481, 484, 485, 486, 488, 492, 493, 494, 495, and 497.

TS497 was the one carrying code block HF/597. All the rest displayed code block HF/590 – 599.

On 4 February 1952, with the case of the troublesome Mosquito TT39 still outstanding, L/C PCS. Bagley RN., took over command of 728 Squadron and immediately inquired why the Mosquito was spending so much idle time at dispersal.

To confirm what many of his pilots had reported the CO finally took it upon himself to fly in one of the aircraft, and as is usually the case the order to have the frame of one of the TT39s stripped down was finally given. Still this came a little bit late for the unfortunate pilot of

PF512 when on 28 April, shortly after taking off from the airfield, for obscure reasons, the aircraft crashed into the sea.

A keen inspection of several parts of these aircraft disclosed that their wooden structure had turned soft and spongy, that was suspected to be caused by the airfield's inherent sea dampness to which the Mosquito was constantly exposed to parked at dispersal.

The TT39s were immediately grounded and were shortly afterwards withdrawn and all target-towing duties taken over by the Sturgeon TT2.

Meanwhile the squadron had in March received the first of its Sea Hornet FR.20s, of which the following were noted to have been taken on charge until they were finally withdrawn in 1956:

Hornet FR.20: TT186, 194, and 197.
VR848, 854, 856, 859, 861 – WE238, 240, 242 – VZY 12.

All aircraft were coded in block HF/530 – 539. WE238 and 242 both carried HF/530 while TT186 displayed HF/532.

On 15 May of that year, with runways at RAF Luqa at the start of a resurfacing program, Hal Far accounted for all air traffic movements and activities in Malta until 6 June. Some forty aircraft types made use of the airfield ranging from civil to military, both British and foreign.

Visit estimates reached 536 civilian and 179 military aircraft with a peak period of 325 movements in a single day, occasionally with more than 150 machines parked around Hal Far airfield.

Whatever Seafires and Mosquitos remained had gradually been getting phased out during 1952 as they were being replaced by the arrival of more modern equipment. Still, at this time, according to some reports all the aircraft that 728 Squadron had on charge by that month were 5 Sturgeons, 2 Vampires and two Expeditors.

Then in December, following the arrival of some Dragonflies, the squadron's strength was increased by the addition of a helicopter section, which was to eventually form the mainstay of Malta's air-sea rescue service.

In 1953 the choice for a squadron to represent all other overseas FAA units at a Fleet Review for the Queen's Coronation being held at Spithead, fell to 728 Squadron. For this event five Sea Hornets were specially prepared for the ceremonial fly-past.

In June of that year the squadron's fleet Requirement role was changed to that of a strike unit just after the Mediterranean Fleet returned to the UK. The Services then had Exercise "Retex" organized, during which one of 728 Squadrons Sea Fury T.20s, WG653, crashed during take off on the 21st of the month.

Early with the dawn of that Summer day two of the squadron's Expeditors were airborne, acting as decoys to some of the Sturgeons and Sea Hornets which were executing dummy attacks on Fleet vessels. Later in the morning Sea Vampires and two Sea Furies joined the fray.

The result of this exercise proved so successful from the squadron's point of view that a second one, "Summer 2", was held the following month.

In this exercise 728 Squadron's fighter aircraft mounted strikes on Neptune patrol aircraft of the RAF.

On 12 January 1954, with the New Year celebrations hardly over, one of 728 Squadrons Sea Hornet F.20s, VR859 ran into trouble during assymetric practice. Striking rocky ground after running short of runway, its undercarriage collapsed.

Shortly after this incident the squadron began to receive the first of its Meteor T.7s, that quite probably, like the Sturgeon TT3, arrived while the unit was operating from Ta' Qali from where it did not return to Hal Far until the early days of October.

Meteors and Sturgeon TT fly past over Hal Far on 15 May 1956 to celebrate 728 Squadron's 10th Anniversary on the airfield.

The Meteor T.7 remained on squadron strength until 1987, throughout which noted examples were: VW446 and 447. WA600, 649, and 650. WL350, 351, and 353, WS106, 111, 112, 114, 115, and 116.

Initially coded in block HF/410-419 these were for long and complicated reasons later changed to code block HF/570-579.

VW446 carried code block HF/570. WL350 and WS111 displayed HF/574, while WS115 was HF/575.

Later still, in 1955, these were to change again, to HF/860- 861, with WL353 carrying code block HF/861 and WL332 displaying HF/860.

On 10 November 728 Squadron was again involved in a military exercise. With Admiral Lord Mounbatten leaving Malta Exercise Famous, a farewell flypast, was organized to celebrate the occasion for which the Hal Far FRU provided three Sturgeons and three Sea Vampires. In this salute were involved 80 aircraft from other units amongst which was the RAAF 78Th Wing.

That same month an additional Expeditor, HD775, reached the squadron from the UK.

At the beginning of 1955 the squadron's inventory was comprised of 5 Sea Hornet FR.20s, 8 Sturgeon TT2s and 3s, 5 Sea Vampire F.20s, 2 Expeditor C.2s and three Dragonfly helicopters.

On 8 February, however, the Admiralty established the squadron's strength by an additional seven Meteors to replace the withdrawal to UK of more of the Sea Vampires.

In April, with repairs to Hal Far's main runway in hand, the squadron's Meteors moved to RAF Luqa for six months.

On 28 May 728 Squadron lost Expeditor FT995, ditching in the sea some 80 miles North-East of Malta due to engine failure while en route from Istanbul. A Whirlwind helicopter of 845 Squadron was immediately dispatched to pick up both passengers and aircrew.

The year 1956 saw the phasing out of more of the squadron's old equipment, particularly the old Sturgeon TT2s. On 23 January the squadron lost a Meteor T7, probably WS112.

Meanwhile it was decided that 728 Squadron should add to its transport element, with the result that Sea Devon C.20s began to arrive. Two of these, XK895 and XK896, were in August flown in and taken on charge by the squadron. It was also noted that XK896 carried code block HF/956.

The Dragonflies in the SAR role were in June 1957 supplemented by Whirlwind HAR3 helicopters, while the Sea Hornets were withdrawn in February.

That year the Admiralty for the first time decided to provide their naval fleet gunners with far more sophisticated a target for their radar-controlled gunnery systems than what 728 Squadron's target-towing aircraft had been offering since 1943.

Tentative tests via the trial and error method on a jet-propelled pilotless target aircraft, the CT10, had been going on for some time. Fired from a fixed site at Benghajsa Point, where a fully rigged firing range, complete with blast-safety walls and a control caravan, equipped with comprehensive plotting gear, was set up.

A CT10, replica of Germany's V.1,
being prepared for launching from Benghajsa Point.

The bright orange-coloured missile leaves its launching pad, a twin-railed 40 degree inclined ramp, trailing fire and brimstone, at a speed of about 70 knots. The two solid fuel rocket boosters attached to the underside of the pilotless monoplane, which propel it into the air, are released from the drone as it reaches a height of some 200 feet.

To avoid damaging these rockets, which are later recovered for further use, a parachute is brought into operation to slow down their descent into the sea.

Weighing a little less than a ton, the CT10 was a product of Nord Aviation of France, carrying designation ARS-5.501.

PTA tracking team about to go into action.
Vice Admiral Durnford-Slater is in attendance on a visit to the site.

Fitted with centrally located square-tipped wing stubs as stabilizers, forming a wing span nearly fourteen feet across, its resemblance to Germany's V.1 of World War Two fame was amazing. Power to the PTA, once the boosters broke away from it, was transmitted via a stovepipe housed petrol operated Arsenal pulse jet engine, developing 396lbs thrust, fixed to a pylon on top of the twenty-feet long cigar-shaped fuselage.

Once airborne and no longer dependent on its two powder rocket boosters, the flight path of the missile was radar controlled from the ground.

Left climbing to a predetermined elevation of some 13,000 feet under its own power, reaching speeds in the region of 300 miles an hour, the PTA was then leveled-off and guided to a pre-determined destination. This was within shooting range of the naval fleet warships

The CT10 is fired off its launching pad.

operating radar-controlled gunnery equipment, most frequently around the island of Filfla.

The PTA was in constant use both by the British and French navies, providing an essential means of exercising for gun crews on warships.

Firing commenced on the rocket until instructions to the contrary were transmitted from control, or a direct hit from the ships' gunners destroyed the PTA.

With the flight of the drone nearing completion all shooting on the CT10 was called off and the ditching procedure began.

As the PTA goes it is tracked both visually and by radar directing it skywards. The engine was then turned off, resulting in a rapid fall-off in speed.

Finally powerless, and in the grip of gravitational forces, the CT10 stalls and begins to fall. A parachute then comes into operation and as the rocket descends seawards, all surplus fuel is automatically ejected from its tanks via a dump valve.

Drained of its fuel the PTA becomes bouyant and floatable on the surface of the sea. Afterwards, its location pinpointed by the several flourescent type markers painted on its fuselage, the missile is recovered, returned to the launching site, and prepared for the next flight.

The PTA could also be brought down on land, for which a steel needle was provided in the nose so that the projectile could dig itself into the ground.

Early in January 1960 the PTA launching site at Benghajsa was moved to another position within Hal Far's perimeter. However, according to a statement by a military spokesman no more of the PTAs could be launched from the new site.

At the Benghajsa Point site maintenance and repair facilities had meanwhile been organized to service and maintain missiles fired at sea from the guided missiles trials ship HMSGirdleness.

Meanwhile, in mid-January 1958, a No. 728B Squadron was formed at RNAS Stretton as a pilotless drone target unit, and equipped with the Firefly U.9, of which some examples used at Malta were amongst the following:

VH130 and VH134
VT364, 370, 413, 430, 462, 463, 470, 481, 485, 487, 493, 497
VX418, 427 and 429.
WB245, 257, 307, 331, 341, 347, 364, 365, 373, 374, 394, 410 and 411.

Aircraft carried code block HF/590-599 with WB341 displaying HF/593.

The squadron arrived at Hal Far late in February, were it

Wingtips missing two Firefly U.9 Drones of 728B Squadron await their fate.

immediately settled in and on 6 March the unit was providing their radio-controlled pilotless aircraft for the trials of the 'Seaslug' Surface-to-Air guided weapon on HMS Girdleness. Shortly afterwards, however, it developed that the aircraft control systems were in need of extensive modifications. These had to be designed, installed and tested by the squadron's own personnel until they turned out in perfect working order, an achievement for which twelve squadron members were all awarded citations, with an MBE going to Lt. Comdr. J.G. Corbell who ended becoming the Navy's expert on radio controlled aircraft.

By October 728B Squadron had nine Firefly drones available, of which WB257 was on the 6th the first of type to be shot down off Malta. A second one, VHI34 was on the 31 October ditched off Hal Far airfield into the sea shortly after take-off.

On 3 November a Firefly U.9, VT370, crashed off Malta while WB394 was on that same day lost to cruiser fire off the island.

The next day WB373 suffered the same fate. Then towards the closing days of November the gunners of HMS Duchess shot down VT441.

Unfortunately on 6 December, one of 728 Squadron's Meteor T.7s, WSI06, while airborne on a test flight, disappeared without trace over open waters.

Meanwhile, however, in March other equipment had been reaching 728 Squadron in the form of Meteor TT20s; with the following examples arriving at intervals during the next few years:

WD592, 610, 612, 643, 711 and 785.
WM147, 151, 160, 255 and 260

From the day of their arrival until July 1965, the aircraft were coded between HF/578 and HF/586, with WD711 carrying HF/579. From July onwards the remaining aircraft were re-coded in blocks HF/862- 866 as follows: WM147 HF/862, WM260/863, WD592/864, WD612/865, and WD785/866.

The following were the aircraft with which 728 Squadron disbanded in 1967 to depart for the UK:

WD785 and WM260 departed on 17 April 1967.
WD612 took leave of the island on 29April 1967.
WD592 and WM147 departed on 4 May 1967.

By the end of 1958 the Meteor TT20 had literally replaced the Sturgeon TT3 of which the last one, TS488, had made its final flight on 1 October, and suffered an undercarriage collapse as it taxied in at Hal Far.

Four days later 728 Squadron lost Lt. Bernard, its test pilot, who was airborne in a Meteor T.7, WS106, that went missing during a sortie.

Sturgeon III, TS488, of 728 Squadron after a landing mishap.

Led by Sea Devon XJ348/795 of 728 Squadron, a Meteor TT20 and a T.7 from the same unit are paired off to its starboard, with a black Seahawk from some other squadron in attendance.

In the summer of 1959 the squadron's Expeditors were scrapped. The Dragonfly helicopters were withdrawn in October with the result that by December of that year 728 Squadron remained with a 'fleet' of Meteor TT20s and T.7s for training and target-towing duties and the Sea Devon C.20 for transport purposes. All the helicopters were gone.

On 10 June 1960 the squadron lost Lt. Pyke who crashed on the outskirts of Safi airfield in Meteor T7, WH-650.

Meanwhile on 8 July 1959 728B Squadron received the first of its Meteor Ul5s, VT.110, carrying code HF/655. These aircraft were painted bright red and yellow all over while the Meteor U16s, of which the first, WF716, coded HF/590, was delivered on 25 May 1960, were painted grey with conventional yellow training markings.

A jet propelled Drone, the Meteor U.15,
also reaches Hal Far airfield and 728B Squadron.

A further three U15s arrived in this order:

VT.104, coded HF/656, delivered on 9 September 1959.
VT310, coded HF/657, delivered on 17 December 1959.
RA375, coded HF/658, delivered on 21 March 1960.

Others, like VW258 – VT243 and VT282 may have also been available but this aircraft type proved problematic in the drone role, a fault these Meteors seem to have arrived with. This forced the 728B Squadron to keep the Firefly on strength longer than expected with the result that VHI30 had a minor incident on 23 July 1959 when the wire of its arrestor hook parted while it was being landed at Hal Far.

Despite the jet's drawback, however, the Meteor U15 still saw limited use with 728B Squadron which lost the first of type, VT.104, to a 'Seaslug' missile fired during radio-controlled target practice on 23 March 1960.

That year drone losses were heavy, indicative of the efficiency of the British fleet's radar-controlled gunnery system.

The losses suffered on 23 March 1960 were on 11 May increased with another two, VT.110 and VT243, when these were both shot down in the sea during radar-controlled target firing practice.

The next day VT310 suffered the same fate. Then on the 25th a Firefly U.9, WB245, crashed during fake off from Hal Far airfield.

On 9 August a further Meteor U15, RA397, was shot down in the sea off Malta during more radio-controlled target firing practice.

Ten days later it was the turn of a Firefly U.9, VT481, to be brought down by the same means of gunfire, which was also instrumental in the destruction yet another Meteor U15, VT417, on the 24 August.

Two more Firefly U.9s, WB.410 AND VT364, having been missed by the ships' gunners, crashed while being landed at Hal Far on the 25th and 26th of the month respectively.

Another Firefly, WB331, was on 26 September written off while it was being landed on Hal Far airfield. This was on 6 October followed by two more of the type, WB365 and WB392, that fell to the ships' radar-controlled gunnery equipment while WB374 was shot down the next day.

At this time Meteor U16s were being received by the squadron which had the first one airborne on 11 October:

The Meteor U.16 Drone follows its predecessor, the U.15, to enjoy some of the island's sunshine under 728B Squadron.

WF716 coded HF/658. Delivered in October.
WK870 coded HF/655. Delivered in November.
WE932 coded HF/656. Delivered in March 1961.

On 14 October 1960 a Meteor U15, VW258, was shot down into the sea by the ships' radar-controlled guns.

VT268, another Meteor U15, was on 7 March 1961 shot down off Malta. In May, however, commenced the delivery of the Canberra D.14:

WH921,	coded	HF/590	was	delivered	on	25 May 1961.
WD941,	"	HF/591	"	"	"	06 June 1961.
WH720,	"	HF/592	"	"	"	07 July 4961.
WJ638,	"	HF/593	"	"	"	09 August 1961.
WH704,	"	HF/594	"	"	"	09 August 1961.
WH876,	"	HF/595	"	"	"	14 September 1961.

By this time 728 Squadron's pilots had flown more than 600 hours in aircraft other than their own so that the Station could fulfill its duties. These included all types of aircraft on FAA strength, from Gannets to Dragonfly helicopters.

Of the batch of Canberras D.14 received by 728B Squadron in 1961, WH921, the first of type in FAA service, was also the first one delivered to the squadron. Ironically, however, it became the first and last Canberra D.14 which was on 6 October 1961 to be shot down by a 'Seaslug' guided missile fired from HMS Girdleness.

The Canberra U.14 Drone, coloured white all over, arrives at Hal Far for 728B Squadron in 1961.

On the 30th of the month the squadron lost another Meteor U16, VZ4I5, to the naval fleet gunners.

But at this time the Seaslug trials were drawing to a close and Meteor UI6, WE932, was flown on one last sortie for HMS Girdleness on 13 November 1961.

With three Fireflies and five Canberras remaining on squadron strength two of the U.9s, VT413 and VT430 were on 23 November 1961 shot down by a Scimitar and a Sea Vixen from HMS Centaur and Ark Royal respectively.

The last remaining Firefly U.9 in FAA service was finally destroyed by the gunners of HMS Duchess on 29 November 1961.

During its few years existence at Hal Far 728B Squadron had no less than 52 aircraft on charge. Although the squadron was kept busy at all times launching drones to meet every schedule, except in bad weather conditions, the period which was estimated to have been most hectic was when the Canberras were available as several thousand extra hours were worked in order to fulfill the program.

Finally, with the service for which 728B Squadron was formed completed, the unit was on 2 December 1961 disbanded.

This squadron number, however, was not immediately lost as the then Hal Far Search and Rescue Flight inherited it, with the result that this number lasted a further fifteen months, until March 1963 when it was finally disbanded for good.

No. 728C Squadron was on 8 January 1958 formed as an Amphibious Warfare Trials Unit. Its purpose was to develop the use of helicopters in lifting Royal Marine Commandos from ship to shore during beach-head assaults. Four Whirlwind HAS22 helicopters were ferried to Malta on board HMS Eagle and Ark Royal to become established at Hal Far on 7 February 1958, right about the time 728B Squadron arrived at the station.

One example was WV218. WV222 was probably another, carrying code HF/622.

Shortly afterwards landing sites were provided at Mellieha Bay, Imtarfa Barracks and St. Georges, the headquarters of 3rd Commando Brigade, with the result that by the end of February the majority of the marines had gained air experience.

In March synthetic assault exercises were practiced, giving the men a good standard of operational knowledge by early April.

On 7 April 1958 the squadron joined HMS Striker for exercises in Libya, but the political situation in Malta led to the curtailing of this activity and immediate embarkation in HMS Ark Royal to return to the island.

After a short rest, however, 728C Squadron was back on Ark Royal enroute to Sardinia where it was to participate in an exercise. However, the opportunity to later enjoy a good time in the old city was once more terminated when, due to the island's internal security, orders reached the squadron to return to Hal Far as soon as possible.

Once these disquiets were resolved, the unit returned to attending to its routine duties until in June, it embarked in HMS Bermuda with units of 46 Commando. The scope for this movement was to assist in watching over the political situation in Cyprus, but the situation there was not as grave as it was at first thought and on 28 July, 728C Squadron returned to the island.

Early in August the squadron was back to its usual duties of which some were of a civilian nature, i.e., ecclesiastical and other mercy missions to and from Gozo.

Later in the month amphibious assault exercises were taken up, keeping the squadron on its toes, then in September two of the Whirlwinds were sent on detachment to El Adem in Libya with half a troop of commandos.

At this time, estimated to have reached a fully competent level in its task, 728C Squadron was upgraded to become 848 Squadron as of 14 August 1958.

The year 1958 brought up with it a strong line of FAA movements and activities at Hal Far as on 13 October Nine Sea Princes T.ls landed on the airfield via Orange in France.

The FAA's Observer School, 750 Squadron, had for several years been based at Culdrose, to the extreme south west of Britain. Weather conditions were unsuitable for the squadron's line of activities in the UK with the result that it was decided to have it moved to the island of Malta, were fairer weather was ideal for training purposes.

From Hal Far 750 Squadron resumed with its routine training of observers but shortly afterwards it was decided that Idris in Libya was more ideal a location for navigational exercises.

Apart from their normal everyday duties aircrews participated in searches for rescue activities. A case in point was that of March 1960 when two Sea Venoms from HMS Albion collided in midair and ditched in the sea.

Early in July 1960 the squadron received its first jet aircraft, Sea

Venoms, which were earmarked for the use of high level navigational training.

The Sea Princes, however, were not relinquished. Navigational exercises to destinations such as Sigonella in Sicily, Palma de Majorca, Idris, Rome and Naples, were carried out in the aircraft.

By January 1961 operations were abandoned due to the shortage of replacement fuel tanks, but this situation had by August improved and five of the aircraft were permitted to fly across to Rome on a land-away navigation exercise.

The Sea Princes were kept busy on low level flying exercises over Sicily. These included radar homings, which absorbed a lot of the aircraft's time during autumn, searching over open waters for fishing boats which might have sailed in areas where Seaslug missiles were being fired from HMS Girdleness.

Both aircraft types combined their naval exercises during 1962 with visiting flights to Pisa, Italy and Hyeres in the south of France.

Over the next three years 750 Squadron remained operating along the same pattern until 1965 when it began the return move back home to UK.

The Sea Venoms were first to depart on 23 June, followed a forthnight later by the Sea Princes.

On 30 June, Meteor T.7 WS115 of 728 Squadron was involved in a minor incident when, during an engine start-up, a fire broke out in its portwheel bay.

However, only by a miracle did the aircrew of two in Meteor T.7 WA600 of 728 Squadron escape with their lives when, on 12 October 1961, they had to unexpectedly abort a take off that completely destroyed the aircraft.

In March 1963, the larger four-engined Sea Heron G.20s, of which the first two to arrive were XR443 and 444, with the latter carrying code HF/794, finally replaced the Sea Devons. Devon XK896, which was the last of type to take leave of the island, departed on 7 March.

In March Whirlwind HAS22 helicopters also returned to ASR duties, to remain operational until August 1965.

Towards the end of 1964, with a surprising shortage in man-power, each pilot ended having two aircraft at his disposal.

At the end of July 1965, one of the Sea Herons, XK444, returned to the UK, leaving XK443 to carry out all transport duties for 728 Squadron. However there was a sharp decline in the amount of work for the squadron, a situation that dragged on into 1966, resulting from a decrease in British naval presence in the Mediterranean.

On 28 March 1967 the remaining Sea Heron finally departed for the UK while the Meteors were early in April prepared for ferrying.

No. 728 Squadron's days were positively numbered now. On 7 April the remaining five Meteors TT20, accompanied by three naval Buccaneers, a Sea Vixen and two Gannets from HMS Hermes, staged a farewell fly-past.

On 11 May, 728 Squadron went into its terminal period prior to its disbanding, which came about on 31 May 1967, after 24 years service to the Mediterranean Fleet.

Chapter XVI

Air Malta

Air Malta - 1947 – Sovereign Military Order of Malta – Malta-Gozo Air Services Ltd – Air Malta - 1973

During the Post-WW2 period travelling by air from Malta was extremely difficult, and seats on scheduled airline flights could only be obtained by devious means via high Government priority. But in the summer of 1946 a local company, Cassar & Cooper, in a joint venture with J.E. Sullivan of London, decided to start chartering aircraft from charter companies based in UK to facilitate civil travel.

The first passengers arrived at Luqa from Croydon on 12 July in an Airspeed Consul, G-AHFT, of Morton Air Services from Croydon. The newlywed couple, who came to Malta for their honeymoon, returned to

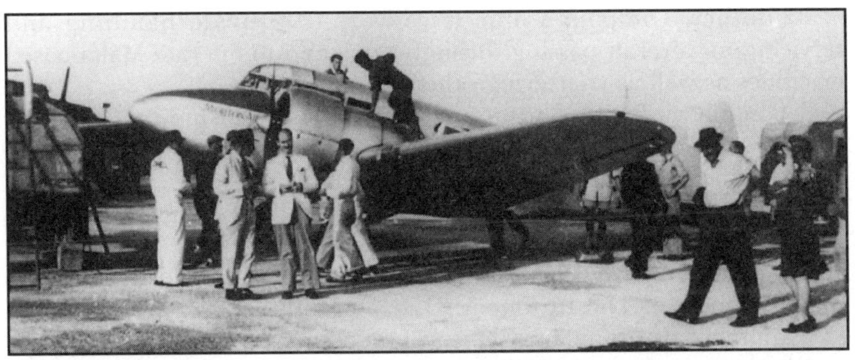

The first Consul, G-AHFT, of Morton Services arrives at Luqa on 12 July 1946. Amongst these first passengers were Mr G. Denaro and his wife.

Mr and Mrs G. Denaro take leave of the island on 26 July 1946 in Proctor G-AHTU.

the UK on the 26th of the month in a Percival Proctor 3, G-AHTU, of A. R. "Tiny" Palgrim at Elstree.

In September arrangements were made with another Charter Company, British Aviation Services (BAS) in London, to become the first associate.

Shortly afterwards this was strengthened further by the association of Silver City Airways Ltd, and on 1 January 1947 British Aviation Services (Malta) Ltd was officially registered.

The new company's objectives were to provide handling and servicing for aircraft passing through Luqa and to operate Malta-based machines as well as chartering others from the UK.

A number of BAS Consul aircraft were used, including G-AHRK, G-AIBF, G-AIKY, G-AJGH, which operated on diverse services to Mediterranean airports.

Meanwhile another Maltese company, W. J. Parnis England Ltd, also decided to charter aircraft at about the same time. These made arrangements with S. Instone & Co Ltd, a long-established British company to form The Instone Air Lines 1946 (Malta) Ltd.

Another UK Company, Chartair Ltd, was taken on as joint associate and between them operated a service of Malta-based Consul aircraft. Nothing more than an adaptation of the wartime Oxford trainer, this aircraft, accommodating six passengers, formed the mainstay of many charter companies at the time.

With the first Directors appointed on 8 November, their registered offices were at No. 60 in South Street, Valletta.

As one would expect the two companies were soon competing with one another to attract prospective customers. They had advertisements in local newspapers announcing that Instone was offering flights to London on four specific days for £25, later increased to £35.

Cassar & Cooper offered Xmas Special Flights to and from London by Avro Lancastrians, probably those of Silver City Airways, as on 10 December their "City of London", G-AHBW, arrived at Luqa; claiming a record London-Malta flight of 4 hours 55 minutes. They also announced that their twin-engine aircraft based in Malta were available for private charter to Europe, the Italian mainland and other destinations in the Mediterranean.

During January 1947 an increase to these chartered flights was again advertised as being available from Malta several times a month on specific dates to cities as far north as London, Rome and Paris, with Tunis and Tripoli in the opposite direction.

First Cassar and Cooper office in Valletta at 12 South Street, in 1948.

A third Company that was registered in the UK on 8 August 1946, Chartair Ltd, was later to form Air Malta. Operations began from the UK flying Proctor G-AHFU but in December Chartair bought four Consuls, G-AIKO, -AIKR, -AIKX and -AIOM.

Just before this purchase the company had merged with British American Air Services that operated h.p. Halifax freighters, leaving Chartair free to continue with its passenger work. Another Associate Company was Airtech Ltd at Thame, a major maintenance organization.

At this time so great was the demand for seats that Mifsud Brothers Ltd., in Valletta, although having no connection whatsoever with the companies, also advertised flights from Malta. These same adverts disclosed that a trip by Proctor aircraft from London to Malta took two days, compared with The Lancastrian's five-hour flight.

The first Chartair Consul to arrive in Malta was probably G-AIOM, during the course of a routine flight from Benghazi and Tripoli on 13 February 1947. This was the forerunner of eleven of the type, which were to be operated from the island by Instone. The second aircraft, G-AIUR, arrived on 4 March, while on a passenger flight from Tunis to Naples. The Consul displayed the 'Instone' name and logo on the nose. The third was expected to reach the island that same week.

Together with the aircraft of BAS they succeeded in establishing services on a charter basis, mainly to Sicily and the Italian mainland as far north as Rome, with Tunis and Tripoli to the south.

So popular had these became during the first quarter of 1947 that services were reorganized on a semi-scheduled basis. This may have been due to the fact that as no others were available the Maltese government gave them permission to continue until such time as a license was issued.

Shortly afterwards Malta Airways proposed that they should take over the interests of the three companies in Malta. Air Commodore Powell opposed this in a letter to the Secretary of State for the Colonies in March, explaining that this would affect badly the orders GAS had placed for a number of Miles aircraft. However, with the demise of Miles Aircraft, it was on 5 April announced that the interests of GAS, Chartair and Instone were to be merged following discussions between their Directors.

The merger came into effect on 1 May 1947, with the scope of providing better services and ensure greater use of the aircraft available under the name 'MALTAIR, which was later in the year changed to Air Malta.

Three of eleven Consuls expected to start operating with BAS at Luqa in 1947.

March 1947. The 1,000th passenger boards Consul G-AHRK for a free trip to Rome.

As a private company, funded through a 50% Maltese holding, with the remainder held by UK shareholders, it was agreed that it would have no connection with any other scheduled airlines.

Applications for licenses were at the same time made to the British and Italian governments, and advertisements announced that services were to operate in the following order:

MONDAYS:	Malta – Tripoli.
TUESDAYS:	Tripoli – Malta – Naples – Rome.
	Malta – Catania – Palermo – Tunis and vice-versa
WEDNESDAYS:	Rome – Naples – Malta – Tripoli.
THURSDAYS:	Tripoli – Malta – Tripoli.
FRIDAYS:	Malta – Catania – Palermo – Tunis and vice-versa.

These were routes which the Italian airlines of the 30s used, with the exception of the weekly service to London via Nice, Marseilles, Lyons and Paris which "MALTAIR" also introduced.

Malta Airways, originally a subsidiary of BOAC, brought a case in the Maltese courts against the use of 'Maltair' in advertisements because of the similarity of name, a demand which was on 24 June rejected after the hearing.

At this time, replacing their wartime twin-engine DC3s with the larger four-engine Avro Yorks, BOAC transferred their services from Malta to Castel Benito after receiving complains made by operating aircrews regarding the state of Luqa airport.

Runways were considered unsatisfactory both in length and surfacing for large- scale day and night civil operations. But this did not seem to be the only reason for their decision. BOAC were also taking steps to reduce costs, relieving the British taxpayer. They also decided to give BEA permission to share their facilities along their respective routes wherever their paths crossed. So BOAC turned to BEA's new associate, Malta Airways, to provide it with the assistance required on those services that still called at Malta.

Ad hock operations took up some of BAS's time occasionally, from flying yeast from Tripoli for a brewery in Malta to Diplomatic Mail for the US Consul in Tunis. However, the largest of these operations was that in which a number of flights had to be made to fly out 52 Norwegian whale hunters to Rome where they embarked in a chartered Douglas C54 Skymaster to Oslo.

Capt. Richards arrives with Dove G-AIWF.

BAS's first D. H. Dove, G-AIWF, of their associate Silver City Airways, was to be used on the Malta-Rome-Tripoli connection.

Arriving at Luqa in the early days of July 1947, in the morning of the 6th demonstration flights were organized for some 30 personalities. Then early in the afternoon the aircraft flew off for a routine flight to Rome and London.

Despite advertisements announcing that the Dove would shortly be operating on scheduled services, whenever it occasionally returned it was always as a visitor.

Instone subsequently disposed of their interests in Air Malta, but continued to act as their agents. Then on 26 November 1947 Capt. Cassar announced a new development in a letter to the Times of Malta. An agreement was reached with Air Cdr. Powell in London where Air Malta intended to establish a 15-minute helicopter services between Malta and Gozo just as soon as a suitable machine became available.

Nine days later the first helicopter landed in Malta from the American carrier USS Midway, at that time anchored inside Marsaxlokk Bay.

Flown by Lt. James Lamm, USN, it was on that same day involved in the rescue of a pilot of a USN Skyraider who ditched in the sea off Malta.

On 10 February 1948, Dove G-AIWF arrived in Malta with Sir Cdr. Powell, Grp. Cpt. Laurence and Mr W. Menzies for discussions.

They departed for Tripoli two days later with Sidney Tennant and Anthony Linney both of BAS.

Meanwhile Air Malta had expanded from one Consul, a licensed engineer and two mechanics to four Consuls and a full servicing and handling staff numbering fifty employees all told. Operated under the management of Capt. Richards wanted to establish Air Malta as a Government licensed company before introducing the Dove. A permit which will give the company the right accomodation space for passengers and their relatives at Luqa's Airport Terminal. At that time, the RAF restricted entry inside the building to passengers only while relatives had to remain outside the aerodrome perimeter.

With Proctor 5 G-AHWX of Dean's Charter Services in Malta in April 1948, the Malta Steamship Co rose to the occasion and had an advertisement in a local newspaper announcing that they were offering a Proctor for charter flights to Italy, Sicily, Tunis and Tripoli. However, this happened to be a short-lived operation for later in the year the owner, Mr C. C. Deane, sold the Proctor to the Italian Air Force.

The air service license Air Malta had been eagerly expecting, to permit them to operate on scheduled services to North Africa, Sicily and Rome, was finally granted on 14 May 1948. At the good news the company confirmed that their Consuls were still in use but expressed their wish to purchase other aircraft.

The appearance of press comments criticizing Malta Airways about their lack of operations, the Managing Director, Mr R. Strickland, replied that British European Airways had commenced operating twice-weekly from Malta in November 1947 flying Vickers Viking to Rome and London at their instigation, a service Malta Airways would take over if a license was issued to them.

BEA & BOAC had not been carrying a great flow of traffic between Malta and the Middle East, so these services had been withdrawn from the island.

Malta's need for Air Services actually lay in the direction of Central and Western Europe, including the UK, and to a lesser extent N. Africa, a need which its own local airlines hoped could be met by European operators. Nevertheless BOAC's undertaking during the war guaranteed the passage of one of its Commonwealth routes via Malta which, for the time being, would be the Lancastrian service to Colombo. To this was included the transit through Luqa of their Skymaster service to the Levant and the Persian Gulf.

Their Dakota services had admittedly brought trade to Malta, particularly to her hotels. The night stops were, however, only a temporary phase, so Malta could not have continued to derive much trade from BOAC after the withdrawal of their DC3.

BOAC's sudden change in their operating program, however, and the issue of two separate licenses to Malta Airways and Air Malta by the Maltese Imperial Government, appears to have confused the interests in the recent development of air services for Malta.

Malta Airways, with the agreement of His Majesty's Government, was the company in which the B. E. A. Corporation was a partner and shareholder. Hence BEA inherited the airline which BOAC started in 1945.

Competition was increasing at this time as Alitalia, for the first time since the war, launched a flying service of their own between Rome and Malta on 12 July 1948 with Fiat G12, I-DALC.

During Autumn BAS Consuls G-AHRK and G-AIBF and Chartair's G-AIKO, G-AIKX and G-AIUR were all noted at Luqa. Estimates at this time concluded that by early November 1948 Air Malta had carried more than 10,000 passengers and flown 4,000 hours over a distance of 520,000 miles. A considerable quantity of freight and mail had also been delivered.

On 12 November the company was issued an official license from the Maltese Government giving it permission to operate scheduled services to N. Africa, Sicily and a stopping service at Rome. So Air Malta claimed a place in history, as the first private company in post-war British civil aviation, not associated with one of the UK nationalized airlines, to be granted such a license. Britain had to be ultimately involved due to the fact that Malta still lacked the authorization to register aircraft locally so the aircraft that the company operated had to retain British registrations coming under the requirement of the UK Air Navigation Order.

At the end of 1948 Chartair disposed of their interest in Air Malta, though the company was in the spring of 1949 advertising excursions to Catania, Toarmina, Palermo and Lugano, but the need for larger and more modern aircraft was at this time evident.

Both the Dove and Percival Prince were being considered for, to operate anything larger on these routes was economically unsuitable. Air Malta was privately owned, operating without any grants or subsidies so any aircraft purchased had to be an economical proposition.

A much-needed addition was Dove G-AKJP, delivered from BAS in the UK in June 1949. The 8-11 seat aircraft was for the planned replacement of the three Consuls the company still had in service.

During the FAA air display held at Ħal Far on 11 June pleasure flights were offered in the Dove for 10/- (50c).

(The proceeds were to go to the Marfa Channel Tragedy Fund.)

To further introduce the Dove to customers His Grace Mgr. Micheal Gonzi, Metropolitan Archbishop, was approached and invited to bless the aircraft.

Named "City of Valletta" by Mrs. Boffa, wife of the Prime Minister, the ceremony was held on 28 June 1949. Assisting were Major L. R. Sammut, Manager of Anglo Iranian Oil Co and The Director of Civil Aviation, Mr F. Menham.

An announcement was made that the Dove was to operate on the Malta-Cairo route and would the next day be joined by another, G-AIWF.

On 11 November, the crash-landing of the latter at El Adem, in Libya, appears to have forced the company to turn to larger aircraft. On 16 December, a Dakota, G-AJAY, leased from Westminster Airways Ltd, was delivered to Luqa from where it was the next day operated on the Cairo service. The aircraft left Malta for Cairo on Mondays and returned on Thursdays. Servicing operations carried out on Fridays and Saturdays served to have trips made to either Catania or Rome.

Probably the second of three Dakotas the company used was G-AIJD of Ciro's Aviation. This aircraft made the first of its three flights on 5 April 1950 as part of the contract held by Air Malta since December 1949 to carry Pilgrims to Catania en route to Rome for the Holy Year celebrations.

The third Dakota, G-AGNG, leased from Eagle Aviation, that replaced G-AIJD, having on display the Air Malta logo with that of Eagle's, made its first trip on 21 June 1950.

With Dakota G-AGNO still in use Dove G-AKJP, as well as Consuls

Last batch of 32 members of the M.U.S.E.U.M. pilgrimage embarking on an Air Malta DC3, G-AIJD on 21 June 1950, bound for Catania.

G-AIKS and G-AIKZ, all seem to have still been in service with the company prior to its demise at the end of 1950.

In June on advertisement by the company announced Special Express Flights to Bermuda with forward connections to New York, Detroit and Chicago, but nothing actually came out of this.

Finally on 26 November, following negotiations between Malta Airways and Air Malta, it was announced that the former would acquire all of the other's shares on 29 December 1950, and on 8 January 1951 the name Air Malta disappeared from the civil aviation scene.

At the same time, pending the issue of the formal Government license BEA has held fort on behalf of Malta Airways. A twice weekly service which, was provided by Viking aircraft between Malta and the UK and Malta and Rome. To meet the demand of the time, in the morning hours of 8 January 1950, BEA inaugurated a flight to Egypt as well.

SMOM

During the early postwar years in the Mediterranean, following the gallant struggle put up by the British air merchantmen during the worst two years of the war in the region, civil aviation progressed at a rate that left little doubt about it becoming the future's main mode of passenger travel. Airfares however, at the time still too expensive to the average man in the street, were undoubtedly against it. Hence several people planning on having a holiday, or otherwise needing to travel, abroad found it cheaper to do so by boat, albeit a time consuming route to take.

Some institutions, however, in favour of air travel, organized group pilgrimages for the purpose of negotiating favourable package deals. Air Malta Ltd, was prepared to offer them acceptable terms on a contract held by the airline on a three flights deal, particularly to transport Societas Doctrinae Christianae (M.U.S.E.U.M) pilgrims across to Sicily.

As far as can be ascertained Dakota G-AIJD made the first of these trips on 22 December 1949.

The second trip was undertaken on Wednesday, 5 April 1950, in which there were 60 pilgrims. With this group was His Lordship Mgr. E. Galea, Bishop of Tralles and Vigor General, accompanied by two nephews and his Chaplain, Rev. Father J. Desira.

It had by this time become clear that, as this aircraft's passenger capacity did not exceed 30 at the most, these had to make consecutive trips between Luqa and Catania according to the number of pilgrims waiting to get cross, in the above case, two.

The third group, organized on 22 June 1950, consisted of 96 pilgrims, all bound for Catania, from where they were to resume with the final leg of their journey to Rome by train, on the occasion of the Holy Year pilgrimage.

As this pilgrimage group was larger than April's, Air Malta's DC3 had to make three consecutive flights between Malta and Catania during the morning to get everyone across.

Organized by Mr J. Schembri these tours were entrusted to the spiritual leadership of the Reverend Fathers G. Briffa Brincat and G. Fenech. However, those who flew on these pilgrimages were individuals who were in some way or another all financially well off.

Others, particularly the poor handicapped and orphans, who were unable to afford the fare, could not even dream about such adventures. Hence, here surfaced the scope for which the Order of the Knights Hospitalliers were originally formed more than 800 years before, caring for those in need.

In 1954, Prof. Dr Coleiro K.M., Prof. Dr Jos. Bugeja K.M., members of the Sovereign Military Order of Malta (SMOM), and Mr A.J. Montanaro-Gauci, Chancellor, made the first arrangements with the Heads of the Italian Knights Association. These were to have Maltese patients admitted on very easy terms into hospitals run by the Order in Italy, a charitable arrangement, which the Maltese Government was to shortly take advantage of, and curtail the activities of the SMOM.

Mr Joseph Portelli, Secretary of the Catholic Travel Association (UTAL), expressed his regret at having to admit that he could find nothing recorded in the Minutes Book for the years prior to 1952. However, he had all the entries considered valuable noted down. But as Mr Montanaro-Gauci's statement indicated that his arrangement with the Italian Knights Association was made in 1954, reports found in the Times of Malta newspaper provided further information with which was expanded this historical civil aviation activity.

Entries in the Society's Minutes Book for 1954 show that on 2 January Rev. Fr Giovanni Briffa-Brincati was elected President of the Society.

The next entry for 14 May, record that Rev. Fr Spiridione Sammut was elected as the Society's Chaplain.

According to part of a report in the Times of Malta of 25 July 1957 Dr Cremona, who was the Union's Medical Officer, had attended all the Union pilgrimages since 1936.

UNITALSI (Unione Nazianale Italiana Transporto Ammalati a Lourdes), however, had the sick ferried by boat from Malta to the Italian mainland for the first time on 29 July 1953.

Shortly after the "Star of Malta" ran aground off Dragonara Point in a a dense sea mist, the Union took immediate steps to suspended this hazardous mode of travel. A report related to this decision is in fact recorded in the Society's Minutes Book for 3 August 1955:

> "Following the wreck of the 'Star of Malta' the Secretary suggests an alternative way of travelling to Italy. He suggests that sick pilgrims should travel by air to Catania."

But the secretary, who dealt with the difficulties sick pilgrims encountered while travelling the exhausting overland trip from Catania all the way up north to Rome, had this entered in the Minutes Book for 11 August 1955:

> "... the best solution will be to travel by air to Rome."

Approval for this proposal, however, was not recorded in the Minutes Book until 21 February 1957:

> "It is unanimously decided to carry the sick pilgrims from Malta to Rome by air."

According to the next recorded entry this was not confirmed until 9 April 1957, more than a month later:

> "Following a secret ballot the decision of carrying the sick pilgrims by air to Rome is confirmed."

On 25 June 1957, it is recorded in the Minutes Book:

> "The Secretary informs the Committee of the offer made by the UNITALSI to transport, free of charge, sick pilgrims to Rome, making use of airplanes belonging to the Sovereign Military Order of Malta."
>
> "The President here reminded the Committee that a similar offer had been put forward to him a year back by the representative of the same Order."
>
> "The offer was accepted."

In acceptance of this offer the next entry recorded in the Minutes Book for 20 July 1957 indicates what the Committee had arranged to honour it:

> "It was unanimously agreed to:
>
> a) Conduct the representative of the SMOM and the crew to the Co-Cathedral of St John and, thence, to His Grace the Archbishop.
> b) Invite them to dinner at the Hotel Phoenicia.
> c) Place four motorcars at their disposal.
> d) Ask Chevalier Vincent Bonello to act as guide."

This entry was made preparatory to the arrival of the aircrew of the first aircraft that the Order was expected to send to Malta before the end of July 1957, and to all others sent to Malta at predetermined intervals.

The first aircraft to arrive to fly out Maltese pilgrims suffering from incurable diseases to Lourdes was an Italian Air Force Savoia Marchetti S.82, serial ZR-73. The insignia of the Sovereign Military Order of the Knights of Malta (SMOM) temporarily fixed over its military roundels on both fuselage sides stood out boldly against its silver finish.

Italian A. Force SM82, 80-ZR with the Knight's Cross –
SMOM leased aircraft.

"This was too good to be true," recalled Dr Cremona, "we could hardly believe our eyes when we saw the plane landing."

With space available for only 27 persons those applying for the pilgrimage had to first fill in an application form. Then, after Dr Cremona personally examined them their names were drawn by ballot.

Dr Cremona, Rev. Father G. P. Briffa Brincat, four Sisters of Charity of the Society of St Vincent de Paule and two male nurses accompanied the sick on this pilgrimage.

The party was flown as far as Rome from where a UNITALSI hospital train, called the 'White Train', proceeded with them overland to Lourdes.

The pilgrims returned to Malta on 2 August 1957.

The Society's new commitment obviously led to the need of extra funds with the result that an annual Dinner Dances, reserved for local VIPs who could afford the expence, were organized for the purpose. These proved successful, raising enough funds to leave the organizers a sound turn over after all expences were paid for.

In his letter dated 14 September 1980, UTAL's (Society for the Transport of the Sick to Lourdes) Secretary, Mr Joseph Portelli, explained that, "... up to 1962 the Society made use of aircraft provided by the SMOM. This could be easily arranged by Don Enzo di Napoli Rompolla, Prince of the Resuttano (SMOM's Chancellor) and General Secretary of the UNITALSI."

The Regia Aeronautica Italiana, who saw to aircraft maintenance and up-keep, as the SMOM could not afford it, used the S.82s. However, whenever the SMOM needed the aircraft they would be put at their disposal complete with Knights' Cross markings masking the Italian AF fuselage roundels and flown by Italian AF pilots.

Mr Portelli explained that these were aircraft taken over from a surplus the Americans had on hand in Rome.

Whether Mr Portelli was referring to the DC3, or the three-motor Sovoia Marchetti S.82s remains doubtful as Mr G. Galea, the SMOM previous secretary, was the one who was directly involved when the latter were first provided.

(However, some reference needs to be raised as, shortly after the end of the war, several S.82s, discovering that their original Alfa 128 850H engines were under-powered, the USAF installed in them Pratt & Whitney 1215HP "Twin Wasps" before pressing them back into service.)

Following the 1957 solitary mercy mission to Rome the loan of further aircraft by UNITALSI did not take place until May 1958 when, from 190 applicants, the 70 sick pilgrims selected waited to be flown to Rome. This was the first leg of their journey to Lourdes, France, where they were to participate in the Centenary celebrations being held there.

According to a report in the Times of Malta of 17 May 1958 UNITALSI provided four S.82s for these pilgrims. This may have well been the case, but it still remains that S.82, serial ZR-80, provided from a Times of Malta photograph, appears to have been the one and only example accounted for. The probability could not be excluded that one, or two, aircraft might have made the four trips consecutively between Luqa and the Italian mainland, as explained earlier.

According to the newspaper report this was the second time that the SMOM had aircraft provided for the sick to Lourdes.

On 6 July 1958 the SMOM were provided with two S.82s, of which one was 86-ZR, to transport 37 boys aged between 10 and 14 years, to Rome for a holiday. This was organized under the auspices of the Medical and Health Department.

Sick and invalids being assisted on board an SMOM SM82, 80-ZR
on their way to Lourdes on 16 May 1958.

More Lourdes-bound pilgrims, suffering from diverse diseases, were on 26 September 1958 ferried to Rome in two S.82s, 78-ZR and 82-ZR, loaned to the SMOM by the Italian airforce, although according to the newspaper report three aircraft were provided.

On 19 July 1959 an SMOM flight, for which 60 children, selected from special families by the Medical and Health Department, were to be taken for a holiday in the Abruzzi mountains in Italy in two Italian Air Force S.82s loaned to the SMOM. Furthermore, according to the newspaper report another group was expected to leave on August 12, two days following the arrival of the first.

Evidently the aging S.82s were after 1959 withdrawn and the C.47, the military version of the civilian DC3, was in 1960 introduced next to accommodate the SMOM services.

The newspaper report of 4 August 1960 indicates that three C.47s provided by SMOM flew a number of children for holiday camps in Italy, again under the auspices of the Medical and Health Department. A scheme the report concludes, that had been in operation for the past four years.

On 3 April 1961 a group of fourty high-ranking Knights of the Sovereign Military Order of the Knights of Malta, several of whom accompanied by their wives and children, arrived at Luqa from Rome in three separate SMOM C47s, ZR-11, -12 and -13.

Some of the pilgrims preparing to leave for Lourdes on two separate SMOM SM82s, 78-ZR and 80-ZR, from Luqa airport on 27 September 1958.

Children for holiday trips to Italy, under the auspices of the Medical and Health Department, were on 20 July 1961 again accommodated by SMOM sponsored C47s.

According to this report, contrary to the S.82s, the C.47's Italian A.F wing roundels were not masked by the Knights Cross Insignia.

One more holiday was organized on 9 August 1961. Fourty-seven children were again to enjoy the fresh air provided by the Abruzzi Mountains, where a SMOM sponsored C47 ZR-16 flew them to.

Some 47 children preparing to leave for a mountain holiday in Italy on three SMOM DC3s, of which one is ZR-16, on 10 August 1961.

"All the aircraft the SMOM provided for our services were not pressurized." Mr Portelli commented, "and could carry no more than 25 persons each. However, space for stretcher cases was readily available due to lack of fixed seats as can be found on present day planes."

Mr Portelli, in a letter dated 11 October 1980, provided information traced from whatever was found recorded in the Union's Minutes Book for the 1960s. However, he stressed that Minutes of meetings held by the Society prior to 1967 could hardly provide any detail.

It seems as if the Government Medical and Health Department gradually monopolized the mercy missions the SMOM had created, since they had their first taste of these free trips in 1957. This resulted that from charitable missions these were turned into Holiday excursions from which it is suspected that more than the poor and needy benefited.

Evidently these holiday trips marred the local SMOM image with the Italian A.F, as will eventually be seen. To keep from further debasement the Society must have omitted all entries related to these activities from their Minutes Book until 1967, by which time irreparable harm seems to have been done by this unrestrained governmental attitude.

By 1963 I had given up further research on this time consuming subject, as these represented no more than one or two trips annually, and turned to other pressing commitments related to diverse outstanding aviation movements and activities on the island.

My last newspaper report entry was for 15 July 1962 in which three Italian Air Force C.47s, SM-13, -14 and -15 were provided to the SMOM so that Maltese children could again be taken for a three week holiday to the Abruzzi mountains in Rome.

From the Society's entries, which began to reappear in its Minutes Book as of 10 January 1967, it seems as if all pre-amicable relations between the Italian Air Force and the SMOM, had for obscure reasons been terminated.

"It was agreed to ask the SMOM, through its local ambassador, for the provision of airplanes for transporting sick pilgrims from Malta to Rome and back."

Air transport might have been provided from 28 July to 8 August, however, entries for 28 March, contradict this:

> "The President states that the SMOM airplanes will not be available in June, July or August."

An entry for 24 April then states:

> "The motion is approved to carry half the number of sick pilgrims to Naples, and the other half to Rome, in BEA flights."

Under closer scrutiny the three above-mentioned entries indicate that the 28 March one was referring to the Italian AF C47s future providement. This is then made clearer still by the entry following it, as BEA aircraft suddenly fill the limelight.

In 1968 one flight was effected from 23 to 31 July, from Malta to Naples and back, undoubtedly by BEA aircraft.

The next brief entry in the SMOM Minutes Book for 6 March 1969 bluntly states that:

> "The SMOM is no longer in possession of any airplanes. Booking through the BEA Malta – Naples – Malta, has been effected."

The entry for 27 March 1969 quotes that:

> "Dr Cachia Zammit, Minister of Health, has approved that the SMOM planes will call at Malta at a later date, so that they would be in time to carry our sick pilgrims to Rome, on their return journey. The BEA has confirmed the booking of fourty seats on the Malta – Naples flights."

Despite the fact that this flight was verified as from 15 to 21 July the minutes at one point stress that the pilgrims traveled in two separate groups. One was from 13 to 23 July and another from 14 to 24 July.

What keeps one wondering is why the Minister had stated; 'SMOM' planes will call at Malta at a later date.

Only one pilgrimage was organized in 1970. This was from 28 July to 6 August.

A couple of further entries in the SMOM Minutes Book for 1970 read:

> 6 February:
> "The President states that he has contacted the Societa' Aerea Mediterrania (SAM) of Ciampino on 28 July 1970."

19 February:

"It is decided to charter the S.A.M. plane for the flight from Malta to Fiumicino on 28 July 1970."

The Italian airline charter was undoubtedly more convenient along this route than BEA, and probably cheaper.

These final few entries in the SMOM's Minutes Book concluded that the appearance of the last of the C47s to appear with the familiar Knights Cross on their fuselage sides in my last entry was on 15 July 1962, something that agrees with what Mr Portelli wrote in a letter dated 14 September 1980.

What is certain is that as of 1967 these aircraft had forever disappeared from sight at Luqa aerodrome.

Air Malta – 1973

The Malta Gozo Air Services Limited was the last company that had tried to have a locally formed airline on a permanent basis, with the scope of gradually expanding this into what the island's National airline, Air Malta, had today become. They had the means upon which a license could be issued for this had been planned in 1969 when a Colonel E. M. Ketley, MBE., decided to develop an inter island air service between Malta and Gozo.

When the Colonel first discussed his plans with a number of local prominent businessmen, and Mr J. K. Arbuthnot, QBE., who was actually in Malta trying to start a flying training school at Hal Far airfield, the island of Comino was also taken into consideration.

Mr Arbuthnot who, having been in 1968 approached with the idea of a Malta International Air Rally by Mr Ken Jones, and became its founder that same year, recalled for my benefit the story behind the Malta Gozo Air Services Limited.

Our meeting was arranged for 11 April 1979, via a close friend of mine, Mr Victor Pisani, to provide me with details regarding the formation of the M I A Rally.

Our talk turned to various local aviation topics, past and present, and the MGAS Ltd was one which Mr Arbuthnot brought up, arousing my interest to an extent that with the MIAR interview concluded I literally implored him to tell me all about the former.

The Malta Gozo Air Services Ltd was formed on 1 September 1969, with Mr Arbuthnot as its first Chief Executive. Offices were set up on the 4th Floor in Airways House, Sliema.

Capital subscribed for the project was £50,000, put up by Colonel Ketley himself, Mr Anthony and Edwin Zammit-Tabona, Mr John Portelli, Mr John Parnis-England EDIM., Mr Malcolm Archer, Malta Airlines, Cassar and Cooper, Mr Sam Simmonds, Mr Arbuthnot and some others.

The company placed an immediate order for the delivery of four Britten-Norman Islander aircraft, of which the first was due for delivery in the summer of 1970.

In March of that year Chief Pilot, Capt. Arthur Milnes, and another pilot, Capt. Edward Carter, were engaged to fly the Islander out to Malta.

A certified aircraft engineer, Mr Harry Gartside, and a qualified aircraft electrical technician, Mr Simon Fenech, were to form part of the Islander's crew when this was requested locally for promotional purposes.

The aircraft, G-AXFC, arrived at Luqa in June, and following several demonstration flights for the benefit of those who were expected to be involved in the project, including the Press, and other important personalities, the Islander was in July allocated a local register, 9H-AAB. However, it could still not be operated commercially due to lack of an Air Operators Certificate, which Mr Arbuthnot was negotiating for with the Director of Civil Aviation, Mr J. Ferro the first one to be granted to a Maltese Airline operating the first commercial aircraft on the Malta Register.

Solitary Islander 9H-AAB of the Malta-Gozo Air Services Ltd at Luqa in the early 1970s.

Reaching an agreement with the D.C.A was more difficult than expected, causing the company diverse problems. Mr Ferro, who had never before been involved in this type of work, was extremely cautious and would not readily commit himself to the grant of an AOC.

"He insisted", recalled Mr Arbuthnot "... that we should at least purchase the first of the four Islanders outright – an unusual policy for a new company to adopt."

This wielded a severe blow to the Company's capital, and was the cause of a cash flow problem from the very beginning.

Hangar accommodation for base maintenance purposes posed a further problem, as none were available at Luqa. A Company request to be given permission to have one built at their own expense was turned down. Neither was the company permitted to make use of one of the hangars at Hal Far airfield. Finally the firm turned to the RAF from whom they rented space at Luqa as, and when, required.

Furthermore, when the Malta Gozo Air Services were finally issued an Air Operators permit, with which the company could operate commercially, they had already missed the opportunity to earn badly needed revenue via pleasure flights over the island during the height of the holiday season.

The Islander, once operations were underway, was used on numerous charter flights to diverse destinations in the Central Mediterranean, to which were included day trips to Pantelleria.

Early in 1970 the British army occasionally chartered the aircraft to support their troops working on flood relief operations in Tunisia.

During all this time the company had been busy working out plans as to where it was best to have an airstrip constructed in Gozo.

When this land was picked out, an uncultivated strip of scrub land about 2 Kilometres SSE of Xewkija, the Gozo Civic Council, all five Gozitan MPs and other influential bodies were in favour of the project.

Meanwhile company representatives had frequent meetings with the Prime Minister, requesting permission to go ahead with the work, with funds which the Malta Gozo Air Services was providing.

When, by the end of 19April 1970, Prime Minister Dr Borg-Olivier had still not given his consent, the Company Board, albeit reluctantly, immediately decided to stop all operations, dismiss the Staff, and have the Islander sold.

The aircraft was shortly afterwards flown back to Gatwick where it was for a few months leased to Loganair, a Scottish operator, and in 1971 it was finally sold to Australian interests.

That year elections in Malta resulted in a change of Government, and the M.G.A. Services again tried to get a permit for the construction of an airstrip in Gozo, so that the Company could resume with their services.

However, the new Prime Minister, Mr Dom. Mintoff, proved to be as uncooperative as his predecessor had been. He explained that he was committed to the Malta-Gozo bridge project and, seeing no future regarding the development of the company, the Malta-Gozo Air Services was in 1972 finally liquidated.

By that time the Malta-Gozo Bridge, having been estimated to be too complex and too costly a project to go ahead with, was abandoned. Another venue opened however, when the Tourist Trade Industry, drew the Government's attention of the benefit which a national airline would accrue to the country's economy.

Although Malta wanted the prestige of having a flag carrier of its own, lack of expertise in this line of business left the Government no alternative and he was committed to issuing tenders for foreign assistance, which only a well established airline could provide.

Pakistan International Airlines who, following negotiations with various other European and American operators, was claimed to have offered the most favourable package deal, was picked to take on the job.

The Airline was finally set up by a Resolution of the House of Representatives on 21 March 1973 with assistance consisting of a wet lease from PIA of two Boeing 720-040Bs for a period of five years, to which was also included a purchase option.

A management team was also provided to assist in running and formalising the Company until such time as Maltese nationals could take over control.

Air Malta was registered on 30 March 1973.

A year later, on 1 April 1974, the first Boeing 720B, PK-AMJ, inaugurated the new Airline's first service to London via Rome.

Meanwhile, however, services by means of chartered Tridents with British European Airways had been launched the previous year.

In spite of having two PIA Boeing 720s, AP-AMJ, in full Air Malta colours, and AP-AMG, on lease, so successful had operational developments become by 1975 that other destinations were included to the Company's route. However, so heavy did air traffic grow that charter flights could not cope with the demand with the result that between 1975 and 1979 Air Malta had to wet lease several different types of aircraft for the purpose.

Western Airlines Boeing B720 AP-AMJ on lease to Air Malta.

PIA's Boeing B720 AP-AMG on lease to Air Malta.

World Airways Boeing B727, N692WA, leased by Air Malta in April 1976.

In April 1975 a British Caledonian BAC 1-11, G-AYOP, was leased for the summer months and returned in October.

A World Airways Boeing 727, N692WA, came next in April 1976, which was kept by Air Malta until November.

On 26 March 1977 a Boeing 727, G-AZTG, was leased from Dan Air. This was released on 3 March 1978, shortly after Air Malta purchased its first aircraft, a Western Airline B720-047B, 9H-AAK, ex-N93143. However, this did not seem to have effectively relieved the load under which Air Malta was operating for by the end of the year the airline was forced to lease three more aircraft.

In April 1978 arrived another Boeing 720, N7513A, from Transanian, which a few days later had its registration changed to 9G-ACN.

In July 1978 arrived an Eagle Air Boeing 720, TF-VLC, which was in December followed by ST-AHG, of Sudan Airways.

(It later developed that Air Malta alternately sub-leased these Boeings to other airlines.)

ST-AHG was again sub-leased from Transanian in February of 1979, but at this time carrying registration 9G-ACO.

Air Malta's first purchase, a Western Airlines Boeing B720-047B, 9H-AAK.

Air Malta purchased a second Boeing 720-047B, 9H-AAL, ex-N93144, from Western on 9 March which was towards the end of the month followed by two more, 9H-AAM and 9H-AAN, both ex-PIA's AP-AMG and AP-AMJ respectively.

In July 1979, Air Malta sub-leased two of Transanian B707-123Bs, G-TJAB, ex-9G-ACN, and G-TJAC which a few months previously had carried registration 9G-ACO.

However, with their own four Boeing 720s on strength Air Malta now ensured that the National carrier was seen in as many countries as they could possibly cover by promoting further successes and gradual growth in the international airline industry, a direction from which the Maltese airline never looked back.

Chapter XVII

R. Aux. A.F. 1952/56

Trenchard's plan – SRU & RAAF – Auxiliary AF Volunteer Reserve – WWII – Ta' Qali Summer Camps

Lord Trenchard visionary plan of a 'weekend air force' in 1920 led to volunteers from all walks of life to gather and form into squadrons from which were established the Special Reserve Unit and the Auxiliary Air Force, who later took an active part in the Second World War. To differentiate the two, the Air Ministry allotted the Auxiliaries with the number 600 series while the Special Reserve Unit was given the 500.

Formed on 25 May 1925, 502 Squadron became the first SRU with a strong compliment of volunteers, but according to a statement by the Ministry of Defence the greatest response drawn was by the Auxiliaries.

The first Auxiliary unit formed, 682 Squadron, came into existence in mid-September 1925, and on 7 October received the first aircraft ever flown by any Auxiliary or SR Unit, DH.9A, serial H.144.

A week later a further three Auxiliary squadrons, 600, 601 and 603, came into force, all equipped with the DH.9A.

A year later, on 5 October 1926, 605 Squadron was established but no further Special Reserve units were formed until 14 October 1928, when 500, 501, 503 and 504 were established simultaneously, squadrons to which there were no more additions in later years. However the Auxiliaries continued to expand when on 17 March 1930, three more units, 604, 607 and 608, were formed.

Six years later, on 10 February 1936, the Auxiliaries gained in strength with the formation of another four squadrons, 605, 609, 610 and 611. This resulted that on 1 May the Air Ministry decided to drop the Special Reserve scheme and embody the few units under it into the former, which gave the Auxiliary AF ultimate recognition.

This led to the incorporation of 500, 501, 503 and 504 Special Reserve Squadrons into the R.Aux.AF in May 1936, but they retained their squadron number. No. 502 Squadron, the founder of all the volunteer units, remained as the last S.R. squadron until it was also transfered to the R.Aux.AF in July 1937.

As if this was not enough, in 1 June 1937, 612, 614 and 615 Squadrons were also formed in Scotland.

On 1st November 1938, due to a fall-off in part-time flyers, 503 Squadron was disbanded and from its few remaining volunteers was formed the nucleus of 616 Squadron Auxiliary, the last unit established under the R.Aux.A.F banner, obliterating the identity of the S.R.Unit.

During the late 1930s, with the constant threat of a Second World War breaking out in Europe ever present, the young men of this volunteer air force looked eagerly forward to the prospect of a probable conflict. This promised them an adventure, with the result that there was hardly any need for the Air Ministry to stress the need for more training. After the war, however, to bring squadrons to high form, due to the cessation of hostilities and the resulting armistice, it became the policy of the Air Ministry to call up to four units for three months of intensive training. Obviously, due to other pressing private life commitments, there were those who did not volunteer and attendance wavered.

In an effort to make the Royal Auxiliary more attractive, overseas detachments were arranged; this was rather in the form of a reward to those squadrons who performed best.

Called Summer Camps these were first introduced in 1952, with 604 Squadron arriving at HMS Bullfinch (Ta' Qali) on 30th May with Vampire jet fighters.

Eventually, however, due to the enormous cost required to keep the Auxiliaries up to modern weapon standards, and the fact that other wars would never again be fought anything like World War Two, in 1957 the Air Ministry decided to disband the R. Auxiliary AF.

Although R. Auxiliary AF units first arrived in Malta for their Summer Camp training in 1952 the Island's connection with some of these squadrons was made earlier than that.

The first two units to arrive at Ta' Qali, 601 Squadron and 603 (City of Edinburgh) Squadron, were in April1942 both ferried to Malta via

Vampire F.3s of 601 Squadron taking off from Ta' Qali airfield in 1952 during the first Summer Camp year for the Royal Auxiliary A F units.

USS Wasp. Earlier still, however, towards the end of 1941, 605 Squadron arrived at Hal Far via HMS Ark Royal. Equipped with Hurricane IIs the squadron remained flying in Malta's defense for nearly three months before moving on to the Far East.

In 1943, preparatory to the invasion of Sicily, two other Auxiliary units arrived in Malta from the Middle East, of which one was again 605, one of the few squadrons still operating Hurricanes, while the other, equipped with Spitfires, was 600 Squadron.

On 14 June, with 604 Squadron's summer tour at Ta' Qali nearly over, 601 Squadron's Vampire jets landed on the airfield to replace the former.

Units flying out of the UK to the Central Mediterranean had to stage through French and Italian stations en route, where pilots were reported having received excellent treatment. In Malta pilots received a glass of cold beer on arrival, something which, undreamed of during the war years, soon became a traditional Ta' Qali greeting to the weekend flyers. Meanwhile all squadrons' ground crews were flown to the Island in aircraft belonging to RAF Transport Command, mainly Dakotas, Vallettas, Vikings, Hastings and Yorks.

In 1952, although flying Vampires like the rest of the other units, 501 Squadron's presence in Malta meant the appearance of the first ex-Special Reserve unit on the Island:

604 Sqdn.	30 MAY to 14 JUNE	VAMPIRE
601 Sqdn.	14 JUNE to 27 JUNE	VAMPIRE
605 Sqdn.	28 JUNE to 13 JULY	VAMPIRE
612 Sqdn.	12 JULY to 28 JULY	VAMPIRE
613 Sqdn.	26 JULY to 09 AUG	VAMPIRE
501 Sqdn.	16 AUG to 30 AUG	VAMPIRE
608 Sqdn.	31 AUG to 13 SEPT	VAMPIRE

In 1953 of the twenty-one Royal Auxiliary flying squadrons in the UK sixteen moved abroad, but only five, two less units than the previous year, were diverted to Malta for Summer Camp training on Ta' Qali airfield. With these returned 601 and 604 Squadrons while the remaining three were first time visitors:

The Meteors of the County of London R Aux. A F 601 Squadron in 1953. Having changed over to the Meteor F.8 in 1953 they are here seen flying past over Grand Harbour in full strength. This unit, with the exception of 1955, did not miss a Summer Camp at Ta' Qali.

No. 616 Squadron at Ta' Qali with its Meteor F.8s basking in the sun.

601 Sqdn.	13 JUNE to 28 JUNE	METEOR
616 Sqdn.	27 JUNE to 12 JULY	METEOR
609 Sqdn.	11 JULY to 23 JULY	VAMPIRE
604 Sqdn.	25 JULY to 08 AUG	VAMPIRE
500 Sqdn.	04 SEPT to 18 SEPT	VAMPIRE

Six Auxiliary units were expected to start arriving for their Summer Camp training in Malta in 1954. Of these three, 500, 601 and 604 Squadrons, had already been at Ta' Qali the year before:

615 Sqdn.	15 MAY to 29 MAY	METEOR
600 Sqdn.	26 MAY to 11 JUNE	METEOR
601 Sqdn.	17 JUNE to 30 JUNE	METEOR
604 Sqdn.	26 JUNE to 09 JULY	METEOR
611 Sqdn.	14 AUG to 28 AUG	METEOR
500 Sqdn.	25 AUG to 09 SEPT	METEOR

In 1955, for obscure reasons, although Auxiliary units moved abroad from Britain, none were diverted to Malta. Then in 1958, due to the then controversial Suez Canal crisis, some squadron's visits to the island had to be cancelled, with the result that only five squadrons, of which only one was a newcomer to Ta' Qali, enjoyed the Auxiliary's final Summer Camp training in Malta:

Meteors of 611 fly past over the island in the summer of 1954.

No. 500 Squadron have their share of summer camping in Malta in 1956.

The pilots of 609 (West Riding) Squadron stand beside one of their Meteors in their lily-whites at Ta' Qali in 1956.

500 Sqdn.	12 MAY to 27 MAY	METEOR 7s-8s
609 Sqdn.	26 MAY to 08 JUNE	METEOR 7s-8s Including two VAMPIRES T.11.
601 Sqdn.	22 JUNE to 06 JULY	METEOR 8s
504 Sqdn.	02 JULY to 27 JULY	METEOR 8s
611 Sqdn.	21 JULY to 05 AUG	METEOR 7s-8s
610 Sqdn.	04 SEPTEMBER	METEOR 7s

Actually 610 Squadron's visit was one of those that had to be cancelled due to the Suez crisis. The main party never came to Malta, with the result that only a detachment of two Meteor 7s and four pilots arrived at Ta' Qali on September 4th, and remained on the airfield for a whole week before flying back to the UK.

Two other squadrons which were that year, expected for Summer Camp training were No. 604, from 1st to 15 September, and No. 615. However, due to the Suez Canal crisis, the Air Ministry cancelled their planned overseas movement to the Island.

Whether by chance or intent, with the exception of 1955 in which all the Auxiliaries missed their Summer Camp in Malta, 601 Squadron remains the only unit that did not miss a tour at Ta' Qali since the first

R. Auxiliary A F overseas detachments began to arrive in 1952. Next, with three tours each, came 500 and 604 Squadrons, followed by 609 and 611, each with two visits, while all the rest came to Ta' Qali once. So, in four summer seasons, fourteen Auxiliary Air Force units made a total of twenty-three separate summer Camp training tours to Malta.

In numerical order the fourteen squadrons, with their places of origin and date of forming were:

500 Sqdn	County of Kent	16-03-31
501 Sqdn	County of Gloucester	14-06-29
504 Sqdn	County of Nottingham	14-10-28
600 Sqdn	City of London	14-10-25
601 Sqdn	County of London	14-10-25
604 Sqdn	County of Middlesex	17-03-30
605 Sqdn	County of Warwick	05-10-26
608 Sqdn	North Riding	17-10-30
609 Sqdn	West Riding	10-02-36
610 Sqdn	County of Chester	10-02-36
611 Sqdn	West Lanchashire	10-02-36
612 Sqdn	County of Aberdeen	01-06-37
613 Sqdn	City of Manchester	01-02-39
615 Sqdn	County of Surrey	01-06-37
616 Sqdn	South Yorkshire	01-11-38

When the Auxiliaries first came to Malta in 1952 they were still equipped with the Vampire jet fighter, however, some of the squadrons were already operating Meteor Mk.7s, modified for target-towing purposes, of which one unit in particular was No. 501.

Then Air Vice Marshall the Earl of Bandon, Air Officer Commanding 11 Group Fighter Command, arrived on an inspection visit of 601 Squadron in a Meteor Mk.7. Flown by a Flt. Lt. Buddin, the jet was escorted by three Meteor Mk.8s in which were Group Capt. Thompson, Flt. Lt. Johnson and a Colonel Tyler of the USAAF.

When asked why the Auxiliaries choose to fly so far away from their home-bases for training purposes Sqdn. Ldr. Chris McCarthy-Jones, AFC., a wartime fighter pilot, replied:

> "Well, the flight to the island makes good navigational training. Furthermore, over Malta there is the room and the right kind of weather to carry out an intensive-firing programme."

Some of the pilots' own comments were:

> "The more flying we get the happier we are."

To help in the training a percentage of regular officers and airmen came to Malta with the weekend squadrons, but all the pilots were part-time flyers while every ground trade was the responsibility of volunteer officers and men. Even clerical, pay and equipment jobs were handled by men who gave each weekend of the year for the love of flying.

"We are a first-line squadron in Fighter Command," said the C O of 601 Squadron in 1953, the year in which, for the first time, all R. Aux. AF units were partly assisted by the men of 78 R. Australian AF Fighter Wing, that the RAF had just allocated to the Station.

It has often been said that a squadron usually operates better when away from its parent station, and so did all the RAF Auxiliaries that came to Ta' Qali between 1952 and 1956, while the serviceability and efficiency rating of all weekenders had also been reported as favourably high.

Each morning there was an air of busy efficiency on Ta' Qali airfield as the first target-towing aircraft took-off, soon after the usual routine drills by every weekend pilot was carried out.

The target drogue, a white banner with a dark bull's eye in the centre, no less than 30 feet in length and about 5 feet deep, measures no bigger than the wingspan of a Russian Mig fighter.

Towed off the runway at the end of a nylon rope nearly 80 feet in length the target-towing Meteor had to be well out over the sea, beyond Gozo, on a northerly heading, before a detail of three aircraft attacked the target drogue in turns.

The first detail was usually airborne at 06.00 hours, a routine that was kept going until lunchtime. Only two of each jet's four 20mm cannons were armed, with rounds daubed by different coloured paints for each pilot, a method by which hits were correctly assessed after the banner was dropped back on the airfield.

Each gun was armed with 60 rounds of ammunition, and half of the 120 rounds carried by each aircraft had to be fired for the score to count. Otherwise, the score was taken only as a percentage of 60.

Over the sea, the target-towing Meteor flies level and its pilot first sees his attacker as no bigger than a speck, its silver finish flashing in the sun as it draws closer to him.

The attacker's procedure was to fly on a course parallel with the Target-tug then swing in with sights moving along the tow rope. When the gyro gun-sight showed that the timing was right buttons were pressed and guns blazed away. Often, several coloured shells pitted the target in the six vital seconds before the pilot broke-off his attack. Keeping to his curving flight path, pulling his aircraft right over the top of the target-drogue, and never under it; this was to ensure that should the drogue be shot down, as often happened, it would not fall on the attacker, causing him disastrous harm with its rod and heavy ballast weight.

(Had the banner been an enemy aircraft in real life combat those six seconds would have sent it down into the sea in flames.)

The attacker then fades away, as fast as he had appeared, into the shimmering azure sky, having executed a task for which pilot, ground-crew and men in obscure faraway offices and factories had devoted years of skill and toil for that one purpose.

The day's work was usually terminated around noon, after which time most of the squadrons' personnel enjoyed the Mediterranean Sea and all it had to offer in relaxation.

The Vampires of the first, and last, Scottish Auxiliary Unit to appear in Malta, No. 612 Squadron, arrived over the island in two waves. The first five Mk.5s flew across RNAS Ta' Qali (HMS Bullfinch) in line abreast, a formation from which each separate aircraft peeled-off smartly, to land on the airfield in quick succession.

The squadron's CO, Sqdn. Ldr. G.W. Cory, was in the second wave, which was shortly afterwards followed by a Transport Command Hastings carrying the ground crew.

No. 613 Squadron arrived with a Vampire missing. However, 'E' for 'Easy' simply had to remain grounded at Istres, France, due to technical problems, where spares were shortly afterwards flown out to effect the necessary repairs.

Two Skyways Yorks and two Vikings of Hunting's in 1953 provided passage to the ground personnel of 604 Squadron. The unit was given freedom of Ta' Qali airfield for the first ten days following the arrival of its Meteors, due to the absence of resident flying units.

However, with the exception of a formation flight for photographic purposes, some Meteor familiarization flights for a new pilot and instrument rating tests, the squadron's entire effort was given over to air firing, a purpose for which three of the squadron's ten Meteor 8s, flown over from Britain, were fitted out with towing shackles for target towing duties. Most of the squadron's pilots led by Sqdn. Ldr. Thomas Turnbull, DFC, were war-timers, veterans of the Burma and North Africa campaigns who had seen service in bombers as well as fighters.

No. 616 Squadron was the first R. Aux. AF unit to equip with the Meteor jet fighter. Numbering more than 110 Officers and men the Squadron's CO, Sqdn. Ldr. Casson, was the only Battle of Britain pilot. A Flt. Lt. Jones, who, professionally, was a test pilot with Rolls Royce, was also a Flt. Cdr. with the unit, responsible for the squadron's every day training program.

To the usual daily intensive air to air gun firing program was also included training flights and formation practice, as well as aerial photography, for new men.

That year, unfortunately, the squadron lost one of their Meteors a few miles off the island's east coast, where only parts of the wreckage were picked up from the sea by a small vessel which was near to the scene of the crash.

It was 11 July, a Saturday afternoon, when eight Meteors of 609 Squadron landed on Ta' Qali airfield. Led by Sqdn. Ldr. Arthur Hudson the unit was on its first 1953 Summer Camp tour in Malta.

It was one of Britain's crack fighter squadrons in the war it was the first unit that accounted for the destruction of the first 100 enemy aircraft in UK. It also boasted of an aerobatic team comprised of a flight of four Meteors. These gave several displays in England in 1955, and the squadron intended organizing one over Malta, but there are no reports of any aerobatic shows over the island during the duration of 609's stay at Ta' Qali in 1956.

That year commanded by Sqdn. Ldr. D. Shaw, the squadron pilots participated in an interesting wet dinghy exercise with the Navy, from where they were all picked up by helicopter and transferred to rescue launches.

In 1953 while 601 Squadron was near the end of its training camp tour, Capt. Michael Birkin, Inspector of the R. Auxiliary AF, flew over from Britain to see how the squadron had got on, and to see whether anything could be improved.

No. 601 had that year already flown 219.15 hours in 343 sorties.

In 1956 it returned to the island sporting some changes. Having given 25 years meritorious service to the country the squadron was in 1955 presented with their colours at a Parade in Buckingham Palace. A change in command was also evident with Sqdn. Ldr. Peter Edelson AFC; who had joined the unit as far back as 1947, as the squadron's new CO

In 1956 Summer Training Camps in Malta for the Auxiliaries 500 Squadron, under Sqdn. Ldr. D. M. Chandler, was chosen by the B.B.C to appear on a television. This programme featured live interviews with

R. Aux. AF personalities in BBC's London Studios, inter-cut with cine-shots of the airmen in Malta flying from Ta' Qali.

No. 611 Squadron that year submitted the military serial numbers of the Meteors with which they executed their Summer Camp tour from the airfield, eight Meteor 8s and two Mk.7.

(In 1954 it had turned up with ten Mk.8s and a Mk.7.):

Meteor Mk.8	*Meteor Mk.7*
WF.758/O	WH359/K WA.718/X
VZ.551/B	WE.899/J WF.770/W
VZ.484/H	WK.852/C
WA.929/L	WH310/J

There remains one particular difference between wartime RAF units and those who came to Ta' Qali during the '50s, although these were in fact working holidays.

Who would believe, that the personnel of just one squadron, would alone consume a total of 4,251 bottles of iced Coca-Cola, a luxury positively undreamed of during the war years.

List of some noted A/C Accidents

Meteor 8, WK.722, of 601 Sqdn. lost the nose wheel during take-off. Pilot had to make a belly landing on returning. (14-06-54)

Meteor 8, WF.714, of 500 Sqdn. undershot while landing and its undercarriage collapsed. (08-09-54)

Meteor 8, WF.713, of 600 Sqdn. suffered from the same mishap as WF.714. (18-06-56)

Meteor 8, WM.421, of 611 Sqdn. Overshot runway and hit a wall.(26-07-58)

Chapter XVIII

REME Hovercraft

Royal visit – REME Representation – Mini Hovercraft – Familiarization trials – Performance at Tattoo – Acceleration Trials at Ta' Qali – Withdrawal to UK

In 1967 an event occured which, chance would have it the event coincided with the 50th anniversary of the launching of the first Malta-built World War One Felixstowe F.3 flying boat.

In 1917, due to wartime exigencies, the Admiralty consented to the construction of a number of these seaplanes at HM Dockyard, Malta. Fifty years later, in 1967, albeit for diverse reasons, there occured the construction of a different type of aerial craft, resulting in adding a further historical chapter to the Island's already large number of aviation events.

Late in 1967 Her Royal Highness Queen Elizabeth II was anticipated to visit Malta, an event which was estimated to result in creating quite a number of unusual activities.

To mark the occasion the combined British services announced that they intended to organize a Searchlight Tattoo, one aimed to surpass any other similar exhibition held previously on the Island, for the benefit of the Royal Family at the Independence Arena, Floriana.

The Royal Electrical and Mechanical Engineers (REME), who were given the task of rigging up the lighting arrangement for the display, were also preparing to represent their engineering division in the forthcoming exhibition as separate participants, by introducing a novelty of their own, preferably something never before attempted by any of the other British units on the island. The outcome was truly outstanding for the organizers could not have made a better choice. Their final decision fell on the construction of a hovercraft, one to their own specific design, which they intended to have ready in time to introduce as their main attraction during the Tattoo.

It was the middle of August when proposals for the construction of a mini-hovercraft were accepted.

Shortly afterwards a comprehensive study of numerous drawings, of which some were featured in the well established British aviation magazine 'Flight', was in progress. With this literature in hand ideas began to build up in the head of Major R. Pearce's, MBE; REME, then a captain, who gradually drafted the blueprints which were finally spread out on the workbench of the 53rd Command Workshop REME, Malta.

Under the guidance of the craft designer, and Capt. J. Jessup, the Maltese artisans and technicians given the task made good use of all the surplus material made available to them during construction work. Tools and all other equipment necessary were supplied free on request from the division's department stores. This was the basis upon which the hovercraft was to be built, a method that would by no means affect REME's normal Army support role on the Island.

The team of Maltese and British workers at REME's workshops, St Andrews Barracks, St Julian's, stand proud beside their finished Hovercraft.

When the machine reached the completion stage it was a truly outstanding achievement; however, no serial number, or any other kind of registration was ever allotted to the hovercraft.

From the planning stage, up to its appearance in public at the Independence Arena on 25 November 1967, the machine had taken its builders approximately ninety days to complete, inclusive of the familiarization trials prior to Exhibition day.

The Hovercraft during its performance at the Independence Arena on 25 November 1967; Tattoo night.

The hovercraft's performance during the Tattoo drew great acclaim.

The public did not fail to praise the military's advancement in technology, but at the Arena, due to the amount of dust raised when too much thrust was applied to reach high speed the pilot, Staff Sergeant R. Steward, was forced to limit this to 30 miles per hour.

At this speed, when skillfully handled, backed by its unique rudder, stabilizer and propeller arrangement, the craft was capable of maneuvering a 180 degree turn over its own 14 feet length.

REME's Hovercraft undergoes operational trials outside the Royal Engineers' own workshop backyard shortly before it was withdrawn to the UK.

Unladen the hovercraft, with a width of 6 feet, weighed 600 pounds, while its six-bladed propeller, also a product of the REME workshop, was capable of producing a thrust in the range of 200 pounds, requiring only a mere force of 5 pounds to move the craft while hovering.

Later acceleration trials were attempted at Ta' Qali airfield, but due to strong variable winds these had to be abandoned just when speeds exceeding 50 miles per hour had been reached. Rudders at this stage had to be held at full lock to maintain straight flight.

Regrettably, before further tests could be arranged to develop the ultimate speeds at which this machine could travel in favourable weather conditions, it was shipped to UK.

For obscure reasons time had unfortunately run out for this Malta-built hovercraft.

The machine was for a time exhibited in the UK, then it was withdrawn to the school of Electrical and Mechanical Engineering in Bordon, Hants, and put in storage.

British Petroleum, with the cooperation of the Manager of B. P. (Malta), Mr D. Bethell, provided the fuel mixtures required to operate the hovercraft in Malta until its unforeseen withdrawal to the UK.

Chapter XIX

Malta International Air Rally

Mr Ken Jones – Mr Arbuthnot OBE; – Hal Far, 1969 – Sir M. Dorman – 1972 Republic Malta – Rally Popularity – Me108 – Luqa, 1979 – Unusuals – T.6 G-ELLY

The idea of a Malta International Air Rally was first out to Mr J. K. Arbuthnot OBE, then Chief Executive of Malta-Gozo Services Ltd, by Mr Ken Jones, the Chairman of the Tiger Club, in the summer of 1968. In the autumn of that same year an advertisement appeared in the local press, asking for volunteers to assist Mr Arbuthnot in forming a committee with the scope of organizing a Malta Air Rally.

Messers Borg and V. Pisani were the first to join Mr Arbuthnot, and the three became the founder members of the M.I.A.R.

Quarters for administration and committee meetings were provided for at Airways House, Sliema. Consisting of Mr Arbuthnot, as Chairman, Mr Borg, Mr Pisani and Wg. Cdr. E. H. Coleman. AFC., C. Eng., F.R.Ae.S., and an additional three members, the organizing committee enthusiastically decided to call the first meeting in 1969. The Malta Tourist Board and the Director of Civil Aviation extended their support while Britain's Royal Aero Club offered their services to this new venture.

Hal Far was chosen as it offered the most suitable site where to rally competitors for various reasons.

At that time the Admiralty had passed on the Station to the RAF who had not yet abandoned it, but, neither had they moved in any of its aircraft to the airfield. Thus it was empty of air traffic, with the exception of some of MIACO's DC3s, recently based to the northeast side of the airfield.

Empty of military air traffic, plenty of space was provided where to park competitors' aircraft, while there was more than ample room to set-up the administrative offices.

Under these circumstances neither would the arrival and departure of these light planes interrupt any flight patterns, as it might have done had Luqa been used, the main reason why the DCA's offer to use Luqa's Civil Aviation facilities was in subsequent years refused by the organizers.

The then Air Commodore C A Winn, CBE; DSO; DFC; agreed to the loan of the old R N A Station immediately he was approached with the request.

Originally the idea was to organize the Rally as a twin event with the Middle Sea Race, but due to the unfavourable weather conditions encountered by diverse competitors in the first two meetings, held in October, the organizers were forced to transfer the Air Rally to the mid-summer months.

Held under the regulations of the International Federation of Aeronautics, the competition rules were those adopted by the Royal Aero Club, and the first MIAR was organized to fall between the 10th and 13th of October 1969.

In his foreword Sir Maurice Dorman, then British Governor of Malta, had this to say about that first Malta International Air Rally meet:

> "I welcome to Malta all those taking part in the first Malta International Air Rally operated under the auspices of the Royal Aero Club of Great Britain. This is a new venture for Malta, but I have every confidence that during your stay here you will enjoy yourselves whether in the sunny skies of these Islands or amongst our friendly people when flying is finished. A weekend is too short a time to see much of Malta, but we hope that this will lead you to revisit us again sometime in the future."
>
> "I would not wish this opportunity to pass without expressing my personal appreciation and gratitude to all those who have had a hand in the organization of this Rally. In particular, the Director of Civil Aviation, the Malta Government Tourist Board, the Royal Aero Club of Great Britain, and the RAF. There are, I know, many other firms and organizations who have supported this new venture. To all I say thank you."
>
> "I hope that this initiative will merely be the start of an annual event bringing together airmen from all parts of Europe and the Mediterranean in an atmosphere of international understanding and

friendly competition. Malta warmly and sincerely welcomes you to its blue skies and its sunny airfields."

The competition agenda prepared for this event consisted of an Arrival and a Pilots competition, a Concours D'Elegance, and a coveted M.I.A.R. Trophy. However, more set on satisfying rallyists, with the scope of attracting greater participation in future meetings, the organizers concentrated their main efforts in making the program as attractive as possible.

Competitors were scheduled to start arriving at Hal Far at 13.00 hours local time, with each successive aircraft to fly in at 10-minute intervals, until they had all landed by 15.40 hours.

Arrivals were provided with refreshments on the airfield soon after immigration and customs clearance, after which hostesses escorted them to their respective hotels.

The last item for the day was a Maltese Specialty Dinner to which all rallyists were treated in the evening.

The next morning, precisely at 09.30 hours, competitors and their guests were driven down to the Grand Harbour from there they were taken to Gozo. En route the motor yacht Kihna was diverted to the Blue Lagoon, Comino, were a leisurely stop was made.

To fill the evening the organizers prepared a barbecue dance.

On Sunday, 12 October, the Malta Government Tourist Board was the host of honour. The day began by a morning sight seeing tour of the island for the benefit of the competitors. This was followed in the afternoon by a drive to Hal Far airfield to attend to the Concours D'Elegance, while in the evening the M.G.T.B. treated their guests to a prize giving reception.

Except for two solitary entries all competitors in this first Air Rally of Malta were British. It is also interesting to note that of these two particular aircraft one, OY-BKI, a Piper Aztek entered by Dr Per. V. Bruel of Denmark, headed the list of that years seventeen applicants.

The other, the only locally registered Cessna 172, 9H-AAA, belonging to Mr M. Falzon, a Maltese, was at the bottom of the list, while the remaining entries, in chronological order of arrival were:

Piper Aztek	G-AWIY	13.10 hours
Comanche	G-ASEO	13.20 hours
Cherokee	G-APVP	13.30 hours
Cessna	G-AWCH	13.40 hours

Cessna 172, 9H-AAA, with another of type -AAD in the background. The two letter gap between the two aircraft were carried by the Malta-Gozo Ferry Islander, 9H-AAB. AAC, however, had not yet been allotted to Piper Cherokee 180E, G-AYIC, as the aircraft went missing over the sea between Malta and Sicily during a bad storm.

Cessna	G-ARLU	13.50 hours
Jodel	G-AVJK	14.00 hours
Jodel	G-AWYL	14.10 hours
Baron	G-ATGR	14.20 hours
Tri-Pacer PA22	G-APZX	14.30 hours
Tri-Pacer PA22	G-AWGS	14.40 hours
Twin Comanchee	G-ATAO	14.50 hours
Twin Comanchee	G-ARFH	15.00 hours
Cessna	G-ARGE	15.10 hours
Jodel	G-ATLB	15.20 hours
Comanchee 18W	G-ARYO	15.30 hours

There were four trophies awarded in this introductory rally. One, the M.I.A.R. Trophy, was sponsored by the Malta Government Tourist Board. Carreras Malta Ltd presented their Rothmans Trophy for the best Arrivals competitor. The Publishers of the magazine Pilot were the sponsors of a Pilot's Trophy, while the Castle Mediterranean Investments Ltd sponsored their Castle Mediterranean Trophy for the winner of the Concours D'Elegance.

Dr Per V. Bruel, in his Piper Aztek PA23, CY-BKI, carried away the first three prizes.

Mr B. P. Irish, owner of Cessna G-AWCH, won the Concours D'Elegance.

In 1970 new names appeared amongst the members of the organizing committee who had pioneered the launching of the first

MIAR. These were Flt. Lt. D. Bell, an RAF project officer, and Wg. Cdr. H.B. Iles MA, AFR.Ae.S, RAF, who like Wg. Cdr. E. H. Coleman was a retired serviceman.

The acclaim received by the organizers for their 1969 achievement was the encouragement they needed to send them to greater lengths to please in 1970, with one scope in mind, to establish the Malta International Air Rally on an international scale.

Very few changes were made to the second Rally program, with the exception of the times of arrival. These were scheduled to fall three hours earlier than those set the previous year.

A growing interest in this new venture was that year shown by other firms and organizations. This resulted to an increase in sponsors and hence more trophies to be won.

The Malta Hilton sponsored a second MIAR Trophy for the runner-up.

A further two in the same category came from Ripard, Larvan and Ripard (Aviation) Ltd and the Malta Government Tourist Board.

Three more were sponsored by Simonds-Farsons-Cisk Ltd., Malta Airways Company

Ltd., and the Bank of Industry, Commerce and Agriculture Ltd.

In 1970 the rally was held between the 3rd and 6th of October.

That year from a total of seventeen entrants three, due to one reason or another, withdrew. Nineteen aircraft owners sent in their application, although two had by September decided to withdraw.

What was noted most in 1970 was the fact that out of the remaining seventeen competitors only eight were British, as can be seen from the entrants list:

Cessna 172	G-AWCH	10.10 hours

The entry, which was expected to arrive at 10.20 hours, failed to turn up.

P. Cherokee 180E	9H-AAC	10.30 hours
Morane Saulnier 880B	G-ASAU	10.40 hours
Sokol Super Aero	G-MAOF	10.50 hours
Auster	G-AIGT	11.00 hours

The next two were the ones who withdrew their applications, then arrived:

KL-107	D-ELUQ	11.30 hours
Cessna 182G	D-EMQI	11.40 hours
Aztek 23	OY-BKI	11.50 hours
Comanchee	OE-DEU	12.00 hours
Cherokee	G-AVBP	12.10 hours
P.149D	D-EBDE	12.20 hours
Dornier Do.28A	G-ASUR	12.30 hours
Cessna 172	G-AVIR	12.40 hours
Cessna 182	OE-DDW	12.50 hours
Aero Commander 680	N99V	13.00 hours
Piper PA28-235	LX-AIR	13.10 hours
Piper PA24-250	G-ARUW	13.20 hours

Mr D. Surridge and his crew who manned an immaculately kept Piper Comanchee G-ARUW carried away the main top honours at this meeting. Not only did they succeed in winning the Concours D'Elegance and the Longest Distance Flown event, but the coveted MIAR Trophy as well.

That year, to elevate the event to greater heights, the RAF's Red Arrows, gave one of their fascinating aerobatic displays over the island at the same time of the rally; the organizers then invited the pilots as guests of honour at one of two barbecue dances held for the rally competitors.

The number of applications received for the 3rd Malta International Air Rally, held on 26th June 1971, were so encouraging that the organizers felt assured that henceforth there was only progress to look forward to.

A typical Hal Far sight during Rally meets.

From an organizing committee of seven in 1969 this had by this time doubled in number. A few had replaced members who, for diverse reasons, felt they should retire.

Capt. P Ripard, probably the most outstanding personality, now filled the post of chairman, which Mr J.K. Arbuthnot had recently vacated. This increase had grown according to the exigencies of the time for the number of competitors had risen to thirty-two in 1971, nearly twice the number of entries received the previous year:

Mooney 20E	F-BNOB	09.15 hours
Beagle Airedale	G-ASAH	09.25 hours
Cessna 172	F-BOQZ	09.35 hours
Piper Aztek	G-ATMU	09.45 hours
Piaggio	D-EBDE	09.55 hours
Cessna 210	G-AYCL	10.05 hours
Piper Cherokee	9H-AAC	10.15 hours
Cessna 172	9H-AAD	10.25 hours
Mooney 21	G-AXZV	10.35 hours
Rhiems Rocket	G-AWWU	10.45 hours
Piper Apache	G-ATJP	10.55 hours
Beagle Pup 100	G-AXUA	11.05 hours
Cessna 172	9H-AAA	11.15 hours
Rallye Commodore	G-AVAK	11.25 hours
Piper Tri-Pacer	G-APWR	11.35 hours
Sud Horizon	G-AWAC	11.45 hours
Cherokee Arrow	G-AYPW	11.55 hours
Cessna 172	G-AVUF	12.05 hours
Mooney 21	G-ATAD	12.15 hours
Cessna 172	F-BOQP	12.25 hours
Dornier 28A	G-ASUR	12.35 hours
Klemm	D-ELUQ	12.45 hours
Cessna 172	G-AVIR	12.55 hours
Mete Sokol	G-APVU	13.05 hours
Cessna 172	G-AVBZ	13.15 hours
Piper Cherokee	G-AXSG	13.25 hours
Piper Cherokee	00-LGH	13.35 hours
B'craft B95A	G-ASIR	13.45 hours
Piper Comanche	G-ARHI	13.55 hours
Mooney 20	G-ASUB	14.05 hours
Cessna 401	G-AWSF	14.15 hours

Piper Comanche	G-ASRA	14.25 hours
Mooney 20	D-EGKE	14.35 hours
Twin Comanche	OE-FPB	14.45 hours
Cessna 182	OE-DDW	14.55 hours
Cessna 182	D-EMQI	15.05 hours
Piper PA.28	G-AVRU	15.15 hours

This increase in the number of competitors also proved that the decision to transfer the rally to the summer months was a wise one.

That year the British entry was strong enough to have carried away every trophy in the 3rd M I A. Rally, but this was almost equally shared between them and the thirteen other European competitors, amongst which were the first three Maltese entries. The final results read:

Arrivals Competition:		
Winner:	Mr O. Sochor	OE-DDW
Runner-up:	Mr H. Hermann	D-EGKE
Flight Planning:		
Winner:	Mr D. Surridge	G-ATJP
Runner-up:	Mr J. McKay	G-AVIR
Concours D'Elegance:		
Winner:	Mr D. Surridge	G-ATJP
Runner-up:	Prince William	G-AYWP
Longest Distance Flown:		
Winner:	Mr T. Tichy	OE-FPB
Runner-up:	Mr D. Surridge	G-ATJP
Piper Trophy:		
Winner:	Mr J. McKay	G-AVIR
Malta G. T. Board Trophy:		
Overall Winner:	Mr T. Tichy	OE-FPB
Runner-up:	Mr D. Surridge	G-ATJP
3rd Place:	Mr J. McKay	G-AVIR

Due to a political disagreement between Britain and the Party recently elected in Government on the island aviation activities in 1972 came literally to a stop. This unavoidably forced the organizers of the M I A Rally to abandon that year's meeting. In spite of this 1972 contretemps, the number of applications received in 1973 did not diminish, demonstrating the popularity the event had gained since 1969.

Arrivals ran in this order:

Thurston Teal 1A	G-BAUL	10.35 hours
Piper PA.28	G-AYRM	10.45 hours
Beech BE.35	G-ATSR	10.55 hours
Dornier 28A	G-ASUR	11.05 hours
Piper PA.28-180	9H-AAC	11.15 hours
Cessna F.172	F-BOQZ	11.25 hours
Jodel DR-360	OO-MAS	11.35 hours
Beech B-90 King Air	G-AWPM	11.45 hours
Sundowner C23	G-BAHO	11.55 hours
Cessna C-337	OO-GCM	12.05 hours
Piaggio P149D	OO-MEV	12.15 hours
Cessna 172	OO-ADO	12.25 hours
Piper PA.28	G-AYWW	12.35 hours
Beech Baron	G-ATGR	12.45 hours
Beech Bonanza	G-APVW	12.55 hours
Beech D95A	G-ASIR	13.05 hours
Piper Arrow	OO-LGH	13.15 hours
Cessna 401	G-AWSF	13.25 hours
Piper PA.28	G-AVWH	13.35 hours

Turston Teal 1, G-BAUL; 1973.

Cessna 340	G-AZRC	13.45 hours
Piper	HB-OHF	13.55 hours
Cessna Skylane	G-AWBV	14.05 hours
Piper PA24	D-ELPY	14.15 hours
Cessna 310Q	G-BARG	14.25 hours
Sud GY80 Horizon	G-AVMA	14.35 hours
Cessna F172G	G-ATNH	14.45 hours
Marchetti SF.260	OO-AHR	14.55 hours
Cessna 414	EI-AWW	15.05 hours
Mooney21	G-AXZV	15.15 hours
Aero Commander	N99V	15.25 hours
Robin CE-25	D-EACB	15.35 hours
Piper 200B	EI-AVH	15.45 hours
Cessna 172	9H-AAA	15.55 hours

Also, due to the change in Government administration in mid 1971, the patronship of the 4th M I A Rally fell to the new Governor General, Sir A. Mamo OBE, QC, BA, LLD, the first Maltese to fill that particular post.

(When Malta became a Republic he was also given the honour of the Island's first Presidency.) So his foreword to the 1973 rally is a must in this historical chapter:

> "It must be gratifying to the organizers of the 4th Malta International Air Rally to look back and see the remarkable progress that has been achieved since this imaginative venture was first launched in 1969. Suffice it to say that from a modest beginning of 37 rallyists in 14 aircraft, in 1971 the numbers rose to 84 rallyists in 32 aircraft from nine countries, including four aircraft from Malta. This is, of course, due to the hard work put in by all the members of the organizing committee and the encouragement and whole-hearted support they received from the Tourist Board, other Government Departments and the Royal Air Force in Malta. But the continued progress of the Rally is also due to the warm friendliness and hospitality shown to the participants by all our people, which has made them wish to come again and to persuade more flying enthusiasts to take part in the competition.
>
> I wish the Rally and all concerned in it further progress and success."

In subsequent years the number of competitors kept on increasing until the organizers of the MIAR were finally forced to limit this to a set number of fifty aircraft.

In 1974 the organizers of the MIAR were proud to declare that their event was considered as a permanent fixture in the International Sports Calendar.

That year, however, due to the monetary exchange rates, arising from the steep prices of fuel, many participants were delayed in Italy with the result that they arrived late at Hal Far, while a few never made it at all.

So little did meetings vary one from another after this date that covering them all here would have unnecessarily extended this episode to the point of monotony; however, some exceptions remain.

The 10th, 1979, MIAR, due to the withdrawal of the RAF from Malta, and the completion of the Luqa airport expansion program, which had been concluded in 1977, was for the first time held on Luqa aerodrome.

Also worthy of note in this chapter is the appearance of some very unusual aircraft which were seen at some of these rallies. Up to the 13th MIAR five drew the attention of every spectator present, and those of the majority of rallyists due to their singularity in structure. The first of these aircraft was an amphibious flying boat. Mr T. Hynett

Fornier RF4D, G-AWBJ; 1974.

The Me108. Forerunner of the famed World War 2 Me109E and subsequent models; 1976.

Rutan Varieze, G-LASS; 1976.

entered a high-wing monoplane with a top mounted single-engine nacelle, British registered Thurston Teal lA, G-ABUL, for the 1973 MIAR.

Like the next two subsequent aircraft G-ABUL, to the disappointment of all those who were expecting its arrival at Hal Far, was for obscure reasons diverted to Luqa airport.

The following year, 1974, a Fournier RF4D, G-AWBJ, a single-seat glider powered by an engine no bigger than a motorcycle's, was entered by Mr D. R. Stevens.

Another, entered for the 7th MIAR, was the forerunner of the Luftwaffe's famous Me109E, a Messerschmidt Me108, D-EDIH, built in 1938. The owner, Herr. B. Klein, a veteran flyer, was as ancient as his aircraft. That year, 1976, to commemorate the occasion, a special prize was introduced, and this Mr Klein won for possessing the oldest aircraft in the rally.

Stranger still was the appearance of a home-built Rutan Varieze, registration G-LASS.

To the superstitious some numbers are considered unlucky, and in the case of the 1982 MIA. Rally, the 13th, this seems to have lived up to that reputation with tragic consequences.

On opening day a competitor landed his aircraft at Luqa with nearly dry fuel tanks. This was one of two Harvards expected to take part in the rally as, due to technical problems, the other was forced to remain grounded back in UK.

Then on 23 June, the day competitors were departing from the island, one aircraft had to fly back to Luqa soon after taking off due to mechanical problems. An insignificant mishap this may have been, but newspapers were filled with news of the previous day's tragic event. One in which, a competitor of the Malta International Air Rally and a passenger were involved. However, this occured after the meeting, though prior to the presentation, so the fact remains that the 13th MIAR ran as smoothly as the previous twelve.

On Saturday, 19 June 1982, Ted White, who had become an immensely popular figure at these rallies, landed the North American Harvard T.6, 1941 model he was flying with Gordon Mills, at Luqa.

The aircraft, in United States Air Force colours, carried registration G-ELLY, but still displayed its original military serial, TA-867 (133867). Maintained by members of the Duxford Aviation Society the T.6 was based at the Imperial War Museum, from where money was provided for its purchase and restoration three years previously.

Harvard T.6; 1982. Parked at Luqa during the Rally meet, destined never to return to UK.

One of these arrivals was a Mike Campbell who, with his wife and another couple as passengers, had flown to Malta in a Cessna 340A piloted by a Mr. Gold. On that fateful 22nd June 1982, the fourth and final day of the rally, Campbell, went up for a flight in the T.6 with Ted White. The latter, 46 years of age, thirteen years Campbell's senior, a pilot with twenty-six years flying experience, possessed a professional pilot's license, and had flown a wide range of different aircraft types.

In 1976 he was declared overall winner of the MIAR and he was one of those Britons who strove to boost local air rally standards since he first took part in 1973.

Campbell, considering his age, was a relatively good Pilot.

The North American T.6 was not the only airplane that took off from Luqa airport for a local flight that particular Tuesday afternoon.

At approximately 14.50 hours the Texan was airborne. Less than fifteen minutes later both White and Campbell were dead, their aircraft a burnt-out wreck.

During an on the spot investigation carried out on 23rd June two officials from the Aircraft Accident Investigation Board in UK were at the crash site, at 'Tal-Virtu' Seminary Buildings, Rabat, assisted by local authorities.

Up to the time of writing what had led to the crash was still considered classified, and will probably remain so for many years to come, with various possibilities pending, i.e., engine or structural failure, although the probability of human error was undoubtedly not excluded.

However, the fact remains that nothing leaked out whether White or Campbell was in control of the aircraft at the time of the crash.

According to two eyewitnesses the Harvard was being flown rather dangerously.

Flying at almost rooftop level the T.6 rose steeply as it passed over the Verdala Hotel. Then leveling out again it went into some fast shallow dives, during one of which, for obscure reasons, whoever was flying the aircraft must have either fractionally delayed his timing, or the controls failed to respond as quickly as was expected.

The evening following the tragedy, the trophy for the Concours D'Elegance was not awarded during the presentation ceremony.

Ted White remained the undeclared winner, while the runner-up of the International Air Rally was none other than Mr D. Gold, the pilot with whom Campbell had flown to Malta from Britain as a rallyist.

Chapter XX

AFM Flying Wing

Independence – Defence Ratification – Malta Land Force – US Patrol Boats – German AF Bell 47Gs – Armed Forces of Malta – Bell Jet Ranger – Libya's Military presence – Italo-Maltese relations – Libyan Aerospaciale SA-319A – Task Force – Oil drilling dispute – Italy pledges to guarantee Malta's neutrality – TF Helicopter Flight fear dissolvement

Recruitment of Maltese personnel with the RAF began in 1918, when this was first formed on 1 April by amalgamating the Royal Flying Corps and the Royal Naval Air Service, after which the number kept on increasing with the years. However, flying of service aircraft was excluded from their contracts, and these youths were primarily engaged as ground personnel.

On 21 September 1964 an Independence Declaration was signed by the Maltese Government, marking the beginning of the end of an association with the British Armed Forces, which was to be terminated after 180 years. This was in the form of a Defence Agreement binding Britain and NATO to remain in Malta for a further ten years, during which they were to provide the island with the necessary protection.

On 1 April 1965 the Malta Government took over control of the three Malta Territorial Units that up till then had been part of the British Armed Forces, the 3rd Light Air Defence Regiment RMA (T), 11th Light Air Defence Regiment RMA (T) and The First Battalion The King's Own Malta Regiment.

By amalgamating the 3rd and 11th Light Air Defence Regiments, in mid-June 1966, the units were reduced to two to become the Light Air Regiment and the 1st Battalion KOMR. These units were then on 1 October 1970 transferred to the Malta Land Force, which had itself emerged by the regrouping of the 1st and 2nd Regiments RMA and the Royal Engineers (Malta). By these means, the MLF gained both regular and territorial units, with the former comprising of the 1st Regiment RMA, RMA Band and the Logistics Unit.

By the 10 year Defence Agreement of 1964 Malta was to be protected by Britain up to 1974, but the defence of the island as of 1975 was not cosidered.

In 1971, following a change in Government, immediate steps were taken to ratify the Defence agreement made with Britain seven years earlier. This was aimed at re-organizing, and upgrading, Malta's national armed forces in expectation of Britain's eventual withdrawal from the Island.

The British were requested to provide Malta's own armed forces with SAR and coastal surveillance capabilities, facilities that they still had available on the island. But this proved to be hard to agree about. Finally, on 26 March 1972, after nearly a year of strenuous negotiations, an agreement was finally signed. Malta got what she had asked for, but she was bound to provide Britain with base facilities for a further seven years, for which Britain and NATO were to pay 14 million Sterling pounds per annum. Nevertheless, the defence of the island had been left out of the agreement signed by the two Governments. This resulted in Britain's final release from this obligation, but the Malta Land Force, now equipped with the necessary means for coastal patrolling, was able to resume with anti-contraband duties.

The United States was the first to offer patrol boats to Malta, and these were almost immediately operated in territorial waters. Germany, however, went one step farther, offering aid in the form of four Bell 47G helicopters. With this equipment plans to form a small helicopter flight, intended to supplement the already active surface craft, were made.

This assistance from West Germany also included the training of Maltese as pilots, to prepare them with the necessary qualifications to fly the helicopters the W.G. Air Force was donating to the country.

Training of Maltese as framework technicians, including technical assistance during the initial period, came with the package.

Maltese nationals, selected from recruits in the Police and Land Forces for training at the West German AF Helicopter Training School at Fassberg, departed from Luqa in October 1971.

In April of 1972 a WGAF team arrived in Malta in two UH-ID helicopters to organize the future base in order at their future base.

On May 24th the eight successful pilots were back in Malta, their course concluded, and with them arrived the first two Bell 47Gs. Five days later the second pair of helicopters were flown over, like the first two, in a Transal of the WGAF.

As a workshop had been set up for the purpose, the newly arrived crated helicopters were immediately moved into a nearby large Nissin hut that had recently been converted into a provisional hangar. It was also decided to keep the Flight stationed there for opposite the hangar entrance had also been prepared a spacious helicopter pad.

Shortly afterwards assembling of the Bells began by the Maltese technicians, assisted by Luftwaffe personnel.

For a time the helicopters' only means of identification remained their constructor's numbers. However a few weeks later, already forming an integral part of the 1st Regiment of the Malta Land Force, the yellow fuselaged Bells, with black airframes and orange day-glo fuel tanks, were issued Maltese civil registrations 9H-AAE, 9H-AAF, 9H-AAG and 9H-AAH.

St Andrew's Barracks helicopter landing pad with Bell G47, 9H-AAF, hovering in to land. No particular colours or insignias appear to have been applied to any of the helicopters.

Bell 47G, 9H-AAF, with floats fitted for duties over open waters.

Libya's donation to Malta, an Augusta Bell Jet Ranger, shortly after arriving at Luqa in a LARAF C130 Hercules. It still carries its original military number and roundels.

Although training continued from St Patrick's Barracks patrol duties for the surveillance of Malta's territorial waters against a variety of illegal activities were immediately launched.

Search and Rescue duties were also included, a role which, in 1975, resulted in the fitting of the first floats on Bell 9H-AAE to provide one of the helicopters with the flexibility necessary in air-sea rescue work. However, it was not long before it became obvious that the Bell 47G, primarily constructed for use as a trainer, was seriously limited in the tasks to which it was being subjected. But the most outstanding being its inability to convey stretcher-borne cases.

For this reason, in the spring of 1973, Malta approached the Libyan Government with a proposition that led Libya to donate an Augusta Bell 206A Jet Ranger to the island.

On 19 April 1973, a change in designation from "Malta Land Force" to that of "The Armed Forces of Malta" was made. At the same time a 5,000 strong Malta Pioneer Corps, was added to the AFM, and organized into four major units.

The Libya donated Augusta Bell helicopter arrived at Luqa on board a LARAF C.130 Hercules on 4 June.

Shortly afterwards, its markings removed, the Jet Ranger had to temporarily retain its constructor's number, 8185, in lieu of a registration.

With this helicopter, the Libyan AF also provided a flying instructor who started the Maltese pilots and technicians on a conversion course.

By the end of 1973 the Flight accumulated nearly 320 operational sorties, totaling some 560 hours flying time.

As expected the Jet Ranger improved the Helicopter Flight's capabilities but, most probably arising from the close relations that had apparently been established between the two countries, since the Labour Government was elected into office, Libyan military assistance went a step farther than that. Late in January 1975, two LARAF SA.321M Super Frelons landed at Luqa airport, an event, that marked the beginning of six years of Libya's military presence in Malta.

One of the large helicopters joined the Malta helicopter Flight at St Patrick's Barracks where, due to its size, it had to use a nearby parade ground as a pad. Flown by Libyan aircrews, AFM personnel were only taken on board as observers during the Super Frelons' normal twice a day patrols.

Meanwhile the unit's main role remained that of round-the-clock surveillance of coastal waters to discourage smuggling and other illegal

A LARAF SA.321M Super Frelon.

Bell 47Gs E and G on arrival from Italy where they were given a major overhaul and a new facelift.

activities. For this purpose all airborne helicopters were in direct radio contact with the Operations Centre, St Patrick's, and any patrol boat at sea, with the result that they could immediately pass on visual surveillance reports to all authoritative centres.

In 1975 thanks to the resumption of Malta's excellent relations with Italy, an agreement to provide for the presence of an Italian technical and military mission, to aid in the islands development, was reached between the two countries. Furthermore, the Italian Government offered to have the AFMs four Bell 47Gs, and the Jet Ranger, overhauled as they were all at this time due for one.

Towards the end of January 1975 the first 47G and the Jet Ranger were embarked in a C.130 Hercules of the Regia Aeronautica and flown to Bergamo. There the 4th Reparto Riparazioni Aviazione Leggera dell'Esercito took charge of them. Shortly afterwards the remaining three ex-German Bells followed.

A year later all five helicopters were returned, with the Jet Ranger now carrying the local registration 9H-AAJ, stenciled in black over its original colour scheme of whites and greens.

Other visual changes had also taken place on the Bell 47Gs. These were painted white all over. However, shortly afterwards, the Regiment's colours of red and blue were applied to all five Bells in the form of a horizontally divided roundel with a white number "1" in the centre. Furthermore, when floats were fitted, these had "AFM Patrol" stenciled on in bold yellow lettering.

Augusta Bell Jet Ranger and two G47s
during the inaugural opening of runway 32 in1977.

In 1977, with the opening ceremony of the extension to Runway 32, the AFM helicopters took part in the air display organized for the occasion.

In the early days of September 1978, the AFM Flight was moved to temporary quarters at Hal Far prior to taking up permanent station at Luqa airport, once the RAF left the island altogether.

Moving the AFM Flight to a former RN hangar on Hal Far airfield seemed to have at first been unnecessary prior to the RAF's withdrawal from the island. However, it later developed that additional Libyan AF equipment was expected to arrive to supplement the Flight, which could not be accommodated at St Patrick's Barracks due to its space limitation.

Three Aerospatiale SA.319A Alouettee IIIs with their associated support equipment and personnel, arrived at Hal Far in two C.130 Hercules of the Libyan A.R.A. Force.

Duly disembarked, the Alouettes joined the AFM Flight and brought it up to peak strength, nine helicopters, the highest ever. However, like the Super Frelons, neither of the Alouettes had their country's colours, or markings, either changed or removed.

Old Sunspot, a site to the southwest of Luqa aerodrome recently used by the Canberras of the RAF's 13 Squadron, was in March 1979 allocated to the AFM Flight.

Quarters close to the airport's Air Traffic Control administrative buildings were finally provided to the AFM Flight. This consisted of two big nissen huts and a hangar large enough to garage not only the Flight's five helicopters but the Alouettes and lone Super Frelon as well.

Never had the AFM Flight a base better suited to its requirements.

On 1 April 1980, the 1st Regiment and other AFM units were amalgamated and placed under a separate command with another designation change, "The Task Force."

The Helicopter Flight, now forming part of this new command, had the colours of their Bell 47s roundels changed to red and white, with the letters 'T.F' stenciled in black, filling the centre.

The summer of 1980 saw the beginning of an oil drilling dispute between Libya and Malta that led to the breaking up of all friendly relations between the two countries.

The Malta Government immediately ordered the Libyan military mission off the island and, in the ensuing hurried departure, all three LARAF Alouettes were left behind.

The Malta Government had no grounds upon which to impound

Bell 47G, 9H-AAG, with wheel-less skids and new TF Insignia.

Italian Augusta Bell AB-204B.

the helicopters. Neither had the Malta Task Force any authority to fly them, so they had to be kept grounded, and in storage.

Following the termination of the amicable relations with Libya, the ties that already existed with Italy were more strongly bonded, with the result that an immediate ratification was made to the agreement signed in 1975. The Italian Government now also pledged to guarantee Malta's neutrality.

Benefiting most from this new clause was doubtlessly the Malta Task Force Helicopter Flight. In 1983 an Italian AF Augusta-Bell AB-204B arrived at Luqa airport on board an A.M.I. Hercules, which served to ease some of the pressure off the light Bell 47Gs.

An Italian AF crewed Augusta-Bell AB-204B helicopter was attached to the Malta Helicopter Flight, however, the training of both Malta Task Force pilots and technicians had previously been the responsibility of the Army Aviation personnel.

The Augusta-Bell proved its worth perfectly to the duties involved and negotiations, with the intent of equipping the Task Force Flight with the type, began.

On 28 July 1983 a second Italian military Hercules brought to the island another AB-204B, one specially equipped for SAR work, and withdrew the first one.

From stated reports it was understood that this particular Augusta-Bell, MM80352, was to be the first one of four earmarked for the Malta Task Force.

Conversion training for the Maltese pilots began in earnest, and four were finally qualified to fly the AB-204. However, although this statement appears to confirm that MTF would soon have the type on strength, except for this one Augusta-Bell no others ever arrived, for reasons reportedly political.

For whatever reason these helicopters were never delivered, an adverse situation that could not have developed at a worse time for the Malta Task Force, because although still operational, for which credit is all due to the ability of the Maltese technicians who maintained them, the Bell 47Gs, which had by this time been on the island for the past twelve years, needed to be replaced by more modern equipment.

Due to this problem there were fears for a time that the Malta Helicopter Flight might have to be disbanded and result in destroying the small, but experienced airborne unit, that had taken more than 13 years to build up to its present standard. Happily this problem was later solved and the Helicopter Flight remains operational to this very day.

MALTA TASK FORCE

Helicopter Inventory

1972 – May		
	Bell 47Gs.	ex-German AF.
	9H-AAE	9H-AAF
	9H-AAG	9H-AAH
1973 – June		
	Jet Ranger	Libyan AAF.
		8185
1976 – April		
	Jet Ranger	ex-Libyan AAF.
		9H-AAJ

The Super Frelons and their crews were alternately exchanged with others from Tripoli every few weeks, and those logged between January 1975 and August 1981 were:

LC151	LC152	LC153
LC154	LC155	LC157
LC158		

Aerospaciale Alouettes SA-316B 2288 – 2295 – 2315 – Ex-Libyan AAF arrived at Hal Far, Malta, in August 1981.

Augusta AS-204B – Italian AF MM15-20. Operated from Luqa from 1982 until 26 July 1983.

MM80352. Arriving in Malta on 26 July 1983, its period of operational flying from the island lasted longer than that of its predecessor.

Bibliography

"Briefed to Attack" – A. V. M. Sir Hugh P Lloyd – Hodder & Stoughton.

"Malta Spitfire" – G. F. Beurling & Leslie Roberts – Arms & Armour Press.

"RAF 1939/45" – Hilary St. C., Saunders & D. Richards – Three Volume Compilation by HM Stationary Office.

"Mediterranean Air War" – Chris Shares – Ian Allan – 2 Volumes.

"Spitfires Over Malta" – Plt. Off. P. Brennan DFC; DFM & Plt. Off. R. Hesselyn DFM & Bar – Henry Bateson – Jarrolds Publication.

"Wings of War" – Laddie Lucas – Hutchinson.

"British Military Aircraft Serials 1911/1971 – Bruce Robertson – Ian Allan.

"Five Up" Laddie Lucas – Hutchinson.

"Malta – The Hurricane Years" – Shores, Cull & Malizia – Grub Street.

"Malta, The Spitfire Year" – Shores, Cull & Malizia – Grub Street

"Tattered Battlements": Fighter Pilot's Diary – Wg. Cdr. Tim Johnston D. F. C. William Kimber.

"Squadrons of the Fleet Air Arm" – Ray Sturtivant & Theo Ballance – Air Britain Publication.

"Mosquito" C. Martin Sharp & Micheal J. F. Bowyer – Faber

"Carrier Operations in WW2" – Vol.1 – The Royal Navy – D.Brown – Ian Allan.

"Luftwaffe War Diaries" – Cajus Bekker – Corgi.

"Faith, Hope & Charity" – Kenneth Poolman – William Kimber.

"War in a Stringbag" – Charles Lamb – Arrow.

"Spitfire Documented History" – Alfred Price – McDonald's & Janes

"Spitfire into Battle" – Duncan Smith – Arrow.

"Churchill's "Second World War" Volumes 1 to 6 – Jerry Scutts – Osprey.

"Military Aviation in Malta 1915–1993 John F. Hamlin – G. M. S. Enf.

"Siege: Malta 1940–1943" – Ernle Bradford – Penguin Books.

"Red Duster, White Ensign" – Ian Cameron – Muller.

"The Air Battle of Malta" – HMSO.

"The Times of Malta" Newspapers.

"Action Stations-Overseas" – Sqdn. Ldr. Tony Fair – Stephen Patrick Ltd.
"Blitzed: But not Beaten" – Phil. Vella – Progress Press Co Ltd.
"After the Battle" (Mag. No.10) – Editor Winston Ramsey – Battle of Britain Prints.
"Warburtan's War" – Tony Spooner – William Kimber.
"Evidence in Camera" – Constance Babington Smith – David & Charles.
"Operaton Bograt" – Donald Stones – Spellmount
"Onward to Malta" – Memoirs of a Hurricane pilot in Malta 1941 – Airlife.
"Spitfire Attack" – Flt. Lt. W.T. Rolls DFC, DFM, AE – William Kimber.
"Maltese Spitfire" – Sqdn Ldr. – H. Coldbeck DFC – Airlife.
"Victory through Air Power" – Major Alexander Seversky – Hutchinson & Co (Publishers) Ltd.
"SO FEW" – The Immortal Record of the RAF – David Masters – Eyre & Spottiswoode.
"In a Now Forgotten Sky" – The 31st Fighter Group in WW2 – Dennis C. Kucera – Flying Machines Press.
"Winged Victory" – AVM J.E. 'Johnny' Johnson CB, CBE, DSO, DFC. & Wg. Cdr. P. S. 'Laddie' Lucas CBE, DSO, DFC. – Stanley Paul.
"Dictionary of American Naval Fighting Ships" – Volume 3.
"Fighter Pilot" – Ed. H. Sims – Corgi
"Fighter Exploits" – Ed. H. Sims – Corgi
"The War in the Air" – (Freedom's Battle 1939/45 – Vol.2) – Edited by Gavin Lyall – Arrow Books Ltd.
Air Britain RAF Monograph Publications.